SAPPHIC FATHERS

Sapphic Fathers

Discourses of Same-Sex Desire from Nineteenth-Century France

GRETCHEN SCHULTZ

UNIVERSITY OF TORONTO PRESS
Toronto Buffalo London

Toronto Buffalo London
www.utppublishing.com

ISBN 978-1-4426-4672-8 (cloth)

University of Toronto Romance Series

Library and Archives Canada Cataloguing in Publication
Schultz, Gretchen, 1960–, author
Sapphic fathers : discourses of same-sex desire from nineteenth-century France / Gretchen Schultz.

(University of Toronto romance series)
Includes bibliographical references and index.
ISBN 978-1-4426-4672-8 (bound)

1. French literature – 19th century – History and criticism. 2. Lesbianism in literature. 3. Women in literature. I. Title. II. Series: University of Toronto romance series

PQ283.S38 2014 840.9′353 C2014-904150-0

University of Toronto Press acknowledges the financial assistance to its publishing program of the Canada Council for the Arts and the Ontario Arts Council, an agency of the Government of Ontario.

University of Toronto Press acknowledges the financial support of the Government of Canada through the Canada Book Fund for its publishing activities.

For Gail Cohee and Jen Rankin, for everything

Contents

Illustrations

All book covers photographed from the author's collection

Acknowledgments

This book has been a long labour that never would have seen print without the help and support of my friends, family, and colleagues. I would like particularly to thank Patsy Baudoin, Gail Cohee, Tamar Katz, Dian Kriz, Rachel Lerner, Henry Majewski, and Lewis Seifert for reading portions of my manuscript and offering invaluable feedback, as well as for their steadfast friendship and encouragement. I also owe a debt of gratitude to Rena Seltzer, who kept me on track through thick and thin.

Brown University provided me with research funding and sabbatical leave, for which I am obliged. Members of my home department of French Studies engaged with my work in the context of our faculty forum. It is a privilege to work with colleagues (*et néanmoins amis*) who are so incisive, and yet still sane and big-hearted. I must also thank my graduate students for reading many of the texts central to this book and illuminating them with lively discussion. In particular, I have more than once called on Heidi Brevik-Zender and Sharon Larson, former students and now accomplished scholars, with questions related to their respective areas of expertise in nineteenth-century fashion and femmes fatales. I would also like to express my appreciation to the participants of the 2009–2010 seminar at Brown's Cogut Center for the Humanities for their intellectual companionship and valued criticism, as well as to the Cogut staff for material support and genial coffee breaks. Dominique Coulombe, Brown University librarian and honorary *dix-neuviémiste*, has generously assisted me in locating and acquiring pertinent texts.

It has been a delight to work with Richard Ratzlaff, my editor at University of Toronto Press, who with great professionalism and good humour supported this project and, ever a calming influence, guided me through the process of turning it into a book. The input of three anonymous peer readers helped me improve my manuscript: my thanks to each of them for their insightful comments and suggestions. Thanks as well to Charles Stuart, sharp-eyed copy-editor, and Barb Porter of UTP's managing editorial department.

Numerous others have supported me through this project in many ways. To my conference klatch and esteemed friends, Philippe Dubois, Dominique Fisher, Melanie Hawthorne, David Powell, and the sorely missed Larry Schehr, among many other habitués of the Nineteenth-Century French Studies, Society of Dix-Neuviémistes, and Rhetoric of the Other conferences, I raise a dry martini to toast our scholarly ramblings on topics related to this project, invariably stimulating and always entertaining. These conferences and their participants have nourished my work.

The members of the Council of the Frog, of which I can say no more, have with their shadowy presence sustained me through my academic endeavours. Others have provided comic relief and the opportunity to take decompressing breaks: thank you, poker ladies, for those magical evenings, which have functioned as a soothing counterbalance to pursuits of the mind. One without the other would be nothing at all.

Many are the dear friends, awesome sitters, and generous neighbours who helped me find time to write by lending a hand with childcare: please know how much I appreciate the time you've given to my boy.

To my son, Julian: this is what I was doing when I was shut up in my study for hours on end. Thanks for being patient and for being such a great kid, even when impatient. I love you more than I can say.

Translations and Permissions

I have relied on published translations where they exist. In most cases, original French quotations from primary sources are supplied in the notes. French poems and their English translations appear together in the text.

Keith Waldrop has generously granted me permission to use his translation of Baudelaire's *Les Fleurs du Mal*, and Norma Cole and Erin Mouré theirs of Verlaine's *Les Amies*. Thank you for your lovely translations.

I also acknowledge Oxford University Press for its kind permission to include the poem "You see, we have to be forgiven," translated by Martin Sorrell and published in *Verlaine: Selected Poems* (1999, p.71).

Where not indicated otherwise, translations are my own.

Portions of two chapters have previously appeared as articles. I would like to acknowledge *Contemporary French Civilization* (Liverpool University Press) for permission to use material from "Transnationalism and Sexual Identity in Literature," which appeared in a special issue dedicated to Lawrence Schehr, edited by Charles Batson and Florian Grandena (37, nos 2–3 [2012]: 193–215). I also acknowledge Edinburgh University Press for permitting use of "Gender, Sexuality and the Poetics of Identification" from *Identification before Freud: French Perspectives*, a special issue of *Nottingham French Studies* (Edinburgh University Press) edited by Joseph Harris (47, no. 3 [2008]: 91–102).

Preface

> Insofar as female homosexuality in France is concerned, the situation may be summed up simply. The Lesbian has little to fear anywhere in France. In Paris, she has license to do virtually as she pleases. And thus Paris has become the Lesbos of modern-day Europe, in truth the Mecca for the female homosexuals of the Western World.
>
> (Hasselrodt, *Lesbianism around the World*)

France, more than any other Western nation, has become associated with sexual intimacy between women due to widespread curiosity about female homosexuality during the second half of the nineteenth century, when a number of Frenchmen produced a large body of literature about lesbians.

Today, fifty years after Hasselrodt's already commonplace assertion of Parisian lesbian licence appeared in print, many North Americans still cling to the cliché of French sexual liberalism, just as the French continue to relish the sport of denouncing Anglo-American puritanism. Such skirmishes about national moral and sexual proclivities have tended to mask a discussion about masculinity. France wins in love (braggadocio and admiration for the potency of Frenchmen, French contempt for prudish Americans), but loses in war. The libertine excesses linked to sexual conquest (from the Marquis de Sade to twenty-first-century presidents and presidential aspirants) become markers of French decadence resulting in moral, and by extension military, feebleness, ultimately trumped by the corrective of American rectitude and might, epitomized by the Allied invasion of Normandy on D-Day.

The above epigraph and the mass-market paperback containing it also regard sexuality as a marker of national difference, while seemingly evacuating masculinity from the equation (see fig. 0.1). Such descriptions of France (and especially of Paris) as a lesbian playground were unremarkable in American pulps of the post-war era, when Colette, Natalie Barney, and Gertrude Stein, members of the turn-of-the-century sapphic literati known as Paris-Lesbos, were still living.

Figure 0.1. R. Leighton Hasselrodt, *Lesbianism around the World* (1963)

But the literary foundations associating France with lesbianism were firmly in place well before these women appeared on the scene. In the following pages, I will trace the antecedents of the equation linking sapphism to continental France. It is an association that has little to do with women and the lives they led and a great deal to do with masculinity and France as a nation, in both love and war. My task is not to delimit and define what has also been called sapphism, tribadism, and female homosexuality or inversion, but to ask *why* interest in it has raged and waned over the last several hundred years. Its experts, detractors, and onlookers, be they prurient or indifferent, have produced contradictory discourses about intimate bonds between women. The result has been a cacophony more ignorant and harmful than elucidating. Is lesbianism a sin or a perversion, inbred or acquired, a predisposition or a choice? Is it exclusive or malleable, an identity or a panoply of practices, unseen or blatantly visible, sexually excessive or sterile and lacking? Until fairly recently, observers rather than persons with a more private investment in the question have dominated this discussion. Novelists and journalists, historians and politicians, theologians and psychiatrists, pornographers and moralists, Hellenists and Pentecostals, the clergy and the literati, penal administrators and marriage counsellors have controlled the parameters of the public conversation about amorous attachments between women. And until well into the twentieth century, these voices overwhelmingly belonged to men.

Much of the noise and even the silence surrounding sapphism, past and present, has produced a rhetoric of insignificance. It is implied that it is, after all, a small thing, a quiet minority within a minority. And a reclusive minority at that, one that is frequently unseen, cloistered, separate or separatist, domestic, ghettoized. A particularity. Insignificant, but also contradictorily ubiquitous or cloaked in beguiling mystery: a rampant scourge, a "strange embrace," a mental aberration, a social ill, an enticing curiosity, a vile practice. Such trivialization and mystification render it all the more important to examine the presumptions and biases of those whose cultural and intellectual capital grant them the authority to dominate the discourse on female homosexuality, all the more important to study the consequences of their words and works for female subjects as they live their own sexuality. Why was nineteenth-century France so expansively invested in constructing lesbianism as a particularity? Why does some of the same rhetoric persist today? Motivating this study is a politics of recognition, a response to those who would consider its focus inconsequential, unseemly, restrictive or exclusionary, identitarian or limiting.

Lesbianism functioned in nineteenth-century France and twentieth-century America as a cipher, revelatory of apprehensions about sex and gender during periods of significant social and political upheaval. As such, it offers fertile ground for investigating dominant ideologies of gender and sexuality at historical moments that positioned female homosexuality at the *centre* of a certain collective vision, even while couching it in a rhetoric of exceptionality or marginality. In the following pages, I document this unprecedented interest by studying an array of authors who lent their imaginations to the contemplation of intimacy between women. I explore the complex of reasons for this episode in French literature and culture at this specific time, attributing it to divergent preoccupations having mutually reinforcing discourses. Male-authored sapphic literature was a generalized phenomenon related to a network of issues. It betrays contradictory motivations, including seduction and denunciation, identification and exclusion, in which the boundaries between pleasure and symbolic violence are sometimes difficult to discern. I consider sapphic constructions in a variety of discursive settings in order

1) to understand why the lesbian became such a prominent figure at this moment, what she represented, and how she signified,
2) to determine what aesthetic, political, and social conditions, practices, and ambitions were involved in constructions of female homosexuality,
3) to explore the afterlives of these objectifying representations and how they reverberated for subsequent writers and readers, and
4) to speculate on what relationship they might have with subjective identity formation.

I conclude by suggesting that, while the explosion of literary interest in female homosexuality was specific to the time and the country, its cumulative force left tangible traces that went well beyond nineteenth-century France.

An introductory chapter provides background on lesbian representations and a historical frame for the period 1850–1900, the main focus of my study, while also presenting some of the literary, political, and sociological elements in play. A survey of the lexicon of lesbianism and an overview of prior literary incarnations of sapphism contextualize the readings that follow. I also show developments in print culture, the vagaries of censorship laws, and the evolving literary field to be features affecting the production of sapphic texts. Civil and international war, rapid regime changes, and the ensuing tumultuous and divisive political scene provided a climate favourable for expressions of sexual panic. And aspects of a quickly modernizing social sphere – technological innovations, industrialization, activism by women and workers, changing population trends, new social categories, among other elements – ratcheted up mistrust of difference and change, thus fostering mentalities of exclusion, which left their imprint on the texts in question.

Chapters 1 through 3 address distinct literary genres in order to illustrate the varying ways that writers harnessed the figure of the lesbian and to consider the different stakes in play in diverse corners of the literary field. Chapter 1 addresses the sapphic trend first launched by a circle of young poets at mid-century. Frequently invoking the lofty literary tradition of ancient Greece, these poets idealized the mythic Sappho as both lover of women and mother of the lyric. This ostensibly apolitical genre's subjective focus and exploration of alterity invited identification and created the possibility of inhabiting the sexual other by adopting her voice. As Paul Verlaine wrote, using a masculine adjective to compare his male speaking subject with the woman poet, "I am like the great Sappho" [Je suis pareil à la grande Sapho].

Charles Baudelaire's *Les Fleurs du Mal* (1857), whose early working title was *Les Lesbiennes*, presents a poetic subject who recognizes himself in his "poor sisters," pariahs like himself who are perpetual "pilgrims of infinity." I read his representation of the sapphic condition as a transposed study of masculine vulnerability and demonstrate its inextricable connection to his broader poetic project. Baudelaire identifies Lesbos as the cradle of lyric expression and lesbians with his poetics of paradox: they are analogous to the malevolent flowers evoked by the title of his collection, subjects upon which to practise the "extraction of beauty from evil." The work of identification in Verlaine's sapphic poetry inscribes not only female, but also male homoeroticism. Whether through identification with exiled femininity, the objectification of a sexually titillating other, or an attempt to find new models for sexualities alien to the lyric tradition, the lesbian provided a rich source for the poetic investigation of sexuality.

Even when largely projective or transitory in their identifications, lyric texts offered the possibility – however problematic – of a sex-positive sapphism, in stark contrast to the dark storylines of popular novels, which overwhelmingly endorsed a traditional socio-sexual agenda. Lesbian prose fiction was a largely modern affair, one reflective of social transformations and concomitant obsessions, set in an increasingly dystopian urban landscape in which abject tribades both incarnated a threat to what was perceived to be a vulnerable social order and, at the same time, enthralled readers and sold books. Chapter 2 contrasts the lesbian plots of mass-market novels with those in erotic fiction, taking the work of Adolphe Belot, author of both popular novels and backroom erotica, as a case study. On one hand, the moralizing rhetoric of his best-sellers, presumably intended for women and the masses, conveyed and rewarded conventional values, decried lax education, and condemned non-normative sexualities. On the other hand, his clandestine pornography, partial to sex scenes between women, was geared to a male audience. Explicit naming replaced the circumlocutions of his popular texts: partners are enjoined to "say all" during their graphically related encounters, which glorify sexual adventuring while serving up a lesbian bacchanal to men. Belot's practice of these divergent genres reveals conflicting motivations for the production of lesbian fictions. They belie a fixed ideological agenda, pointing instead to a nexus of socio-literary factors (financial gain, professional networking, sexual curiosity) whose analysis sheds light on the economic and sexual politics of non-canonical fiction, defined by one critic as that which is "rejected [refoulé] by official literature" (Migozzi, "Littérature(s) populaire(s)," 97).

In chapter 3 I turn to representations of female homosexuality in the fin-de-siècle novel. High literature of the early Third Republic exhibited a greater ideological investment than did popular fiction. "Serious" writing increasingly reflected contemporary political divisions as government censorship ended. This chapter studies artistic and ideological differences between naturalist and decadent authors. Their sapphic novels invariably converged with reflections on social disarray and the perception of increasingly precarious class distinctions. They depicted tribades as abject or fatal women from the upper or lower classes, figures that encapsulated a social menace, repositories of fears and fantasies deriving from political and social tumult. Naturalism followed a purportedly scientific method as it strove to uncover previously unrepresentable social disease, with authors such as Zola and Maupassant gravitating toward working-class lesbians (prostitutes and criminals). Decadent authors (Péladan, Mendès), aesthetes in flight before such proletarian preoccupations, tended to focus on a degenerate nobility, extravagant and sublime even in decay. Despite a deeply antagonistic relationship, both camps shared a fervent interest in sapphism and a reliance on recent theories of heredity and degeneration. Each carries traces of the Darwinian revolution and attendant advances in medical research.

Across Europe, early research on homosexuality coincided with the rapid diversification of scientific disciplines driven, like naturalism, by the positivist creed. Curiously, while doctors and criminologists across Europe increasingly turned their attention to male homosexuality, often in the context of forensic medicine, the topic remained taboo for novelists just as their interest in tribadism intensified. Chapter 4 shows the scientific treatment of male and female homosexuality to be dissimilar, despite repeated claims of their equivalence. In contrast to the forensic focus on male homosexuality, other medical professionals having different agendas laid the foundation for the construction and regulation of female homosexuality: physicians and social hygienists writing about marriage, masturbation, and prostitution.

Fictional and medical representations of tribadism cross-pollinated. Just as the aesthetic doctrines of decadence and naturalism relied on vulgarized medicine, so did medical researchers invoke literature. I survey European scientific texts that bring literature to bear on the discussion of female homosexuality and then turn to the work of Julien Chevalier, a doctor of legal medicine and author of *L'Inversion sexuelle: Une maladie de la personnalité* (1893). Chevalier concluded that education corrupted more women than did tarnished heredity and called for the containment of non-congenital lesbianism, whose social sources he enumerated. These included same-sex spaces, life in large cities, feminism, the breakdown of traditional values – themes already present in novels – and sapphic literature itself.

Chapter 5 takes U.S. pulp novels as a potent example of the distance travelled by constructions originating in France. The first lesbian pulp, *Women's Barracks* (Torres, 1950), recounts the erotically charged lives of women of the Free French Army in London during the Second World War. It sold millions of copies in North America and gave birth to the genre. Overwhelmingly male-authored, ranging in tone from sympathetic regret to sensational exploitation, these inexpensive paperbacks with lurid covers were coveted not only by their intended male audience, but also by women for whom they provided the first access to lesbian representations. The pulps themselves show women discovering their sexuality in books in which references to French texts figure prominently. Scenes of self-recognition in literature are echoed in interviews with historical readers of pulp novels, for whom the discovery of lesbian characters, however abject, introduced them to models for their own sexual and affective desires. These unintended readers allow one to imagine a parallel consumption of male-authored sapphic fictions by women readers in nineteenth-century France. Numerous points of contact demonstrate both the role of France as a signifier in subsequent lesbian fictions and the lasting and wide-reaching power of French writing for the self-fashioning of female sexuality.

We can never know how many women had access to such texts or with what investment they read them, whether they sought themselves in these occasionally titillating, often pathological and dystopian creatures, the only available models to approximate their own desires. These were the figures that, nonetheless, entered the dominant cultural landscape and informed the ways in which it perceived and marginalized intimacy between women.

SAPPHIC FATHERS

Introduction: Backstories

The sapphist fathers, [...] brothers who preach of counterfeit love and artificial ecstasy.[1]

(Jean Lorrain, *Dans l'oratoire*)

In the United States of the 1950s, as the American homophile movement began tentatively to form, a fledgling lesbian group in search of a name turned to a book written sixty years before by a Frenchman. Pierre Louÿs's *Chansons de Bilitis* (1894), a cycle of prose poems recounting the life and loves of a fictional contemporary of the ancient Greek poet Sappho, gave birth to the Daughters of Bilitis (DOB).[2] While one present-day critic has called the *Chansons* "a popular source of voyeuristic thrills," in 1955 the DOB contended that "it presents a sensitive and searching picture of Lesbian love."[3] DOB members chose to associate themselves with what today appears blatantly to be an objectifying portrait, one that exploited its subject in order to titillate readers, which suggests that models of same-sex desire, both real and fictional, were in short supply. Until relatively recently, this was an insufficiency that socially marginalized and often deeply closeted lesbians, having a limited ability to contribute to social discourse or sway public opinion, could not themselves do much to correct. Accordingly, in the literary column of its newsletter, *The Ladder*, the DOB regularly recommended a selection of books featuring female couples, supplying titles that its largely isolated readers coveted and eagerly consumed. These were written by men and women, fictional and non-fictional, in English or in translation, derogatory and (more rarely) heartening, dated and contemporary. The column, called "Lesbiana," notably included a number of writers representing a good part of the nineteenth-century French literary canon, from Balzac to Zola.[4] Their visible presence illustrates both the volume of sapphic texts produced in France during the period and, I would propose, the cultural capital they had accrued. These titles were invoked to validate or ennoble a reviled group, one composed of disparate subjects linked by an amorphous, mutable underground culture. Such hints of the social and aesthetic power of these texts invite further consideration of the impact that the literature of the "sapphist fathers" had on subsequent readers.

We owe this expression to the decadent writer Jean Lorrain, who with great irony thus named those men who preached sapphism, the "pagan religion [...] of inventive and sterile caresses."[5] *Sapphic Fathers* considers the broad and deep interest in female same-sex desire apparent in France during the nineteenth century, over the course of which what were then called *tribades* or *saphistes*, among other designations (when they were named at all), grew increasingly to be visible literary icons. While it has become customary to trace the emergence of homosexuality to the medical and legal pathologizing of minority sexual behaviour near the end of the nineteenth century, in fact the idea of women choosing other women as intimate partners enthralled French men of letters long before attracting the attention of medical researchers. With great frequency, the scientific community turned to fiction for evidence of sapphism that was unavailable in the clinic.

This study asks why lesbian literature, written nearly exclusively by men, proliferated in France during this time, and what impact it might have had on the lives and self-perceptions of women motivated by desire for other women and, more broadly, on the culture and its stereotypes. The sheer quantity of French writing about female homosexuality eclipses any comparable corpus in English, evincing France's profound fascination with the subject.[6] Writers of all genres devised plots, diagnosed symptoms, detailed traits, described milieus, and imagined couples and couplings of women. Given the weight of these accumulated images, women who engaged in same-sex practices became a familiar type, begging the questions: what stake did French male writers have in female homoeroticism, and what kind of heritage did these sapphic fathers bequeath to subsequent generations of readers?

As the following pages aim to demonstrate, the phenomenon of the phantasmal lesbian must be attributed to a complex of issues rather than reduced to one. A number of interconnected circumstances created a fertile terrain for the representational overgrowth of perilous women in general and lesbians in particular. The trend took place during a politically tumultuous century buffeted by revolutions (1789, 1830, 1848, 1871) and coups d'état (1799, 1851), with the shifting and unstable social, cultural, and economic landscape that such upheaval can engender. I will delve into the social and political environment of the Second Empire and early Third Republic below, necessary background to understanding why it was then and why in France that this sapphic explosion occurred.

Reading across genres, it becomes clear that there were in fact multiple types of engagement with the figure of the lesbian. The texts engaged here are by no means uniform: the tribade meant different things and was variously interpreted according to an author's position and status in his field and his allegiance to specific political positions and social milieus. And those meanings shifted across time. Discursive context largely determined the aesthetic and ideological stances invested in the figure of the lesbian, which functioned as a lightning rod towards which writers gravitated to work through assorted and sometimes unrelated literary, scientific, social, and political issues having to do with gender and sexuality. Regardless of their initial context, over time these representations interacted with, echoed, and built upon each other, in so doing creating what were often arbitrary cultural references. Motivated or accidental, they amounted to a kind of landscape of lesbianism that has come down to us today. This is the topography that the following pages will explore.

Sapphic Fathers addresses discursive practices and constructs having little or no correlation with historic persons or lived reality. Male perceptions of lesbianism, imaginary products bound to particular ideological agendas, nonetheless quite likely contributed to the formulation of identities. These authors held the power to disseminate arbitrary or inauthentic images that became naturalized through repetition, only to be imposed upon or adopted by subjects having proclivities analogous to the objects of representation. This body of literature represents primarily a conversation among men, one driven by sometimes obsessive curiosity about women together. The seductive lesbian couple, typically a complementary pair of blonde and brunette beauties, served to entice readers by offering the voyeuristic pleasure of exploring anomalous or forbidden sexualities. To a certain extent, lesbianism functioned as allegory for wayward femininity and responded to a lurid fascination with the sexual unknown. However, these representations frequently did double duty: they warned readers just as they excited them. Lesbian sexuality also connoted excess and menace, dangerous not only for other women (seduction, corruption), but also for men (unrequited fatal attraction, unbridled jealousy). These works policed sexuality by cautioning their readers, inculcating norms, and condemning aberrance. They were seemingly motivated by desire and its opposite impulses, repudiation and control.

Whether prurient or cautionary, male-authored lesbian texts of the period were overwhelmingly dehumanizing and symbolically destructive, even as they contributed to the establishment of a cultural repertoire. They inflicted representational violence upon those they purported to portray by manipulating an imagined type as an instrument, thus denying the autonomy, individuality, agency, and subjectivity of women who desire other women, both singularly and as a group.[7] I would add that exclusion is a direct result of such objectifying practices, and that representing *as* excluded contributes to exclusion in the real.

Words

The lexicon of same-sex desire varied and was variously employed according to the type and context of the literature in question. The overwhelming majority of mainstream poetry and fiction avoided naming altogether, while a rich vocabulary was used liberally in erotic and scientific literature. In fact, most of the fiction in question eschewed both labels and any mention of sexual activity. They favoured periphrasis, allusion, and euphemism. Some writers, as did Lorrain, turned to religious metaphors: "I will never again change sects" (Belot).[8] Others associated tribades metonymically with particular places, often same-sex spaces (convents, prisons, brothels, dormitories, factories), with occupations (prostitution, acting, singing, teaching), or manner of dress (cross-dressing, short hair). Some sapphic couples were marked simply by virtue of their constant companionship: Zola's *La Curée* (1872) features a couple who, having met in a convent, are described as "inseparable."[9]

Particular, inexplicable, and unmentionable, female homoeroticism was nonetheless thought to be widespread. Of the synonym *tribaderie*, one lexicographer wrote, "The word is less common than the thing itself," and a contemporary doctor concurred that, while "the word sapphism [...] might seem new, the act that it defines is ancient."[10] The core vocabulary – lesbian, sapphist, tribade – is Greek in origin and primarily associated with a single figure, the poet Sappho. As David Halperin has indicated, the word *lesbian* is both very old, "originally the adjectival form of the Greek place-name Lesbos" dating to the tenth century BCE, and, in its "standard designation for 'female homosexual,'" rather new (49). Between its earliest geographical and more recent sexualized meanings, *lesbian* acquired other significations, largely through association with Sappho, who lived on the island of Lesbos during the seventh century BCE. These associations were sometimes poetic, becoming more frequently related to sexuality and gender expression. *Lesbian* as noun and adjective has been employed without sexual implications to designate women poets (such as Louise Labé), and it has signalled heterosexuality in reference to the legend of Sappho leaping from the Leucadian cliffs into the sea when spurned by the boatman Phaon. The word's increasingly homosexual implications relied on Sappho's supposed relationships with female students. Halperin suggests that it has also signified "gender deviance or sexual role reversal," which is substantiated by erotic lexicographer Alfred Delvau's definition of the masculine noun *lesbien*: "What English thieves call a *gentleman of the back-door*."[11] Halperin dates its synonymity with "female homosexual" to "sometime after 1923." And yet he also writes that, by the end of the eighteenth century, "'Lesbian' had become virtually interchangeable with 'tribade,'" which more specifically and consistently had long since signified what Delvau describes as "a woman who has her way sexually [qui abuse de son sexe] with another woman" (*Dictionnaire érotique*, 359).

Whatever date one wishes to place on the current definition of the word, it is safe to say that in France, by the nineteenth century, *lesbienne* could be used interchangeably with *saphiste* and *tribade* to refer to women who engage in sexual activity with other women. For example:

1836: "Sappho bequeathed her name to the vice of tribades: it is called *sapphism*";
1851: "they say that, in her depraved youth, she even shared the rather lesbian bed of the voluptuous Ninon";
1866: "[they were] entwined together like young Lesbians";
1881: "in women, [homosexuality is called] tribadism, clitoridism, lesbianism, etc., without mentioning the popular expressions that have no place here";
1884: "the two lesbians locked themselves in the atelier";
1891: "A woman who loves women is called a 'sapphist.' She is also called a 'tribade' or a 'lesbian,' because the inhabitants of Lesbos were accused of this depravity."[12]

These words and their derivatives (*tribader, tribadiser, tribadie, tribaderie, tribadisme, saphiseuse, lesbique, lesbiennerie, lesbisme, lesbosisme*) designated female homosexuality in a general fashion, but were employed with greater precision in scientific language. In nineteenth-century medical literature this vocabulary refers to specific sex acts and those who engage in them. Lesbianism and sapphism are typically synonymous with cunnilingus: "lesbian love" is defined as "the act which brings on the orgasm by the licking of the genitals" and sapphism as "oral coitus."[13] Tribadism is usually true to its etymology, meaning frottage, although "several authors reserve the name of tribadism for a special designation, *clitoris in vaginam alterius.*"[14] More frequently, *clitoris in vaginam alterius*, or vaginal penetration by a hypertrophied clitoris, is termed clitorism (or some variant thereof): "the vaginal intromission of an inordinately long clitoris, which has grown anomalously."[15]

Popular expressions, which Dr Julien Christian contended "have no place" in medical treatises, can be gleaned from erotic literature and argotic and erotic dictionaries, although these words rarely if ever appeared in mainstream fiction before the turn of the century. Here is a sampling of expressions used to name women of various gender expressions who engage, exclusively or occasionally, in sexual activity with other women: *accouplées, anandrynes, anti-physiques féminins, dames pour dames, femmes-hommes, femmes sodomites, filles de Lesbos, fricarelles, fricatrices, frictrices, frotteuses, gougnottes, gouines, gousses, gousses d'ail, gratteuses, gunophiles, gynandres, lesbiennes modernes, petites agenouil-lées, ribaudes, saphiseuses, schismatiques, subigatrices, titilleuses, vrilles*. Some of these are specifically sexual terms, but others can also refer to affective preference or social grouping (*anandrynes, gynandres*). The verbs that describe sexual acts were sometimes conveyed by derivatives (*clitoriser*), sometimes by other formulations: *faire minette, gamahucher, glottiner, gomorrhiser, lécher la plaie, sucer*. These words and idioms, some of which had long been in use, others newly minted, were known to fiction writers, as evidenced by personal writings (Flaubert's correspondence, the Goncourt journals) and preparatory notes (Zola). As we shall see in chapter 2, pornographic literature brought out the verbal painters in writers who practised the erotics of naming.

This is a varied and colourful vocabulary indeed.[16] But I would contend that women readers who could in some fashion identify with those represented in this body of literature were and are more interested in the same-sexuality of it than in the words that describe homoeroticism in all its permutations and activities, that delimit it, that fix upon it. In fact, in the past certainly and perhaps to a certain extent even today, some readers were repulsed by or afraid of overly raw or explicit naming, for their own sake or for the sake of how others saw them. Naming is and has always been both highly personal and highly political, and quite changeable as well (as evidenced by reclaimed terms such as *dyke, fairy, queer*).

Subjects in History

Although my focus with regard to this literature, whether explicit or oblique, is on the *production* of same-sex characters and scenarios, I will also speculate about its *reception*, about the extent to which individual subjects sought out these representations, consumed them, and perhaps identified with them. I am interested in the relationship between discourses of exclusion and how the texts that embody them were perceived. While there is simply no way of knowing how nineteenth-century women readers might have reacted to the works of the sapphic fathers, there is more information to go on in the twentieth century. This is one of the reasons that I jump to the age of the Daughters of Bilitis in the final chapter, in which I consider female interest in the largely objectifying body of pulp fiction as analogous to (although not necessarily the same as) how Frenchwomen might have read the sapphic fathers a century earlier.

While the texts in question are disparate, they have one thing in common: they have attracted an unanticipated audience that in some way has recognized itself in them. This objectifying literature drew readers into encounters that were in some sense subjective, which is also to say enormously variable and context-specific. We can imagine such accidental readers as being either naive or sophisticated; projecting themselves onto characters, borrowing something from them for themselves, or being repelled by abject characterizations; taking in representations at face value or from an analytic or ironic distance; thunderstruck by their novelty or blasé before their repetitiveness. Such women, whom Jeannette Foster called "variant" in the 1950s and who today might call themselves lesbian, bisexual, transgendered, queer, or perhaps nothing at all, sought out books about women together in order to be able to see their lives and desires acknowledged in print.

The juncture of history and homosexuality is fraught with problems to which, not being a historian, I cannot pretend to do justice.[17] Changing idioms of and identifications with same-sex desire present greater complications for historians, who consider how people lived, than for literary critics, who worry about how people expressed in words their perceptions and imaginings of lives lived. And yet we encounter similar problems when venturing into the thorny terrain of reception. Who were these reading subjects, and how can we know about them?

The establishment of any kind of profile of such subjects is troublesome given the inability of one designation to convey an ever-shifting entity or sense of self. As historian Martha Vicinus has noted, "When we can't even claim a specific sexual expression as a key to our past, we must accept a fragmentary and confusing history."[18] Sally Newman concurs, adding that "The notion of 'fact' or evidence is an issue that is fraught with theoretical and definitional uncertainty in lesbian historiography" (53). Indeed, the impressive amount of fictional material (and here I include scientific work in this category) does not reflect a wealth of historical data on same-sex affinities during this period; on the contrary, imaginary lesbians figure much more prominently in the arts and sciences than do empirical signs of such subjects. Vestiges of any kind of social history of female homosexuality can be found primarily among elite populations, those most likely to leave behind recorded traces.[19] The reliance on archival evidence tends in particular to preclude lesbians of the working class and the petite bourgeoisie, who left few marks, although some fascinating work on these largely invisible populations has lately begun to emerge.[20]

Largely the result of speculation or invention, rather than personal observation of a notoriously misunderstood, censured, and therefore hidden population, sapphic literary portraiture entailed a great deal of conjecture, projection, and disparagement. Whether sanctimonious or salacious, French authors portrayed lesbians as outsiders to the middle class (foreigners, criminals, members of the working class, aristocrats). These characters were excessive both in their sexuality (prostitutes, deviants, predators) and in their affect (jealous, raging, seductive, murderous), as well as eccentric in their appearance.

These were, then, real and imaginary figures of exclusion. Historically powerless and so without access to the discourses that defined them, lesbians had no other social identity than the primarily demeaning ones imposed upon them until the turn of the century, when women living in Paris began to write about their own sexuality in a context that has been referred to as Sappho 1900, to which I return in my final chapter. During the nineteenth century, literature and science placed them at the margins, imagined their sexual practices, and, through association with other outlaw groups, created profiles of them as sexually deviant women.

However far they were from any concrete reality, sapphic fictions raised public awareness about same-sex eroticism and provided models for women who preferred women as intimate partners, as well as for the general public. Given the visibility and near-exclusivity of objectifying images in a climate of repression, women who gravitated to women for intimate fulfilment had few other examples to look to, raising the probability that, if to an uncertain extent, they absorbed such subordinating cultural references. Philosopher Diana Meyers has examined how "culturally entrenched tropes, mythic tales, and pictorial images that depict women serve as a kind of shorthand in which group norms are crystallized" (25). Her analysis of the contribution of such tropes and tales to the elaboration of female self-perception in general, in which convention is naturalized, I would argue, could not be more pertinent to a discussion of minority sexualities.

It is perhaps impossible to say, with respect to the assimilation of sexuality and gender into a sense of self, what role is played by images projected by exterior cultural manifestations, or by conscious recognition of difference, or by unmediated urges. Relative to identity construction, historian Alain Corbin has asked "how much of self-representation is determined by personal formulation and how much by some pre-established model available for adoption, a patchwork of existing roles and models refashioned in keeping with the inner life of an individual?" (*Harmonie*, 419). Corbin looks to the role of reading in how women who are attracted to each other view themselves, taking the nineteenth-century Englishwoman Anne Lister as an example. A dedicated diarist and affluent landowner from Yorkshire, Lister left volumes of journals, some written in code. She exemplifies the freedom that her wealth and the privilege of her station granted her to act upon her inclinations, a privilege later enjoyed by Renée Vivien, Natalie Barney, and other women associated with Sappho 1900. And yet Lister was largely isolated from others who were similarly disposed: "[she] participated in no institution associated with a lesbian subculture." Corbin contends that Lister's journals reveal the importance of classical literature to her development of a sense of sexual self. Although hers is an exceptional case, it is nonetheless revelatory of the force of literary representations, which offer unprecedented but nonetheless recognizable formulations to subjects grappling with the articulation of their sexuality and gender expression. Lister's journals suggest that literature plays a role in self-determination, in how subjects think about themselves and present themselves to others. In a very different historical framework and social register, some American women readers of the 1950s recognized themselves in an analogous fashion in pulp novels that, for the first time, offered them glimpses of same-sex relations.

Objects in Literature

I start with poetic production at mid-century, not because it marks the first apparition of literary sapphism in France, but because it inaugurates a break from earlier representations and marks the germination of the vogue.[21] The bulk of these representations are to be found in the novels of the late nineteenth century, commercial best-sellers as well as loftier works. But the varied network of interpenetrating texts analysed within the temporal confines of this study, roughly 1850–1900, drew on previous fictions dating back at least to Denis Diderot's *La Religieuse* (1796). Sapphic novels such as his were routinely referenced by later authors seeking to situate their work in a tradition. Because I read sapphic fiction as existing on something like a chain that stretches into the past and, eventually, reaches into the future, some literary context is appropriate here.

The phenomenon of male interest in female homosexuality, which has been referred to as male lesbianism, was neither new to the nineteenth century nor particular to France.[22] There is much to say about literary precedent in the circulation of lesbian representations in and beyond France: those from the period that concerns us are not only echoed in later, sometimes distant contexts, but they carry as well shadows of preceding fictions that date back to ancient texts (in addition to Sappho, we could name Ovid, Juvenal, Lucian).[23] Early French precedents, which I note here in passing, include "Élégie pour une dame, enamourée d'une autre dame" (1573) by Pontus de Tyard, Renaissance poet of the Pléiade; the racy "Tribades, ou Lesbia" (1646) by poet, politician, and one of the first members of the Académie française, François Maynard; *Vénus dans le cloître* (1683), erotic and anticlerical dialogues between two young nuns, attributed to the abbot Jean Barrin; and *Vies des dames galantes* (1666) by Pierre du Bourdeille, seigneur de Brantôme, which claims that "in France today, such women are rather common" (114).[24]

French interest in female homoeroticism became more noticeable towards the end of the eighteenth century, and this fixation grew in intensity as the nineteenth century dawned and moved forward. The eighteenth century, age of both the Enlightenment and libertinage, experienced an intellectual, cultural, and political climate propitious for sustained interest in tribadism. Marie-Jo Bonnet has identified "the appearance of tribades as a group identity" at this moment, and further argues that "never before had an era been so tolerant of women who are 'wild about their gender'" (203–4). Bonnet writes that "nonconformity in love stops being an object of indignation and becomes a subject for admiration," but suggests that this freedom ended with the Revolution.[25] The presence of an entry for *tribade* in Diderot's encyclopedia is but one indication of its appeal for the *philosophes*: "woman who has a passion for another woman. Type of odd depravity as inexplicable as that which inflames a man for another man." But Diderot's most memorable contribution to the sapphic discussion was his anticlerical novel *La Religieuse*, which tells the tale of an unfortunate young woman, Suzanne, confined against her will by her family to a series of convents. A different variety of institutional hypocrisy or corruption is represented by each mother superior encountered, from mysticism to sadism to homoeroticism.

Sapphic episodes also proliferated in the libertine literature of such authors as Restif de la Bretonne and the Marquis de Sade. Other prominent examples include Mirabeau (*Erotika Biblion*, 1783) and Pidansat de Mairobert (*Confession d'une jeune fille*, 1784). Whether one considers libertinage to have liberated or stigmatized tribades (both arguments have been made), it is curious to note the coincidence of progressive political change and sexual repression that followed the fall of the old regime, a pattern that would be echoed a century later by the social and sexual conservatism of the dawning Third Republic.

Rumours swirled around historical persons, such as Marie Antoinette and her entourage, in pornographic pamphlets.[26] Much was made of the mysterious "anandryne" sect that appears in the literature of the period and over which the actress Françoise Raucourt was said to preside.[27] A great deal of frequently clandestine writing revolved around Raucourt and the singer Sophie Arnoux, who were notorious for their public dalliances with other women.[28] One could speculate that actresses figure prominently in later novels (Belot, Péladan, Zola) because of Raucourt's prominence. A number of subsequent fictional representations relied on historical figures or found models in the world around them. According to Bonnet, a certain Mademoiselle de Chartres was the model for the abbess d'Arpajon in *La Religieuse*, and Gautier's Mademoiselle de Maupin was based on the cross-dressing lesbian actress Madeleine d'Aubigny (1670–1707). The Italian Princess Belgiojoso (1807–71) purportedly served as model for both Balzac's Marquise de San-Réal and Péladan's Princess d'Este.[29]

The romantic period produced a number of works interested in gender indetermination.[30] Balzac's *Père Goriot* signals this curiosity for non-traditional gender expression, later designated as "the third sex," with a sign advertising rooms in a "Private boarding house for both sexes and others." Balzac was perhaps the most daring explorer of gender and sexual nonconformity in a series of texts published in the 1830s.[31] His *Sarrasine* revolves around the secret of Zambinella, a feminized castrato. *La Fille aux yeux d'or* unravels another mystery, that of Paquita, a young woman kept cloistered by the Marquise de San-Réal and seduced by the Marquise's brother, Henri de Marsay. The novel ends in a bloody mess, but not before Paquita convinces Henri to dress as a woman in order to add piquancy to their lovemaking.[32]

Théophile Gautier's *Mademoiselle de Maupin* (1835) famously features a cross-dressing woman who is believed to be a man and ultimately beds another woman, Rosette (who is not displeased to discover a female body under the masculine dress), as well as the male narrator, d'Albert (who is relieved to find that the object of his desire is not, in fact, another man). This period's valorization of androgyny is also exemplified by George Sand's *Gabriel* (1843), which tells the story of a girl raised as a boy in order to inherit the throne, and the ensuing conflict that results from Gabriel/le's attempts to unify a masculine persona with female heterosexual desire. Sand's play questions the meaning of difference for both biological sex and gender. Its tragic ending might be read as feminist pessimism in the face of the cultural abjection of women.

A number of other literary texts of the period represent polymorphous sexualities in plots featuring characters of unclear gender. Hermaphrodites appear in J.P.R. Cuisin's *Clémentine, orpheline et androgyne* (1820), Henri de Latouche's *Fragoletta* (1829), and Balzac's *Séraphîta* (1835). While some of these portraits were salacious (Cuisin) or scandalous (Sand's startling male attire is thought to have contributed to literary interest in transvestism), the merger of male and female attributes was frequently prized during this period. Androgyny and hermaphroditism are sometimes likened to angelic perfection. For example, Gautier's poem "Contralto" (*Émaux et Camées*, 1852) admires the beauty of a Greek statue, comparing its indeterminate sex to a contralto voice. And Théodore de Banville's "Hermaphrodite" (*Les Exilés*, 1867) relishes the uncertainty of a "beautiful Being" [bel Être] whose torso resembles that of a "heroic young man," but whose breasts are like those of a "pale virgin."[33] Works such as these played out an interest in sexual uncertainty, which differed in important ways from later sapphic literature. Chiefly, they tended to be more interested in the *ambiguities* of gender and sexuality, whereas beginning around the mid-century, polarized gender expression and distinct sexualities became increasingly prevalent.

Even though same-sex plots underwent a noticeable modulation at mid-century, these precedents remained inescapable models and intertexts for those that proliferated during the century's second half. References to prior novels are frequent. For example, beautifully bound copies of *La Religieuse*, *Mademoiselle de Maupin*, and *La Fille aux yeux d'or* appear on a bookcase in Adolphe Belot's *Mademoiselle Giraud, ma femme*. No explanation is needed: their mere presence informs the reader of the proclivities of their fictional owner. Throughout the century, references to sapphic novels continued to serve as clues to a character's sexual inclinations, and character names themselves became code words for lesbianism. In Jean Lorrain's *La Maison Philibert*, Bilitis stands for all manner of lesbian excess: "girls in couples, no, we can't have that. They bring war and craziness into the brothel, it's an insane asylum. [T]here's always a crisis; there's drama, fits of jealousy, fake suicides, and threats of murder! I tell these ladies, none of that in my establishment. *I don't want any Bilitis in my employ*" (14, emphasis added). In the twentieth century, Louÿs's *Chansons de Bilitis* figured in works by Tereska Torres. Literary taste reflects sexual disposition in her memoir: "We toast bread on the radiator, sometimes she reads us pages from Proust, Colette, [...] *The Songs of Bilitis*." Sapphic works and authors are also descriptive of lesbian types in her fiction: "The second type of 'women for women' is more refined, more wicked. Their debauchery is gloved in white, inspired by the *Songs of Bilitis* or by Renée Vivien."[34]

Politics

The early limits of this study coincide with the Revolution of 1848, whose disillusioning aftermath, involving the violent repression of a workers' uprising, the coup d'état led by Louis-Napoléon Bonaparte, and his proclamation of the Second Republic in 1852, had the effect of decoupling literature and political engagement. These had been closely aligned during the romantic era, epitomized by the social novels of Victor Hugo, George Sand, and the later Eugène Sue. Disenchantment with politics was exacerbated by heightened censorship under the Second Empire, which cracked down on printed matter from its inception. Particularly during its more authoritarian first decade, the Empire produced a chilling effect on the press and literature, exemplified by a number of prominent trials, notably those of Baudelaire and Flaubert, both in 1857.[35] Censorship, and with it anti-government sentiment, encouraged a retreat into a pure art stance, witnessed by Parnassian poetry's refusal of political engagement. These formalist poets, nurtured on the aesthetic doctrine of art for art's sake, closed their windows to the revolution and were instead inclined to look to the past. Théophile Gautier placed this apolitical *ars poetica* as "Preface" to his *Émaux et camées*:

As Goethe at Weimar delayed
And dreamed in the fair garden closes,
And, questing in sun or in shade,
With Hafiz plucked redolent roses,

I, closed from the tempest that shook
My window with fury impassioned,
Sat dreaming, and, safe in my nook,
Enamels and Cameos fashioned.

[Comme Goethe sur son divan
À Weimar s'isolait des choses
Et d'Hafiz effeuillait les roses,

Sans prendre garde à l'ouragan
Qui fouettait mes vitres fermées,
Moi, j'ai fait *Émaux et Camées*.]

Redolent of the recent turmoil, this poem bespeaks the consciously isolationist stance taken by many writers, reflecting a retreat from the here and now with its reference of the fourteenth-century Persian poet Hafez. The sapphic poems and plays written in this environment similarly looked to the past and the elsewhere, be that of the orient or of antiquity. Ancient Greece, home to the muses (Mount Parnassus) and birthplace of lyric poetry, evoked a particularly idyllic past in which allusions to Sappho served poetic idealism.

But the manner in which the lesbian was positioned would soon change again, and at the end of the Empire, she took a turn towards the modern and the dystopian. With its liberalization, the government relaxed censorship laws in 1868, thus loosening its control over the printed word. Best-selling fiction increasingly drew upon motifs of sexual excess and deviance, particularly by women, to lure readers. This created the conditions for Belot's landmark sapphic novel, *Mademoiselle Giraud, ma femme*, which was met with great interest when published in 1870, the year the Empire fell. The sapphist became a visible personage in best-selling novels, a media figure that offered various and sometimes conflicting visions to the reading public.

The emergence of this figure coincided with the complex national upheaval that erupted in 1870, when Napoléon III declared war on Prussia. In a matter of six weeks, the French imperial army was devastated at the battle of Sedan, a commune on the north-eastern border with Belgium, Napoléon III was taken prisoner of war, the Empire collapsed, and the Third Republic was proclaimed. Paris soon fell under a siege that lasted a gruelling four months. With Parisians under heavy bombardment and starving for lack of food, the provisional French government at Versailles voted to surrender and negotiated an armistice that relinquished the Alsace-Lorraine region to a newly united Germany. Estimates place the total death toll of the war at over a quarter of a million, but there was more bloodshed still to come. This time, the French killed their own.

By universal male suffrage, the French elected a conservative Parliament, which chose Adolphe Thiers as chief executive. And yet in Paris, a radicalized National Guard refused to disarm or recognize the newly formed national government, forming an insurrectional municipal government that came to be known as the Paris Commune, an extraordinary if short-lived experiment in collective governance. Now Parisians were besieged by their own army, which after two months reclaimed Paris, killing thousands in the process. Thousands more were then condemned to prison terms or deported to penal colonies. This mayhem, both international and domestic, had an enormous effect on national sentiment. France had lost tens of thousands of its citizens to the Prussians, who pillaged its land and left its contours deformed. The German enemy emerged stronger and united after the war, while France suffered a period of decline. A hunger for revenge or *revanchisme*, a term coined after the war, took hold and festered into a new nationalism by the end of the century, spurred on by the Dreyfus Affair, of which I will have more to say in chapter 3.

Born of war and civil unrest, the Third Republic (1870–1940) would prove to be the longest-lived regime in a century having already cycled through two republics, a restored monarchy, and two empires. It witnessed technological advances leading to innovations in medicine, travel, communications, and industry. And yet until the Great War, it was enshrouded in an atmosphere of what historians regularly refer to as national anxiety and crisis. While its developments were hailed as progress in some quarters, their consequences were condemned in others. Industrialization and new markets meant an evolving economy as well as demographic and social changes brought about by an expanding urban working class. Workers organized against the abuses of industrialism, buoyed by Marxist thought and rising socialism, while the right pushed back against proletarian activism. Women, too, intensified demands for equal education and work opportunities, among other goals. Traditional measures for gender expression and class standing were challenged and became increasingly unreliable. These political and social disturbances contributed to a pervasive perception of threat coming from various quarters. Historians of the period have identified crises of the family, marriage and divorce, the birth rate, the economy, criminality and prostitution, education, and publishing, all background elements at play in the flowering of lesbian literature.

Although the nation suffered anxieties under the Third Republic that went beyond questions of women's legal and social status, it has been argued that a crisis of masculinity figured prominently in the environment of unease at the end of the century.[36] Wounded national pride and a sense of emasculation in defeat had a direct bearing on reinvestment in normative gender expression and sexual conduct. Moreover, alarming depopulation trends became ever more evident thanks to the new science of demography, which owed a great deal to Jacques Bertillon, chief statistician for the city of Paris. Bertillon would go on to found the National Alliance for French Population Growth at the end of the century, which ironically had as its goal "the purpose of encouraging republican *men* to father large families."[37] The low birth rate was a national concern that affected policy for decades, with the explicit goal of producing more children in order to bulk up the population of France and strengthen its army.

Following Thiers, Patrice de MacMahon, who served as commander of the French Army during the Franco-Prussian War, was elected president. During his term (1873–9), this royalist was biding time in view of a re-established monarchy. He favoured repressive policy and a return to the strict censorship that had been eased during the final years of the Empire. MacMahon's policy of "moral order" reflected the conservative desire to return to a familiar, disciplined social and political organization. Self-willed subjects endangered national discipline and lawfulness, while a strong Republic relied on acquiescent women to fulfil prescribed roles of wife and mother and thus to repopulate the nation and function as lynchpins of harmonious homes. MacMahon's policy perpetuated the mistrust and exclusion of marginal and non-conformist elements.[38] This context of suspicion contributed to the enactment of repressive laws. It also undoubtedly emboldened writers and encouraged the symbolic violence that they lavished on women and minorities, violence that would progressively be directed towards a variety of non-normative sexualities, of which tribadism was but one.

Towards the end of the 1870s, elections broke the monarchist majority, cemented a parliamentary republic, and moved the government to the left, facilitating renewed activism and making possible a number of important legal reforms. Censorship continued to ebb and flow until it was finally relaxed under the Loi sur la liberté de la presse du 29 juillet 1881, setting the scene for the proliferation of risqué literature.[39]

Male Rivalries

Other developments related to the publication, dissemination, and consumption of literature would have a considerable impact on the propagation of sapphic fictions during the second half of the century. These had to do with the production and policing of literature and what sociologists have described as a restructuring of the literary field. Increasing literacy and a modernizing publishing industry created new demands that contributed to the rise of sapphic fictions. The gradual democratization of education led to new populations of readers, particularly among women and the working class, and new print technologies created books and formats that were more affordable.[40] The literary marketplace witnessed an explosion of printed material and new vehicles for disseminating novels, chiefly the *roman feuilleton*, or serial novel. The volume of novels published yearly surged, with writers deploying sapphic characters as enthralling and increasingly complex expressions of disquiet during a time of rapid change.

While mass-market fictions that touched upon female homosexuality continued to attract a wide audience, the literary novel began to do so as well, at the same time as it grew in prestige and diverged from popular texts, owing to what Pierre Bourdieu has identified in *Rules of Art* as the emergence of a dual structure in the literary field. This progressively polarized structure reflected hierarchies of taste (symbolic value) in directly inverse relation to commercial success (economic value). Divergent genres were also associated with different reading publics. Popular novels were commonly marketed to women, such that Anatole France quipped, "it is mostly only women who read novels these days."[41] Sociocritical theorist Marc Angenot has argued that nineteenth-century popular novels bore traces reflecting the gender of their intended audience, that writing was "*marked* for women's use and produced for them."[42] Traits associated with the "woman's novel" included a formulaic plot, melodramatic style, focus on domesticity, didactic and moralizing tone, and the goal of entertaining its intended audience. It bore many features of the popular novel, which focused on current events in contemporary urban settings, and had plots in which realism and unlikely coincidence coexisted.

But if popular novels were ostensibly written for women, avant-garde literature distinguished itself as an art form dominated by men and targeting a male audience: "It is for men that the naturalist or modernist novelist claims to write."[43] These are the novels that have come down to us today. They are taught in universities, published in scholarly editions, and lavished with critical attention. Considered to be of higher quality, their plots are more tightly woven, their characters more complex, their prose fresher, their rhetorical devices less conspicuous, their undertaking more theoretical. And yet they echo many of the preconceptions and preoccupations of popular novels.

The presence of an aesthetic agenda validated literature, even novels that delved into unseemly topics, as consequential and distinct from mere profit-driven entertainment. While popular and pornographic works suggest writerly motivations that are financial and prurient in nature, the tradition of the high-art novel ostentatiously – if perhaps disingenuously – disavowed pecuniary interests and dismissed their commercial counterparts as hacks. Even in the face of often withering criticism, intellectual writers of the period contended that the pursuit of such noble goals as scientific exactitude, ethical inquiry, social criticism, literary originality, or aesthetic refinement elevated their novels. Zola maintained that "we are far distant from the novel that our fathers were acquainted with. It was a purely imaginative work, whose sole end was to charm and distract its readers. [...] Serious men disdained novels, abandoned them to women, as a frivolous and compromising recreation."[44]

Whether associated with high or low, literature or paraliterature, nineteenth-century novelists produced lesbian fictions in an interactive context, building on past representations to which they alluded in their own work. And they did so in a polarized political environment reflected in the divide between naturalist and decadent writers. At the apex of the moral and sexual panics of the Third Republic, the figure of the sapphist functioned as an allegory for all manner of threat to the cohesion of this tender regime.

Female Trouble

The tribade thus played a multifaceted role in the culture wars of the period. She at once joined other derided female figures and encapsulated them. A symbol of female independence, she attracted male writers opposed to women's changing relation to both public and private domains. Novels represented sapphists in a number of contexts and a variety of guises: associated with the Church as schoolgirls and nuns, they served as an outlet for anticlericalism on the left; associated with Jews, a pretext for anti-Semitism on the right ("Jewish neuroses [...] have fostered tastes formerly honoured by Lesbos alone," Drumont 394–5). Frequently said to dwell on the margins, among the criminal underclass, in bohemian milieus, or in the company of a degenerate aristocracy, tribadism provided a channel for class warfare from all sides. Aligned on one hand with prostitution, it justified sexual policing; on the other with professional women and feminists, it provided an outlet for antifeminist sentiment. Seen in all its manifestations as a sure sign of sexual perversion, female homosexuality incarnated the dangers of non-reproductive sexuality.

Enormous advances in access to education coincided with the new law granting freedom of the press: the Camille Sée law (1880) created high schools for girls and the two Ferry laws made primary education for both sexes free (1881) and then mandatory and non-secular (1882).[45] The Civil Code, written under the regime of Napoléon Bonaparte, had stripped married women of the right to financial independence. Marriage reform and divorce were therefore important concerns for women, so it was a milestone when in 1884 the Naquet law sanctioned divorce (first authorized during the Revolution, then disallowed in 1816 under the Restoration).[46] These issues were at once part of a feminist agenda and tools in the movement for laicization; in other words, their proponents did not necessarily share the same agenda, with feminists provoking deep suspicion.

This remained a puritanical and patriarchal Republic whose promotion of women's issues was self-serving. Its anticlericalism muddied the waters for progressive women: while republicans supported education reform for girls, they did so less out of a desire to further the emancipation of women than to wrest education from the control of the Roman Catholic Church, which shared a bed with backward-looking monarchists. Secular republicans similarly supported divorce reform in the context of a broader conflict that opposed the political and cultural influence of Catholicism with secularism and the increasing intellectual authority of science. But following this logic, they also opposed voting rights for women under the presumption that women were more inclined than men to follow Church doctrine and political positions.

In fact, feminist activism had relatively modest goals during this period. In a climate of fragile republicanism and national paternalism, the majority of feminists continued to hew to the centre, in contrast with greater outspokenness across the Channel. The "woman question," which dominated social policy in the decades following the war, ushered in an era of "familial feminism" whose goals were often conditioned by the reformist agenda of republican politics (increasing natality, secularization, parliamentarianism). A number of social programs intended to benefit women and families grew out of a national desire for increased production of healthy, socially integrated children. While some measures unquestionably benefited women (maternity leaves, paternity suits, and health care for unmarried mothers), others were seen as paternalistic and limiting (such as reducing work hours for women, which lowered their earning potential). The argument of Alexandre Duverger, a respected law professor at the Faculté de droit de Paris, exemplified the fear that women's rights endangered the family. He based his opposition to civil equality for women on "natural laws": "Political law must not impose upon women duties that would divert them from their natural mission in the family and in the State; civil law must not interfere with the natural subordination of women in marriage" (iii).

The success of the Republic relied on women remaining subordinate and fulfilling their domestic duties, childbearing first among them.

Bourgeois feminist objectives, as announced at the first International Congress on the Rights of Women (Paris 1878), focused primarily on equal access to secular education and professional schools, equal pay, the right to unionize, the authorization of paternity suits for unwed mothers, marriage reform, the legalization of divorce, and the suppression of prostitution. Republican feminists did not seek suffrage or political representation, since they placed the security of the state before women's rights. Only a marginalized minority campaigned for these rights and for birth control and abortion, considered the most radical of goals. Neo-Malthusians' fight for women's right to reproductive control was particularly threatening: they were perceived to be intent on driving an already underpopulated country towards extinction.

Republican feminists thus tended to be sexually conservative. Maria Deraismes condemned the double standard that allowed men sexual licence but punished unmarried women and prostitutes for illicit sex. She wrote that sexual inequality created "an entire system of corruption" targeting poor women.[47] In order to curb prostitution, she preached the honour of sexual restraint as practised by women and demanded self-control from men. Rather than calling for an end to the hypocrisy that punished women for sexual activity, she adhered to dominant constructions of female sexual reserve, a vision of femininity that reinforced the republican ideal of motherhood. Social order demanded that "each being play the role that nature has assigned," with women having a "natural tendency to devotion" and thus being destined to "represent the family, the home, the house."[48] Disagreeing with the utopian feminists of the romantic era, Deraismes held that "Free love is a fiction [...] the worst kind of chain and the family's annihilation. Liberty becomes meaningless when passion is ascendant."[49] Republican feminists were ultimately caught between a rock and a hard place: pragmatically adhering to viable political positions, in doing so they condemned themselves to sexual repression and the imperative to procreate voiced by their political allies and enemies alike.[50]

Political activism by women, even in this moderate form, fuelled acrimonious discussions about women's role in the public and private spheres, discussions often characterized by misogynist invective. All those who had a stake in opposing feminist demands or in co-opting them for a particular agenda participated in this hue and cry. Public debate involving women's issues incited opposition from a growing number of quarters and was increasingly clamorous. The journalist Edmond Texier remarked upon the imminence of the "woman question," which would grow more heated still as the century progressed: "The woman question becomes weightier day by day; it has become a true social question" (ii). Texier's alarmist book, entitled *Les Femmes et la fin du monde* (1877), claimed that there were fewer and fewer real women left, that soon civilization as it had been known ran the risk of disappearing.

Memories of the Commune added fuel to this fire, and the menace of radical feminists loomed threateningly before those on the right who, without great conviction, held the reins of the new republic. Women who had taken active roles in leadership and battle during the Commune (including André Léo, Louise Michel, Paule Mink) were vilified as bomb-throwing *pétroleuses*.[51] Following the bloody resolution of the Commune, they were deported to the penal colony in New Caledonia. *La communarde* became identified in literature and the press as a type characterized less by political activism than by frenetic sexuality, "a veritable Hydra who is obscene, sadistic, hysterical, and cruel."[52]

Even as workers' rights gained traction on the left, feminist demands continued to meet with often fierce resistance from all points on the political spectrum. Appeals for equal rights and opportunities were perceived as attacks by men hostile to incursions into heretofore male-only domains and met with retaliation. Feminist novelist André Léo noted with irony that increased democracy coincided with renewed anti-feminism: "Has the *necessary* subjugation of women to men ever been declared so frequently as in these democratic times? Has women's claim to self-sovereignty ever been more universally and constantly mocked? It must be that the danger is becoming menacing" (47). The far right, in particular, contended that the battle for women's rights was unpatriotic, equating feminist demands with the falling birth rate. Others on the right associated feminism with the left, saw it as an attack on the nation, and considered it a precursor to decadence. Antifeminist sentiment was equally poisonous on the far left, where feminism was denounced as a bourgeois movement in its call for incremental change – and as an unnecessary crusade, since the revolution would naturally bring with it equality for all. The labour movement marginalized women workers and opposed their attempts to unionize.[53] Socialist philosopher Pierre Proudhon held notoriously regressive views about women in the public sphere: "Nature and conjugal law have dedicated woman to purely domestic functions. To allow her to exercise public functions, which makes of her a *public* person, is an attack on familial modesty. It is a de facto proclamation of sexual confusion, of the abolition of the family, of an absolutist State, of the servitude of people and the infeudation of property."[54] Of considerable influence in the workers' movement, Proudhon's antifeminist rhetoric contributed to the divorce of socialism and feminism, movements that had close ties during the era of utopian socialist feminism earlier in the century.[55]

Antifeminist backlash against enhanced civil rights became evident in literature as well as in political debate and public policy. As fiction began increasingly to reflect the socio-political climate of the moment, it gave birth to new female types and revived classics (the femme fatale, the masculine woman writer, the prostitute) in response to feminist demands and evolving social roles for women. Also ripe for vilification were professional and working women, adulterous wives and divorcées, the New Woman, athletic women, those wearing trousers and riding bicycles, women freed from reproductive duties by birth control, and sexually active women uninhibited by the intimidating marriage laws of the Code. The lesbian showed up to take her place among these unconventional, ambitious, autonomous, overtly sexual female figures, each representative of specific perils to the social fabric.

Intellectualism in a woman masculinized her and rendered her sexually unappealing: "when a woman possesses the kind of vigorous mind that makes her resemble the strong sex, men are not attracted to her. This is a matter of instinct. Men do not seek out masculine women" (Duverger, 21). The sexuality of women who were masculine in appearance or bearing, self-possessed, or feminist was suspicious: "the epithet *virago*, which refers to ambiguous creatures of manly appearance and the temperament of a soldier, is not well received: they are suspected of having wicked habits. The qualifiers *loose* [*coureuse*] and *emancipated* are even worse by virtue of the same analogy between the moral and the physical" (Proudhon, 24). The Margueritte brothers provide an exemplary portrait of a stereotyped feminist with a character designated as "the president of the League for the emancipation of women." She is not only masculine, she is representative of a distinct and unattractive breed: "She's a type! Short, flushed, thickset, *a mannish face, the shadow of a moustache*, she is the standard-bearer of intolerant feminism."[56] Feminists were themselves all too aware of the tactic of portraying assertive, active women as unsexed, hypersexual, physically grotesque, or deviant: "Opinion is swayed against [the strong woman] in order to isolate her. *She's crazy, hysterical, scheming, a prostitute, a lesbian!*"[57] The success of such lesbian-baiting is evident in another feminist's defensive safeguarding of her femininity: "Feminism must not be [...] *a trend toward virility. We must not strive to imitate men, but to equal them.* It is absolutely useless to cut our hair, to flatten our chest and square our hips in order to become an orthodox feminist."[58]

The spectre of the tribade reinforced normative femininity and conjugal reproductive sexuality with the threat of moral condemnation. As an alluring if poisonous emblem of forbidden female sexuality, she attracted and excited readers under the cover of this moralizing agenda. While female homosexuality was not illegal in France, it became symbolically so through her association with the underclasses and the wayward aristocracy. Women who were sexually deviant, declassed, criminal, or in breach of social expectations became broadly associated with one another: sex workers were criminalized, female offenders were sexualized, and homosexuality was ascribed to women guilty of any number of transgressive acts. The sapphist became both a single example of the aggression directed towards non-normative femininity and emblematic of all manner of female menace to an apprehensive populace. She implied the refusal of marriage and maternity and a disregard for social conventions. Fictional texts increasingly associated lesbians with masculine comportment, describing their manner of dress and gender expression as aberrant or indecipherable: "In truth, that outfit could cast some doubt on the lady's sex." Female homosexuals were thought, moreover, to have their own language, vulgar and riddled with slang: "they speak to each other in an impertinent sort of jargon."[59] They corrupt innocent women, ruin marriages, and usurp masculine privilege. Insofar as the female homosexual conjoined deviant, non-reproductive sexuality and independence from men, she doubly cast the shadow of ungovernable femininity.

Science

As the century neared its end with a growing number of sapphic models entering the public consciousness through literature, the sense of what intimacy between women connoted socially and interpersonally grew more complex, even as the physical and psychological profile of the tribade began to ossify. Such portraits were confirmed by the rapidly developing and diversifying scientific fields. Although the Republic shifted to the left, the tendency to mistrust and exclude groups deemed undesirable prevailed. Criminals, prostitutes, the mentally and in certain cases physically ill, the indigent and homeless, religious and sexual minorities, to name the most obvious targets, increasingly became the focus of political and scientific attention and public obsession. And homophobic sentiment intensified. The impact of theories of heredity, the rising prominence of a scientific discourse of pathology and degeneration, the growing authority of medical doctors, and the trend towards specialization all contributed to this fixation on sapphism.

Charles Darwin's work on natural selection and Bénédict-Augustin Morel's treatise on degeneration (which held that the decline of tainted bloodlines led to physical, sexual, and social pathologies) appeared in the late 1850s. Both these men had an enormous effect on the research-based fields that defined homosexuality as a congenital or acquired disease at the end of the century. Across Europe, medical men began in earnest around 1870 to study homosexuality and, more generally, sexual deviance. Notable physicians and criminologists, including Richard von Krafft-Ebing, Cesare Lombroso, and Havelock Ellis, whose works would form the basis for the new field of sexology, focused their analysis on sexual pathology. Several French psychiatrists and forensic doctors, to be considered below, also contributed significant articles and monographs on the topic. But while the medical attention devoted to homosexuality encompassed female homosexuality, it did not define it. Medical and forensic professionals largely based their findings on male homosexuality, treating female inversion as ancillary or as a simple variation. The burgeoning body of lesbian fiction stood in for case studies, as medical doctors oftentimes documented the existence of lesbianism by referring to literary models drawn from the French tradition. One specialist, Julien Chevalier, to be taken as our own case study in chapter 4, went so far as to suggest that literature *created* lesbianism. Deploring the "veritable inundation of a specifically lesbian pornographic literature," he maintained that the surfeit of sapphic novels placed women readers in danger of succumbing to temptation or curiosity.

Genealogies

> I really don't like these books, but the girls are all crazy about them here. That Willy is an evil genius! He's capable of corrupting the entire brothel!
>
> (Lorrain, *La Maison Philibert*)

Echoing Chevalier's theory of "sapphism by literature," these words are spoken by a brothel owner who refuses to allow his prostitutes to read Colette's novel, *Claudine s'en va* (initially published under her husband's name, Willy), for fear of depraving his house of prostitution. This passage, from Lorrain's *La Maison Philibert*, attributes a great deal of power to fictional representations of nonconformist sexuality. While highly ironic, it nonetheless captures the fear, regularly and sincerely expressed in fictional and scientific literature of the period, that reading contributed to sexual contagion.

Although books and visual images have been held accountable for all manner of corruption, the rapport between representation and human behaviour can never ultimately be known. We cannot measure the countless silent ways that living persons looked to and either shrank or borrowed from the texts to be considered in the following pages. It is of course easier to establish that fictions model themselves after historical figures or contain seeds of prior representations than to confirm Chevalier's cause-and-effect linkage of exposure to literature and the adoption of behaviours.

But the notion that discursive constructs in some way affect a subject's sense of her own sexuality is one that I maintain. The great quantity of lesbian fictions spawned in France during the nineteenth century did not so much move women to turn to each other as it gave narrative shape to erotic pairings of women and bequeathed these depictions to future readers, regardless of biological sex, gender comportment, or sexuality. Exchanges among the real, the putative, and the fictional resulted in an amalgamation, such that literature pointed indiscriminately to living persons and to itself, science to literature, and literature back to science as various discourses worked to capture portraits of women who engaged intimately with other women. Cultural archetypes might be seen to be the product of distinct elements that act upon each other – fantasy, fiction, non-fiction, historical persons, public opinion, state policy, historical context, cultural obsessions. Precedent, context, and ideology interact with the literary to shape perception and representation, and representation in turn works on its audience in myriad ways. The resulting mix provides a context for succeeding models that subjects reject, embrace, endure, or absorb as they do the work, conscious or unconscious, of assuming, delineating, naming, and enjoying their sexuality.

Bequest and exchange therefore mark the various discourses that grappled with female homosexuality in nineteenth-century France, and the voluminous, if dubious, body of representations they left for readers then and now. These representations, be they fictional or scientific, playful or damning, erotic or repulsive, objectifying or identificatory, contribute and unavoidably belong to our cultural heritage, for better or for worse. Instead of following Chevalier's linear thinking or a Darwinian model of genealogical descent, we might consider these texts to be participants in an orgy of elements, each one taking something from the past, each one leaving something else for what is next to come, in a meandering, culturally infused but unmotivated process of selection. This view is more Foucauldian than Darwinian:

> Genealogy does not resemble the evolution of a species and does not map the destiny of people. On the contrary, to follow the complex course of descent is to maintain passing events in their proper dispersion; [...] it is to discover that truth or being do not lie at the root of what we know and what we are, but the exteriority of accidents. (*Language*, 146)

Such a sinuous genealogy constitutes a heritage with which subsequent generations must necessarily contend, but to which they are not beholden.

1 The Poetics of Lesbian Identification[1]

LESBIAN. A woman who prefers Sappho to Phaon.

(Delvau, *Dictionnaire érotique moderne*)

De la mâle Sapho, l'amante et le poète.

(Baudelaire, "Lesbos")[2]

At the mid-century, a circle of young poets moved on from the romantic flirtation with androgyny and transvestism, exemplified in works by Honoré de Balzac, George Sand, and Théophile Gautier, and began to write about same-sex intimacy between women, around which a literary fixation rapidly developed. Sapphic legend was to a large extent responsible for opening the lyric to such possibilities: the double association of lesbian and poet invited affiliation with the ancient Greek poet. As a result, poems of the period that feature female homoeroticism frequently take place in an idealized ancient setting – Lesbos, Sappho's birthplace – and allow for idyllic, heroic, or tragic renderings rather than the dysphoric figures associated with the corrupt modern city that would later become typical in novels and medical texts. In the mid-1840s, Charles Baudelaire advertised a forthcoming collection entitled *Les Lesbiennes*, which would eventually see the day in 1857 as *Les Fleurs du Mal*. Arsène Houssaye and Philoxène Boyer both published plays entitled *Sapho* in 1850, and through to the end of the century a number of others, including Paul Verlaine, Théodore de Banville, Pierre Louÿs, and Henri de Régnier, wrote lesbian poems set in ancient Greece, featuring both historical figures (Sappho, Erinna) and fictional characters (Bilitis). Such male-authored sapphic poetry, in sharp contrast with prose fiction and scientific treatises, stands out for its engagement with a variety of subjective stances.

The sapphic poetry of Symbolism mainly avoided the vilifying representations of female couplings typical of novels, but was not for that devoid of symbolic violence and objectification. Louÿs's *Chansons de Bilitis* is illustrative, as is Régnier's response to Louÿs in this second of the "Three Sonnets for Bilitis":

> To praise Love, Bilitis, you gathered two roses from a single bush that bears double blossoms, holding one as the other in its rich blooming redness. Their blood sprays in petals.
>
> From two amphorae borne by a single slave, you pour the wine of one vine, both aged side by side. Your gesture fills an onyx coupe for the god you implore.
>
> The Eros you serve on the delicate Isle is not one who seeks a varied embrace, such as that of a virgin who succumbs to man's might;
>
> Bilitis reveres the love she resembles, whose caresses are subtle and supple her motions, and appears in another to be true to herself.[3]

[Bilitis, pour louer l'Amour, tu as cueilli,
Sur le même rosier qui fleurit double et porte
L'une et l'autre en sa pourpre épanouie et forte,
Deux roses dont le sang en pétales jaillit.

Dans la coupe d'onyx que ton geste remplit
Aux deux amphores d'or qu'un esclave t'apporte,
Tu verses pour le dieu vers qui ta voix exhorte
Le vin du même cep en même temps vieilli;

Car l'Éros que tu sers dans l'Île délicate
N'est pas celui qui veut l'étreinte disparate
Où la vierge succombe à l'amant musculeux;

Bilitis est pieuse à l'amour qui, comme elle,
Subtil en sa caresse et souple dans ses jeux,
Semble être dans une autre à soi-même fidèle.]

This poem relies on the trope of mirroring, conventionally attributed to same-sex couples and later reinforced by Freud's linkage of homosexuality to narcissistic object choice ("On Narcissism," 1914). Régnier focuses repetitively on sameness and doubling, conjuring up identical lovers who are interchangeable with each other and have no distinguishing features. The adjective *même* (same) appears three times, and the poem's objects are presented in duplicate: "two roses," "two amphorae." Bilitis seeks a love characterized not by the recognition of difference ("varied embrace"), but by the search for oneself in another, "in another to be true to herself."

Frequently objectifying and voyeuristic, sapphic literature, whether celebratory or damning, overwhelmingly disavowed or invalidated female homosexuality as a viable identificatory position. And yet Naomi Schor has described a literary investment that is "not male *fascination* with female lesbianism but a more subtle, imaginary *identification* of nineteenth-century French male authors with lesbians" (391, emphasis added). While she locates such identification in Flaubert, I would suggest that it is predominantly the *poetry* of the period that offers the most striking examples. Alongside poems like Louÿs's *Chansons* or Régnier's sonnet, one occasionally encounters texts that present a masculine surrender of subjectivity to sapphic figures, male quests for selfhood that take detours through lesbian personae. Baudelaire and Verlaine, authors closely associated with both literary lesbianism and poetic modernism, present two such cases. Their sapphic work is exceptional for its *sincerity*, and by this I mean for its lack of irony or for its critique thereof (rather than the earnest and sentimental sincerity of romanticism). The approach to otherness discernible in their lesbian cycles offers keys to understanding the role of gender and sexuality in Symbolism's double project of unsettling identity and dismantling prosodic conventions. Albeit having disparate poetic and political agendas, the works of Baudelaire and Verlaine, to which I return below, are central to this project's investment in difference.

The history and conventions of lyric poetry contributed to rendering such identifications possible. Poetic voice directs the genre's inclination, or at least explains its receptivity, to identifications with others. In contrast with descriptive fiction's focus on surface, the lyric text stakes its claim on interiority.[4] Lyric poetry is arguably among the most subjective of genres, since the first-person subject's encounters are highly personal and interpersonal: the poetic *I* speaks overwhelmingly either in the context of an intimate relationship with another or through internal monologue. And yet the specificity of lyric conventions, particularly the tradition descending from Petrarchan love poetry, has informed, indeed limited, the shape and tenor of the lyric subject in relation to the beloved. Because of the genre's predominantly male authorship, and because of what Adrienne Rich has named compulsory heterosexuality, lyric poetry is broadly biased towards the opposition of male subjectivity and female objectification, in which the female figure is constructed as desired other. While largely absent as subjects in male-authored texts, female figures have nonetheless always played a central role in poetry. Muse, beloved, addressee, interlocutor, siren: "woman" in multiple guises could be said to motivate the poetic text in relation to its male voice. The gender politics of poetic intersubjectivity produces an authorial slant towards the masculine speaking subject, the objectification of the feminine *thou*, and their inherent lack of reciprocity.

This is not to suggest a transparent relationship between authorial and poetic voices (in which heterosexual male poet = heterosexual male lyric subject), but rather to examine poetic voice as what Elisabeth Cardonne-Arlyck has called a *disguise*: "The lyric *je*, cut loose from its referential moorings to the writing subject and yet answerable to that subject across its various disguises, puts the split between authorial person and voice to the test. Indeed, by exploring the fluid and uneven boundaries of the split between person and voice, the lyric *je* works to define it" (167). The lyric *I* could thus be called an exploratory subject, one that is neither autobiographical nor wholly fictional, neither reflective of a historical author's lived existence nor entirely the product of invention. Poetry grants free reign to manipulate the first-person singular as a site of investigation for a variety of identificatory subject positions: the lyric voice is theoretically as malleable and as multifaceted as its author's imagination is supple and broad. The poet can write as, among other things, lover, recluse, visionary, soldier, activist, victim, flora, fauna, and, of course, poet.

But could the nineteenth-century male poet write as a woman? Male poetic identification with women is unusual. There have certainly been moments in which "woman" has been heralded not only for her beauty and allure, but also for traits worthy of adoption. The romantic cult of sensibility comes to mind. The rhetoric of romanticism entailed the adoption of privileged qualities conventionally associated with femininity, such as compassion, intuition, sensitivity, and emotionality: "Though a man, he is gentle like a woman" (Hugo); "I borrow a woman's voice [...] My sighs, as they travel through your soul, carry more tears and incense" (Lamartine).[5] Rather than constituting an identification with women, however, romantic poets' espousal of "feminine" characteristics involved the projection of predictable attributes onto women. These poets were not attempting to pass as women, they were adopting gendered traits as a mantle: rather than *identifying* with women (whatever that might be), they *invested* women with dominant expectations of orthodox femininity. Indeed, romantic poetic masculinity was never placed in question; it concerned instead, to borrow Judith Butler's lens, a performance of femininity.

Ultimately, the feminization of poetry that led to such impersonations was repudiated by the Parnassians. Following the mid-century, Parnassian poets began to eschew romantic tone and style: "there is such an absence of virility in this continual moaning [...] its language is soft, effeminate, and inexact; its poetic line lacks muscle" (Leconte de Lisle).[6] Identifying rigorously with masculinity, they abandoned the romantic focus on intersubjectivity and championed instead a more objective and "muscular" approach to poetry, one that valued technical and descriptive prowess. Whether celebratory or misogynist, both romantic and Parnassian poets continued to rely on convention in their constructions of and identifications with polarized gender positions.

While the symbolist emancipation of the subject loosened the hold exerted by preceding conventions and gave licence to examine other identities (Rimbaud's claim that "I is an other" [Je est un autre]), the gender of the speaking subject nonetheless remained largely unavailable for exploration.[7] The heterosexual compulsion sheds light on the lack of creative invention and self-imagination with respect to gender and sexuality in male-authored poetry of the period, since the construction of female desiring subjects posits, in a heterosexual context, male objects of desire. Indeed, one could speculate that, in addition to their hesitancy to relinquish subject positions, many male poets resisted writing about longing for men and male bodies, which lyric fictions in female voices would entail. The virtual absence of homoerotic literature by and about men during this period of intense interest in female homosexuality is symptomatic of social interdiction. (Only a few male poets began, towards the end of the century, to write homoerotic verse, including Verlaine, Robert de Montesquiou, and Jean Lorrain.)

Stéphane Mallarmé's "Hérodiade" and Paul Valéry's "La Jeune Parque," lengthy symbolist poems that posit female speaking subjects, are significant exceptions. These are fascinating poems and worthy of attention for their enactment of female voices. While beyond the scope of this study, they do suggest directions of inquiry with respect to male-authored constructions of female subjectivity. Let us note in passing Cardonne-Arlyck's estimation of Valéry's failure to inhabit his female character, indicative of the difficulty of inhabiting the other: "'The feeling of the body' which, among other mental impulses, Valéry wishes to figure, is presented from an external perspective, in accordance with conventional representations of the female body [...] The feminine *je* is a theatrical voice; however close it may be to the poet's adventure, it remains self-circumscribed, bound up in the recognizable codes of feminine identity" (168). It is furthermore notable that the salience of Mallarmé's Hérodiade is her refusal of desire. While these remarks do not do justice to such rich and complex poems, they point to questions one could ask more broadly of male-authored, female-voiced poems. To what extent have they succeeded in transposing female objects of desire into desiring subjects? In what kinds of intersubjective relations do these subjects engage? How do they speak of their own embodiment? Are male identifications with female figures reflexive or projective? If one thinks of such poems as mirrors that male authors hold up to their own perceptions of femininity, what kinds of reflections do they disclose? Can such poems inscribe or inspire self-recognition in the other?

And what, then, of the lyric male lesbian? Even in poetry, such identifications occur in varying guises and are easily artificial: an impersonation or parody, an appropriation or conquest. Male lesbian poetry bypasses the unseemly obligation of inscribing longing for male bodies, which heterosexual female voices oblige, even as it provides an opportunity for cross-gendered male fantasies. Louÿs's *Chansons* are nothing if not voyeuristic. And yet alongside such appropriations of female voices, male lesbian poetry *can* represent an ingenuous attempt to inhabit the other and speak from within her, to the extent that this is possible. I propose to pursue this premise by considering poems by Baudelaire and Verlaine. What are their perceptions of lesbian subjectivity, and what does their investment in it say about their poetic practice and the process of lesbian identity construction?

Baudelaire's Rhetoric of Antithesis

Lesbienne, s. f. Fleur du mal, – *et non du mâle.*

(Delvau, *Dictionnaire de la langue verte*)

Walter Benjamin famously identified the lesbian as Baudelaire's "heroine of modernity." While there is much to admire in Benjamin's reading of Baudelaire, there remains room for argument with his analysis of the lesbian as symbol of resistance to mercantile capitalism. Benjamin reifies the lesbian as "a woman who signifies hardness and virility," when in fact this description finds no equivalent in Baudelaire's cycle (*Writer*, 119). Benjamin's assimilation of lesbianism and mannishness leads him, erroneously I believe, to presume that Baudelaire's lesbian serves to reflect capitalism's masculinization of women ("Baudelaire affirms these traits," 144). This socio-realist analysis lacks coherence, unreflective as it is of the work of gender in *Les Fleurs du Mal* and of Baudelaire's sexual politics more generally. To my mind Baudelaire's interest in sapphism is more obviously related to psychic and poetic issues than to economic critique. In fact, Baudelaire's lesbians are clandestine creatures markedly removed from public spaces and urban settings. Far from enlisting the lesbian to represent "the protest of 'modernity' against technological production," far from the urban modernity on display in a text such as *Peintre de la vie moderne*, which praises commodified femininity, Baudelaire associated them instead with unidentifiable and timeless places. He figured them against an ancient backdrop ("Lesbos"), located them in a sumptuous interior ("Delphine et Hippolyte"), or sent them wandering across barren landscapes ("Femmes damnées").

And yet I agree with Benjamin's assessment that the lesbian is central to Baudelaire's modernist aesthetic, but central as a figure of *femininity*, as a vehicle for identification, and as an emblem for the trope of antithesis, the cornerstone of his oxymoronic poetic practice. Benjamin has noted that "for Baudelaire modern life is the reservoir of dialectical images" (134). More broadly, his work presents a world view rigorously constructed with rival terms (among them: spleen/ideal, evil/beauty, hell/heaven, nature/culture, feminine/masculine). The figure of the lesbian is privileged for her role in both encapsulating and undermining antithesis, as I hope to demonstrate in the following pages.

To fully appreciate Baudelaire's aesthetic investment in female homoeroticism and its implications for the gender and sexual politics of his work, I will discuss his lesbian poems in the broader context of his œuvre, beginning with a consideration of some of his essays. Baudelaire's interest in and representations of sexuality vary broadly across the fictional and non-fictional genres he practised. Although his work is largely heterosexual in its frames of reference, it offers a significant exception with the lesbian cycle (and, to a lesser degree, with scattered and dismissive references to "pederasts"). And yet, whether hetero- or homosexual, Baudelairean objects of desire are overwhelmingly female. While his investigation of sexuality (its presentations, contexts, and associations) necessarily centres on female sexuality, this is not to say that male sexuality is not in play; on the contrary, female embodiment and sexual expression ultimately serve as foils for the exploration of male subjectivity.

Baudelairean accounts of sexuality intersect with but cannot be limited to discourses of love, lust, and platonic admiration. His poems often place material bodies and their functions in representation and, as if in parallel, show aestheticized bodies to be abstractions divorced from physical contact. In his intimate journals, Baudelaire's vision of *amour* is contradictory, described in either highly idealistic terms or graphically physical ones. Love is either "the sole thing which merits the turning of a sonnet" or likened to the sordid manipulations of copulating bodies: "There is, in the act of love, a great resemblance to torture or to a surgical operation"; "What is annoying about Love is that it is a crime in which one cannot do without an accomplice"; "Thus all Love is prostitution."[8]

It is with what has been called his "double postulation" that Baudelaire spells out with greatest clarity the antithetical world that structures so much of his writing:

> There are in every man, always, two simultaneous allegiances, one to God, the other to Satan.
>
> Invocation of God, or Spirituality, is a desire to climb higher; that of Satan, or animality, [a joy] in descent. It is to this last that love for women and intimate conversations with animals, dogs, cats, etc., must be ascribed. The joys which derive from these two loves are appropriate to the nature of these two loves.[9]

These contrasting urges operate on a vertical plane, with human intercourse occupying the lower, satanic, animal regions and spiritual concourse the upper, godly, ethereal sphere. It is worth noting that the transcendent postulation is a striving but unachieved one ("a desire"), whereas Baudelaire represents the slide into animal (sexual) love as accomplished ("a joy"). He opposes a one-way appeal ("*invocation of* God") to intimate exchange ("intimate *conversations with* animals"). With this opposition, he affirms the dichotomy between the solitary man of genius and the base subject who loses (prostitutes) himself to physical love ("the need to emerge from oneself").[10] In the latter instance, femininity is a siren song and an impediment to triumphant masculine genius. And yet this passage's final sentence applies the vocabulary previously reserved to speak of carnal love to both registers ("The *joys* which derive from these two *loves*"), as if a reminder that these diametrically opposed impulses are in some way, at the same time, equivalent facets of a single thing.

Whether spiritualist or animalist, Baudelaire's representations of sexuality establish contradictions and raise questions that both exemplify the author's dualistic thinking and reveal the unravelling of antithesis in his work. In the pages to follow, I will examine his sexual double postulation in some of his non-fictional prose and then turn to his verse to consider the fate of this binarism in the more complex linguistic and rhetorical setting of poetry. Baudelaire's fascination with antithesis – oppositions, contradictions, doublings, oxymorons, incompatibilities – necessarily calls to mind the pairing of masculinity and femininity, constructed as radical opposites in his work. As such, by examining the deployment and functioning of antithesis, particularly in representations of female figures, we will alight upon the poet's own exploration of sexual otherness. One might then consider the various and competing sexual discourses in his work as so many flirtations with otherness. Such toying with difference is sometimes prudent and done from a (frequently disrespectful) distance: this is the case of the essays, which are adamant but (or therefore) self-protective. At other times, and particularly in Baudelaire's poetry, the proximity between self and other becomes close enough to risk the effacement of difference and, so, the undoing of antithesis.

Prosaic Oppositions

Baudelaire's essays present natural chaos and artificial organization as the two extremes that define his divided vision of female sexuality in its carnal and aesthetic implications. His venomous, subjective prose, in particular the vituperative personal journals (*Fusées, Hygiène, Mon cœur mis à nu*) and notes on Belgium, unambiguously displays a sexualized natural world with all attendant negative connotations. In contrast, Baudelaire's art criticism, in which he praises synthetic beauty (*Peintre de la vie moderne*), depends upon an internal logic in which the refinements of surface and adornment negate the possibility of bodies in concourse.

Baudelaire drafted notes for a book to be called *Pauvre Belgique!* over a two-year period in the mid-1860s when he was living in Belgium, although he died before he was able to finish it. Within the context of his bicameral universe, *Pauvre Belgique!* is without a doubt governed by the trope of descent. It describes the country and its inhabitants as lowly, dirty, and obsessed with physicality and materiality. Baudelaire's expressions of loathing derive not from nationalistic chauvinism (elsewhere he lavishes French culture with disdain), but rather function to elaborate a metaphor for hell on earth: France's neighbour is Satan's lair, whose many circles are peopled by animals, criminals, philistines, savages, sex offenders and, above all else, women. From start to finish, *Belgique!* associates Belgium with the ignoble yearnings for what is animal, female, and carnal that are evoked in the double postulation.

These notes are outspoken and provocative, undoubtedly due in part to their non-commissioned provenance and unpublished form. As they come to their readers today, however, in their formal rawness they mirror the crudeness of their invective and their obsession with excrement, smells, and prostitution. Love is the loss of self, both physical (ejaculate) and intellectual: an expenditure, a prostitution. Women, into whom man expends himself, are compared to latrines (as is George Sand in *Mon coeur*). Stylistically, the notes on Belgium are as fragmentary as Baudelaire's journals. They are terse, repetitive and, finally, unfinished. Like the animal excess and human excretions they describe, these texts are disorganized, vociferous, and chaotic.

However the unrestrained and hyperbolic invective of *Belgique!* produces a lusty violence, a kind of textual gratification that comes from a repetitive pleasure in naming. Without moderation, it revels and rolls in what it repudiates: unadorned bodies, animal couplings, filth and excrement, hatred and brutality. Its sexual discourse (defined as heterosexual intercourse) resides in what editor Claude Pichois disapprovingly calls Baudelaire's *failure* ("this pamphlet was not a part of Baudelaire's essence" [n'appartenait pas à (sa) nature profonde]), which he attributes to the poet's deteriorating physical and mental condition as he succumbed to the final ravages of syphilis (2:1473). And yet, for all its excess and disorder, I take it as a triumph of erotic delight rather than a failure, insofar as it partakes of what Baudelaire elsewhere describes as the thrill of the abject: "delight in ugliness proceeds from a still more obscure sentiment – the thirst for the unknown and the taste for the horrible."[11]

In the telegraphic style of these unadorned notes, then, Baudelaire enumerates the country's loathsome traits: "Belgian coarseness"; "baseness and domesticity"; "ferocity, stupidity, greed, and bestiality combined"; "Belgian impiety."[12] Although Baudelaire maintains that "It is difficult to assign a place for the Belgian on the scale of beings," he enumerates national qualities and situates Belgians according to animal categories and through animal metaphors: "the Belgian man is a worm that one has forgotten to squash. He is completely idiotic, yet sturdy as a mollusc"; "the Belgian temperament is indistinct, hovering between the mollusc and the monkey"; "Belgians are *Ruminants* who digest nothing"; "Frog people who emulate cattle"; "their bestial curiosity, like ducks flocking to a view."[13] After having established the thoroughgoing animality of the Belgians, Baudelaire hyperbolically suggests that their homeland offends even beasts of nature: "even the animal flees these accursed lands."[14] In keeping with the scathing association of female sexuality and nature found in his journals ("woman is *natural*, that is to say abominable"), he expands, in particular, on female animality: "the tyranny of the weak. Women and animals"; "facial features, general type analogous to the sheep or ram"; "legs of an elephant and the strut of a pigeon; hens and stuck-up butcher birds."[15]

Pauvre Belgique! feminizes the country and its inhabitants in this parallelism that opposes them to the masculinity of the French: "Just as [moralist Joseph] Joubert thanked God for having made him a man and not a woman, you will thank him for making you not Belgian, but French."[16] In a section entitled "Les femmes et l'amour," Baudelaire asserts that neither exists in Belgium: "No *women*, no *love* [...] There are only *females* here." Women are products of nature having animalistic bodies whose functions Baudelaire catalogues in repetitive detail. Although the country is loveless, primitive sexual coupling is rampant: "What they call love here is unequivocal animal gymnastics"; "Belgians think that gallantry means bestiality!"[17] Female sexuality is generative and therefore repugnant, and a materialistic and utilitarian affront to Baudelaire's art-for-art aesthetic. Indeed, the animality of women derives from their reproductive capacities, one of many excretory operations of the body ("we can only make love with our excretory organs").[18]

Belgique! is intensely scatological and seems to relish enumerating the ways in which the country is awash in waste: "prodigious love of excrement observable in old paintings"; "excremental jokes"; "poor neighbourhoods and naked children rolling around in droppings, although I don't think they eat them"; "Belgium is a *shitty stick*." Baudelaire's Rabelaisian associations place maternity on stage with elimination: "Belgian mother in the privy (door open) plays with her child"; "pisspots and shithouses of Belgian women [...] Six ladies pissing in a narrow street, some standing, others squatting."[19]

And yet waste elimination is only one aspect of a more general interest in the body's excretory functions. Belgium and its inhabitants are governed by an economy of corporal expenditure, be it of feces, urine, infants, semen, or vomit ("How Belgians express grief. Drunkenness, pissing, vomiting").[20] The intimate journals provide keys to reading waste in Baudelaire: living in one's body means the loss of self; it is likened to prostitution, to vaporization. The expense of bodily fluids represents the loss of intellect ("think as a pack, piss as a pack") and signals a lack of depth: "No mystery or profundity, like Nothingness!" Systemic expenditure coincides with moral turpitude and aesthetic primitivism. Belgians are animalistic morally as well as physically, and their criminality expresses itself as sexual violence: "the bestial nature of Belgian intoxication: drunken father castrates his son."[21]

As animality is opposed to spirituality, expenditure to containment, vaporization to centralization, so sexuality is to the pursuit of beauty and nature is to artifice. These associated dyads suggest a sublimated sexuality, a repudiation of the body to the profit of Art. Aesthetically, then, Belgium represents the antithesis of beauty, "Hatred of Beauty." Rather than as a chauvinistic diatribe against a neighbouring country, *Belgique!* should be read as an *ars poetica* in the negative, as a compendium of aesthetic and ideological judgments in which "Belgian" is an arbitrary signifier of the abject: "The debased man would admire himself and consider beauty to be ugliness. Witness the deplorable Belgians."[22]

In fact, *Belgique!* presents itself both literally and analogically as art criticism. Baudelaire recounts museums visited, catalogues collections, and ruminates on Belgian artists ("No artists, save [Félicien] Rops" – who furnished the frontispieces for a number of risqué or banned books, including Musset's erotic novel, *Gamiani*, and Baudelaire's *Épaves*). Baudelaire devotes a chapter to "les beaux-arts" ("National taste for what is foul"), another to architecture, and includes a poem entitled "The lover of fine arts in Belgium." He presents Belgian art in as negative a light as he does its population, offering, for example, this assessment of Flemish painting: "No composition, or absurd composition. Vile subjects, people pissing, shitting, and vomiting. Disgusting and monotonous foolery."[23]

But his discussion of architecture is much more nuanced and, in fact, stands in sharp contrast to the abuse he heaps on the citizenry and art more generally. Here Baudelaire drops the invective, expresses admiration, and offers a more restrained analysis. Indeed, he allows himself to be moved: "The beauty of painted sculpture [...] my tenderness [...] the church of Saint Catherine. Exotic fragrance [parfum exotique] [...] Painted virgins, rouged and adorned." While the Belgians lack coyness ("no coquetry in the women"), in the pomp of religion Baudelaire discovers a "Religious coquetry. The cult of Mary is beautiful." Although Belgian women have no interest in adornment ("No attention to appearance"; "hideous animality of their clothing"), "the communicant in her robes" captures his attention.[24] What Baudelaire finds to appreciate in Belgium resides in its *artifice*, the same quality that his art criticism praises. Beauty, surface, and adornment are at the centre of *Peintre de la vie moderne* in particular, in direct opposition to the bald vulgarity of the Belgians and to the repulsion they incite.

In contrast, *Peintre de la vie moderne* praises an artificial femininity, one defined by graceful surfaces of – rather than vile outpourings from – the body. In *Peintre*, Baudelaire admires an aestheticized woman, her apparel, coquetry, and mannerisms. This is the visual rather than olfactory version of city living, idealized as opposed to vulgarly realistic, aristocratic instead of common. Polished *toilette*, polished prose: *Peintre*, like the woman described in its published pages, is recherché, organized, understated, complete. Insofar as it concerns relations between the sexes, Baudelaire's art criticism partakes of a discourse of love rather than one of sexuality. Woman, as object of beauty rather than physical receptacle, offers an exercise in containment, not expenditure – in centralization, not vaporization.

In the section called "In Praise of Cosmetics," Baudelaire writes that "Everything beautiful and noble is the result of reason and calculation. Crime, of which the human animal has learned the taste in his mother's womb, is natural by origin. Virtue, on the other hand, is *artificial*."[25] This passage summarizes Baudelaire's hierarchy of values, in which the human animal, reproductive femininity ("his mother's womb"), and uncivilized disorder (crime) – subjects all aligned with nature (not to mention worthy of Zolian naturalism) – provide a foil for the virtues of the artificial and the reasoned, which inspire "philosophic pleasures" [voluptés] rather than animalistic intercourse (29). He describes woman as a goddess rather than an animal, as "the source of the liveliest [. . .] and of the most lasting delights," rather than the inspiration for "delight in ugliness." She is deified by virtue of her beauty, rather than reduced to her hideousness: "a divinity, a star, which presides at all the conceptions of the brain of man." In other words, woman's pleasing exterior makes her a muse for poets and calls for decoration: "for whom, but above all *through whom,* artists and poets create their most exquisite jewels."[26] Here, "through whom" names female objectification. Woman is surface, a lovely surface both worthy of adornment ("most exquisite jewels") and equated with it: "Everything that adorns woman, everything that serves to show off her beauty, is part of herself [...] above all she is a general harmony, not only in her bearing and the way in which she moves and walks, but also in the muslins, the gauzes, the vast, iridescent clouds of stuff in which she envelops herself."[27] It is impossible to distinguish between innate beauty and embellishment, between body and clothing: "what poet [...] would venture to separate her from her costume?" Men (poet or man in the street) are responsible for this assimilation. As they gaze upon her, they are "making thus of the two things – the woman and her dress – an indivisible unity."[28] Indeed, embellishment becomes a requirement for beauty: "as an idol, she is obliged to adorn herself in order to be adored."[29]

Baudelaire explicitly repudiates nature (which "teaches us nothing") to the profit of artifice, a repudiation based on a moral system in which beauty holds the highest value: "Evil happens without effort, naturally, fatally; Good is always the product of some art."[30] In contrast, nature recalls the body, its needs ("to sleep, to eat, to drink"), self-protection, and violence against others, inciting man "to murder his brother [son semblable], to eat him, to lock him up and to torture him." In *Peintre*, Baudelaire uses restrained language for what he spells out in *Belgique!*: "It is this infallible [nature that] has created patricide and cannibalism, and a thousand other abominations that both *shame and modesty prevent us from naming*."[31] The purpose of cosmetics, then, is to repair and improve upon nature's work, it "is successfully designed to rid the complexion of those blemishes that Nature has outrageously strewn there" – but never to emulate it: "Who would dare to assign to art the sterile function of imitating Nature?"[32]

The refined, artificial sexuality represented in *Peintre* is therefore civilized (the lure of beauty rather than the craving for physical union) and aristocratic: "I am thus led to regard external finery as one of the signs of the primitive nobility of the human soul." Although he attributes the association of nature with beauty and goodness to "the eighteenth century's false premise in the field of ethics," Baudelaire's view of women as measures of refinement nonetheless harks back to Enlightenment France.[33] His writings on feminine beauty anticipate a chapter from the Goncourt brothers' *La Femme au XVIIIe siècle* (1862), if only the one on beauty and fashion. However, unlike the Goncourts, who cast "woman's domination and intelligence" in a positive light, Baudelaire resolutely refuses to appreciate intelligence in women. Baudelaire longs nostalgically for lost sophistication and demonstrates an elitist protectionism that aims to preserve former distinctions (both in the sense of excellence and of difference) from what he saw as the reigning stupidity of the nineteenth century and the vulgarity of his contemporaries. Analogous to his double postulation, which represents a vertical hierarchy (Satan/God, "from deep abyss to highest heaven"), Baudelaire's art criticism ideologically codifies the erotics of femininity according to moral and aesthetic values, placing aristocratic cultivation on a higher plane far removed from the coarseness of the instinctive, reproducing masses ("We have climbed down [...] to the femina simplex").[34] Prescient of Pierre Bourdieu's *La Distinction*, which studies the relationship between class and taste, Baudelaire shows social value to rely on the smallest of differences, as in his description of a hypothetical woman "who lacks practically nothing to make her into a great lady – that 'practically nothing' being in fact 'practically everything,' for it is *distinction*."[35]

The double postulation – and by extension the dualisms that structure Baudelaire's thought and work – thus governs his representations of the female body, from its repugnant animal excretions to refined surface embellishment. But such starkly drawn contrasts beg the question of what these poles might share. The poem “Hymne à la beauté,” which asks whether Beauty's provenance is diabolical or heavenly, provides elucidation. Following a lengthy string of antithetical associations (depth of sky/abyss, sun sets/sun rises, dark void/stars, joy/disasters, Angel/Siren), it replies “who cares?” [qu'importe?], concluding that it does not matter whether Beauty is lofty or hellish, since her effect on the speaking subject is identical in either case: “you render the universe less hideous and less heavily laden.”[36] The diametrically opposite poles that Baudelaire took such pains to establish in this poem, as he did in his essays, essentially amount to the same.

With respect to his essays, I would argue that the grotesque female body from Belgium and the refined, civilized body in art are the same in this regard: they share a thoroughgoing materialism. They take the body as object, either in its surfaces or in its expulsions; in either event, it is or moves towards exteriority. And regardless of the value assigned to these bodies – high or low, cultivated or vulgar – woman finds her equal in man. The female animal has her mate in the sexualized male: “Only the brute is really potent” [bande bien].[37] Moreover, the dandy (“this doctrine of elegance and originality”) and the pomp of “military coquetry” provide mirrors with their costumes and gallantry for the adorned and embellished woman.[38]

Baudelaire's invective and his art criticism also share this: they inscribe relations of power and, specifically, of masculine domination. In *Belgique!*, Baudelaire proclaims that nation's cultural (social, moral, artistic) inferiority while associating – and *by* associating – it with women. Because Belgium is “weak” like women, children, and animals, power is implicitly invested in masculinity (and, undoubtedly, in French culture). Similarly, the relation of the male artist or critic to representations of women entails an aesthetic division of control between the active maker and the passive object.

Whether through repudiating disdain or proprietary admiration, Baudelaire therefore maintains a distance from the female object in the prose pieces considered here, a distance that his lyric poetry frequently broaches. There is a noticeable turnabout in *Les Fleurs du Mal*, in which female figures dominate the speaking subject. Baudelaire's heterosexual poetry represents women as coldly menacing (“Je t'adore ...,” “Avec tes vêtements ...”) or cruel (“La Beauté,” “Tu mettrais l'univers ...”). Female figures are overpowering, sensual, exotic (“Parfum exotique,” “Sed non satiata”), and sometimes devouring (“Le Vampire”). They also appear as idealized and maternal, but irretrievably lost (“Le Balcon,” “La Géante”). While these femmes fatales vary in profile, they are equally dangerous for their ability to draw in the speaking subject and render him powerless. And regardless of the judgments placed upon them, the female characters and feminine symbols that people *Les Fleurs du Mal* exist in close proximity to the speaking subject and, in so doing, inspire fear and attraction.

Far different from the sexualized relations of power found in his prose, Baudelaire's lyric poetry is a place of masculine vulnerability and feminine power, of dangerous women. Instead of surface or ejection, it explores depth and interiority: this is where Baudelaire's lesbians reside.

Femmes damnées: *Lesbian Sexuality and the Undoing of Antithesis*

From its oxymoronic title to the first poems of "Spleen et idéal," *Les Fleurs du Mal* brings antithesis to mind more readily perhaps than the non-fictional prose. But as I hope to demonstrate, the poems ultimately confound the rigidly oppositional vision of female sexuality revealed in his essays. Indeed, by refusing prose and the prosaic and thus escaping the materialism of his essays, Baudelaire's lyric poetry offers a murky and messy, but nonetheless tightly refined vision of female sexuality, which emerges here in its greatest complexity.

The degree of proximity or distance between male subject and female object is suggestive of the degree to which the object is recognized as worthy of integration. Baudelaire's poetry presents an array of intersubjective possibilities, from repudiation of the feminine other, to impersonation, to incorporation. As we have seen, loathsome femininity is a well-worn theme in Baudelaire. Elsewhere, as in "La Beauté," he becomes a ventriloquist and speaks for a female figure, constructing her through projection: "O mortals, I am beautiful, like a dream in stone" [Je suis belle, ô mortels, comme un rêve de pierre]. In this sonnet, Baudelaire does little more than parody the personification of beauty as both alluring and dangerous to poets: "and my bosom, bruising all comers, is such as to inspire in the poet a love silent and eternal" [Et mon sein, où chacun s'est meurtri tour à tour, / Est fait pour inspirer au poète un amour]. This figure recalls Baudelaire's frequent representations of cold women who are fatally attractive to men: "And [I] cherish, O cruel implacable brute, even that coldness that makes you more beautiful!" [Et je chéris, ô bête implacable et cruelle! / Jusqu'à cette froideur par où tu m'es plus belle] ("Je t'adore ...").

But in his lesbian poems there seems to be a different kind of relationship at work, one closer to affinity than hostility or struggle. Here the female figures are not represented strictly as objects of male desire, but rather function as subjects of masculine identification. The contradictory network of associations found in "Lesbos" and the two "Femmes damnées" poems ("Femmes damnées," "Femmes damnées: Delphine et Hippolyte") points to recurring images and the sexual obsessions that traverse the collection, and to a poet excavating the lesbian persona for traces of a masculine self in a poetic quest for identification. This cycle is revelatory for Baudelaire's investigation of sexual sameness and difference, which implies his questioning of antithetical rhetorical figures.

At the heart of *Les Fleurs du Mal* lies the eponymous section "Fleurs du Mal," whose lesbian poems critics since Proust have treated as keys to the collection's primitive title, *Les Lesbiennes*. One can interpret both titles as referring to the same aesthetic program, which Baudelaire summarized as "the task of extracting *beauty* from Evil" [d'extraire la *beauté* du Mal] (1:181). The lesbian would be, for Baudelaire, a kind of malevolent flower.

In the "Fleurs du Mal" section Baudelaire brings such associations alive, translating his baleful flowers into lesbians, unnatural but alluring women of barren sexuality, doomed to lead lives of social exile. These poems present lesbians as allegory and offer a means of access to the sexual politics of a poetic collection that runs the gamut between misogyny and idealization, repulsion and attraction. The lesbian content of these poems is inextricably linked to Baudelaire's poetics of paradox. A subject upon which to practise the extraction of beauty from evil, lesbianism is a locus of aesthetic interest for Baudelaire and, perhaps, of considerable psychic significance as well. "Unnatural," thus linked to the cult of the artificial, feminine yet containing its opposite, lesbianism is crucial to Baudelaire's fascination for the coming together of opposites.

An analysis of the lesbian poems necessitates a certain amount of reconstruction. For all the notoriety they garnered during the 1857 trial, Baudelaire's lesbians remain shrouded in a mystery of the poet's own making, a mystery compounded by the legal judgment, which resulted in the censorship of "Lesbos," "Delphine et Hippolyte," and four other poems. Let us recall the order of the lesbian trilogy in the 1857 edition: "Lesbos" came first, then "Delphine et Hippolyte," followed by the shorter "Femmes damnées." I read "Lesbos" and "Delphine et Hippolyte" as a contradictory pair, another demonstration of Baudelaire's penchant for antithesis. After pursuing this contrast, I'll consider how "Femmes damnées" mediates between them.

While nubile girls frolic on Baudelaire's idealized and bucolic isle in "Lesbos," in contrast, "Delphine et Hippolyte" unfolds in a modern-day, darkly lit, sumptuously upholstered, languid scene later to become so familiar in the interiors of decadent fictions. While "Lesbos" paints a multitude of jubilant pubescent girls in a frisky sunlit romp, "Delphine et Hippolyte" sounds an earnest, claustrophobic, tragic toll for two lovers, one tentative and the other eagerly persuasive, both embarking on a descent into hell. Ancient versus modern, euphoric versus dysphoric, exterior versus interior, idyll versus tragedy: these are just the most obvious of the contrasts between the two poems.

"Lesbos" is set in ancient Greece and thus away from modern associations of sexual corruption and the Christian morality that condemns the "femmes damnées." In fact, it is largely celebratory: Lesbos is the site of a joyous love fest, and Sappho surpasses even the heterosexual Venus ("More beautiful than Venus rising on the world" [Plus belle que Vénus se dressant sur le monde]). Rather than hurtling lesbians down to hellfire, as in "Delphine et Hippolyte," Baudelaire presents an apologia wrapped in the incantatory repetitions that structure his quintains (five-line stanzas):

> What would we want with laws for just and unjust? Lofty-hearted virgins, pride of the Aegean, your religion as august as any: love will hoot at Hell and at Heaven. What would we want with laws for just and unjust?
>
> [Que nous veulent les lois du juste et de l'injuste?
> Vierges au cœur sublime, honneur de l'archipel,
> Votre religion comme une autre est auguste,
> Et l'amour se rira de l'Enfer et du Ciel!
> Que nous veulent les lois du juste et de l'injuste?]

The "religion" of female homoeroticism trumps the laws of man. The tone of these poems could not be more sharply distinct when the question of judgment arises. We encounter male moral authorities in both poems: Plato in "Lesbos" and a nameless, condemnatory voice in "Delphine et Hippolyte." While similarly disapproving, they are varyingly successful in their condemnatory rhetoric. The speaking subject of "Lesbos" brushes aside philosophical censure: "let old Plato wrinkle his austere brow; you gain your pardon from excess of kisses" [Laisse du vieux Platon se froncer l'œil austère / Tu tires ton pardon de l'excès des baisers]. But the thunderous denunciation with which "Delphine et Hippolyte" ends promises eternal suffering in hellfire reminiscent of Dante: "Down, down, sorry victims, down the path to eternal hell!" [Descendez, descendez, lamentables victimes / Descendez le chemin de l'enfer éternel].

"Spleen et idéal," lesbian-style, these two poems suggest contrasting circumstances as much by their composition as through the words that their characters utter. The soothing five-line stanza of "Lesbos," with its lullaby repetitions, is reminiscent of other nostalgic maternal poems such as "Le Balcon" ("Mother of memories, mistress of mistresses" [Mère des souvenirs, maîtresse des maîtresses]) and "Moesta et errabunda" ("innocent paradise, full of furtive pleasures" [Innocent paradis, plein de plaisirs furtifs]). In contrast, there is something unsparing about the severe quatrains, expository organization, and hortatory tirades of "Delphine et Hippolyte." Rhetoric and argumentation preoccupy the latter poem not only in its closing invective, but also in Delphine's persuasive oratory, with which she exhorts Hippolyte to embrace her love. While Delphine and Hippolyte's exchanges are strictly verbal, the hypersexualized inhabitants of Lesbos get down to business: "kisses are like cascades! [...] girls [...] caress the ripe fruit of their nubility" [les baisers sont comme des cascades! / ... / Les filles [...], / Caressent les fruits mûrs de leur nubilité].

I have argued elsewhere that "Delphine et Hippolyte" stages an identification between the poet and the passive Hippolyte, while Delphine stands in for the fatal woman.[39] One can read the poem as an examination of male vulnerability, which offers a relationship of submission to female dominance analogous to the one found in "La Beauté." As Diana Fuss has suggested in a different context, "Identification is not only how we accede to power, it is also how we learn submission" (*Identification*, 14). Ultimately, "Delphine et Hippolyte" permits an identification with what Baudelaire saw to be the poet's and the lesbian's shared social marginality and moral abjection, rather than with women or love for the same. Like Sappho, the poet writes verse to and loves women. But Baudelaire's "femmes damnées" also permits him to slip on the mantel of passivity or vulnerability associated with femininity, while avoiding doing so in what would constitute, for the authorial male poet, a veiled homoerotic voice by writing of love for a man.

It is interesting to note that the textual poet does not empathize with the nubile virgins of Lesbos the way he does with the tortured and abject women of the two "Femmes damnées." There is no implicit interconnection because these pre-modern lesbians exhibit no noble desolation with which to identify. It is instead the dolefully heterosexual Sappho who, as poet and as victim, provides the possibility of identification. "Lesbos" ends with this Sappho's death, her tragedy provoked by her love for a man, not a woman, and thus by her renunciation of the lesbian creed that she founded: "Sappho [died] the day of her blasphemy [...] insulting the rite and the contrived cult" [Sapho [...] mourut le jour de son blasphème, [...] insultant le rite et le culte inventé]. The male voice of "Lesbos" is instead chosen as a kind of bard: "For Lesbos chose me above any on earth to sing the secret of its flowering maidens. From childhood I was admitted to the dark mystery" [Car Lesbos entre tous m'a choisi sur la terre / Pour chanter le secret de ses vierges en fleurs, / Et je fus dès l'enfance admis au noir mystère]. His position is paternal rather than identificatory: "And, ever since, I keep watch on the summit of Leucadia, like a sentinel with keen and steady eyes" [Et depuis lors je veille au sommet de Leucate, / Comme une sentinelle à l'œil perçant et sûr].

"Femmes damnées," to which I now turn, admires and identifies with the titular creatures, reviled yet fragile: "poor sisters, I love you as much as I pity you." Pariahs like the poet, they are "pilgrims [chercheuses] of infinity" whose sexuality Baudelaire associates with a wounded heart:

> Like pensive cattle lounging on the sand, some turn their eyes to the marine horizon and, feet seeking foothold, hands folded, are subject to mild languors and cold shivers.
>
> Some, deep in groves by murmuring brooks, hearts smitten by long confidences, spell out their timid childhood love and carve out the green wood of young shrubs.

Others, like sisters, walk slow and serious across the rocks teeming with apparitions, where Saint Anthony saw surge like lava the naked purple breasts of his temptations;

some there are, in the gleam of crumbling resins, in the mute hollow of antique pagan caves, who call to you for help from their raging fevers, O Bacchus, you who muffle old remorse!

And others, whose breasts take to scapulars, who hiding a whip under their long gown, in dark woods and lonely nights, mix the spume of pleasure with tears of torture.

O virgins, O demons, O monsters, O martyrs, grand spirits disdainful of reality, pilgrims of infinity, devotees, sirens, now laden with cries, now with tears,

you I have pursued even to your hell, poor sisters; I love you as much as I pity you, for your dull pains, your unappeased thirst, and the urns of love your great hearts hold.

[Comme un bétail pensif sur le sable couchées,
Elles tournent leurs yeux vers l'horizon des mers,
Et leurs pieds se cherchant et leurs mains rapprochées
Ont de douces langueurs et des frissons amers.

Les unes, cœurs épris des longues confidences,
Dans le fond des bosquets où jasent les ruisseaux,
Vont épelant l'amour des craintives enfances
Et creusent le bois vert des jeunes arbrisseaux;

D'autres, comme des sœurs, marchent lentes et graves
À travers les rochers pleins d'apparitions,
Où saint Antoine a vu surgir comme des laves
Les seins nus et pourprés de ses tentations;

Il en est, aux lueurs des résines croulantes,
Qui dans le creux muet des vieux antres païens
T'appellent au secours de leurs fièvres hurlantes,
Ô Bacchus, endormeur des remords anciens!

Et d'autres, dont la gorge aime les scapulaires,
Qui, recélant un fouet sous leurs longs vêtements,
Mêlent, dans le bois sombre et les nuits solitaires,
L'écume du plaisir aux larmes des tourments.

Ô vierges, ô démons, ô monstres, ô martyres,
De la réalité grands esprits contempteurs,
Chercheuses d'infini, dévotes et satyres,
Tantôt pleines de cris, tantôt pleines de pleurs,

Vous que dans votre enfer mon âme a poursuivies,
Pauvres sœurs, je vous aime autant que je vous plains,
Pour vos mornes douleurs, vos soifs inassouvies,
Et les urnes d'amour dont vos grands cœurs sont pleins!]

This poem is difficult to qualify and, in fact, appears to mediate between the contrasting visions offered by "Lesbos" and "Delphine et Hippolyte." It contains references to both an ancient deity (Bacchus) and a Christian saint (Saint Anthony). Closer to the spareness and dysphoria of "Delphine et Hippolyte," it nonetheless shares a kind of other-worldliness with "Lesbos," akin to the "nonhistorical past" that Leo Bersani identifies in "La Vie antérieure": "the deliberate unreality of the languid, voluptuous, [...] past" (30). Temporally unfixed, "Femmes damnées" is interested, like "Lesbos," in a community of women rather than the tête-à-tête of the Delphine and Hippolyte couple.

Indeed, one can read "Femmes damnées" as a poem that in a sense contains both of these two other contradictory poems and allows for their cohabitation: in essence, "Femmes damnées" *is* internally antithetic, a confrontation of polarized terms within the context of Baudelaire's sexual discourse. As such, it goes to the heart of Baudelaire's poetic practice, which negotiates between heaven and hell, good and evil, love and hate, masculine and feminine, and it works to explain such oppositions.

That is to say that "Femmes damnées" is *at least* double and, indeed, goes beyond dyads. One of the most marked grammatical traits of the poem is its preoccupation with plurality. Its rhymes are exclusively plural, as are most of its internal nouns, suggesting plenitude or excess. The poem reflects a concern for the group; its lesbians are seen as part of a class. Neither a window onto a contemporary homoerotic relationship ("Delphine et Hippolyte") nor a nostalgic return to the cradle of Sapphic poetry and lesbian love ("Lesbos"), "Femmes damnées" presents a timeless, floating landscape across which a multiplicity of female figures passes.

The poem's strict organization suggests an obsession with categorization, which serves to diversify the "femmes damnées" into clearly delineated subsets, signalled by a series of pronouns with which each of the four expository stanzas begins: "some," "others," "some there are," "and others." After the introductory stanza, these four central ones offer four renderings of the lesbians. The final two quatrains succinctly recapitulate the inventory presented in the body of the poem: "O virgins, O demons, O monsters, O martyrs." This line also enumerates figures prominent elsewhere in *Les Fleurs du Mal*: virgins ("À une madone"), demons ("La Destruction"), monsters ("Le Monstre"), and martyrs ("Une martyre"). And then comes a drive to an enigmatic conclusion, to which I will return below.

Baudelaire is almost Balzacian here, with his taxonomic interest in species and their variations. But in fact what we find are further examples of very Baudelairean antithesis, less interesting for their redundant clichés about lesbians than as an illustration of Baudelaire's aesthetic priorities. Based on stark contrasts, the four central stanzas offer vignettes that progress from youth to old age, from innocence to sordidness. The second stanza considers the category of virgins through a vocabulary of youthfulness: "timid childhood," "the green wood of young shrubs." Such idyllic associations are quickly lost in the third stanza, devoted to demons who wander across "rocks teeming with apparitions." The reference to Saint Anthony is ambiguous: are the "femmes damnées" meant to resemble the hermit, beset by temptation, or rather the apparitions that entice him? The fourth stanza resolves the uncertainty in favour of depraved monsters – "in the gleam of crumbling resins" – who beseech the Roman god Bacchus for forgetfulness. Finally, the fifth stanza returns to Christian imagery with martyrs "whose breasts take to scapulars." Baudelaire's inventory of "femmes damnées" ends with a conflation of pleasure seeking and self-punishment reminiscent of Diderot's nuns, who "mix the spume of pleasure with tears of torture."

This movement from blamelessness to decay, from clear day to dark night, from "green wood" to "dark woods," unfolds on a changing natural landscape in preposition-filled verses intent on fixing location. Indeed, the poem is nearly as obsessed with prepositions as it is with plurality, prepositions that serve to position Baudelaire's "femmes damnées" on various natural terrains: "deep in groves," "across the rocks," "in the mute hollow of antique pagan caves," "in dark woods."

Baudelaire's preposition of preference, *in* [*dans*], which is repeated four times in "Femmes damnées," focuses the poem on interiority and clandestinity. The language of the poem reinforces his prepositional insistence on concealment: "deep in," "carve out the green wood," "in the mute hollow," "antique pagan caves," "urns of love," "hiding a whip." It is replete with recesses, cavities, hollows, and repositories, forms that suggest surreptitiousness and, I would suggest, point to vaginal imagery. In the midst of temporal imprecision, then, Baudelaire's spatial specificity more often than not places the accursed women in hidden or obscure settings, far removed from cityscapes or others than their own kind. The lesbians that Baudelaire took pains to render visible are ultimately clandestine creatures, darkly hidden by the poem's language. The virgins are secreted away in hidden groves; the demons isolate themselves like Saint Anthony in uninhabited regions; the monsters hide away in the recesses of pagan caverns; and, finally, the martyrs take to the shadowy woods.

Indeed, although seemingly placing multitudes of lesbians before us, naming them, typing them, multiplying their kinds and their numbers, drawing back the branches to give us a glimpse or parading them across barren landscapes, at the same time Baudelaire represents them as hidden from view. Such concealment is consistent with Delphine and Hippolyte, who are sheltered from the outside world in close quarters: "Let our closed curtains shut us off from the world" [Que nos rideaux fermés nous séparent du monde]. Similarly, Sappho's lesbians are exiled on an island far from prying eyes: "drawn from us [...] glimpsed vaguely on the edge of other skies!" [loin de nous [...] / Entrevu vaguement au bord des autres cieux]. All these figures are shrouded in clandestinity.[40]

Of course, the theme of secrecy and mystery is a constant in sapphic literature, whether written by nineteenth-century men, from Balzac to Belot, or by twentieth-century women.[41] The hush-hush of lesbian love reinforces associations of shame and illicitness. But the play of concealment and revelation, in Baudelaire and elsewhere, also serves to heighten the voyeuristic erotic thrill. Pubescent girls surprised during their titillating games (Verlaine's "Pensionnaires") or filthy secrets revealed (naturalist writers' association of the lesbian and the prostitute): these are two poles of representation in sapphic literature from Baudelaire onward.

What, then, are the secrets of "Femmes damnées"? What does Baudelaire conceal under his poem's proliferation of lesbian types and the insistent plurality of its nouns? We might follow a lead from "À une madone," another poem evocative of inner spaces, in which the speaking subject expresses the desire to "carve out a niche [...] in the darkest corner of my heart" [creuser (une niche) dans le coin le plus noir de mon cœur]. That is to say, we might dig into the blackest corner of the heart of "Les femmes damnées" to uncover its hidden secrets. Here lies "the dark mystery," as the poet of "Lesbos" describes the sapphic condition, the darkness of the sexualized heart.

At the heart of "Femmes damnées," then, in its central fourth stanza, lies a curious image, which seems doubly to insist upon concealment: "in the mute hollow of antique pagan caves." Baudelaire places the lesbian monsters not simply in an old cavern, but within its silent hollow: a soundless hole within a hole. This quiet is striking after all the (often unintelligible) clamour emitted by the panoply of lesbians who "spell out their [...] love," "call to you for help," "now laden with cries, now with tears." When we peel away the noise and the numbers, at the centre of this poem there is a single crevice within a hollow: a total, final, soundless void.

Hearts are named twice within the poem. The first instance evokes girlish exchanges: "hearts smitten by long confidences." But the second occurrence, in the final line of the poem, is less transparent and, indeed, difficult to visualize: "the urns of love your great hearts hold." Antoine Adam's gloss on this line attributes its peculiarity to carelessness on the part of the poet. He invites the reader to "notice the incoherence of this metaphor, hearts full of an urn of love."[42] But rather than being incoherent, this image of hearts filled with a receptacle in fact mirrors the image we uncovered in the central stanza: a container of emptiness, or nothing within nothingness.

Baudelaire focuses on one organ here, the heart buried deep within his poem. But his images invite us to imagine a second organ as well: Baudelaire's heart of darkness looks strangely vaginal. Visual associations go to his contemporary, the painter Gustave Courbet, an admirer of Baudelaire and another lesbophile responsible for such sapphic representations as "Le Sommeil" and "Les Deux Amies" (pictured on the pocket edition of *Les Fleurs du Mal*, fig. 5.15). His "Origine du monde" captures, much more explicitly, the female sexual organs hidden at the poem's centre. Baudelaire's curiosity for female sexuality is covered in bushy undergrowth ("deep in groves"), concealed in the recesses of his poem ("in the mute hollow"), drowned out by noise, shrouded in lesbian secrets.

The phonetic texture of the poem likewise points to female genitalia: its proliferation of bilabial consonants [b, p, m] summons the doubling of lips through its sound structure. From start to finish, lips are joined to sound out the poem: /p/: "pensif, pieds, rapprochées, pleins d'apparitions, pourprés, païens, appellent, scapulaires, plaisir, pleines de pleurs, poursuivies, pauvres, plains"; /m/: "mers, mains, amers, amour, remords, larmes des tourments, démons, monstres, martyre, mon âme"; /b/: "bétail, sable, bosquets, arbrisseaux, Bacchus, bois sombre" – and, one might add, Baudelaire. I hasten to make clear that this is no claim for a proto-Irigarayan celebration of lips speaking together. Indeed, as we've already seen, these hollows are mute and cannot speak their name.

If woman is the hole, nothingness, the lesbian is doubly so. It is certainly not arbitrary that Baudelaire chose metaphorically to evoke female genitalia in a poem about lesbians, since women who bypass phallic sexuality are especially privy to the secrets of female sexuality. A text such as Alphonse Daudet's *Sapho* confirms this, since its title character, a primarily heterosexual courtesan, is nonetheless associated by her name with both lesbianism and sexual excess. The hypersexualized lesbian is to this day frequently represented as intensely feminine, as opposed to the desexualized mannish lesbian.

But there is clearly much more to Baudelaire's "Femmes damnées" than voyeurism and objectification of lesbian sexuality. In fact, the frame of the poem looks elsewhere and points to identification rather than to objectification. In the introductory, somewhat hallucinatory stanza and the final two, the speaking subject comes out to play and finds a point of contact with the subjects of his poem. In contrast with the game of hide-and-seek evident in the central four stanzas, where the poet leads us to obscure corners and dark crevices, here we find animalized women – perhaps reminiscent of Baudelaire's Belgian women – gathered in full sunlight, "lounging on the sand." Their horizon opens up completely: they "turn their eyes to the marine horizon." No longer secreted away, secluded, or veiled in obscurity, the "femmes damnées" are now defined by an insatiable thirst for the infinite. Named "pilgrims of infinity," they are closely associated with the work of the poet.

In fact, all three lesbian poems link these doomed women to the poetic act. Hippolyte, too, is represented as a visionary: "She looked [...] toward blue horizons." The speaking subject exhorts her, along with Delphine, to "flee the infinite that you carry within" [fuyez l'infini que vous portez en vous]. The infinity of the broadening horizon and infinity within both suggest the boundless expansion of the aesthetic quest, a sign of plenitude that coexists alongside evocations of emptiness. Emptiness, exile, social isolation, and ridicule are traits that also associate lesbianism with the well-worn poetic persona evident in such early poems as "Bénédiction" or "L'Albatros," which find the outcast poet spurned for his difference: "The Poet is like that prince of clouds [...] exiled to the ground, jeered on all sides" [Le Poète est semblable au prince des nuées / [...] / Exilé sur le sol au milieu des huées].

Moreover, Baudelaire identifies Lesbos as the cradle of lyric expression and, by extension, lesbians with the poetic act: Sappho is double, both "lover [amante] and poet." The male poet is drawn to the insatiability of lesbians, like him always thirsting, like him never full: "you I have pursued even to your hell." Baudelaire lets us know in "Lesbos" that he has been admitted into its secret: "For Lesbos chose me above any on earth to sing the secret of its flowering maidens." Looking for plenitude in emptiness and absence, his poems seem both predictably to associate femininity with lack and revel in an incompleteness defined as exile, solitude, castration, and sterility.

But it is in this very emptiness that Baudelaire finds lesbian distinction, in her barrenness that he locates her fullness. In his repugnance for feminine fecundity – "laden with the heredity of vicious motherhood and all the hideousness of fecundity!" [Du vice maternel traînant l'hérédité / Et toutes les hideurs de la fécondité!] – Baudelaire privileges lesbian sexuality, which he represents as being divorced from reproduction: "the ruthless sterility of your [sexual pleasure]" [L'âpre stérilité de votre jouissance]. Lesbian sterility also resonates in his poetic persona's repudiation of social convention, for he too is an "enemy of families." Anti-utilitarian, unnatural, free from the materiality of reproduction and childbirth, lesbians rise to a new status and acquire a female nobility that is rare in Baudelaire's work. In their repudiation of materiality and therefore of "reality" lies their greatness: they are "grand spirits disdainful of reality."

"Femmes damnées" ends in a jumble of contradictions: virgins and demons, monsters and martyrs, devotees and sirens, cries and tears. Baudelaire seems to offer the lesbian as the antithetical image par excellence: full and empty, devoted to a cult and yet debauched, wild both with passion and with anguish, hypersexualized but barren, overwrought and under-satisfied, a manly woman and the emblem of female sexuality.

This modulation between incompleteness and grandeur, between nothingness and plenitude, is particularly apparent in the closing stanzas of "Femmes damnées," where the adjective *plein* (full) appears three times, recalling the plurality of the rhymes and the multiplicity they suggest. Its final line, worth quoting again, links vaginal emptiness to a full heart: "the urns of love your great hearts hold." Elsewhere in *Les Fleurs du Mal* Baudelaire represents the heart as a container. More than once described as an abyss [abîme], it also becomes a hole within a hole, falling into a "dark pit" [gouffre obscur]. "In my heart" is also an oft-repeated phrase, and within this heart lies a multitude of things: tears, funereal images, temples, ardour, and so forth. "Le cœur plein," the full heart, is common enough as well, sometimes full of light but more often of dreams of death. But it is only in the poetic lesbian heart that fullness and emptiness come together.

A look at the concordance is instructive about Baudelairean hearts and helpful in teasing out the importance of female homoeroticism in his work. It shows that throughout *Les Fleurs du Mal,* hearts are remarkably fragile and usually associated with violence. This list samples the adjectives used to describe the many hearts that appear in his poetry: *torn out, swollen, gnawed upon, drunken, withered, irritated, frightened, drowned, bleeding, cursed* [*arraché, gonflé, rongé, enivré, flétri, irrité, effrayé, noyé, saignant, maudit*]. Among the many brutal associations to the wounded heart, let us note one in particular: that of violent penetration. Satan instils "the cult of sores [...] in the hearts of whores" [le culte de la plaie [...] dans le cœur des filles] ("Litanies"). Knives enter, and the heart – a "target" – bleeds: "You who, like a knife, entered my groaning heart" [Toi qui, comme un coup de couteau, / Dans mon cœur plaintif es entrée] ("Le Vampire"). The hemorrhaging vaginal heart is a violated one; it does the poetic work of explaining the fragile male lover of *Les Fleurs du Mal.*

Alongside the preponderance of images of tender, afflicted hearts we find much rarer images of an *afflicting* heart: "a heart of snow," "indifferent hearts" [un cœur de neige, les cœurs indifférents]. Indifferent or frozen, it is a synecdoche for the cold, castrating heterosexual woman, typically heartless and cruel to the masculine speaking subject, who nonetheless seeks her out: "I cherish [...] that coldness that makes you more beautiful" [Je chéris [...] cette froideur par où tu m'es plus belle] ("Je t'adore ..."). Barbara Johnson has unveiled the masculine masochism pervasive in Baudelaire's work, in such poems as "Le Vampire," suggesting that "In Baudelaire's anatomy of ambivalence, the part of phallic torturer is played by a female figure" (174).

The Baudelairean heart, a fragile, hemorrhaging organ, is indeed the target of rampaging femininity, and in the heterosexual poems the male victim is feminized by this brutality. The importance of the lesbian poems lies in their ability to unite in one figure the female victim (who gives rise to scorn and derision) and the feminine predator (a model for acts of violation). As such, they serve as a stand-in for the poet and recast the wounded male heart as violated female sexual organs. Annihilation of the other and self-destruction, "the wound and the knife" [la plaie et le couteau], plenitude and nothingness: this is the sublime unity of the *femme damnée*, and the founding contradiction of Baudelaire's poetic quest.

The Lesbianization of Paul Verlaine

… soyons deux jeunes filles …

(Verlaine, "Ariette oubliée")

Paul Verlaine – poet and prisoner, savage and voluptuary, abusive husband and scandalous lover of young men, devout Catholic and addled absinthe devotee, homeless wanderer and aging doyen of decadents – produced a body of work whose incongruities mirrored his dishevelled life. Author of an influential series of portraits of "accursed poets" (*Les Poètes maudits*) and erotic poems, he also produced religious verse and delicate refrains. Much of the force of his work emanates from the attempt to reconcile these fluctuations. Innocence and lust, masculine and feminine, delicacy and obscenity, among other contradictions, all provided fodder for his representations of sexuality and informed his pendular poetic practice. Verlaine's investment in sapphism, in addition to its aesthetic import, was much more immediate than Baudelaire's. Instead of shying away from male homoeroticism, he looked for socially acceptable codes with which to express it.

Verlaine's corpus covers a broad sexual spectrum. It includes heterosexual poems, representations of both male and female homoeroticism, and a handful of poems in which the genders of subject and object are unclear. His erotic triptych – *Les Amies*, *Filles*, and *Hombres*, each collection devoted to a differently configured couple – is indicative of the pansexuality of his œuvre. While I will focus on Verlaine's lesbian poems, it is illuminating to note the differing intersubjective models proposed by these three cycles. I will explore below the often objectifying and distanced observer in *Les Amies*, a primarily third-person voyeur. The speaking subject in *Filles*, Verlaine's homage to prostitutes, is perhaps equally objectifying, but actively implicated in the first-person voice ("Brunette, whom I have yet to have, I want to have you nearly nude" [Brune encore non eue, / Je te veux presque nue]).[43] While *Hombres* also privileges specular appreciation, which leads to reification ("Let's admire this splendid body" [Admirons cette chair splendide]), the relationship between speaking subject and erotic partner retains a certain reciprocity, a "care for pleasing and being pleased" [souci de se plaire et de plaire].[44]

Verlaine was nourished on Baudelaire's poetry: his first collection, *Poèmes saturniens* (1866), owes a great deal to Baudelairean spleen. The young Verlaine also followed Baudelaire's sapphic example. *Les Amies* (1867), his second collection, is a series of six sonnets, most featuring titillating encounters between young women. It was first published in Belgium by Baudelaire's publisher, Auguste Poulet-Malassis, under the name Pablo de Herlagnez, in order to avoid the French censors. It is Verlaine's earliest and most explicit foray into sapphic poetry, to be included much later in his collection *Parallèlement* (1889).

Significantly, the poems in this series are written in exclusively feminine rhymes, a startling break from prosodic convention, which until Verlaine's innovations consistently alternated "masculine" and "feminine" rhymes. The latter are composed of words ending in a silent *e* or *es*, as opposed to all other rhymes, classified as masculine. These seemingly arbitrary designations are rooted in archaic pronunciation practices and had thus been a merely formal distinction for centuries.[45] Historically, the gender of rhymes is unrelated to the condition of being male or female, and in fact has little to do even with grammatical gender. A feminine rhyme could very well join a grammatically masculine word (such as *un idiome*) with a grammatically feminine word (*une pomme*), or even two words that are both grammatically (and even semantically) masculine: *idiome/homme*. With these sonnets, Verlaine both jolts his contemporary readers with his iconoclastic prosody and infuses unmotivated rhyme gender with intimations of biological sex: the masculine is evacuated and the feminine vividly, exclusively present.

The poems focus on the young women's appearance, in particular on their complementarity. They are alike, but with distinguishing traits: "One at fifteen, the other at sixteen years"; "One pale with hair of jet, the other pink / And blond").[46] The décor is dominated by beds and mystical evening darkness ("The dishevelled Bed, opening in shadow," "mysterious, indolent shadows"), and the sinuous, translucent fabrics of their clothing and bed curtains ("long curtains of white muslin") that invite prying eyes.

Although these sonnets are partial to the visual, they are also interested in orality, more specifically in cunnilingus: "In frenzied tumult where her mouth yet yearned, / Dove into blond filigree to discover shadowed grey"; "Let me, among the bright leaves of grass, / Drink of the tiny drops of dew." But they move beyond simple curiosa and suggest an empathetic interest in sapphic sexual difference. The young women of *Les Amies* are both sensual and pitiable, lusty and noble. And beyond the voyeurism of this sonnet series lies a quest for verbal orality, for a voice. Its architecture reveals a movement from objectification to something resembling compassion for suffering. The sonnets' progression from longer to shorter metres coincides with this evolution in voice, and the final sonnet, which stages Sappho's suicide, is clearly distinguishable from the erotic content of the first five.

On the Balcony

They both watched butterflies rise in flight:
One pale with hair of jet, the other pink
And blond, their light lace peignoirs waves
Undulating, as clouds might, round them.

And both, with the asphodel's languor,
While the heavens lifted a soft, round moon,
Savoured long draughts of evening's deep
Feeling, and the wan joy of true hearts.

Thus, arms pressing close and moist their supple waists,
Strange couple in sympathy with other couples,
Thus, on the balcony the young women in reverie.

Behind them, in the dark deeps of their sumptuous lair,
Grand as a melodrama's throne and full of scent,
The dishevelled Bed, opening in shadow.

[Sur le Balcon

Toutes deux regardaient s'enfuir les hirondelles:
L'une pâle aux cheveux de jais, et l'autre blonde
Et rose, et leurs peignoirs légers de vieille blonde
Vaguement serpentaient, nuages, autour d'elles.

Et toutes deux, avec des langueurs d'asphodèles,
Tandis qu'au ciel montait la lune molle et ronde,
Savouraient à longs traits l'émotion profonde
Du soir et le bonheur triste des cœurs fidèles.

Telles, leurs bras pressant, moites, leurs tailles souples,
Couple étrange qui prend pitié des autres couples,
Telles, sur le balcon, rêvaient les jeunes femmes.

Derrière elles, au fond du retrait riche et sombre,
Emphatique comme un trône de mélodrames
Et plein d'odeurs, le Lit, défait, s'ouvrait dans l'ombre.]

Boarding-School Girls

One at fifteen, the other at sixteen years;
They both slept in the same room.
It was on a ripe and humid September's eve:
Delicate and blue-eyed, a strawberry's blush,

Each, for her comfort, had pulled off
Her thin blouse, with a scent of amber.
The younger's arms held out in gentle camber,
And her sister, touching her breasts, kissed her,

Then fell on her knees, wildly turned
In frenzied tumult where her mouth yet yearned,
Dove into blond filigree to discover shadowed grey;

And all the while, the child counted up
On adorable fingers the promised waltzes,
And, in blushing innocence, smiled.

[**Pensionnaires**

L'une avait quinze ans, l'autre en avait seize;
Toutes deux dormaient dans la même chambre.
C'était par un soir très lourd de septembre:
Frêles, des yeux bleus, des rougeurs de fraise.

Chacune a quitté, pour se mettre à l'aise,
La fine chemise au frais parfum d'ambre.
La plus jeune étend les bras, et se cambre,
Et sa sœur, les mains sur ses seins, la baise,

Puis tombe à genoux, puis devient farouche
Et tumultueuse et folle, et sa bouche
Plonge sous l'or blond, dans les ombres grises;

Et l'enfant, pendant ce temps-là, recense
Sur ses doigts mignons des valses promises,
Et, rose, sourit avec innocence.]

The first two, most objectifying sonnets are in the third person, allowing no possibility of interaction with the figures they describe. The first in alexandrines (twelve-syllable lines) and the second in decasyllables, they form a pair that represents a chronologically inverted love scene. “On the Balcony” begins with an afterglow and ends with a visual recollection of lovemaking (“the dishevelled Bed”), while “Boarding-School Girls” moves from a sleeping scene to a sexual encounter. They are scantily dressed (“their light lace peignoirs”) or not at all (“Each, for her comfort, had pulled off / Her thin blouse”). The retracted curtains unveil intimate acts: “And her sister, touching her breasts, kissed her, / Then fell on her knees, wildly turned / In frenzied tumult where her mouth yet yearned.”

Per Amica Silentia

The long curtains of white muslin
Undulating in an opaline wave
By the nightlight’s pallid gleam
In mysterious, indolent shadows,

The full drapes of Adeline’s high bed
Have heard, Claire, your laughing voice,
Your silvery, sweet, seductive voice
Shot through with another, stormy.

“To love, to love!” they said, entwined,
Claire and Adeline, adorable victims
Of the noble promise of your sublime souls.

Love, then, oh love! dear Isolate Girls,
For in these days of misery, yet and still,
The glorious stigmata anoint you.

[***Per amica silentia***

Les longs rideaux de blanche mousseline
Que la lueur pâle de la veilleuse
Fait fluer comme une vague opaline
Dans l’ombre mollement mystérieuse,

Les grands rideaux du grand lit d’Adeline
Ont entendu, Claire, ta voix rieuse,
Ta douce voix argentine et câline
Qu’une autre voix enlace, furieuse.

"Aimons, aimons!" disaient vos voix mêlées,
Claire, Adeline, adorables victimes
Du noble vœu de vos âmes sublimes.

Aimez, aimez! ô chères Esseulées,
Puisqu'en ces jours de malheur, vous encore,
Le glorieux Stigmate vous décore.]

"Per Amica Silentia," written in decasyllables, speaks directly to the couple and is less sexually explicit. The poem opens with a scene similar to those described in the preceding two, in the softly lit evening on an inviting, curtained bed. But instead of interlacing limbs, the reader hears the speaking subject directly addressing the couple as their voices commingle: "your laughing voice, / Your silvery, sweet, seductive voice / Shot through with another, stormy." Despite the silence evoked in the title, the lovers briefly employ the first-person plural so rare in heterosexual love poetry of the period: "'[Let's love, let's love!' they said, entwined." And the speaker is admiring of them: "adorable victims / Of the noble promise of your sublime souls." Echoing their words, he exhorts and emboldens them: "Love, then, oh love! dear Isolate Girls, / For in these days of misery, yet and still, / The glorious stigmata anoint you." The incongruously plural "Isolate Girls" [Esseulées] places them, like Baudelaire's "femmes damnées," on the social margins. They suffer in their difference ("days of misery"), yet are glorified by their commitment ("the noble promise of your sublime souls") to their non-reproductive sexuality, seen as a nearly religious sacrifice of social integration and familial inheritance. Calling female homosexuality a "ritual" in the final poem, here Verlaine compares their social stigma to the crucified Christ's stigmata. He has confounded his readers' expectations for another arousing scene, and delivers instead a vindication for and sacralization of homosexuality.

Spring

Gently the red-head,
Excited by such innocence,
Says to the younger fair-haired girl
These words, in a soft, sweet tone,

"Sap that rises, bloom coming into its own,
Your childhood is an arbour:

Let my fingers roam in the carrageen
Where the rosy button flowers,

"Let me, among the bright leaves of grass,
Drink of the tiny drops of dew
Sprinkled upon this tender blossom –

"Until, my dear, delight illumines
Your spotless brow anew,
As dawn the sky of timid blue."

[**Printemps**

Tendre, la jeune femme rousse,
Que tant d'innocence émoustille,
Dit à la blonde jeune fille
Ces mots, tout bas, d'une voix douce:

"Sève qui monte et fleur qui pousse,
Ton enfance est une charmille:
Laisse errer mes doigts dans la mousse
Où le bouton de rose brille,

"Laisse-moi, parmi l'herbe claire,
Boire les gouttes de rosée
Dont la fleur tendre est arrosée, –

"Afin que le plaisir, ma chère,
Illumine ton front candide
Comme l'aube l'azur timide."]

Summer

And the child answers all aswoon
Beneath the urgent wet caress
Of her breathless mistress:
"I'm dying O my dearest!"

"I die: Your flaming, unrelenting
Breast intoxicates and presses close
Your vivid flesh, a strangely scented
Drunkenness released.

"It has, your flesh, the somber charms
Of summer's ripeness –
The amber of it, its umber hue,

"Your voice sounds clear in the blast,
And your blood-red hair
Flees suddenly in night's slow fall."

[**Été**

Et l'enfant répondit, pâmée
Sous la fourmillante caresse
De sa pantelante maîtresse:
"Je me meurs, ô ma bien-aimée!

"Je me meurs; ta gorge enflammée
Et lourde me soûle et m'oppresse;
Ta forte chair d'où sort l'ivresse
Est étrangement parfumée;

"Elle a, ta chair, le charme sombre
Des maturités estivales, –
Elle en a l'ambre, elle en a l'ombre;

"Ta voix tonne dans les rafales,
Et ta chevelure sanglante
Fuit brusquement dans la nuit lente."]

"Spring" and "Summer" form another narrative pair, this one shortening to octosyllabic lines, in which each lover is given her turn to speak: in "Spring," a woman expresses her desire for the innocent and spring-like "fair-haired girl," who in "Summer" responds in kind to her intimate partner, a redhead in her sexual prime ("summer's ripeness"). While these poems return to the voyeurism of the first two, it is pertinent to note that, like "Per Amica Silentia," they again linger on voices, now rising in volume, from "These words, in a soft, sweet tone" ("Spring") to "Your voice sounds clear in the blast" ("Summer"). The arc of the series presents the increasing use of the lesbian first person, albeit in quotations, which coincides with a progressive thinning of the sonnets through the shortening of its metres: a visual diminuendo overlapped by a crescendo of voices.

Sappho

Frenzied, hollow-eyed and stern of breast,
Sappho, troubled by languorous desire,
Like a she-wolf, she tracks cold furrows,

She dreams of Phaon, forgetting all Ritual,
And, just then seeing her tears disdained,
Tears out her hair in huge handfuls;

In remorse unassuaged, she then recalls
Those times when shone so pure the youthful glory
Of her loves, sung in verse that soul's memory
Will murmur soft to virgins as they sleep:

And see now she lowers her sallow lids
And leaps into the sea where her Fate calls her –
While, in the skies, igniting the black water, bursts
Pale Selene who avenges girlish Loves.

[Sappho

Furieuse, les yeux caves et les seins roides,
Sappho, que la langueur de son désir irrite,
Comme une louve court le long des grèves froides,

Elle songe à Phaon, oublieuse du Rite,
Et, voyant à ce point ses larmes dédaignées,
Arrache ses cheveux immenses par poignées;

Puis elle évoque, en des remords sans accalmies,
Ces temps où rayonnait, pure, la jeune gloire
De ses amours chantés en vers que la mémoire
De l'âme va redire aux vierges endormies:

Et voilà qu'elle abat ses paupières blêmies
Et saute dans la mer où l'appelle la Moire, –
Tandis qu'au ciel éclate, incendiant l'eau noire,
La pâle Séléné qui venge les Amies.]

Ultimately, these poems are more invested in looking than in listening. The final sonnet gives its reader a cold shower in a number of ways: tragic rather than erotic, ancient rather than atemporal or modern in setting, it breaks the visual rhythm of the preceding five with its return to alexandrines and inverted form: a visual confirmation of Sappho's return to men. Ironically, Verlaine applies the trope of inversion, which contemporaries used to label homosexuality, to heterosexuality. Sappho, having forsaken other women ("forgetting all Ritual"), kills herself for love of Phaon, yet remains remorseful for the loss of what Verlaine presents as idealized love between women: "Those times when shone so pure the youthful glory / Of her loves, sung in verse." Disidentified with homoeroticism, Sappho dies, and yet the sonnet ends with the moon goddess's promise of succour, "Pale Selene who avenges girlish Loves."

These youthful poems, while veiled in gauzy descriptions inspired by the sapphic fad, already exhibited a certain affinity with their subjects, encompassing Baudelaire's appreciation of their poetic worth and tragic nobility. Verlaine's insight into homoeroticism would soon be deepened in a manner both material and literary by virtue of his relationship with Rimbaud. *Romances sans paroles* (1874) followed their meeting, and it bears the traces of their physical as well as poetic partnership. Ethereal and impressionistic, the poems of *Romances* do not name, as the titular reference to wordlessness suggests, so much as evoke their subjects. This collection, nuanced and innovative, contains the seeds of what Mallarmé claimed almost two decades later to be pioneering about symbolist poetry: "To *name* an object is to take away three-quarters of the pleasure of a poem, which comes from deducing it bit by bit: to *suggest* it, now that's ideal."[47]

"Ariette oubliée" IV of *Romances* accomplishes just this. While less explicit than *Les Amies*, it invokes female homoeroticism as a cover, I would suggest, for male homoeroticism:

You see, we have to be forgiven things;
This way happiness lies,
And if our life goes through gloomy times,
Why then, we'll be a pair of snivellers.

How good if our twin souls could blend
Vague desires with the infantile joy
Of walking free of women and men,
Backs turned on persecutors.

Let's be children, let's be two young girls
Free as air and full of wonder,
Who grow pale in simple groves of trees,
Not knowing even that they've been forgiven.

[Il faut, voyez-vous, nous pardonner les choses:
De cette façon nous serons bien heureuses
Et si notre vie a des instants moroses,
Du moins nous serons, n'est-ce pas? deux pleureuses.

Ô que nous mêlions, âmes sœurs que nous sommes,
À nos vœux confus la douceur puérile
De cheminer loin des femmes et des hommes,
Dans le frais oubli de ce qui nous exile!

Soyons deux enfants, soyons deux jeunes filles
Éprises de rien et de tout étonnées
Qui s'en vont pâlir sous les chastes charmilles
Sans même savoir qu'elles sont pardonnées.][48]

A self-described "feminine" poet – "je suis un féminin" – (and arguably model for the "foolish virgin" of Rimbaud's *Season in Hell*), Verlaine offers with this poem his most thoroughgoing identifications with femininity.[49] Like the sonnets of *Les Amies*, it is exclusively feminine in its rhymes, which Christine Planté has fittingly called "homosexual rhymes." Moreover, it employs the uncommon hendecasyllabic (eleven-syllable) metre, which is also referred to as the sapphic metre for the line employed by the Greek poet. Verlaine's use of it also references romantic poet Marceline Desbordes-Valmore, who resurrected it earlier in the century, and whom Verlaine discovered with Rimbaud.[50]

Written in the first-person feminine plural, "Ariette oubliée" IV offers a vision of reciprocity more akin to *Hombres*, even though, in comparison to the candid eroticism of *Hombres*, the couple's childlike innocence ("the infantile joy," "let's be two young girls") renders it seemingly sexless. And yet the poem suggests a fault with the insistence on pardon with which it opens and closes. While much remains elliptical – what is to be pardoned, the reason for their exile – it is the poem's very elusiveness that provides the answer. Baudelaire's forgiving "Lesbos" offers an intertext and a key. Coded prosodically as homosexual, "Ariette oubliée" IV can be read as an implicit reference to a same-sex couple. The fault ("things"), the girls' distress ("gloomy times"), their imprecise vows ("vague desires" [vœux confus]), and their common banishment also echo the language of *Les Amies*, whose exiled "Isolate Girls" make a "noble promise" and suffer in kind ("these days of misery").

The poem echoes, moreover, the unspoken commitments and social rejection of same-sex couples. Their isolation and distance from heterosexuality ("walking free [loin] of women and men") and their search for different ways of and places for living ("backs turned on persecutors" [dans le frais oubli de ce qui nous exile], "in simple groves of trees" [sous les chastes charmilles] – recalling "your childhood is an arbour" [charmille] of "Printemps") suggest the search for new, yet-to-be-located existential models. This is Verlaine's version of Rimbaud's oft-cited exhortation that "love must be reinvented." The use of the female first-person plural veils a homosexual love poem in which innocence, evocative of youth, is above all indicative of blamelessness. Ultimately, these bewildered playmates suggest lesbianism as a cipher for male homosexuality.

Verlaine returns to the ancient poet in *Parallèlement*, a collection notable for its polysexuality. In addition to *Les Amies*, it includes *Filles* and poems of both male and female homoeroticism. The title of the collection can be read as a reference to loves parallel to or outside of the norm. It opens and closes with lesbian poems, from *Les Amies* to "Ballade Sappho." The latter is in a lighter vein than the "Sappho" of *Les Amies*. A startling poem for the sapphicization of its male speaking subject, it suggests an identification with a lesbian Sappho in a seemingly heterosexual context: "Je suis pareil à la grande Sappho" is its refrain. Verlaine's poem recalls Baudelaire's description in "Lesbos" of Sappho as both female lover and poet ("la mâle Sapho, l'amante et le poète"). And yet while Baudelaire presents as speaking subject a male poet *annointed* by Sappho ("For Lesbos chose me above any on earth to sing the secret of its flowering maidens"), Verlaine's "I" *identifies* with the female lover of women as well as with the poet. The poem's adjectives establish the speaking subject's maleness, and yet he nonetheless refuses strict gender assignment ("Prince or princess") or sexual identity. He speaks of his desire to please his female lover as a woman or a man: his "gentle hand" might belong to either ("Ma douce main de maîtresse et d'amant"). The poem describes oral sex using language similar to that found in *Les Amies*: "Let my roving head lose itself in a wild and aimless quest for shadowy scents, a dreamy effort toward the sweet taste of your secret glory" [Laisse ma tête errant et s'abîmant / À l'aventure, un peu farouche, en quête / D'ombre et d'odeur et d'un travail charmant / Vers les saveurs de ta gloire secrète]. But his body is clearly male: "Your skin pressed against my athletic body, which grows taut and, at intervals, softens" [Toute ta chair contre mon corps d'athlète / Qui se bande et s'amollit par moment]. The poem is particularly attuned to the other's pleasure: "My hand steals laughingly over your dear and joyous body, laughing and delighting in its delight. You know it was made to serve you" [Ma main … / Passe et rit sur ta chère chair en fête, / Rit et jouit de ton jouissement. / Pour la servir tu sais bien qu'elle est faite]. With its direct address and search for reciprocal pleasure, "Ballade Sappho" places the male speaking subject in a sapphic body, just as "Ariette oubliée" IV provided a lesbian voice for the omnisexual Verlaine.

As these poems suggest, Verlaine's engagement with female subjects and lesbian figures varies from youthful emulation of Baudelaire's precedent to erotic exploration and the attempt to find new models for as-yet-unrepresented sexualities. A poem like "Ariette oubliée" IV presents an identification with female homosexuality and a representation of same-sex love rendered in a form acceptable to – even marketed by – literary men. Verlaine's impressionism and ambiguity, his deliberate equivocations between masculine and feminine, between heterosexuality and homosexuality, suggest a queer poetics *avant la lettre*.

With a view to dissecting and understanding moments of male identification with female homosexuality, poetry written during the second half of the nineteenth century offers a particularly fertile terrain of inquiry. Vastly different from consistently objectifying prose texts, the poems studied here nonetheless remain largely projective or transitory in their identifications. Baudelaire tried on and cast off identities in order to flirt with femininity and, at the same time, remain clear of male love objects, while Verlaine perhaps did so as a cover for expressions of love between men. Although homosexuality was less central to Baudelaire's interest in sapphism than Verlaine's, to a certain extent their enactment of it was propelled by homophobia, whether imposed by the culture or the poet's own. But we find here as well an identification with Sappho, masculine and feminine, homosexual and heterosexual and, above all, the idealized pre-modern poet and mythic figure who offered and permitted a fluid array of subject positions.

Is identification with lesbian subjectivity possible when the author is male and when lesbianism does not yet exist as a consolidated identity? When the nature of self-perception is often fluid, something taken on or invented, evolving or subsequently abandoned? Perhaps not. But even attempts to do so are profoundly significant for the representations they produce, which in turn become models for women in search of images that reflect their own invisible lives and unarticulated sentiments. Indeed, male authors who toy with lesbian voices offer prototypes to their readers and to younger poets; the impact of their texts on subsequent identifications by women is a subject to which I will return in the final chapter.

2 Tribades for Sale: Popular Fiction and Backroom Books

Tribade: from the Greek word *tribas*, meaning Sapphist, which derives from the verb *tribein*, to rub.

(Taxil, *La Corruption fin-de-siècle*)

The 1870 publication of Adolphe Belot's serial novel *Mademoiselle Giraud, ma femme*, which relates the story of a man who unwittingly marries a tribade, was a watershed event in the history of the sapphic novel. A scandalous success that went through forty-five editions in five years, it was translated into several languages and forever linked Belot's name with lesbian plots. *Mademoiselle Giraud* both inaugurated a wave of novels representing female homosexuals and anticipated the psychiatric discussions of homosexuality soon to follow. Although forgotten by the turn of the century, the novel's immediate cultural import was felt in France and beyond, becoming, like *La Religieuse*, *Mademoiselle de Maupin*, and *La Fille aux yeux d'or* before it, a point of reference for later sapphic fictions. Never destined for canonization, Belot is exemplary of the uses to which popular writers put lesbian plots in order to attract readers and sell copy.

Most of Belot's readers were unaware that alongside his many fast-selling titles, he authored and anonymously published a number of erotic novels, directed at an entirely different audience, that also featured female homosexuality. The juxtaposition of these two bodies of work, the popular and the pornographic, brings to light some glaring incongruities and illustrates to what extent the moral tenor of Belot's work was shaped by the diametrically opposed contexts in which he wrote and published. On one hand, the judgmental discourse of the widely available popular novel, generally assumed by critics to be directed to women readers, condemned same-sex intimacy using euphemistic language. Belot's clandestine erotica, on the other hand, was geared towards a male audience and celebrated explicitly recounted sex acts between women.

The popular novel prescribed conventional sexuality for women, while erotic literature served up a lesbian bacchanal to men.

But were these polarities so consciously intended and so strictly observed? And what did such dissimilar incarnations of the female homosexual imply? These contradictions raise a number of issues about Belot's contribution to the chain of sapphic fiction and the production of lesbian identities. His inconsistent investment in the figure, which involved such disparate elements as sexual curiosity and careerism, belies a rigidly ideological agenda. It points instead to a nexus of sociological, commercial, and literary historical factors whose analysis sheds light on the uses of lesbian plots in non-canonical literature, on the relationship between reading and gender, and on the sexual politics of literary genre.

Print Culture: Adolphe Belot, the Literary Field, and the Rise of the Sapphic Novel

The nineteenth century witnessed significant changes in print technologies and the demographics of literacy, which effectively revolutionized the production, diffusion, and consumption of printed matter.[1] Popular fiction and serial novels played pivotal roles in the establishment of a mass print culture, the vehicle for the dissemination of the lesbian novel.

Thanks to advances in paper-making and print production, the number of newspapers and books in circulation expanded considerably and their price dropped, thus making them accessible to new populations of readers. While colportage (book peddling) waned, the proliferation of bookstores, libraries, and kiosks satisfied the demand for more efficient means of distribution. A growing railway network facilitated the transportation of books and papers to the provinces, and train stations created additional points of sale (in 1853, the publishing house Hachette inaugurated the *roman de gare*, novels sold at train stations). France was becoming a nation of readers who came from all walks of life and were drawn to a broadening array of novelistic genres, be they sentimental or suspenseful, sensational or salacious.

As inexpensive collections and series multiplied, so did newspapers, which since the early century had increasingly exploited serial novels to attract larger audiences and boost sales. The rise of the popular novel is typically associated with the birth of the feuilleton, which dates to 1836, when Émile de Girardin brought out his newspaper *La Presse* at half the price of previous dailies.[2] The *roman-feuilleton*, or serial novel, functioned as a lure to attract readers, with serialized fictions by authors such as Balzac, Eugène Sue, and Alexandre Dumas *père* contributing to the growth of the daily press. Other new modes of diffusion allowed novels to reach still more readers, including weeklies, journals sold in installments, and inexpensive editions that came to be known as *romans à quatre sous* (penny novels).

The readership of newspapers grew exponentially over the course of the century. Bowing to government censorship, in 1863 the daily *Le Petit Journal* stifled political coverage in favour of entertaining *faits divers* (sensational news items) and serial novels. With this new format and at an even lower price, circulation continued to rise. At the same time, democratization and education reform significantly increased in literacy rates, first among the bourgeoisie, then the working class, and increasingly among women.[3] The Falloux law (1850) allowed public education for girls and, shortly after elections that shifted France's political landscape to the left, the Sée (1880) and Ferry (1881–2) laws mandated public, non-religious schooling in secondary and primary education, respectively. Like the press itself, the *roman-feuilleton* continued to evolve with the expansion of its readership, and new popular genres such as the *roman de mœurs parisiennes* (novel of Parisian manners), *roman scientifique*, and the *roman policier* (detective novel) came into being.

The feuilleton was responsible for a new industry of writers, new genres, and a new approach to reading. Although serial novelists were increasingly dismissed as hacks, most nineteenth-century writers now considered canonical initially published their works serially in newspapers or journals: writers from all points on the spectrum of high to low depended upon the feuilleton to attract a broad audience. Those associated with realism and the naturalist school were themselves ambivalent about appearing in the mass press, but they nonetheless profited from it as they did from contacts with commercial writers such as Adolphe Belot: "The attitude of naturalist novelists in relation to the feuilleton is divided. On one hand, they rely on it to circulate their own works (in search of sales and readers); all of Zola's work appeared in feuilletons. […] On the other hand, they criticize and reject successful serial novels written by 'storytellers' in the name of a higher aesthetic."[4] Belot numbered among such "storytellers" who wrote for the consumption of the greatest number of readers. His work fulfils this succinct definition of popular fiction: "novelistic production that combines public success with the symbolic relegation to lowly genres."[5] Belot's novels are also largely consistent with the more elaborate description offered by a historian of the popular novel, Yves Olivier-Martin, who defines it as a melodramatic, often sensationalist genre, moralistic in tone, directed towards and reflecting the preoccupations of the petite bourgeoisie, of the newly emerging literate working class, and in particular of women readers. Olivier-Martin describes the popular novel as a reassuring genre that upholds bourgeois values with plots designed to defuse dangers to the status quo. Belot's novels tend to be formulaic and have stock characters, such as the lesbian seducer, her victim, and a hero who acts to re-establish socio-sexual equilibrium. They function in a simplistic moral universe in which good triumphs over evil; indeed, sexual evil is punished in nearly all of Belot's novels: his tribades go insane, die of disease, or are murdered with the blessing of all concerned.

Following Belot, many other authors grasped the financial possibilities of sapphic plotlines and went to work composing their own, quickly consumed and most as quickly forgotten.[6] In addition to the foundational nature of *Mademoiselle Giraud*, Belot's eager pursuit of profitable venues and bankable story lines render him a consummate case study.[7]

While celebrated during his lifetime, Adolphe Belot is poorly known today. He was born in 1829 into a banking family in Pointe-à-Pitre, Guadeloupe, and became so famous that upon his death in 1890, his obituary appeared on the front page of the leading daily, *Le Figaro*. As a young man, he studied law in Paris and passed the bar in Nancy, but soon abandoned the law to write. He published his first novel in 1855, a year after becoming a lawyer. Belot's second profession as a man of letters relied on a skill associated with his first: the ability to size up an audience and manipulate it rhetorically. In the words of a contemporary, Belot knew how to "captivate the crowd."[8] A man of impressive entrepreneurial capabilities and a facility with the pen, his success depended upon the ability to anticipate the desires of his readers and to satisfy them with judiciously chosen plotlines.

Accounts by Belot's contemporaries and in recent studies point to his opportunist investment in the literary field. One critic has called him "a precursor of literary marketing" and noted that Belot's manoeuvring is reflected in his own fiction: "In *Le Drame de la rue de la Paix*, he has his protagonist, Dumouche, say 'I want to write novels, serial novels, legal thrillers (*romans judiciaires*). This type of literature is in vogue right now. These are the kinds of titles that appear in newspapers below the fold.'"[9] (Daily instalments of serial novels generally began in a band across the bottom of the first page.) An American reviewer at the turn of the twentieth century caustically labelled Belot an "enervating disciple of commercial lubricity."[10] Value judgments aside, Belot was incontestably adept at choosing topics that already held an avid public interest and at painting his novels with the brush of fashion while spinning a captivating tale. He selected material for maximum impact by drawing on already sensational stories either "ripped from the headlines" or borrowed from other writers. Contemporary references supply one of the most interesting aspects of Belot's fiction: his work contains a gold mine of ephemeral detail about cultural trends and events and is richly indicative of what captured the public's imagination during most of the Second Empire and the first two decades of the Third Republic. He gleaned lucrative material from a number of sources, including new laws that altered

France's social landscape, inventions and medical breakthroughs, and, of course, newspapers. According to contemporary accounts, female homosexuality was an increasingly visible part of this landscape, and by introducing it as a leitmotif in his work, Belot helped render it even more prominent.

Alphonsine (1887) is illustrative, providing several examples of Belot's ability to capitalize on current debates and topical subjects including, but not limited to, sapphism. The novel tells the story of an aspiring young actress, kept by an older and more established woman, who is arrested for murdering a wealthy man under mysterious circumstances. Its plot development relies on the controversial subject of divorce, legalized only three years prior to the novel's publication. The Goncourt journal recounts Belot's own 1885 divorce, whose orchestration belies the sanctification of marriage espoused in his novels: "This morning Mrs Daudet told me about Belot's divorce, which he and his wife cooked up and plotted together, in which Belot was caught in the act by the police commissioner. You could say they turned their own lives into a theatrical production. And they did so for the pleasure of dramatic intrigue, to satisfy their lowly inclinations and amuse their histrionic imaginations."[11] The novel also reflects current interest in hypnotism, attributable to the popularization of Jean-Martin Charcot's recent work, *Contribution à l'étude de l'hypnotisme chez les hystériques* (1881). As historian Ruth Harris has remarked, "Hypnosis in the 1880s and early 1890s was at the confluence of almost every major cultural trend" (158).

Belot was, moreover, an extremely versatile writer who practised a number of styles and genres. He used material from his legal training in his fiction, which reveals a fascination with laws and their transgression, with crime and punishment, and with various kinds of detective work – themes all present in his sapphic novels. Belot's corpus includes several successful examples of the legal novel (*roman judiciaire*), and a good deal of his domestic fiction shares characteristics of the newly emerging detective novel (*roman policier*).[12] Above all, he was known for stories of transgressive passion, including but not limited to sapphic plotlines.[13] Examples include *La Vénus de Gordes* (1866), in which a woman and her lover murder her husband; *La Femme de feu* (1872), about a woman willing to commit adultery in order to recover money stolen from her husband by her father; *La Femme de glace* (1878), a novel of revenge; *La Bouche de Madame X* (1882), which I will touch on below; *Adulter* [*sic*]: *Dernière aventure parisienne* (1885); *Une affolée d'amour* (1885); *Courtisane, roman parisien* (1886), in which a former prostitute marries her daughter to a baron. Like his popular novels, Belot's erotic texts illustrate his fascination with marital misconduct and sexual taboos such as, in addition to lesbianism, adultery, impotence, frigidity, high-end prostitution, orgies, incest, and a variety of non-reproductive sex acts.

For its great commercial success, *Mademoiselle Giraud* stands out as Belot's trademark novel of sexual marginality, although it was by no means his only venture into the subject of lesbianism, which would play a significant role in his abundant literary production. Following it, Belot published a number of books with suggestive but misleading titles that employ the feminine plural. For example, *Hélène et Mathilde* (1874) has nothing to do with same-sex eroticism, but instead relates the story of a woman who takes her daughter's fiancé as her lover.[14] Although attempting to capitalize on the notoriety of *Mademoiselle Giraud* with such suggestive titles, Belot's next real foray into lesbian content followed a wave of sapphic texts by a host of other writers, with *Alphonsine* and, more centrally, *Mélinite* (1888).

Belot began his literary career primarily as a playwright, often writing in collaboration. His first triumph came in 1859 with a three-act comedy, *Le Testament de César Girodot*, which had an impressive run at the Odéon theatre and eventually entered the repertory of the French national theatre, the Comédie-Française. Following *Mademoiselle Giraud*, he largely abandoned original playwriting for the greater profitability of the novel, in newspaper feuilletons and in book form. Henceforth, the few plays he wrote were frequently recast from earlier novels, a common practice among novelists during this period, while he vastly increased his production of novels.[15] According to several sources, despite his success he was frequently in debt because of a penchant for gambling, and reportedly turned to writing serial novels to cover his financial obligations. Gambling plots inevitably joined other themes culled from lived experience, in novels such as *L'Article 47* (1873), *Une joueuse* (1879), *Le Roi des grecs* (1881), and *Une lune de miel à Monte Carle* (1887). The Goncourt journals reveal that Belot's notoriety earned him a pension in exchange for frequenting the gaming tables of Monte Carlo's casino ("gaming establishments subsidize journalists and some men of letters with disgraceful stipends").[16] Whatever the state of his finances, one could say that, for better or worse, handling money was in the blood of this banker's son.

All told, Belot wrote and saw produced nearly thirty plays and published fifty commercial novels in about thirty years.[17] He earned a great deal of money from his writing: his plays broke production records, and his novels outsold those of Zola and other authors having loftier literary aspirations. Belot cultivated relationships with contemporary writers; he appeared to be as attuned to the use value of literary relationships as he was to the desires of his readers. By signing his name to lesbian fictions, which circulated at an ever-increasing speed among authors of all stripes, Belot successfully penetrated a network of "serious" writers to which he clearly aspired, but with mixed results. He gained popular renown, literary connections, and the marks of professional success, including being named Chevalier of the Legion of Honour in 1867.[18] But he was also subject to resentment and scorn by his peers.

Perhaps not surprisingly, Belot's easy successes infuriated his more intellectually ambitious contemporaries. His popularity enraged Gustave Flaubert: "Public mentality seems to sink lower and lower. To what depths of stupidity will we descend? Belot's latest novel sold eight thousand copies in fifteen days. Zola's *La Conquête de Plassans* [1874] sold seventeen hundred in six months."[19] Ironically, Zola was one of a relatively small number of avant-garde authors who achieved popular success. Jules Barbey d'Aurevilly, among many others, derided Belot for the facility with which his works attracted public attention: "Mr Belot is a literary manufacturer. He makes serial novels and plays like someone intent on selling products and becoming famous. As long as his engines are more or less working and grab the public's crass curiosity, all is well" (*Théâtre*, 70). The Goncourt brothers also questioned his talents as a writer: "when he writes, this man is absolutely devoid of literature and has no idea, not the slightest, how to bring beauty to a book."[20] Symbolist poet Stéphane Mallarmé disdained him as well, calling him an "author of uninteresting and obscene novels" (*Correspondance*, 81).

Belot's professional contacts and borrowings were motivated by commercial concerns and the desire for social capital as much as by collegial respect. He regularly took material from novels recently published by other authors, profiting from and often outstripping their sales. For example, although many critics credit *Mademoiselle Giraud* with initiating the wave of realist lesbian fiction that authors high and low churned out from 1870 through the turn of the century, Ernest Feydeau is also deserving of some recognition for his 1868 novel, *La Comtesse de Chalis*, which flirts with "vile rites," a euphemistic reference to female homosexuality and echo of Verlaine.[21] (Feydeau's subsequent *Histoire d'une cocodette* treats it explicitly.) *Mademoiselle Giraud* and *La Comtesse de Chalis* both portray honest and earnest young men who arrive in Paris and encounter sexually deviant countesses whose sapphic proclivities contribute to their loss of innocence and ensuing psychological disintegration. In fact, Belot alludes to Feydeau's precedent in the text of *Mademoiselle Giraud*. So while the germ of *Mademoiselle Giraud* lies in Feydeau's novel, Belot had the flair to better frame its formula by placing the lesbian intrigue at the centre rather than at the margins of the plot.

Although Flaubert begrudged Belot for surpassing Zola in sales, the latter two profited from professional exchanges with one another.[22] At different points in their careers, they appealed to each other for favours in publishing, theatrical productions, and promotion. In 1865, young and as yet undiscovered, Zola spoke of the older Belot in obsequious terms to a literary critic: "I am attached to [Mr Belot], and even owe him my gratitude."[23] But twenty years later, he counselled Alphonse Daudet to avoid collaborating with Belot: "Why work with a man of no talent like him?"[24] And when Daudet did indeed turn to Belot to recast his novel, *Sapho*, as a play, Daudet did so not out of respect for Belot's talent as a writer, but because of his theatre connections – and, undoubtedly, due to his association with the sapphic subject matter. For his part, Belot was thrilled by the play's success, exclaiming "yes, yes, we have at least fifty performances to go, which will make money!"[25] Such borrowings and favour sharing were and remain typical of professional networking; indeed, Belot rode many times on the coat-tails of writers more respected and who would enjoy longer-lasting renown than he.

Belot's patterns of collaboration and citation thus align him with popular authors who wrote for rapid consumption as well as with intellectual writers engaged in an enterprise whose goals were presumably more aesthetic than financial. Tellingly, he appears both in Compère's *Dictionnaire du roman populaire français* and in Hamon's *Dictionnaire thématique du roman de mœurs*, which treats primarily canonical writers. The difficulty in precisely locating Belot on the spectrum from low to high literature points to the hybridity of his work as well as to the overly rigid imposition of genre distinctions. The divide between paraliterature and literary fiction, commercial fiction and "serious" novels, is notoriously arbitrary, although, as Jacques Migozzi reminds us, "the division between literature and popular literature rigidifies and becomes more emphatic over the course of the 19th century."[26] It is with writers such as Belot, whose ideas and representations circulated both below and above, that the fault lines in such overdetermined categories become evident.

Keeping this in mind, we can see how Belot sometimes slips through the critical and generic cracks. On one hand, his upper-middle-class background and professional education, the serial publication of *Mademoiselle Giraud* in *Le Figaro* (a daily paper addressed to more sophisticated readers than, say, *Le Petit Matin*), and his fruitful contacts with more highly regarded authors would seem to place him outside of Olivier-Martin's category of popular novelist. And yet Belot remains a mere footnote in studies of authors prized by scholars of realist and naturalist French literature: Daudet, Flaubert, the Goncourt brothers, and Zola.

The publishing context in which Belot's work came to prominence helps illustrate the difficulty of pigeonholing his novels. This history shows the marking of territory and the hardening of divisions between transient popular fiction and enduring literature, between the pursuit of profit and the ostensibly disinterested quest for literary innovation, between unsophisticated readers and more cultured ones. It leads to questions about audience and literary status since, ultimately, the reputation of a novel or an œuvre is determined by its readers, and the value accorded to different reading sectors is heavily weighted by ideology. By shifting the focus from the highly subjective criterion of quality to a consideration of readership – both intended and actual – we can perhaps place Belot more accurately. Anne-Marie Thiesse shows that the classification and hierarchy of subgenres were directly related to the gender, education, and social situation of both the reader and the writer, and Marc Angenot further analyses presumptions about readers and identifies what he calls the ghettoization of three discursive sectors: children, the working class, and women.[27]

While Belot's works fulfil expectations for the popular novel, then, his relationship to the genre is far from straightforward. His versatility also contributed to his success. Belot's deployment of the tribade traversed genres, resulting in a cross-pollination that mixed theatre and fiction, crime and sex, prurience and didacticism, high and low, best-selling and clandestine. The genius of this generic and discursive mélange was to direct related plots to different publics using different linguistic and moral registers. The viewpoints of his disparate texts shuttled between attraction and repulsion, arousal and denunciation. The condemnatory language of best-sellers, often taken at face value in the nineteenth century, in fact provided a cover for delving into a subject considered reprehensible: it protected the writer from accusations of obscenity and provided his readers with a morally upstanding message as rationale for their racy readings. While Belot exploited sex for profit, his novels were also busy policing desire by bending love plots into detective fiction. His fictional male characters invoked laws, decried lax education, and urged men caution for their vulnerable sexuality. In contrast to the euphemistic language of his best-sellers, his erotic novels revelled in explicit naming. Between the lure and the loathing of sexual excess, Belot attracted a great number of readers.

Mademoiselle Giraud, ma femme: Reading Between the Lines

Tribade: love of a woman for another, widespread among girls in boarding schools and women in convents.

(Delvau, *Dictionnaire érotique moderne*)

Introducing Sapphism

As one of the first sapphic fictions of the post-romantic period, *Mademoiselle Giraud* marks a turning point. Published at the end of the largely authoritarian and prudish Second Empire, its subject matter, no matter how veiled and genteelly delivered, was susceptible to strong reaction, subject to censorship, and therefore rarely raised in print. However, Belot's text undoubtedly benefited from the liberalization that took place during the Empire's final years. The censorship laws that were invoked to bring *Les Fleurs du Mal* to trial were relaxed in 1868, as were strict controls on the right of assembly. These developments led to, among other things, an expanded and democratized press and renewed feminist activity, which will be considered in greater depth in the following chapter.

The daily newspaper *Le Figaro* began printing *Mademoiselle Giraud* in 1869, but discontinued publication of instalments before reaching the end of the novel, purportedly due to reader complaints about the dubious morality of its subject matter:

> The serial story we are currently running, *Miss Giraud, My Wife*, has offended some susceptibilities. People feel as though it is based on an extremely delicate matter, and that it is dangerous for a journal to raise such indecent issues. Mr Adolphe Belot has preferred to stop publication rather than to modify his work.
>
> We are informing those readers who have not been overly alarmed by the *Adventures of Miss Giraud* and who wish to know how it ends that it will appear in book form next month. This novel, which is recommended for its exceptional qualities and highly appealing intrigue, will doubtlessly enjoy very successful sales. (*Le Figaro*, 22 December 1869)

There is reason, however, to doubt the motives behind this abrupt cessation. In fact, the feuilleton was interrupted well before the disclosure of the title character's lesbianism and at the very moment when the government abandoned administrative control of the press. *Le Figaro*'s overreactive censorship proved fortunate for Belot; indeed, it has been implied that the discontinuation was fabricated as a publicity coup that worked to the author's advantage by increasing sales. Within a month, the fashionable publishing house Dentu brought out *Mademoiselle Giraud* to great success, as *Le Figaro* had predicted, even amidst the chaos and devastation of war and regime change.

Six months after *Mademoiselle Giraud* arrived in the bookstores, in July 1870, France declared war on Prussia. This was a disastrous move for Napoléon III, leading to his downfall and the end of the Second Empire. The novel reached twenty-five editions within a year of its publication, during which time the Third Republic was declared, Paris was besieged and fell to the Prussians, and an armistice was signed resulting in the annexation of Alsace-Lorraine by the German Empire. Shortly after the fall of Paris, workers established the Commune in defiance of Adolphe Thiers, whose army brutally repressed the rebellion. A conservative government was formed under the leadership of President Thiers. Surely the country was in need of some entertaining fiction!

In its notice of discontinuation of *Mademoiselle Giraud*, *Le Figaro* proposed two readings of the provocative subject matter: it was an awkward topic unsuitable, even dangerous, for a daily newspaper ("it is dangerous for a journal to raise such indecent issues") and a novel of considerable interest commended to its bolder readers ("this novel is recommended for its exceptional qualities and highly appealing intrigue"). This oscillation, between an ostentatious concern for readers who could be harmed by exposure to the subject matter and a dispassionate endorsement to those inured to its scandal but not unaffected by its appeal, became typical in subsequent fiction and non-fiction alike, which would treat tribades as both shocking and intriguing, unspeakable and commonplace.

Mademoiselle Giraud itself treats female homosexuality as a topic at once dangerous and alluring, a dichotomy that encapsulates paternalistic attitudes towards women readers and male sexual fascination with tribadism. Because the popular novel was presumed to be directed to and consumed primarily by women, it was obligatory to moderate language that might otherwise offend or corrupt and to leave readers with an edifying lesson. But Belot writes to and for both innocent and worldly readers, which is another way of saying both women and men, and he offers something else to his curious male readers: a splash of titillation. Belot's dual address corresponds to what Angenot has called the "double reading" of the popular novel, which combines "one that is sentimental and melodramatic, the other thoughtful and pessimistic. Chaste in words and immoral in theme, it indulges women readers without annoying men."[28]

Belot's cautionary foreword, which responds directly to *Le Figaro*'s notice and borrows its language, illustrates the diversity of the public he wants to reach. He grants the sensitivity of his topic: "it is true that the subject of *Mademoiselle Giraud, My Wife* is a delicate one."[29] In his defence, he emphasizes the propriety of his language: "[the novel's] form was rigorously attended to, in order to avoid any evil-sounding expression, any excessively vivid depiction, any indiscreet detail." The vocabulary of lesbianism is, in fact, absent in his novel: Belot maintains the reticence of his literary predecessors, refusing to name the vice. The word *tribade* is not uttered; neither are *saphiste, lesbienne, fricarelle, fricatrice, frotteuse, ribaude,* or any of the many other scientific, argotic, metaphorical, genteel, or vulgar terms used to designate the female homosexual during the nineteenth century. Instead, he relies on periphrasis and euphemism to indicate the nature of the relationship between his two female characters: "The author often preferred to err through excessive obscurity." Belot imagines an innocent reader in need of gentle handling: "[the author] is convinced that if this novel were to fall into the hands of young readers, it would remain enigmatic for them." The book therefore presents no danger to the young, and yet sophisticated readers will grasp the plot without difficulty: "As for those persons who are *used to reading between the lines* and understanding what is implied, they can't reproach us for having chosen a subject already chosen by well-respected authors, notably Balzac" (9, emphasis added).

By invoking Balzac as precedent to justify his treatment of topic, Belot covers himself with the mantle of great literature. His multipronged defence is vigorous, although not particularly coherent. On one hand he claims literary licence, on the other hand, linguistic restraint. Failing those justifications, he points to his novel's pedagogical value: "[readers] will at least have to concede that this book was written in a serious fashion and that it contains useful lessons" (10). Seriousness, Angenot has shown, numbers among the pretensions of novels directed to male readers, didacticism among the burdens of those written for women.

Belot's 1866 feuilleton, *La Vénus de Gordes*, itself based on a *fait divers* about adulterous lovers who murder the cuckolded husband, inspired Zola's *Thérèse Raquin* (1867).[30] In turn, Zola wrote an appreciative review that (rather ironically) defended the morality of *Mademoiselle Giraud* against its detractors. It was added as a preface to the novel in 1879 and carried some weight since it was authored by an innovative if controversial writer whose talent had by then been recognized by his peers. Zola's motivations for writing the piece are dubious, given his pronounced disrespect for Belot's literary integrity. In fact, Zola – who signed his preface "Th. Raquin" – might just as well have been defending himself against the accusations of immorality levelled at *Thérèse Raquin*, also a *succès de scandale* and instrumental in launching Zola's career. He responded to his own critics as he does in writing about *Mademoiselle Giraud* that "the dirty word of *immorality* [is] devoid of meaning with respect to literature," even while announcing that "the moral of the story is blinding" (4, 7). Zola takes umbrage with those who attack novels based on content while overlooking the intellectual ambitions of their authors. (In Zola's case, of which more below, "scientific method" and sociological realism were central to the naturalist project.)

In essence, Zola excuses Belot's novel for its very success, claiming that readers were attracted by their "prurient curiosity" and that, hypocritically, they accused the author of having "tried to cash in on the more shameful tastes of the day" (3, 4). Zola insists that in doing so, they misread a highly moral book whose goal is not to inflame, but rather to condemn: Belot is "a moralist who has had the great courage to point out one of the scourges of the education of young girls in convents" (4). This justification of Belot's morality is reminiscent of Baudelaire's defence of his lesbian poems, in which he claimed to represent sapphism only in order to condemn it. As was the case with Baudelaire, the sincerity of Zola's rationalization is questionable, since all indications in fact point to Belot's having speculated on the public's tastes.

Zola's preface offers several indications of the use value of the figure of the lesbian in nineteenth-century French literature. While Belot's moralizing bombast satisfied the requirements of popular fiction, as a toll paid in order to enter into the subject, Zola's (and, by extension, other high-art writers') pronouncements about female homosexuality carried ideological implications that were less specious. In Zola's case, same-sex female eroticism would become a vehicle for attacking the Church. Accusations that convent education posed a danger to the sexual purity of girls furthered his own anticlerical agenda at a time when progressive secularists were doing battle with the conservative Church, a battle played out in part through the hotly debated topic of education for girls.[31]

While Zola's anti-lesbianism covers for anticlericalism, it also contributes to the novel's pattern of male collusion. Christopher Rivers has convincingly argued that *Mademoiselle Giraud* is as much about male homosociality as it is about female homosexuality. Indeed, Zola's preface is addressed to men and carries a warning about the corruption menacing their daughters: "if you have daughters, may your wife read this book before she chooses to have those dear creatures leave her and be sent off to a convent" (5). Might readers' wives also succumb to "the leprosy of Lesbos" (7)? Zola exhorts men not to hide the book, but rather to have their wives and daughters read it as a warning. Zola's preface finally raises the question of knowledge that is central to the book itself. Differing with the author's claim that one can read the novel innocently, Zola suggests that there is no such thing as ignorance about sapphism: "Belot hasn't told anyone anything he didn't already know [...] It's a story that has already made the rounds in this society of ours, rotten to the core" (5).

Narrative Blindness

In fact, the novel relies on its narrator's naivety and blindness to his wife's lesbianism. The plot concerns the eligible Adrien's courtship of and marriage to a young woman, Paule Giraud, who – inexplicably – refuses to consummate their vows. But it opens proleptically with a chance meeting that prompts a prematurely aged Adrien to tell his story. Pale and melancholic, he encounters an old school friend, Camille, in the sex-segregated smoking room of a masked ball, a setting charged with the symbolism of secrecy and vice. Camille's expression of concern for Adrien's well-being elicits a response that comes later in the form of a lengthy written confession, which he authorizes Camille to publish anonymously "if you think that it might be useful to someone else" (19). In it, Adrien unveils the secret of his woes to the reader as he recounts his protracted and tortuous discovery of his wife's lesbianism. Ironically, the manuscript reveals that Adrien himself is incapable of "understanding what is implied" by clues with which he peppers his own narrative. He is in a sense feminized by his lack of knowledge, an impotence that is only symbolically corrected when he finally learns the truth about Paule's sexual proclivities.

The novel thus posits an internal audience, the fictional Camille, who provides the narrative's first instance of homosocial bonding, and an external one that crosses gender lines. It relates the unravelling of two parallel secrets: Camille discovers the cause of Adrien's despair as Adrien recounts how he solved the enigma of his wife's sexuality. Adrien's story reads more like a journal than a retrospective account of his adventures, since he reports his attempts to bed

Paule without sharing the knowledge he would later gain.[32] Using this device, Belot builds suspense, thus serving the purpose of maintaining reader attention, a necessity for successful feuilletons, which depended on a faithful readership. It also facilitates a double reading, allowing, on one hand, perspicacious readers to have greater insight than the narrator himself, since they are able to deduce Paule's secret while watching Adrien struggle to learn it. But on the other hand, Belot also addresses the hypothetical ideal of woman ("la femme idéologique," Angenot) who, it was imagined at the time, is enticed by sentimental plots, private drama, and gauzy prose, but is as uninformed as Adrien about female homosexuality.

Adrien begins his tale by describing the frustrations of his search for a wife, in which he is introduced to countless women but taken with none. He has nearly given up hope, but then by chance sees Paule Giraud, to whom he is immediately drawn. She is appealingly feminine, and yet her description carries suggestions of a different, perhaps dangerous sexuality:

> her breasts are voluptuously developed, and her hips, pronounced like those of a Spanish woman, emphasize all the more her slender and elegant waist. Her arched feet, nervous, flirtatiously shod in little boots with heels, graze the ground. [...] Pungent and mysterious perfumes emanate from her and intoxicate me. [...] her voice – resonant, emphatic, almost masculine [...] Such sensuality on her red lips, a little thick, curled back on themselves, and topped by a provocative patch of light down! (24)

The evocation of Spain, hypersexualized in other sapphic novels (*La Fille aux yeux d'or, Histoire d'une cocodette*), Paule's strong and mysterious scent, her masculine voice and the down above her lip, all point to a heightened sexuality and atypical femininity.

Moreover, Paule appears to have no interest in men: "[she] indulged in none of those innocent flirtations that certain young girls, even some of the most virtuous, tend to indulge in." But at the same time she betrays something other than indifference towards women: "The only time I did see a spark of interest in her was when she watched a rather pretty young blond woman walk by. The woman's eccentric clothing had no doubt caught her eye, and Paule turned in order to continue looking at her" (25). Adrien deduces nothing amiss from his own observations just as, to believe Belot, his innocent readers will turn the page unenlightened. However those worldly readers "used to reading between the lines" are able to pick up on the indicators of Paule's sexual orientation that punctuate the narrative: looks exchanged, seemingly innocent gestures, physical traits, eccentric manner of dress.

Just as *Mademoiselle Giraud* represents a genre in formation – the lesbian novel – its main characters Berthe and Paule are emergent figures in their physical typing and other codes with which the novel assigns them sexual identities. *Mademoiselle*

Giraud makes literal and allusive references to earlier texts and contributes new elements that would become standard tropes, signs of deviant sexuality and conventions of lesbian appearance entrenched in subsequent novels. Later writers would add detail to the "eccentric clothing" meant to signal the passer-by's sexuality. Jean Lorrain wrote in 1888 that novelists themselves recognized and perpetuated a number of "distinctive signs" attributed to sapphists, here enumerating those contributed by Catulle Mendès:

> an unusual pressure of the fingers, a nibbling at the edge of a fan, penetrating eyes that stare unhurriedly into a neighbouring blue eye [...], Mendès noted the gait, gesture, scent; not only did he describe the smile and respiration, he decreed the outfit, head-covering and stockings, short hair, [...] dress tailored in an androgynous fashion, the slight, straight collar of a valet, man's jacket, woollen outfit, provocative expression reminiscent of Narcissus, flat chest and narrow hips. (*Dans l'oratoire*, 53)

Several of these signs are clearly not yet in circulation in 1870. As does Paule's, the portrait of her "best friend" Berthe de Blangy carries a number of attributes that are particular rather than general:

> As blond as her friend Paule was dark, Berthe de Blangy had a charm all her own: her big blue eyes revealed her to be both guileless and audacious; her voice was infinitely sweet; her mouth was almost exceptionally small but contained lovely teeth, set close together; her round and plump chin, with its little dimple, would have set a physiognomist dreaming. Even other women had to admire her perfectly formed shoulders. (*Mademoiselle Giraud*, 27)

Berthe betrays no particular mark of deviance or masculinity, and neither she nor Paule yet represents the coalescence of a physical type. The only sign of difference in Belot's description of Berthe is the repeated use of the adjective *eccentric*: "her manners were a bit eccentric" (29). Adrien notes that she is seductive to women as well as men, yet another hint of her sexuality. Adrien's own preference would appear to be for homosexual rather than heterosexual women: after refusing to choose a bride from among the "batches of heiresses" presented to him, he is dazzled by both women, whose friendship charms rather than troubles him: "Berthe and Paule, the two convent-school friends, the two inseparables, the blonde and the brunette [...] The contrast between their respective styles of beauty was truly alluring; each brought out the other and they thus complemented each other [...] Between the two of them, they possessed all the charms possible and achieved the most complete perfection" (21, 28, 52–3). Their physical complementarity, especially that of their hair colour, already present in Verlaine ("One pale with hair of jet, the other pink and blond"), quickly became stock in trade of lesbian fictions. The singularity of Belot's couple is to attribute indicators of weakness and femininity to the older, pernicious lesbian (her softness, myopia, and blondeness) and of masculine vigour to Paule, who would become her victim. By the early 1880s, the masculine brunette and feminine blonde had become requisite types.

Although Berthe, who has known Paule since their days together in convent school, has repeatedly warned Adrien not to proceed with the marriage, he is enraptured and takes the rather indifferent Miss Giraud as his wife. Here is another clue missed by Adrien: convents and boarding schools, as well as more tawdry same-sex spaces (prisons, brothels, harems), are rife with lesbian activity, already a common feature in libertine fiction. Belot's novel shares the warnings of Diderot's *Religieuse* that girls are potential prey to older girls and women in convents, and that boarding schools present dangerous temptations to the innocent. Paule suffers the same fate as sapphic characters, from Musset's pornographic *Gamiani* (1833) to Verlaine's *Les Amies* and Dubut de Laforest's clinical novel, *Mademoiselle Tantale* (1884): "the boarding school dormitory had corrupted the lesbian" (44). Subsequent writers would increasingly attribute lesbian contagion to such spaces.

After their marriage, Adrien is at first discreetly patient with what he identifies as his wife's timidity. He respects the locked door to their bedroom, even though Paule's sophistication seem incompatible with the reticence of a blushing young bride. Adrien wonders whether he "was dealing not with an ingénue, not with a schoolgirl, but with a marvellously experienced young woman" (60). At this point in the novel, Adrien's innocence is securely intact, and Paule appears to be closer to the pole of experience, although by the end of the novel they will exchange these positions. Eventually Adrien's understanding turns to incomprehension of her perpetual coldness and impatience at her refusal of sexual intimacy. He endures "acute nervous pains," "nervous overstimulation," "nervous fits," "nervous tension," all attributed to his sustained state of unsatisfied arousal – as well as indicative of the interest in nervous illness that patterns the text and a further manifestation of Adrien's effemination. He furtively removes the lock, only to be outwitted by Paule. The novel's preoccupation with locks and keys transparently represent Adrien's impotence and failed attempts at literal and intellectual penetration. When he resorts to violence, Paule delivers a cold shower with her derisive laughter. At the end of his rope, Adrien first confides in Berthe and then determines that she is a bad influence, forbidding Paule to see her.

Policing and the Law

The novel's itinerary, from ignorance to knowledge, begins at this point to read like a detective story in which Adrien pursues the truth about a crime and subjects the criminal to the law. As in Gautier's and Balzac's work, lesbianism is a secret to be revealed either to other characters, the reader, or both. To the established device of the lesbian secret, Belot adds the suspense of the detective novel. *Mademoiselle Giraud* conforms to Todorov's definition of the genre, whose double plot depends on a crime and its inquest.[33] I would suggest that the influence of detective fiction went beyond Belot's work to, more generally, the body of lesbian representations of the period, in which the secret to be revealed or the crime to be solved is ultimately linked to sapphic activity. Lesbianism is the mystery, that which is illicit and hidden, if not literally illegal.

In despair, Adrien considers using his authority to force his wife to submit sexually. When he suspects another man, he wonders "who had dared take my property from me, who had seized my rights?" (100). Adrien bases his claim to authority over his wife on the French Civil Code, which did indeed make a married woman the legal property of her husband. Feminists had already begun to militate for marriage reform and the right to divorce when Belot was writing *Mademoiselle Giraud*; Adrien comes down clearly on the side of traditionalists intent on upholding the Code. The novel employs a legal vocabulary throughout, and even Zola's preface likens Belot to a judge and his novel to "the transcript of a [criminal] trial" (7). Adrien surreptitiously tracks his seemingly obedient wife across the city in an attempt to discover her secret, comparing himself to an officer of the law: "jealousy had just transformed me into the most expert of policemen" (95). Belot presents Paris not only as background landscape, as did Balzac in *La Fille*, but also as an actor complicit in the enactment of tribadism, thus anticipating later fictions and non-fictional pronouncements of squalid as well as luxuriously decadent quarters teeming with homosexual women. Journalist Léo Taxil claimed that "in Paris, the number of women partial to women is incalculable."[34] Whereas the literal and social cloistering of Diderot's Suzanne and Balzac's Paquita make them vulnerable to predatory lesbians, freedom of movement and the anonymity of the modern city allow the women in Belot's novel to carry on their affair: it is "always in the great capital cities that one encounters these women."[35]

Adrien determines that Paule has taken a lover and stages an elaborate surprise visit to the apartment that she regularly visits. He is dumbfounded and perplexed to find only Berthe with his wife. Not even her small library, which includes sapphic classics by Diderot, Balzac, Gautier, and Feydeau, helps to clarify the situation for Adrien. While Adrien fails to deduce Countess de Blangy's sexual inclination from the novels lining her bookshelf, it is less clear what the reader is expected to grasp. Do these titles reflect the degree of cultivation expected of his intended "sophisticated" audience, men and women of a certain socio-economic stature? And yet Belot could not have presumed that the majority of women imagined as consumers of popular novels would have been familiar with them. Such references were both winks from the author, details noted but whose implications are not initially grasped by the narrator, and part of the project, suggested in the author's preface, to opt for tact and obscurity.

Berthe's apartment carries orientalist trappings reminiscent of *Gamiani* and of Paquita's boudoir in *La Fille*: "One of those huge Turkish-style sofas [...] a rock-crystal goblet full of Turkish cigarettes" (*Mademoiselle Giraud*, 108–9). More peculiarities appear in the décor of Berthe's flat: "No eccentricity on her part would have surprised me." She is associated with male habits ("she had rented that apartment to lead the life of a 'bachelor,'" 120), and thus more clearly begins to emerge as the seducer and active force behind Paule's sexual behaviour.

Exhausted and defeated, Adrien remains unenlightened: "I found myself alone with the enigma that tortured me day and night" (121). He leaves to travel and, in Nice, he meets the Count de Blangy, Berthe's mysteriously absent husband, in a far-fetched coincidence typical of popular novels. They become fast friends, another instance of the male complicity running through the novel, and exchange confidences as Adrien had with Camille ("your secrets in exchange for mine," 144). Even the name of the hotel – Hôtel des Princes – reinforces the novel's focus on male homosociality. After a great deal of pleading from Adrien ("I want to know that secret, I demand it!" 142), Blangy explains the nature of their wives' relationship.

With difficulty, Adrien finally grasps that Paule and Berthe are lovers: "The light had shone through!" (154). The biggest obstacle to his understanding is his naive belief that "those ills," of which he was only vaguely aware, belonged to the lower classes alone: "among the working class, among the peasants, the morals leave something to be desired, but among the better classes of society, among the bourgeois" (148, 130–1). However the disillusioned count, as seasoned as Adrien is unworldly, spares no detail as he instructs him about the corruption endemic in modern France: "In this nineteenth-century Parisian society of ours [...] vices of all sorts [...] insinuate themselves into our mores" (150).

This turning point in the text, the moment of illumination in which secrets are revealed, is marked by a series of changes, not least of which is the realignment of character traits that leads to the settling of scores. Adrien's new-found knowledge masculinizes him and stirs him to action, while Paule devolves from sophisticate to victim and Berthe from sly rogue to fiendish femme fatale. In Blangy's account of his marriage and his wife's relationship with Paule, Berthe emerges as a seductress, while Paule begins to resemble more of an ingénue than a cunning woman: "Paule, as a young girl would, blushed, went pale, and ended up having a nervous fit" (149). We learn that Berthe herself pursued Blangy "to convince him to give her his name and his fortune" (148).

The novel's title underlines the narrow relationship between identity and naming. Although married to Adrien, Paule is designated by her maiden name because their marriage has not been consummated. Although we never learn Adrien's last name, Berthe de Blangy carries her husband's surname and title since, despite her repugnance, she consents to "fulfilling her wifely duties."

Adrien grants the count this "incontestable advantage": "he had been a husband to his wife" (148). And he concludes that Paule's only hope for a cure is to fulfil her sexual duty to him.

This moment also finds Adrien altering the tone of his narrative in a fashion corresponding with his change in perception. Disabused of his innocence, Adrien's style hardens. He abandons the language of love and imagination ("the poetic turn," "stylistic flourishes"), adopting instead an objective tone: "I will return to the land of prose, never to leave it again." The very subject matter obliges him to be frank:

> When confronted with certain vile things, one cannot remain silent; one is obliged to speak, so as to condemn them. Indifference, disdain, or silence encourages them; the shadows that surround them give them hope for impunity [...]. They must be combatted wholeheartedly, with no fear of offending delicate ears or awakening dangerous ideas. It is because of people's ridiculous prudishness, because they thereby end up sparing vice and neglecting to stigmatize it, that vice manages, eventually, to pass itself off as virtue. (127)

The narrative voice sounds more like Zola's preface here than Belot's foreword in which, let us recall, he called for obscurity over clarity of language in order to protect innocent readers when treating delicate topics.

One of the central conceits of *Mademoiselle Giraud* – as of many subsequent sapphic fictions – is the danger of uncontrolled homosexuality among women, which men are helpless to contain without the assistance of the law. Not only are girls and women potential prey, but here, for the first time, men also appear as victims to the lesbian femme fatale, a victimology symptomatic of the crisis of masculinity that became widespread at the fin de siècle. Although Adrien and Blangy identify sapphism as a morally condemnable offence, it is not legally punishable as a crime: just as it remains unnamed by the narrator, it is unrecognized by the law. The Count de Blangy laments the Code's silence on the question of female homosexuality: "'The law,' he told me, 'would obviously have refused me any help; lawmakers have failed to foresee certain misdeeds, which are thus granted impunity. I could barely obtain a separation from the courts: Mme de Blangy's wrongdoings toward me were of such a nature that judges often refuse to admit them as evidence'" (149–50). Although the Code states that "The husband may ask for a divorce in the event of adultery on the part of his wife" (article 229), it recognizes only heterosexual adultery. The medical doctor Julien Chevalier would later echo Belot in writing that same-sex activity between women was a "transgression that the Code did not foresee, an infidelity that the police commissioner would refuse to report, should he uncover its secret" (*Maladie*, 229).

In the name of morality if not love, the two men plot to separate their wives. Although the law does not consider the affair between Berthe and Paule to constitute adultery, their husbands realize that it does give them power over their wives: "The law protects us, let us use it! […] The Code requires [your wife] to follow you wherever it pleases you to take her, [and] it offers you the means to oblige her to do so" (*Mademoiselle Giraud*, 152–3). Paule is legally free to couple with Berthe, but proscribed by laws applying to married women: "The wife is obliged to live with her husband and to follow him wherever he deems appropriate to reside" (article 214 of the Code civil).

With new-found authority backed up by the Code, Adrien returns to France and whisks his wife away from Paris, the site of contagion. Paule recognizes that "the law gives you rights over me" and submits to Adrien's orders (159). They go south to Oran (the Maghreb would later be associated with sexual deviance and excess), where they engage a doctor to treat her illness, now physical as well as moral. She has contracted "chloroanaemia," which is attributed to female sexual fragility: "young women […] should never be loved too passionately. Although passion charms them, it also kills them, because they're not prepared for it" (169). The irony of having the doctor blame his sexual ardour for Paule's illness is not lost on Adrien. The reader is left to surmise that it is in fact homosexual, not heterosexual lovemaking that endangers Paule's health. Just as Paule begins her cure, the pernicious Berthe discovers her whereabouts and draws her away. Now an unwilling victim rather than a strong-willed participant, Paule is too weak to resist. She has in essence exchanged places with Adrien, abandoned her haughty independence, and recovered such normative feminine traits as nervousness ("neuralgia and heart palpitations"), passivity, and contrition (157).

More plot twists follow, and Paule's chloroanaemia (in fact an iron deficiency common in adolescent girls) develops "cerebral complications" (170). She is dying of "a brain disease […] pachymeningitis" (199). Belot's use of medical language (Adrien himself refers to the doctor's "excessively technical terms") and flirtation with theories of causality are noteworthy. Despite the patently illogical suggestion that anaemia could lead to inflammation of the cerebral membrane, Belot's naive use of technical terminology serves the reality effect and anticipates scientific interest in the aetiology of sexual perversion and speculation about co-morbidity, which would become increasingly prominent in the decades to follow.

When Adrien reaches Paule's side, she is delirious and repentant, redeemed by a deathbed repudiation of lesbianism, another trope of later fictions. She dies as victim of the perverse ministrations of Berthe, who by the end of the novel is portrayed as a soulless sexual predator: "how she dominated me[!] how she had subjugated me[!] […] how extremely dishonest she was" (192, 196). At this point, Adrien takes the law into his own hands. He encounters

Berthe by the ocean, "accompanied by one of her friends, Mlle B., that ravishing young brunette" (204). A *fait divers* recounts the scene: she swims too far to return, the current carries her, Adrien goes to rescue her, to no avail: "Alas! [...] he was unable to save the poor woman" (205–6). Blangy *reads between the lines* of the newspaper article and writes to absolve Adrien: "I understand what happened, and I thank you, *on my own behalf and on behalf of all decent people*, for having rid us of that reptile" (206, emphasis added). Adrien's life and health are ruined, but the novel's dénouement is nonetheless reassuring: the scourge has been stopped thanks to the collaboration of the two men, who are implicitly presented as agents for society's greater good in the parallelisms of the previous and following quotations: "*we owe it to society, we owe it to ourselves*, to challenge reprehensible aberrations!" (154, emphasis added).

There are several morals to this story: of the hazards of convent education as a breeding ground for corruption ("men don't ruin women, women ruin each other"), the dangers of independent women, the perils of sexual frustration for men and sexual excess in women, the insufficiency of the law to punish lesbianism (178). The pretence of moral outrage takes hold in *Mademoiselle Giraud*, which represents lesbianism as an established blight for which there is no legal remedy. All this was to be confirmed by succeeding legal and medical treatises: same-sex spaces are perilous; older, experienced women prey on innocent girls; women left to their own devices are at risk and therefore in need of oversight; moral decay and physical feebleness are interrelated.

Mélinite: Telling Stories

Tribade. Woman who has a passion for another woman. Type of odd depravity as inexplicable as that which inflames a man for another man.

(Diderot, *Encyclopédie*)

Tribade. Term to avoid. Woman who takes sexual advantage of other women.

(Littré, *Dictionnaire de la langue française*)

Eighteen years of political and social upheaval separated the publication of *Mademoiselle Giraud* and *Mélinite* (1888). Accustomed to novelistic transgressions in general and to sapphic plots in particular, the public was not so easily shocked as before. Belot's writing, more urbane in the later novel, bears traces of this accumulation and evolution of representations. In the context of greater liberty of expression and a more sophisticated readership, Belot forged a reputation for tantalizing plots that never crossed the line into vulgarity.

Mélinite fuses the figure of the lesbian prostitute with that of the lesbian maid, both members of the pantheon of sapphic types. Its plot revolves around a chambermaid turned courtesan, Louise Bauquet, who drives a man to suicide due to sexual frustration. She then becomes a servant to his unsuspecting widow, Olga, whom she tries to seduce. In addition to its lesbian content, the novel shares a number of similarities with *Mademoiselle Giraud*, particularly in narrative structure and plotting, and develops several of the tropes found in the earlier text (lesbian appearance, somatization and sexual deviance, sapphic orientalism). Key preoccupations include the proprieties of storytelling, female sexual curiosity, and the relation between deviant sexuality and social mobility.

Presented as Olga's journal, *Mélinite* is framed, like *Mademoiselle Giraud*, by a device that, through circumscription, might be said to control its subject matter. In this instance an offer of marriage to the desirable widow ("a journalist declared that I was not only the prettiest woman of Paris, but of the world," 35) generates her lengthy response. If you really want to marry me, she replies to her aspirant, you must know my history first. So Olga sends him her journal, which recounts the death of her husband, Gontran, up through Olga's unmasking of his fatal seducer, Mélinite. The novel, then, is about storytelling. It relates Olga's quest to understand her husband's death, a mystery that once again depends upon lesbian secrets, and it recounts Louise's transformation from a chambermaid to a wealthy courtesan, and back again.

By telling the story of a servant who aspires beyond her station, *Mélinite* explores the consequences of social mobility for those with whom she comes in contact. In fact, Louise shows disdain for at least two social institutions, class hierarchy and heterosexuality, and in so doing presents a clear and present danger to structures indispensable to maintaining the status quo. If previous fictions represented the lesbian menace as coming from above in the form of degenerate aristocrats (the Countesses Gamiani, Chalis, Blangy; Balzac's marquise), here and in many subsequent novels we see it coming from below, a dichotomy particularly pertinent in naturalist and decadent fiction.

The novel's plot is pulpy and far-fetched. After several weeks of uncharacteristic agitation, the normally sedate Duke Gontran succumbs to what his doctors identify as "an acute episode of delirium caused by idiopathic damage to brain functioning," a condition that leads to his eventual death (15). The bewildered duchess investigates her husband's alteration, his death, and the disappearance of a considerable sum of money, and learns of a certain Mélinite, a courtesan who knew the duke under a false name, the Baron de Virmeux. Olga suffers from the idea of her husband's betrayal but, characteristically curious, wants to know who this woman could be. This is the first instance of what will become a refrain repeated over the course of the novel: "oh! I am excessively curious about everything, even when it is better not to know" (6).[36]

In one of many improbable coincidences, Olga's socialite cousin, Arthur de Blazac (his name a transparent anagram of Balzac and, by association, reference to *La Fille aux yeux d'or*), knows Mélinite. While Olga lives at the centre of Parisian high society, Blazac circulates on its shadier periphery, the demimonde, speaks its suspicious language [sa langue verte], and runs with a "carousing band of men and women" [sa bande de viveurs et de viveuses], having escaped his proper family to "live it up" [mener la grande vie] (43). Blazac is, in fact, the one who introduces Mélinite into Parisian society, having frivolously chosen her for her hair colour: "long since tired of hearing only about blondes [...] I wanted to prove that men could also find brunettes appealing" (50, 51). He finds her "living with a blond woman whom she serves as chambermaid" (51). Blazac is also the author of her sobriquet, Mélinite, so named for picric acid, an explosive whose military potential was recognized and put into service only a few years prior the novel's publication. With the defeat of 1871 still a recent memory, the importance of a substance many times stronger than dynamite was not lost on the public.[37] Blazac describes melinite as "a *fairly powerful, slow-working* explosive" that is easy to handle. It aptly characterizes his protégée, who is "absolutely inoffensive in ordinary conditions" but highly volatile when provoked (54). Like a slow-burning explosive, this beguiling and intelligent adversary plots both the downfall of Duke Gontran and the seduction of his widow, the Duchess Olga.

On a warm evening, Olga goes for a ride in the Bois de Boulogne and stops for an ice cream along the Allée des Acacias, "a fashionable spot" in the 1880s and 90s. In *Bois de Boulogne, Bois d'Amour*, the novelist Pol Prille wrote that "society women and others would come parade along the famous avenue" (58). The Bois is a popular destination for Parisians of all stations. A woman dressed in a masculine fashion, none other than Mélinite, attracts Olga's attention: "What a funny little woman and what unusual clothing! A high straight collar and necktie; her spindly body encased in a white silk waistcoat and tailored jacket of black serge; on her head, a soft felt hat like the ones men wear in summer, partly covering very short black hair curled with an iron [...]. In truth, this outfit could cast some doubt on the lady's sex" (*Mélinite*, 60). Mélinite's manner of dress recalls the "eccentric clothing" of the passer-by noticed by Paule, although here Belot has fleshed out the description with specific details, some (short hair) in agreement with Jean Lorrain's assessment.

Long known to be a rendezvous for romantic and illicit sexual encounters, especially after sundown, the Bois de Boulogne appears as a backdrop in numerous novels of manners of the period, including other lesbian fictions, such as Mendès's *Méphistophéla*. Prille details the variety of amorous and sexual meetings that take place under cover of the park. In his chapter "Dames pour Dames" he specifies that "the Bois de Boulogne encompasses all humanity and its varied vices, including saphism" (168). Here, too, the author's description resembles that of Belot: "there are women who are masculine in appearance, wearing broad felts hats, short tailored skirts and fitted coats, high boots or gaiters, commanding gestures [...]. [In the Bois de Boulogne,] the secret joy [of lesbians] is to play the role of a man" (170).[38]

Olga senses that Mélinite is as intrigued by her as she is by this unusual creature. Blazac, coincidentally passing by as well, tells Olga that Mélinite, who does not know that the duchess is none other than the widow of the man she knew as the Baron de Virmeux, has admired her from a distance: "She saw you several times since you became a widow, and she finds you even more lovely in your mourning attire" (64). In spite of herself, Olga finds "her rival" appealing:

> her eyes are small, but what a gaze! Eyes of a bird of prey, which first entrance their victims to more easily get the better of them [...]. Her very white teeth are expressive precisely because they are uneven and a bit pointed. Oh, how they must bite! Her body certainly is thin, the body of a girl more than of a woman [...]. I understand her success, her fortune, her irresistibility. (65–6)

The androgynous Mélinite is likened to a predatory animal with vampiristic teeth.[39] This portrait highlights a nature both seductive and dangerous: Mélinite is a femme fatale to both men and women. By the time Prille was writing in the 1920s, these traits had become generalized: "not a pretty face, but having a kind of strangeness capable of seducing" (173). Although not classically beautiful, the lesbian predator is unusual ("eccentric"), bewitching, treacherous.

When later Olga seeks to hire a chambermaid-cum-companion to accompany her while vacationing at her country estate, a blonde named Louise Bauquet applies who looks astoundingly like Mélinite: "teeth I thought I had seen before [...] that face, those features [...] the same deep and fascinating eyes, nostrils flaring each time she inhaled, her lips parted lasciviously" (81–2). Troubled and obsessively curious ("how eternally curious I am!"), Olga verifies Louise's impeccable references with her former mistress, Madame de la Bère, whose blondeness sets off Mélinite's brown hair, as her "very full bust" and "submissive tendencies" [tendance à s'amollir] do the "narrow forms" and taught energy of the latter – complements that have by the late 1880s become established marks of the lesbian couple (91, 98, 60). Olga finds Madame de la Bère as bland as Mélinite is alluring, "an unoriginal, conventional beauty," although there is something decidedly different, "oriental" about her: "She approaches me with the gait of a weary Oriental harem woman" (98, 99). Her other traits betray emotional turmoil: her eyes "burning as if they had cried," her skin flushed as if after "a heated discussion" (97, 98). From this the reader is meant to deduce the pain of an impending separation, although the narrator deduces nothing. She concludes that the blond Louise could not possibly be Mélinite the brunette.

Although highly attentive to social standing, Olga is at first unable to place Madame de la Bère, whose furnishings, like her appearance, give no indication of "her true social position" (96). At several points in the novel, the high-born Olga discourses at length on social divisions, revealing herself to be staunchly elitist at every turn. The very inability to situate Madame de la Bère is an indication of a society run amok by democratization: "since department stores began to sell furniture, one no longer knew where one stood: respectable women and disreputable women shopped in the same places" (96). As in *Mademoiselle Giraud*, lesbianism is related to this blurring of lines between the classes: "little by little, all kinds of vice [...] permeate our customs" (*Mademoiselle Giraud*, 153). Paule, the issue of an honest middle-class family, is corrupted by an aristocratic temptress. *Mélinite* offers the viewpoint of a haughty duchess who is quite cognizant of her social position and its boundaries. The Duchess Olga is higher on the social hierarchy than the Countess Berthe, and she aspires to be the wife of a prince, whose breeding meets her approval: "we are equal by birth, in social status and relations, almost by kinship" (*Mélinite*, 2–3).

Madame de la Bère recommends Louise highly, although "with a touch of bitterness," and assures the duchess that she will execute her work faithfully: "She will be seduced by many things that I am unable to offer her [...] a new mistress has an appeal that the old one no longer has." Instead of grasping that Madame de la Bère is relinquishing her lover to her, Olga finds that she "was giving too much importance to a chambermaid" (106). But Olga herself has lavished time and attention on the task of choosing Louise as her live-in companion: "This is the first time I've taken so much trouble for a chambermaid" (109).

Olga then retires to her chateau in the country, at Boulogne-sur-Mer, a name reminiscent of the Bois de Boulogne and, consequently, evocative of its mixed associations of genteel privilege and depraved trysting. It also confirms the leitmotif of doubling threaded through the novel, beginning with Paris, both respectable and disreputable, and the Bois, aristocratic and working class. Alone with Louise to wait on her, Olga discovers that her servant possesses superlative qualities: skill, discretion, intelligence. Here begins the work of seduction, of which Olga remains unaware, despite her weighted descriptions of Louise's attentions to her body. As Louise fixes her hair, Olga grows somnolent "under the comb's caress": "Such drowsiness and languor, which I had never before experienced in similar circumstances, gave me a feeling of well being, offered me small sensual pleasures, allowable ones, and I gave myself over to them" (136–7). The pleasure is reciprocal: "leaning over me, she seemed to admire me as if in ecstasy. For my part, half asleep, I couldn't help but find her most gracious in all her movements, in all her poses" (137–8).

Like *Mademoiselle Giraud*, this novel is written in the first person from the point of view of a narrator confronted with the mystery of another's lesbianism.

Through Adrien's perspective, the reader could not penetrate locked doors; Olga's journal, however, regales the reader with scenes of lesbian seduction. The novel is more titillating in its representation – perhaps the result of the banalization of its subject matter – and yet it maintains the same pretence of narratorial ignorance, which makes the reader's position all the more voyeuristic: we witness what Olga herself cannot recognize. Even after Louise kisses Olga's hair ("suddenly, contact with something burning, slightly damp"), Olga accepts a feeble excuse and scolds her, "half smiling, half serious" (138–9).

Louise becomes indispensable to Olga, reading her books she chooses herself. The description of Louise's reading preferences allows Belot to repeat his homily concerning the limits of audacity in fiction and the moral usefulness of novels for women. With this lesson intended for women, he excuses and counterbalances the voyeuristic descriptions his novels address to men. Speaking through Olga, Belot reaffirms his formula, which marries a daring subject matter with restrained language: "modern novels, new publications, authors who are audacious, but tactfully so" (171–2). Olga's self-description resembles Belot's intended reader: "a woman who is well-bred and honest, but curious, a seeker and searcher who is determined to educate herself." Here Belot makes female curiosity into a virtue, since such a woman dares to instruct herself "at the risk of a few small sacrifices to modesty" in order to "flee all dangers or fight them and, despite vice's appeal, to remain consciously virtuous." This is indeed a delicate balancing act. Will Olga herself, forever curious, explore the mysteries of Louise's sexuality without succumbing and emerge strengthened by her travails and lessons learned? Will Belot's readers, eagerly and bravely following Olga's tale of illicit love, remain virtuous despite the attraction of vice? Will they take away from the experience "a good and important lesson" (172–3)?

The novel posits an analogy between literary curiosity and sexual curiosity, concluding that it is the author's task to entice women readers with suggestive but always delicately phrased material, only to lead them to reject the very transgressions that capture their attention: "morality must emerge from what appears to be immoral." Women readers can take their pleasure and triumph over it, too, all without guilt and in the name of self-improvement.

Louise anticipates her mistress's every need and lavishes her with attention, the cumulative effect of which is a kind of submissiveness and a pleasant, but mind-numbing, languor: "long mornings in bed, baths, massages, naps, good meals, all my wants anticipated, all my caprices satisfied" (173–4). Her maid's attentions are to blame ("it's Louise Bauquet's fault") for inciting in Olga a passivity that impedes activity, including her habitual journal-writing. Olga begins to resemble the languid Madame de la Bère, and she reintroduces references to the East used earlier to describe her predecessor: "it's completely oriental" [C'est du pur Orient] (161).

Louise is "a submissive slave who is intelligent and capable, unlike any slave ever found in the harems of Egypt or Turkey," and Olga likens herself to "a sultan's wife, or at least the favourite mistress of a pasha" (160, 162). Louise introduces Olga to massage, a habit enjoyed by "most Turkish ladies," a skill learned by Louise "from a Negress at a Turkish bath" (162, 163). Such foreign, exotic, and sumptuous settings evoked here and in other lesbian fictions associate homosexuality with the foreign, which is at once appealing and treacherous. Olga's descriptions are more than suggestive as they linger on her nudity ("the satiny whiteness of my skin"), her pleasure, and Louise's excitement (164). She justifies her immodesty: "I am never ill at ease with [my chambermaid ...] I pay no mind when a woman looks at me, especially when she is in my service and has the duty of undressing me" (167).

But Olga's luxurious overload explodes one stormy afternoon after a bath. Both women are enervated by the tempest ("the storm was affecting her as it was me, and it was making her a bit agitated") when Louise begins to massage Olga and, in so doing, lulls her to sleep (176). The dozing duchess awakes to feel Louise's head on her knees: "suddenly I felt a light tickling on my skin from contact with hair [...] and at the same time a kind of weight, a warmth" (179). Olga recoils in horror and sends Louise away. She agonizes over the reasons for the kiss, torn between outrage and the desire to understand. Olga is unable to conceive of a non-platonic love between women, an idea she associates with the transgression of social boundaries: "love cannot exist between one woman and another, between a servant and her mistress" (191). She concludes that the kiss is a sign of Louise's subservient admiration ("this is how a slave kisses its master") and decides to keep her in her service, but at arm's length (187). She puts a stop to the massages, which are "too irritating for both masseuse and client" (188). Olga links this renunciation to the repudiation of the orient, which is also a symbolic return to heterosexuality: "I am also giving up my oriental life. I want to become once again a woman of the Occident, a woman of the North."

Just as Olga resumes the activities – walks in the country, journal-writing – of her life as an "occidental woman," she learns finally that Louise and Mélinite are one and the same from an unwitting Blazac. In her ramblings, she once again bumps into her cousin, who tells of his displeasure in learning that Mélinite is "a false brunette" who wears a wig to please Madame de la Bère, "her blond mistress who likes contrasts" (204, 230). Blazac adds that she lived as a maid with Madame de la Bère even after becoming rich, and he shares some details of their odd relationship, which ignores social distinctions ("they serve each other in turn"), but is discreet on other points (210). Echoing Belot's and Olga's recommendations for narrative restraint, Blazac insists on sanitizing his own storytelling: "I know how far I can go with a woman who isn't overly prudish, like you, and when to stop with a respectable woman" (209).

Horrified at having been served by her husband's murderer, although still unenlightened about Louise's sexuality, Olga confronts Louise with the knowledge of her double identity, which the latter does not deny, but rather confirms with a change in expression and affect: "Mélinite, the courtesan, was re-emerging along with her shamelessness, her audacity, her cynicism" (222). A change in linguistic register accompanies this metamorphosis, and in her diary Olga strives to recall not only the sense, but also Mélinite's "words themselves, in all their crudeness" – so different from Louise's "usual delicacy," which rivals that of Belot's ideal novelist, who "employs innuendo to say difficult things" (227). Mélinite offers to tell her story, which "is no more immoral than a novel" (224). Olga encourages her to do so in the hopes of learning her husband's fate and in order to satisfy her curiosity: "Go ahead and tell your story, don't hold back. [...] At least I will learn something, I'll have read one more bad novel, but a real, living novel. I'll satisfy my unhealthy curiosity that, to our shame, torments some of us!"

With "stark enjoyment in baring herself before a respectable woman," Mélinite recounts her ambitious rise, her hatred of men, and her liaison with the Baron de Virmeux, whom she still does not know to be Olga's husband (225). At first drawn to him, then angered by his refusal to treat her as an equal, she vows to act as a consummate courtesan and take him for his money. Mélinite bewitches him, then maddens him into impotence by withholding the ultimate favour, thus emasculating him despite the manliness suggested by his chosen name, *Vir*meux: "you aren't a man!" (265). He is left in a state of constant agitation in which his only option is to go back to her and try again. Male hysteria due to sexual withholding emerges as a common theme in Belot's work: "He died of shame for having loved me, of nervous irritation for not having possessed me."[40] The duke's naivety makes him particularly vulnerable to Mélinite's manipulations, and in this he resembles Adrien, "a naive man without much experience in life" (267). Olga pardons her husband, the victim of a lesbian femme fatale whose only crime is one they share: "he is only guilty of a moment of unhealthy curiosity" (274).

Mélinite shows herself to be at least as class conscious as Olga, having extravagant aspirations of social mobility. She refuses to consort with other servants: "My fellow servants, the house help, don't matter to me. I place my affections higher" (220). She singles out Olga precisely because of her rank: "a noble lady was all I was missing" (229). When introduced to the duke by his pseudonym, she reacted with disappointment, "What? he was only a baron" (244). Mélinite even remarks on the hierarchy of prostitution, and prides herself on occupying the highest echelon: "We are all co-workers, but to different degrees [...] there's no resemblance between those of us who have arrived, the high-class ones, and the lowly ones who never will" (247).

Olga is appalled, but suffers Mélinite's familiar and shocking language in order to hear her confession to its conclusion. When Mélinite finally declares her love for the duchess, Olga has difficulty grasping the concept: "Can a woman love another romantically? It's obvious that you're mad" (280). The worldly Olga's ignorance of and shock at homosexuality is harder to swallow than that of the naive Adrien, especially given her reading preferences and admission that "a few books skimmed through" had brought "this monstrous thing," "this sacrilegious love," to her attention (284–5). As if it were something that existed only in literature.

Olga desires vengeance and plots to treat Louise as Mélinite had treated her husband: to let her serve her for a price, but never to cede to her desires. As did Mélinite, Olga drives a hard bargain: "a woman like me must be worth more than a woman like you" (286). Like Adrien, she invokes the law: "the Code punishes murder with death" (289). The arrogant Mélinite is again transformed into the increasingly abject Louise and, as time passes, Louise gradually pays the duke's million back to the duchess (which she subsequently donates to widows and orphans).

After weeks of tormenting Louise, as Mélinite had the duke, with enticement and withholding ("a long, nerve-wracking intimacy only increased [Louise's] madness"), Olga's writing turns introspective (308). Is she harbouring a desire for Louise and might she succumb? "Perhaps, yes, I'll risk confessing it, for a second I became aware of my desire" (297). She finds herself guilty of thought crimes, "latent, passive sins" provoked by her imagination, "the real offender" (296). Although repulsed by the sexual expression of tribadism ("an abhorrent, unnatural longing"), Olga resumes the massages and takes pleasure in flirtation: "I'm not beyond coquetry [...], I dress up [...], I too make myself beautiful for her" (302–3). Olga is moved by Louise's devotion and quiet suffering and blames herself: "I was behaving badly, it was unworthy of me" (307). She vows to stop the charade, protect herself from temptation, and send Louise away. In a confrontation in the ruins of the old chateau, Olga tells Louise that she must leave and explains why a woman of her moral stature could never love another woman: "We are not made for your depravity; it revolts us" (320). She uses a vocabulary of both disease ("repugnant illness") and vice ("your perversions"), expressing "an instinctive aversion for all that appears unnatural" (321).

At the novel's melodramatic end, Louise learns that the Baron de Virmeux was in fact Olga's husband, that she is responsible for his death, and that consequently Olga is unattainable to her. Once again assuming the role of the other of her own vicious game, Louise throws herself into the (rather Baudelairean) abyss, dying, like the duke, for her unattainable desire: "He killed himself for me! I will kill myself for her in turn!" (324).

The novel's frame, recounted in the third person, closes with the marriage of the duchess and the prince. A new narrator speculates about the prince's reactions to Olga's journal, imagining his fear that she be lead astray: "he was doubtlessly unnerved to see the duchess, after having gone so far and become so aroused, stop without satisfying her curiosity" (326). Then follow two contradictory programs for keeping her in the fold, one libertine and the other paternalistic. In the first case, the husband himself instructs his wife in sexual technique in order to satisfy her curiosity. The narrator claims that men are more expert at sexual instruction since they can demonstrate both heterosexual and homosexual activity: "in this kind of education, men are superior to women: they can teach everything women teach and also what they will never teach" (327). Female homosexuality is thus reduced to the mastery of a sexual act, presumably cunnilingus, which, once known to the wife, renders lesbianism superfluous: "Girls with golden eyes, Maupins, Miss Girauds, and Mélinites are not really so dangerous." Belot has added his own work to the chain of lesbian fictions.

But in his second scenario, the narrator cautions against such marital sexual experimentation and delivers a sententious warning to all husbands about the dangers of introducing their wives to "the refinements of love." To do so is to show a lack of respect for the institution of marriage, already diminished by divorce, and to defile "the lawful wife and mother" whose purpose it is to "make beautiful, healthy babies who are free from the neuroses of our time" (328). Non-procreative matrimonial relations were frequently referred to and broadly condemned as "conjugal fraud." Such sexual acts, whose slippery slope inclines towards sapphic love, were thought to be contagious and a threat to marital stability and family formation. Female sexual curiosity places sexual fulfilment before the imperative to reproduce. Moreover, even the "latent, passive sin" of fantasy or homosexual practices learned from a husband can lead to sapphism proper: "the female imagination does not know how to stop itself [...] women run toward the unknown." The novel's final sentence, which contradicts the earlier claim that sapphism is "not really so dangerous," alerts readers to the explosive and insidious peril of female homosexuality for both men and women: "Mélinites are equally dangerous for both sexes" (329).

Like *Mademoiselle Giraud*, *Mélinite* does its part in conveying normative values by raising the spectre of female homosexuality. Female curiosity can lead to moral ruin; lesbianism is a foreign, unnatural, and nefarious curse to both men and women; and class mixing is as undesirable as sexual segregation. And yet, despite their similarities, *Mélinite* trumps *Mademoiselle Giraud* in audacity with its deliberations about sexual technique. The vibrant and curious duchess doubles for the naive Adrien in seeking answers to lesbian mysteries, and yet by virtue of narrating her own seduction rather than a fruitless pursuit, she offers the gift of greater detail to the voyeuristic reader (both the prince and the reading public). Olga is, moreover, a much more interesting character than Adrien, since she demonstrates greater introspection. She is also a stronger adversary than her own husband, who more fully embodies the weakened and victimized fin-de-siècle man. Despite its melodrama and forced coincidences, the plotting of *Mélinite* is, like Olga, more sophisticated and thoroughly rendered, reading less like a meandering feuilleton written in instalments. Finally, although the lesbian character is to a certain extent more formulaic, given that the signifiers of lesbianism were more entrenched by the end of the 1880s, she is nonetheless more fully drawn and evolutive. Called a viper, as was Berthe, she moves towards redemption as did Paule, from the socially pretentious and murderous Mélinite to the increasingly abject and compliant chambermaid, Louise Bauquet. Her changeability, as we will see in the next section, could be applied to Belot's writing itself: "I know how to disguise myself, to transform myself quite well" (317).

Naming and Knowing in Belot's Erotic Fiction

Tribade: How strangely the word rang in the ear. What images it summoned up: of voluptuous pleasures, of lusts carried to the ultimate degree, of endless foreplay, of releases which, once achieved, led only to greater but even less achievable delights.

(Musset, *Gamiani*)

Tribadism, incest, flagellation, refined depravity [...] such foul language to label what has throughout the ages been considered natural, and which today is publicly condemned by the hypocritical bourgeoisie alone [...] while they commit such things in private.

(*Sélect luxure*)[41]

Belot's sapphic best-sellers pay explicit attention to the proprieties of storytelling. They insist on the importance of what remain unsaid and on the necessity of refined language: "it is true that the subject of *Mademoiselle Giraud, My Wife* is a delicate one, but its form was rigorously attended to, in order to avoid any evil-sounding expression, any excessively vivid depiction, any indiscreet detail" (*Mademoiselle Giraud*, 9). In doing so, these novels condemn verbal liberties, such as Mélinite's "enjoyment in baring herself" (*Mélinite*, 225). They might be said to practise and preach the linguistic equivalent of the secret, in which the bounds of language and knowledge are coextensive. The Duchess Olga refuses familiar or coarse language and, despite her curiosity, remains ignorant of homosexuality ("a monstrous idea") until told of it plainly, literally, unreservedly by Mélinite, who uses words "in all their crudeness" (285, 227) – comparable to Blangy's delivery of the uncensored truth to Adrien: "I will tell you everything I know" [de la façon la plus précise] (*Mademoiselle Giraud*, 147). In contrast with Olga, the omnivorous Mélinite speaks without restraint and brooks no limits to experience or understanding: "I wanted to know everything" (*Mélinite*, 229).

Belot's heterosexual blockbuster, *La Bouche de Madame X* (1882), functions in an intermediary fashion with respect, on one hand, to the sententious lesbian best-sellers, whose linguistic reticence it shares, and, on the other, to his erotic fiction, which invites libidinal exploration and pleasure. This novel allows the heterosexual transgressions it recounts to escape vilification, and in doing so condones the disconnection of language and experience, of style and content. Whereas in *Mademoiselle Giraud* the elevated linguistic register is purportedly cautionary (the evil is gingerly portrayed in order to warn and edify), the equivalent language in *Madame X* is *permissive* of its arguably more audacious content. *Madame X* introduces itself as a bold tale whose refined language and aristocratic characters render it acceptable reading for well-bred but sexually curious women: "although risqué in certain respects, it is written with great discretion" (14). It tells the story of the Countess Gabrielle (Madame X), who goes to a "trysting house" [maison de rendez-vous galant], a brothel for aristocratic women in search of pleasure as well as gain, where she commits adultery because her impotent husband cannot satisfy her. It is recounted from the point of view of a well-bred man who meets her there and becomes infatuated with her particularly voluptuous lips.[42] Similar to Olga's quest for Mélinite's identity, the narrator is obsessed with determining who this woman is, her name, and her social standing.

Madame X is framed as a first-person manuscript-confession that makes its way into the hands of another party who then publishes it, a device we have come to see as typical of Belot's fiction. It contains three levels of storytelling:

(a) the first-person narrator, Count D (a well-travelled and well-known Parisian bon vivant), recounts his conquest of Madame X in a manuscript prepared at the request of
(b) W, a Hungarian princess, described as "good looking, witty, utterly elegant," but also as having "cosmopolitan tastes and habits [...] an independent character, and a rather uninhibited appearance" (4). She gives the manuscript to her friend X, a Frenchman travelling in Hungary. In turn X passes it along to his best friend,
(c) the ostensible editor and unnamed narrator of the frame, who opens the novel by explaining the provenance of the story and relating the meeting of Princess W and X in Budapest, at which they discuss literary style and the needs of sophisticated women readers.

These multiple narrative layers establish a decorous distance between the indecencies of the plot and its recounting – this in sharp contrast to techniques used by Belot to heighten the immediacy of his erotic texts (such as the adoption of the present tense in graphic passages). The frame establishes doubles for the central characters: Madame X and Princess W are sophisticated, sensual women in search of fulfilment (sexual and literary), while still careful to safeguard their reputation. Count D and X are worldly men linked by the princess and their interest in Madame X's story. Of greatest interest to my argument is the double role played by Princess W, who, as both the intended reader of Count D's story and literary critic, weighs the readability of Madame X's tale. The princess compares it favourably to contemporary treatments of sexually daring subject matter. Although she does not name naturalism, which was characterized broadly in the press of the day as crude of language and obsessed with sordid environments (a naturalist preoccupation), it bears the brunt of her negative criticism.

The literary playing field had shifted considerably since Zola defended Belot in his preface to *Mademoiselle Giraud*. No longer a young man appealing to a more successful writer, Zola had profited financially and professionally from the scandalous successes of novels called "pornographic" by some critics. The "physiological" novels of naturalism sold in previously unimagined numbers, and as broadly as they were consumed, they were just as broadly condemned by critics and moralists. So in the case of *Madame X*, Belot calls upon Zola as a foil rather than as a defender. The novel opens by mimicking the ambient repudiation of naturalism that grew along with Zola's success.

The prologue of *Madame X* thus takes pains to distance the story that follows from naturalist representations. The Hungarian princess calls on novelists to write for "women who would happily stray beyond their moral milieu, but on the condition of remaining in their physical milieu" (28). She claims to appreciate a story that is both audacious and discreet – not unlike herself – but which avoids seamy settings: "Why have us descend into basements and cellars [...] when one could instead open doors to unexplored drawing rooms, boudoirs, and bedrooms into which we would willingly peek, timidly and furtively, but also probingly?" (17). In other words, Belot provides sexual escapades without slumming, for even while *Madame X* might be said to tell the story of a woman who leaves her physical environment for a brothel, this is a bordello *comme il faut*.

In addition to repudiating indecorous milieus, the princess prefers linguistic restraint over "le mot tout cru," language that is coextensive with such unseemly settings (14). Women readers like herself "allow all liberties save that of language" (27). She blames contemporary novelists for their vulgarity: "Truly sirs, you novelists fail to engage those women who are curious to see all there is to see and avid to learn as much [...] you allow your rather vulgar tastes to spill over [...]. You throw yourselves headlong into unseemly details and daring expressions" (17, 21–2). In spite of this risqué subject matter and of the rash of censorship trials against naturalist and decadent authors in the 1880s, the censors left *Madame X* alone: could this have been because of the author's ostentatious repudiation of indecency? [43]

Belot's advocates included the outspoken feminist Olympe Audouard.[44] Audouard had a prior history of defending women writers, having responded to Barbey d'Aurevilly's misogynist invective (*Barbey d'Aurevilly: Réponse à ses réquisitoires contre les bas-bleus*, 1870). Adopting a discourse similar to that of the Princess W, Audouard condemns Zola (and by extension naturalism) and takes Belot as an ally for women in pursuit of a language of refined sensuality. In an 1883 portrait of Belot, she contrasts the two: "Zola is a pornographer. [...] Adolphe Belot strikes me as a sensualist [whose] works, while sometimes suggestive, retain the language of a man of the world who would like to speak openly, but in the words of a well-bred man" (*Silhouettes*, 308).

Belot accomplishes several things with the framing structure of *Madame X*. He mocks the now-consecrated naturalist writers with whom he had regularly collaborated. At the same time he flatters his women readers by associating them with the upper classes and cultivated tastes: they can read about sexual exploits without encountering the squalid settings or clinical language attributed to naturalist fiction. Belot gives them permission to read on by disassociating his novel from the kind of literature labelled morally offensive – a calculation that paid off, since *Madame X* appears to have been an even bigger seller than *Mademoiselle Giraud*, with fifty editions in its first year.

Although addressed to women, the suggestive intrigue of *Madame X* undoubtedly also appealed to heterosexual male readers. Whatever the actual composition of Belot's audience, something that can never be known with certainty, his novels, and the popular novel in general, were presumed to rely on a largely female readership, hence the obligation to employ euphemistic language and remain within the bounds of the socially acceptable. But Belot's anonymously published erotic works were ostensibly written for men, and their language is another matter entirely: these forbidden books ("livres de deuxième rayon") were all about licence.

Baring It All in the Back Room

> both women, half naked and rolling around in each other's arms, abandoned themselves to tribadism's most exquisite pleasures and lesbianed each other [se lesbianisèrent] repeatedly.
>
> (Belot, *La Canonisation de Jeanne d'Arc*)

Lesbian pornography has a much longer history than does the more reticent popular novel. Eighteenth-century libertine authors (notably, Pidansat de Mairobert,

Restif de la Bretonne, Sade) relied to a considerable extent on same-sex intrigues. According to Bonnie Zimmerman's *Lesbian Histories and Cultures*, "Half of the titles of eighteenth-century French pornography contain lesbian sex scenes" (270). Marie-Jo Bonnet has suggested, moreover, that eighteenth-century erotica was responsible for renewing literary sapphism: "Sappho re-enters literature through libertinage."[45] Erotica was widely produced if strictly prohibited in nineteenth-century France, and even following legislation in 1881 that overturned prior censorship laws, there remained a clause prohibiting immoral works ("offence of gross indecency"). In addition to those by Belot, noteworthy nineteenth-century erotic texts include Alfred de Musset's *Gamiani* (1833), Henry Monnier's *Deux gougnottes, Dialogues infâmes* (1864), Gustave Droz's *Un été à la campagne* (1868), and a number of titles by others such as Effe Géache, Pierre Louÿs, and Hugues Rebell.[46] Many French authors of erotica published anonymously in Belgium where laws were less stringent, their books then sold under the counter or in the back room ("sous le manteau" or "dans l'arrière-boutique") in France. Although they avoided the censors in this way, an unsigned text effectively nullified authorship rights: writers of erotica could not reliably profit from sales or the publicity that otherwise accrued to signed works.[47] Under these conditions, sex sold, but one could speculate that the takings benefited publishers much more than authors. Belot's signed novels, risqué but within bounds, earned him his keep, while he wrote pornography for reasons other than financial gain.

At least ten explicitly erotic texts have been ascribed to Belot, each one featuring sapphic content.[48] Most were signed A.B. or accredited to "the author of *La Maison à plaisirs*." Attribution of anonymously published erotic material is notoriously difficult, added to the fact that most of those associated with Belot were published posthumously. Those likely written by him are *L'Éducation d'une demi-vierge* (1883), *La Maison à plaisirs, ou La Passion de Gilberte* (c. 1888), *Les Heures érotiques modernes* (1890), *Les Péchés de Minette* (1890), "L'Art de payer sa couturière" (1890), *La Canonisation de Jeanne d'Arc* (1890), and *Stations de l'amour* (1896).[49] There is some suggestion that other authors signed works as A.B. in order to capitalize on the success of previous erotic novels so signed.[50] The analyses in the following pages rely on similarities with Belot's popular fiction, which I believe substantiate his authorship of the novels in question.

What remains to demonstrate here is the antithetical but complementary nature of Belot's two œuvres, the popular and the pornographic. The trope of secrecy and the guarded language of the popular novels give way to unveiled sexual encounters, explicitly recounted. Several of the erotic texts read like novels of sexual education, sometimes within the context of a conjugal relationship, casting marriage in a much different light than that found in his popular fiction. Indeed, one could interpret them as liberatory in their celebration of female sexuality in general and of lesbian eroticism in particular (although, as in *Gamiani*, the male gaze is never far from the peephole). There is also a certain amount of mirroring at work here, with personages (their names, their elevated social status), preoccupations (particularly domestic arrangements), and plotlines of the mainstream novels either recycled or reconsidered in the erotica.

In contrast to Belot's popular novels, which have no explicit sexual content and, according to Zola, are "chaste in the extreme" (*Mademoiselle Giraud*, 7), his erotic production names sexual acts and relies on their verbalization by the actors. *Les Stations de l'amour* is an epistolary novel framed as the erotic correspondence of a husband and wife discovered years after the fact. During a separation forced by the husband's travels, they give each other permission to pursue sexual liaisons under the condition that they tell each other everything, "in detail and without reserve" (45). Cécile complies faithfully with these rules as she relates her sexual encounters with her chambermaid, Thérèse, to her husband Léo.

Naming sexual acts and players is also central to the lesbian scene in Belot's one-act play, "L'Art de payer sa couturière" ("The Art of Paying One's Dressmaker"), in which the profligate Madame du Rény works off her debts in exchange for sex. She turns three tricks in her dressmaker's back room, her encounters becoming progressively more daring, with a sapphic episode placed at the climactic end. Here the respectably married Madame du Rény is initiated by the alluring Marquise du Château-noir, who quickly triumphs over the former's hesitation. As Madame du Rény's curiosity gets the better of her, it is to positive effect, in direct contrast to the shameful consequences of Olga's untamed inquisitiveness: "I'm curious, just like Eve [...] I feel a new kind of desire: this marquise is quite lovely!" (625). When the two get down to business, the Marquise du Château-noir's sexual excitement depends on hearing Madame du Rény describe her preceding encounter in graphic language: "Tell me he put his cock in your cunt [...] say it with dirty words" (626).

While *Mademoiselle Giraud* and *Mélinite* avoided the vocabulary of lesbianism, suggesting a character's sexuality instead through portraiture, comportment, or association, that which goes unnamed in mainstream novels appears liberally in erotic fiction: "tribades" and "lesbiennes" describe the sapphic couple in Belot's *Gilberte*. Even the vulgar slang "gougnottes" is a word that "is not unfamiliar to the fair sex": "here, here's my cunt; come and suck it my sweet, lick me, my darling dyke" [gougnotte] (*Maison*, 69; "L'Art," 627). Verbalization functions both to arouse the sexual partners portrayed in the text and to excite the voyeuristic reader.

Belot's erotic novels reuse the daring but delicately delivered material of his bestsellers. The physical description of the Marquise du Château-noir combines elements of portraits found in *Mademoiselle Giraud* and *Mélinite*: "swarthy, with searing eyes; a light down descends from her hairline onto her cheeks" ("L'Art," 624). She is typical of many representations of dominant lesbians for her masculine attire, brown hair, and – a detail perhaps gleaned from contemporary physicians – her unusually large clitoris ("it's like a man's thing!"). The sign of complementarity appears here as it did in *Mademoiselle Giraud*, with the marquise remarking to Madame du Rény, "how white your skin is; see how mine is darker" (625). Adrien's pleasure with contrasting women is also echoed in *Maison*, whose male narrator admires the two women who join him for a threesome: "Here I am between two lovely women, one blond and the other chestnut, almost brunette, a pleasant contrast" (47). The author attributes this penchant for contrasting skin and hair colour to his female characters as well. For example, the narrator of *Les Péchés de Minette* ponders that "blondes have a predilection for women with dark hair, while brunettes always prefer blondes: a quirk of nature that physiologists can explain perfectly" (56).

The common elements shared by *Madame X* and *La Maison à plaisir* invite one to read the latter as an erotic variation of the earlier popular novel. Both are written from the point of view of a man who enters a "maison à plaisirs" and is delighted to find himself serviced by a well-bred woman. The narrator of *Madame X* describes, in general terms, the heterogeneity of visitors attracted to the brothel. In *Maison*, however, the clientele, male and female, and their proclivities are described explicitly: "for those who practised lesbian love, it provided a discreet place to meet with a sweetheart and, together, abandon themselves to guilty pleasures; or, failing that, to be paired with young women who understood and shared their penchant, who liked to give and receive the lingual caresses that drive tribades wild" (7–8). Unlike the secrecy that surrounds lesbian sexuality in his popular fiction, Belot's erotic novels require openness. Even the racy *Madame X* relies on the secret of an identity that remains a mystery, building suspense until its final revelation; in *Maison*, however, there is no suspense, and the woman is immediately revealed to be the surprised narrator's cousin. Transparency instead of cloaking rules in the erotica: "would you really do that in front of me?" (*Maison*, 69). The illicit voyeurism of the popular novels, in which male readers are enticed to search beyond the edifying facades erected for women in order to catch glimpses of forbidden sexuality, is replaced with an explicit invitation to look.

In the popular fiction, secrets cloak forbidden knowledge revealed only under duress. But characters of the erotic novels hold secrets of coveted sexual knowledge, which they generously impart to one another in scenes of initiation. In *Les Péchés de Minette*, the title narrator shares with her female lover the secret to marital fidelity ("Read [my diary]; it holds my *secret*," 82): husbands remain faithful to wives who behave like mistresses and are sexually adventuresome ("*to become the mistress* of one's husband"). A woman who makes love "*out of duty* and flat on her back cannot expect to keep [her husband] faithful forever" (51). The irony of Minette's own infidelity is unintentional, since faithfulness is defined heterosexually, and since her husband, the Baron Gontran (who shares the sexually evocative name [*con, gonorrhée*] of Olga's husband), is not threatened by her women lovers: "I'm not saying that I wouldn't be jealous if you shared your heart or gave yourself to another man; but it's not the same thing with a woman. I will always be your only male, and you will only have *friends of your sex*" (53).

Throughout his work, Belot associates lesbianism and insatiability, suggesting that there is something lacking: "as tired as I am, I don't feel satisfied; there's something still missing" (*Minette*, 67). Even after Gontran gives Minette a dildo to use with her lover, the Marquise Marguerite B (a friend from boarding school), Minette opines that "I don't think that it could favourably replace a husband's jewels" (106). Gontran does not interfere in their lovemaking, since he profits both in hiding during the women's trysts and after them. As he looks on from the neighbouring room, Gontran functions as a stand-in for the reader who follows the exploits of Marguerite and Minette. Likewise, Gontran's actions after his wife is done with her lover presumably mirror the reader's fantasies of satisfying what remains to be satisfied with the benefit of the "husband's jewels."

Even while asserting the supremacy of heterosexual intercourse, Belot betrays a fascination with oral sex, most blatantly in *Les Péchés de Minette* in which the narrator is coached in the art of oral sex, or *faire minette*. If the fantasies that involve the alluring mouth of *Madame X* go only as far as a kiss, several of Belot's erotic novels involve an experienced woman instructing a neophyte on the art of cunnilingus. Let us recall that cunnilingus is implicitly identified as the sexual technique constitutive of lesbianism in *Mélinite*, where the husband proves to be a more apt instructor than a female lover. In *Gilberte*, which spends a good deal of time describing both cunnilingus and fellatio, the question is rephrased: "who does it better, a man or a woman?" (73). Gilberte is asked to judge as the narrator and another woman take turns, and yet "the question remained unanswered, with the result that many ladies delight in repeating this comparative study of tongues" (74). Elsewhere in the novel, however, it is suggested that women are the more experienced teachers: "It's true that ladies are initiated into the most ingenious refinements of sensual delight by other women, much more frequently than by men" (34). The reader can again detect an echo from the moralizing *Mademoiselle Giraud* – "men don't ruin women, women ruin each other" – which decries instead of celebrates such initiations.

It is notable that several of Belot's erotic texts are written in the female first person (Cécile's letters, the authors of the journals in *Minette* and *Canonisation*) and address women readers. Direct addresses frequently reference transgressive language: "to use an expression that women readers will forgive" (*Canonisation*, 677); "an odd expression, isn't it ladies?" (*Maison*, 67); "If ever these secrets should fall into the hands of a prude, she would surely wonder how a lady bearing a title of nobility could write of such improprieties, could indulge in such ghastly language" (*Minette*, 76–7). Even while asking how her reader would react to such accounts, the narrator invites her to cast off prejudice and embrace sexual freedom: "following a fine meal, which flames the fires of desire in our womanly thoughts, what matter could social propriety and society's hypocrisy be to us?" (*Minette*, 69). Instead of enforcing the sexual double standard, as do Belot's popular novels, the erotic novels condemn such hypocrisy: "I then grasped the injustice of the social position allotted to women, obliged by absurd conventions to cloister themselves and suffer in silence, while men …" (31). The women of Belot's erotica take charge of their sexuality, whether under the tutelage of a husband (*Stations*, *Minette*) or freed from the restrictions of marriage by the newly acquired right to divorce (*Éducation*).

I do not mean to suggest that Belot's use of women narrators and narratees, or his critique of social convention, make of him a crusader for female sexual liberation. The disjuncture between female narratee and implied male reader in fact enables male voyeurism of female homosexuality. The homonarrative relationship between Minette and the women to whom she recounts sexual acts between women intensifies the feminine intimacy on display. On one level, Belot supplies sexually uninhibited and insatiable women to people the fantasies of heterosexual male readers for whom lesbianism functions as a potent lubricant. On another, Minette shares it all with Marguerite and the unnamed prudes she imagines will read her. One finds the inverse in such popular novels as *Mademoiselle Giraud* and *Mélinite*, in which the narratees are male, but the implied readership is arguably both male and female, and the novel itself is angled towards a double reading.

Given the unbridled sexuality of Belot's erotica, the moralizing of his popular novels must be taken with a grain of salt. In their competing discourses, the choice to inscribe sexual excess or sexual repression depended upon the rules of the literary field rather than an inherent, consistent moral or political stance regarding female sexuality. Logically then, genre divisions, insofar as they can be clearly marked given the kind of cross-pollination we have seen, owe a good deal to niche marketing, to the necessity of conforming to the expectations and desires of a specific readership as key to authorial success. Whether condemning or arousing or both at once, Belot's best-sellers aim to flatter bourgeois sensibilities while placating the authorities in order to turn a profit. His pornography aims to arouse male readers while bypassing censors.

In addition to studying the nuances that separate narratee from implied reader, perhaps we also need to question the *actual* readers of these texts and the potential readings they might produce. We could then accept the possibility that, just as *Madame X* permitted women to read about marital infidelity,

Mademoiselle Giraud and Belot's other lesbian novels unintentionally provided his female readership with the opportunity to envisage a different kind of sexual expression. If we take for granted that erotic lesbian fiction sexually aroused its male readership, could we not conclude as well that Belot's female readers also read out of desire? Did some women have access to Belot's erotica and use it as a source of fantasy and identification as they undoubtedly did the popular novels that made him famous?

Sarane Alexandrian, surrealist, art historian, and devotee of erotic literature, has praised the "finesse" and "sincerity" of Belot's writing, concurring with this anonymous assessment: "This fin-de-siècle erotomaniac brings *sincerity* above all to his libidinous tales, but retains all the illusion of *tasteful debauchery* for his reader."[51] Alexandrian dismissed Belot's popular novels ("the fundamental insipidity of literature […] that conforms to the taste of bourgeois readers"), but would canonize the erotica: "only that which springs from a writer's deepest desire renders him interesting for posterity" (608). It is debatable whether indeed Belot's libidinally invested pornography emanates *sincerely* (> Latin *sincerus*, meaning clean or pure) from his deepest desires, in contrast with his unprincipled best-sellers, calculated to please the public and make money. One could imagine that Belot *sincerely* enjoyed different kinds of pleasure (sensual, financial, perhaps even literary) while practising these seemingly antithetical genres. Regardless of whatever benefits Belot's writing afforded him, the contrasting lesbian intrigues in his best-selling novels and in his furtive erotic fictions illustrate the arbitrary nature of many constructions of female homosexuality. This arbitrariness, coupled with the supposition that actual women readers attempting to name their *own* pleasures consumed Belot's work, raises more questions still about identification and the power of literature, in all its genres.

3 Dystopian Sapphism: Anti-Feminism, Class Warfare, and the Elite Novel at the Fin de Siècle

The two conditions of womanhood: prostitution and aristocracy, the Whore and the Lady.

(Mendès, *Méphistophéla*)[1]

"Fin de siècle" denotes the end point of a period of time dominated by a pessimistic political and philosophical outlook. It also refers to an aesthetic stance, whose relation to the idea of cultural decline is anything but straightforward. In his widely read book *Degeneration* (1892), the German journalist and physician Max Nordau asserted that, although international in its application, "*Fin-de-siècle* is French, for it was in France that the mental state so entitled was first consciously realized" (1). His work both exemplifies the cultural divide that pivoted on the idea of decline and encompasses the inconsistencies of the period. Nordau championed scientific progress while he decried artistic innovation, which he believed to be the product of physical degeneration and social decay. Such cultural conservatism was not atypical of liberal positivists of his day who placed faith in the ability of science to usher rational nations towards a new age. Nordau believed that progress relied on order and sobriety, but was undermined by the fin-de-siècle ethos, in which he discerned "emancipation from traditional discipline [...], unbridled lewdness, [and] the unchaining of the beast in man" (5). The Darwinian concept of the "beast in man," or as Zola called it, *la bête humaine*, was a central tenet of naturalism.

Nordau took each school of French writing in turn and denounced it for its contribution to cultural decomposition; he was indiscriminately critical of movements that were antithetical to each other both in their literary programs and in their philosophical outlook. Nordau's rhetoric alternately resembled those who derided naturalism ("the filth of Zola's art," 13) and the naturalists themselves, literary champions of scientific rationality. In his defence of bourgeois conventions, Nordau presented an argument strikingly similar to those *supporting* idiosyncratic exceptionality: "The ordinary man always seeks to think, to feel, and to do the same as the multitude: the decadent seeks exactly the contrary" (306). Many decadent authors and the characters they created have taken such a vision of conformity as an invitation to eccentricity. According to the men of letters incriminated by Nordau, the rise of the tribade as fin-de-siècle icon inhabits *both* the multitude and its contrary.

This chapter will consider the impact of political, cultural, and social change on the representation of the sapphist in the literary novel of the century's divisive final quarter. No longer exclusively the stuff of poetry, pornography, and commercial literature, same-sex female eroticism came under the critical eye of writers who had a much greater investment in both literariness and politics. Although female homosexuality was no less sensational a presence in highbrow fiction, it served less to boost sales (although it nonetheless continued to do so) than it did to epitomize cultural disarray. The tribade first became fodder for naturalist writers, and soon after decadent authors began to feed from the same trough. By 1880, the literary lesbian was more than ever a measure of social turmoil.

Let us recall the salient factors contributing to the upheaval and the great transformations of the period: the effects of France's defeat at the hands of the Prussians in the war of 1870–1, a new political landscape created by the fall of the Second Empire and establishment of the Third Republic, the march of industrial progress and the demographic and social changes that ensued, the creation of a workers' movement, and the rise of first-wave feminism. These elements were involved in the nation's increasing polarization, in which the secular was pitted against the religious, republicans and radicals against monarchists and Bonapartists, confidence in scientific and social progress against the fear of decline, and democratic ideals against nostalgia for aristocratic ascendency. These political and ideological differences were paralleled by those dividing the major novelistic trends at the end of the century. They too defined themselves against each other, but their quarrels were more than simply aesthetic. As we shall see, naturalist and decadent literature represented distinct world views that reflected contemporary politics and social issues. One important commonality was this: both told stories of dystopian sapphism.

The proliferation of tribades in literature coincided with the consecration of the novel as an intellectual endeavour in both naturalist and decadent camps. A frightening figure of female independence and excess during a tumultuous and disorienting time, the lesbian provided a trope for those seeking literary ascendancy, through which they voiced the fears and desires of beleaguered masculinity. Representations of lesbian abjection can be read as defensive, reactionary posturing from the right and the left, both intimidated by the prospect of growing numbers of independent women. And yet an antithetical response accompanied the disciplinary and punitive obsession with lesbianism as allegory for wayward femininity: a lurid fascination with the sexual unknown. Without overlooking the similarities and points of contact and exchange between naturalism and decadence – and their common reaction to "the woman question" will be of primary concern here – the following pages will focus on their competing political leanings and aesthetic agendas, a rivalry evident in their contrasting treatment of female homosexuality.

Serious Novels Rising

Cultural historian Christophe Charle has suggested that the political investment of writers changed drastically in the early days of the Third Republic, that following a period of apathy and "absolute separation between political and literary domains" during the Second Empire, France witnessed "the invasion of politics in the literary field" (*Crise* 147). Not only had the political climate and social battles evolved into something very different, the emerging literary tendencies could also stake out their territories with greater freedom when the era of moral order ended (1879) and new legislation relaxed the grip of the censor (1881). What follows will review the history and evolution of the literary field that paralleled political changes: these supplied the backdrop against which literary lesbians, hand puppets for great novelists, enacted scenes of social strife.

The first inklings of naturalism's success appeared in the 1860s, with novels such as the Goncourt brothers' *Germinie Lacerteux* (1864) and Zola's *Thérèse Raquin* (1867). These and other authors placed themselves in the realist tradition of Stendhal, Balzac, and Flaubert, although the emerging naturalist doctrine differentiated itself by its interest in scientific method and its "documentary" approach. *Thérèse Raquin*, a novel about a woman whose lover murders her husband, was, let us recall, inspired by Belot's 1866 feuilleton, *La Vénus de Gordes*, itself based on a *fait divers* that took place in the southern village of Gordes.

Zola's reimagining of Belot's novel is instructive about the development of naturalist theory. He moved the setting from the countryside to a Parisian arcade, for Walter Benjamin the quintessential emblem of nineteenth-century modernity, allowed the crime to go unpunished by the law, and, after a time, married the adulterous couple. The pair, which had been driven by desire for one another to commit the crime, avoids legal reckoning but is tormented by guilt-induced hallucinations of the dead husband, too frightened to continue their relations but doomed to sleep in the same bed. Zola's stated goal, which involves the human animal anathema to Nordau, was, "given a powerful man and an unfulfilled woman, to look for the animal in them, to see only the animal, to throw them into a violent drama and scrupulously observe their feelings and actions."[2] Taking a banal story following a conventional arc of betrayal, murder, and retribution, Zola reworked the plot into a cutting-edge study of modernity and lust, one that attracted virulent criticism in spite of its claim to objectivity and empiricism: "my aim was above all scientific [...] I did no more than practice upon two living bodies the analytic work that surgeons practise on cadavers."[3] In a diatribe that appeared in *Le Figaro* targeting *Germinie Lacerteux*, *Thérèse Raquin*, and *La Comtesse de Chalis*, Louis Ulbach (writing as Ferragus) called Zola's novel "a puddle of mud and blood that all too faithfully sums up the putridity of contemporary literature" ("La Littérature putride").

Three years later, Zola published *La Fortune des Rougon*, the first instalment of his twenty-volume novel cycle *Les Rougon-Macquart*, which would attract even greater critical censure than *Thérèse Raquin*. Predicated upon the idea of a hereditary taint that descends from one generation of a family to the next, each novel addresses a different social problem or milieu, but the backdrop of degeneration remains ever present. The task that Zola set for himself was to resolve "the double question of temperament and milieu," the interrelation between nature and social environment.

By the late 1870s, naturalism had produced a good number of other controversial blockbusters and become the reigning literary trend. In an "impartial review," *Le Figaro* likened Zola to Sade and wrote of *L'Assommoir* (1876), "This is not realism, it is filth; it is worse than crudeness: it is pornography." This did not, however, prevent the critic, Millaud, from quoting the novel at length. He condemned the work for its subject matter ("writing in which abjection does battle with abnormality") and its author for his politics: "Zola is the apostle of democratic and social literature." These two faults are ultimately interrelated, it is implied, for only an author with socialist leanings would choose to portray the ravages of alcoholism in a working-class neighbourhood. Similar accusations were regularly repeated in the press: 1880 was dubbed *l'année pornographique*, partly in response to the publication of Zola's *Nana*, which features a man-eating courtesan and her prostitute lover.

This was also a defining year for Zola's group as a movement: 1880 saw the publication of both *Le Roman expérimental* and *Les Soirées de Médan*. The first, a collection of essays, established the theoretical basis for naturalism in analogy to physiologist Claude Bernard's *Introduction à la médecine expérimentale* (1865), whose project Zola characterized as "virile," an attribute of central importance to his conception of naturalism.[4] Zola claimed to apply Bernard's scientific method to the novel in order "to prove in laboratory experiments laws that appear to hold true in nature." He envisaged the naturalist writer as a scientist, less a creator than an observer, not one who invents but rather relates findings based upon inquiry and documentation. Formal issues were of negligible importance to the naturalist project, whereas *method* was primary. In fact, Zola considered preoccupation with style to be an affectation: "contemporary writers exaggerate the importance of form [...] these days we are overloaded with poetry."[5] Stylistically, naturalism was essentially conservative, favouring omniscient narration, linear plotting, and unadorned prose. Despite his brutal plotlines and inelegant language, Zola nonetheless reached for rhetorical figures (hyperbole first among them) and was not reticent to invest his works with symbolism, the tell that revealed what Barthes would later call the reality effect.

Les Soirées de Médan, named after the locale of Zola's country home where he often entertained young writers, is a collection of short stories, each set during the Franco-Prussian war, by Zola and five disciples (Guy de Maupassant, J-K Huysmans, Léon Hennique, Henry Céard, Paul Alexis). Under the tutelage of Zola, the Médan group, which had been gathering since the mid-1870s, consecrated the style as a literary movement. These writers produced controversial novels that incurred critical indignation. The eminent critic Ferdinand Brunetière lambasted naturalism for its subjects, language, and immorality: "it is an art that sacrifices form to subject matter, picture to colour, feeling to sensation, and the ideal to the real. It does not shrink from triviality, nor even brutality, but speaks its language to the crowd, finding it easier to make art beholden to the basest instincts of the masses than to raise their intelligence to the level of art."[6] Brunetière accused Zola of having "denigrated bourgeois customs" with "the obscene and grotesque visions of his agitated imagination" (324, 326). Clearly, naturalism had struck a chord with its representations of sex and violence, and for the light it shined on poverty, class antagonism, and bourgeois complacency. While distasteful, it was not considered far-fetched to represent the working classes as drunken and debauched; indeed, the *real* scandal was to suggest that the middle class was, like them, driven by base instincts.

Zola's defence against his many detractors was as vitriolic as their condemnation of him, be they right-wing proponents of "official criticism" or republican moralists suffering from "a ridiculous attack of prudishness."[7] Naturalism refused to moralize against sexuality, which was no more or less than a fact of life and a viable object of scientific scrutiny. To imagine otherwise was puritan hypocrisy, which Zola associated with Protestant republicanism.[8] With truth on his side ("literature shares the summit with science"), Zola rebuked those who called his work obscene, declaring that he refused to join "speculators in virtue" who pander to women readers, "those who specialize in not making women blush and those who profit from doing just that." "Real artists," continued Zola, "do not write for a specific audience [une classe], they have the ambition to write for posterity [...] without worrying whether their boldness will provoke scandal."[9]

Naturalism's explosive subject matter and the critical controversy that it provoked nonetheless assured its commercial success, a triumph that in turn vindicated its literary program. And yet, because of their negative critical reception, naturalist authors failed to win institutional approbation, a doubly difficult task since they were exposed to the "discredit attached to commercial success."[10] We saw in Belot's case to what extent market success was equated with literary inferiority. Naturalism thus struggled to differentiate itself from the popular novel – "industrial literature" as critic Sainte-Beuve famously called serial fiction – which was meant to entertain and motivated by financial gain. The evolution of the literary field led to the stratification of low and high, or commercial and "serious," literature.[11] Flaubert's stylistic exactitude in such works as *Madame Bovary* (1857) and *L'Éducation sentimentale* (1869) transformed the novel, elevating it to a genre that could be considered and practised as art. Naturalism carried the added gravitas of a theoretical program having scientific ambitions. The intellectual aspirations of realist authors marked their works for male readers, as did their engagement with political issues, considerably less prominent in commercial literature. Naturalists, admirers of Flaubert (who nonetheless kept his distance from them), sought to distinguish their work from the sentimentality of popular fiction ("to preserve the novel from degenerating into a 'feminine' genre," Angenot, *Le Cru*, 130) with provocative subjects and a hard-driving style.

As divisions between high and low literature became increasingly marked, schisms among those competing for literary renown also became apparent. Reaction to both the strictures of the neoclassical Parnassian school and the unadorned scientism of naturalism resulted in new literary platforms in which the words "decadent" and "symbolist" were generously bandied about, beginning in the early 1880s. Decadent poetry appeared as a short-lived offshoot of Symbolism, itself a loose clan of splinter groups formed during this inventive period when manifestos and small poetry journals proliferated.[12] The writer Anatole Baju claimed his fifteen minutes of fame in 1886, when he coined the term *décadisme* and consecrated it as a movement by founding the review *Le Décadent littéraire et artistique*. The lifespan of the school, as of the review and Baju's celebrity, was brief.

Théophile Gautier and Paul Bourget had already used the word "decadent" to describe Baudelaire's work, which did indeed have an enormous impact on the young poets who pursued a liberatory aesthetics. Mallarmé described the headiness of the moment, its spirit of experimentation and refusal to conform: "At this moment, we are witness [...] to a truly extraordinary spectacle, one that is unique in the entire history of poetry: each poet is retreating to his own corner to play the melodies that please him upon his very own flute."[13] Under the influence of

Mallarmé, young poets fractured syntax; following Verlaine, they rode roughshod over prosodic conventions; and in the wake of Rimbaud and Marie Krysinska, they began to use free verse for the first time in France. Verlaine played the role of elder, his collections *Jadis et naguère* and *Parallèlement* and essays on the *poètes maudits* eagerly received by the younger generation (the satirical *Deliquescences* by Adoré Floupette also contributed mockingly to Verlaine's stature).[14]

Literary decadence was linguistically esoteric, disdained convention, and exhibited a penchant for the elegant and the strange. This poetics of emancipation took decadence to be an aesthetic rather than a defeatist world view. At first an insult launched by critics, "decadent" was subsequently adopted by an eclectic bunch who associated the word with artistic refinement and anti-materialism. Although not necessarily political, some decadents aligned their poetic practice with leftist politics: Baju, for one, had socialist leanings, and Jules Laforgue, among the most talented of the decadent poets, was influenced by anarchist thought.

Iconoclastic poets and novelists, both symbolists and decadents, rejected naturalism on aesthetic grounds. The anti-naturalist critique would, however, evolve into something quite different. This was especially so among novelists who, while similarly reacting to the artistic implications of naturalist materialism and approving the aesthetic values associated with decadence, dug in their heels to defend French traditions they saw to be under attack by positivism and its spawns: naturalism, yes, but secularism and republicanism as well.

It should be noted that the terminology of the period does not neatly correspond to literary categories employed today. In *Enquête sur l'évolution littéraire* (1891), a series of interviews with contemporary men (and one woman) of letters, Jules Huret reserved the label "decadent" for poets, while those whom we now, rather loosely, designate in this way also include novelists whom he divided among a number of other categories, including the "psychologists" (Barrès), "occultists" (Péladan), "independents" (Richepin), or housed with earlier affiliations (Mendès is Parnassian, Huysmans naturalist). Huret himself remarked on the arbitrary and changing nature of such affiliations. For the purposes of this study, the term "decadent" will designate those who reacted against realism's investment in the social and its refusal to honour an "objective hierarchy of subjects" (Bourdieu, *Rules*, 105). The banal and undignified subjects of naturalism (chiefly the contemporary urban moment and its excesses: sexuality, crime, poverty, corruption) repelled decadent idealism in its quest for beauty. While naturalism sought objectively to extrapolate general truths from the scrutiny of the quotidian, decadent aestheticism privileged the unusual and the particular, voiced by subjective viewpoints. Charle aligns the authors of this "pessimistic wave" (*Crise*, 88), some destined to be elected to the conservative Académie française (Bourget, Richepin, Barrès, Maurras), with dominance in the literary field. Although the naturalist novel sold better than the psychological novel (*roman psychologique*), novelists associated with *l'art pour l'art* received critical approval and thus accrued greater cultural capital.[15] According to Bourdieu, the artistic hierarchy of literary genres is "almost exactly the inverse of the hierarchy according to commercial success" (*Rules*, 114).

As foundational decadent texts began to appear in the mid-1880s, naturalism in general and Zola in particular came under attack not only by the critics, but by their own as well. Joris-Karl Huysmans's classic decadent novel, *À rebours* (1884), is a case in point. Typically seen as the debut novel and "breviary" of the decadence, it sold well, thus making Huysmans's defection from naturalism all the more visible.[16] In the novel's second preface (1903), Huysmans took issue with naturalism's monotonous focus on the general at the expense of the unusual (and in doing so sounded like Nordau's counterpoint): "in theory at least, [the naturalist school] never allowed for special cases [l'exception]. It limited itself to portraying shared existence and, under the pretext of being true to life, made a point of creating characters as similar as possible to average people." Huysmans found the very vigour of naturalism's style and platform to lack nuance: "those of us who were less audacious [moins râblés], preoccupied with making subtler and more genuine art, had to wonder whether naturalism was heading for an impasse."[17]

A few years after the publication of *À rebours*, a group of five young naturalists published an article, later known as "le manifeste des cinq," that condemned Zola's novel *La Terre* (1887). *Le Figaro* headlined this open letter to Zola on its first page. It was signed by Paul Bonnetain (author of *Charlot s'amuse*, indicted for alluding to masturbation) and four others of his cohort, whom Huret designated as "neo-realists." This group kept its distance from Zola, accusing him of vulgarity ("it's like reading a scatological collection") and commercial interests. Going beyond these familiar complaints, the letter's signatories in essence dethroned and unmanned Zola. They accused him of self-importance ("full of Hugolian pomposity"), ineptitude ("the Master's profound ignorance in medical and scientific matters"), and, lowest blow, erectile dysfunction: "the irremediable and morbid depravation of an abstinent man." Marshalling the language of medicine against him, they suggested that Zola suffered from a malady that was either physical ("an illness of the lower organs") or mental: "Perhaps Charcot, Moreau de Tours, and those other doctors at the Salpêtrière [the Parisian psychiatric hospital] who exhibited their coprolalic patients before us could evaluate the symptoms of his illness." They also used the language of degeneration against Zola ("the decadence of his talent"), adopted for themselves the virile pose ("we are protesting in the name of healthy and virile ambitions") that Zola proclaimed inherent to his own method, and cast aspersions on his "competence in matters of love." Finally, they made it clear that, unlike Zola, nobility, propriety, and artistry ("our supreme respect for *Art*") were among their core literary values, thus sliding "neo-realism" that much closer to the decadent aesthetic. The conservative mystical writer Léon Bloy nailed the naturalist coffin shut with *Les Funérailles du naturalisme* (1891), published a year before Zola's final novel in the *Rougon-Macquart* cycle.

Decadence was proudly brandished by many, if not all, of those who came to be associated with it. While chiefly reliant on the despairing trope of decline, it is a contradictory notion that sometimes posits a creative beginning born of decay. The texts themselves frequently walk the line between condemnation of perceived political and moral corruption (the flamboyantly anti-flamboyant Max Nordau) and proud embrace of artistic and sexual distinction. Critics have explored both sides of this contradiction between what one has labelled "negative decadence" and the aestheticism of a "positive decadence."[18]

Paul Bourget, one of the first to theorize the idea of decadence in literature, acknowledged the bipolar perspective imbedded in its world view. Tracing its roots to Baudelaire and beyond to the Roman Empire (important points of reference for other decadent works), he proposed two visions. The first, reflecting the reasoning of politicians and moralists, saw the decline of a nation or a people to be the result of hedonism and a lack of virile investment in the social. Interestingly, he referenced low birth rate as a cause of Rome's decline. But it is safe to say that he also had France's underpopulation in mind in this analysis: "A society survives only if it remains capable of vigorously fighting for existence in the competition among peoples [concurrence des races]. It must produce many robust children and form many courageous soldiers. [...] Ancient Rome produced few children and reached the point of no longer maintaining a national army. Its citizens were little concerned with issues of paternity. They detested the ruggedness of camp life" (14–15). Bourget's second and preferred interpretation, which he attributed to "the pure psychologist's viewpoint," saw the decadent sensibility not as a cause of social decay, but as its result. Aesthetic refinement might lose out to the invading hordes, but it nonetheless represented an advanced state of civilization. In this analysis, the gifts of the individual artist took precedence over the duty of the masses: "Even if the citizens of a decadent society are inferior workers [and] poor progenitors, is it not true that their profuse and subtle emotions, their exquisite and uncommon impressions, make them refined, albeit sterile, virtuosos of voluptuous pleasure and pain?" At odds with Nordau's Everyman, Bourget shunned the multitude.

What we can take away from the debating positions posited by Bourget is a set of values that privileges the uncommon and the particular, correlatively disdaining the many, be they workers or bourgeois, and rejecting broad social panoramas in favour of personal portraits of distinctive protagonists. Decadent ideology confirms the association of high art with elitism: "high culture is founded upon rarity and exclusion" (Lidsky, 32). Like Des Esseintes of Huysmans's *À rebours*, the decadent aesthete is frequently of noble birth, but the last gasp – *la fin de race* – of a degenerating nobility. Isolated by his misanthropic exceptionality, rendered impotent (in both body and will) by his solitude and heredity, the artist played a key role in the obsessive quest for distinction and refinement in a context of perceived decline. It becomes clear that the oppositional nature of fin-de-siècle literary agendas were political as well as artistic: the first naturalists tended towards positivist republican optimism and the decadents towards dismayed legitimism. Ironically, as Bourdieu has pointed out, "Political progressivism is more associated with aesthetic conservatism" (*Rules*, 118).

Politics and Literature

Charle and Bourdieu have demonstrated the social determination of judgments of taste and convincingly argued that social standing and political inclinations reflect a writer's position in the literary field. In *La Crise littéraire à l'époque du naturalisme*, a social history of late nineteenth-century literary movements, Charle illustrates the narrow association between political and literary affiliations, asserting that literary groups "have a coherent social meaning" (21). His work considers writers "as a function of distinctive features of their social, cultural, and economic capital" and explores "the political stakes of rivalries between literary tendencies" (21, 150). The tangled ties between naturalist and decadent literature during the last third of the century were coloured to a goodly extent by the political antagonism that increasingly characterized France following the Franco-Prussian War. While most writers stayed clear of active involvement in politics until the Dreyfus affair, patterns of belief ran parallel in politics and literature and produced a similar rhetorical opposition: a narrative of progress on the left competed with one of decay on the right.

Zola's intellectual foundation (and by extension the cornerstone of naturalism) belonged firmly to the rationalist, secular tradition, traceable to Auguste Comte's philosophy of positivism, which provided optimistic models for those invested in a transformative agenda, be that political, scientific, social, or literary.[19] A detached, sociological intellectualism characterized Zola's school, whose pretence of scientific objectivity favoured an ostensibly empiricist vision of the observable world. And yet Zola was ambivalent about political involvement, an ambivalence fuelled by the negative criticism he received from republicans who rejected his work as vulgar. Nonetheless, naturalism, the dominant school by the early 1880s, was clearly "classed to the left."[20] Zola's disapproval of imperial and religious power and his disdain for social hierarchy are evident in the Rougon-Macquart cycle, whose subtitle (*Histoire naturelle et sociale d'une famille sous le Second Empire*) points to the object of both his interrogation and his contempt: the authoritarian and intellectually flaccid Second Empire.

Naturalism's trust in the ability of science to explain the unknown and in so doing to confer order, it is safe to say, ran counter to the "sense of futility" that led decadent writers to abandon rationalist inquiry for aesthetic quests.[21] On the right, monarchists lamented the losses brought by the revolutions that ended their various incarnations, as Bonapartists did the fall of empire. Aristocracy and legitimism provided contemporary refuge, thanks to their distance from the many, the sordid, and the modern. Disdainful of the putrescent present, decadents on the right took refuge in the past. These factions saw decline in the advances trumpeted by the left: secularism, parliamentarianism, republicanism. Analogously, decadent writers fled from scientism and the social towards an introverted, frequently cynical, and highly subjective poetics of refinement, thus repudiating with political apathy the social critique implicit in the works of many naturalists.

The polarization of the political and social aspirations of the French came to a head at the end of the century with the Dreyfus affair, during which there were only two possible positions to take: *for* or *against*. Unjustly arrested and condemned for treason in 1894, then sent to the penal colony on Devil's Island, Captain Alfred Dreyfus, a Jew, was found guilty in a second trial in 1899, despite clear evidence of his innocence. He was pardoned and subsequently rehabilitated in 1906.

Zola became an important voice in support of Dreyfus, famously publishing an open letter to President Jaurès in the newspaper *L'Aurore*, which carried the words "J'accuse" as its headline and refrain and denounced the complicity of the government and the press. At the same time, the virulently anti-Semitic right saw in Dreyfus all the marks of difference (religious and national among them) that threatened France. The nationalist novelist and politician Maurice Barrès claimed that Dreyfus's religion alone was grounds for conviction: "I conclude from his race that Dreyfus betrayed his country."[22] One of the effects of the Dreyfus affair was to harden lines of demarcation already in place and to prompt greater involvement on both sides of the literary divide.[23] Many men of letters became active in the associations founded at the very end of the nineteenth century in reaction to the Dreyfus affair: the Ligue française pour la défense des droits de l'homme et du citoyen defended Dreyfus, while the Ligue de la patrie française and the Action française condemned him. Both Bourdieu and Charle credit the Dreyfus affair with marking the birth of the public intellectual.[24] It also favoured what sociologist Gisèle Sapiro has called "the literary field's importation of political divisions as a pertinent means of classification" (25). If nothing else, it made the cleavage patently visible. As Charle demonstrates, the anti-Dreyfusard camp included many names associated with literary decadence (Barrès, Bourget, Huysmans, Loti, Louÿs), while naturalists were split between opponents (Céard, Daudet, Hennique) and proponents (Paul Adam, Alexis, Zola) of Dreyfus.[25]

A schematic of political, social, and literary associations and allegiances would look something like this:

Naturalism	**Decadent Literature**
low	high
active	passive
masculine	feminine
formally conservative	stylistically ornate
descriptive, empirical	lyrical, abstract
stalking the real	questing beauty
literal	ironic
ostensibly objective, analytical[26]	subjective, imaginative
amoral	moralistic, immoral
left	right
secularist	clericalist
Dreyfusard	anti-Dreyfusard
anti-Protestant[27]	anti-Semitic, xenophobic
positivist	cynical, anti-science
invested in progress	the product of decay
materialistic	idealistic
physiology	psychology
study of pathology	expression of pathology
sociology	fine arts
the social	the individual
the general, the typical	the particular, the unusual
the masses	the few, the aristocratic

This is a simplification whose exceptions and nuances have long caused debate among critics. The relationship between naturalism and the much less coherent and organized literary tendency of decadence has given rise to significant differences of opinion, with some finding continuity where others see rupture.[28] Ultimately, the boundaries between the two camps were to a certain extent porous, with a number of fin-de-siècle novelists displaying traits from both sides of the divide.[29] Decadence and naturalism were products of the same moment and imbued with similar points of reference. While they tended to differ in the objects of their inquiry, writers associated with them shared an impassioned interest in heredity, social stratification, and sexuality. And this is where we circle back to lesbian plots, since the novels in question placed female homosexuality at the juncture of these three obsessions. The infiltration of ambient scientific theories fed interest in female homosexuality, which itself served as a vehicle for talking about class differences.

I would argue that decadent authors were just as marked as naturalists by the new sciences, although others have affirmed the contrary.[30] They were particularly consumed by dissident sexualities, preoccupations beholden to recent theories of degeneration and Darwin's work on heredity and natural selection. The tenets of both circles made homosexuality a particularly appealing object of inquiry, although they approached it from different angles. In contrast to naturalism's ostensibly empiricist vision of the observable world, decadent literature's propensity was for subjective viewpoints. Informed by the work of early psychiatrists, decadent writers paid more attention to individual psychologies and frequently denigrated naturalism's engrossment in a physiology of the masses. Zola and his disciples took licence from the naturalist credo that no subject was taboo, not even sexual inversion, and they answered the imperative to lift the most sacrosanct veils of secrecy with what they professed to be scientific objectivity.

At least as far as *female* homosexuality was concerned. Indeed, despite such pronouncements, naturalist writers refused to go near male homosexuality, whereas decadents revelled in it. One would be hard-pressed to name a major decadent author who failed to touch upon deviant sexuality and gender expression in both male and female characters. Rachilde's work, from *Monsieur Vénus* and *Madame Adonis* to *Les Hors nature* and *L'Heure sexuelle*, epitomizes the panoply of sexual and gender nonconformity represented in decadent literature. The treatment of masculinity presents a significant difference between naturalist and decadent texts. This is a vast topic in itself and beyond the scope of the present study; however, it is relevant to note the central role played by decadence in the emergence of a gay male literary tradition and culture at the end of the century.

The path to an emancipated homoerotic literature took very different courses for men and women. Although awash in contemporary medical literature, gay male authors had no unsolicited literary tradition equivalent to what the work of the sapphic fathers would present to lesbian writers. With only a few exceptions, male homosexuality was virtually ignored in post-revolutionary French literature until the end of the century, when writers first began to explore unconventional male sexuality and gender expression in the context of the decadent movement.[31] Decadent writers often engaged reigning constructions of male homosexuality as disease and as a manifestation of the corruption and excess rampant in fin-de-siècle cities. Profiles of enfeebled masculinity are common, of men suffering from nervous exhaustion or neurasthenia, which were given as symptoms of emasculation, since "a woman's soul resides in the nerves."[32] But this literature also pushed back by creating often ironic homoerotic tropes from discourses of perversion and by affirming the exceptionality of homoeroticism.

Decadent culture has long been associated with male homosexuality, not least because of a number of openly gay writers active in France and England during the Belle Époque. The subjective articulation of non-normative sexualities first came of age with such writers as Verlaine, Lorrain, and Georges Eekhoud, who contributed to the increasingly overt presence of atypically gendered male characters, which blossomed at the turn of the twentieth century, most notably in the work of André Gide and Marcel Proust.[33] These authors engaged in culture building through the writing of the sexual self; their work can be seen as a coming-to-writing for gay men, whose lesbian equivalent would soon follow. There is much to say about the homoerotics of the decadent aesthetic, its refinement and hyperbole, and the recherché dandyism with which it is associated.[34] The very visibility of some public figures (Oscar Wilde, Robert de Montesquiou) and their performance of effete elegance were central to this aesthetic, which in turn informed gay self-perception and cultural traditions. Lesbian self-perception has more crucially relied on the vast body of literary representations composed by men who viewed their subjects with a gaze that was typically objectifying and heterosexual.

Just as scientific theories informed perceptions of physical, psychological, and collective pathology in naturalist and decadent camps, their import for judgments about the social were also central. Class and its transgressions provided a predictable topos when concern for hierarchy and social movement collided (the new working and middle classes, the infiltration of the *monde* by the *demi-monde*). Both inclinations provided a politics of class as backdrop and offered various scenarios of social conflict in their plots. Naturalism's interests lay in the milieu of the popular, lower, and marginal classes while the decadents, dismayed by democratization, fled from banality to focus on the beleaguered aristocracy. Cross-class lesbian relationships in both movements reflected anxiety about a porous class system and symbolized social decay.

The fate of the bourgeoisie is somewhat more complicated, at times playing victim to corruption from above (the decadent aristocracy) and other times below (the dissolute masses). But, as Bourdieu argues, both movements defined themselves *against* the bourgeoisie, if for very different reasons. I would contend that this was particularly so for the aesthetes, who portrayed the new middle class as a burgeoning mass of philistine vulgarians ("democrats are boors designed for obedience") who challenge and usurp the power of a traditionally privileged class ("races made to command") waning in influence.[35] From a naturalist perspective, a novel like Zola's *Pot-Bouille* peoples the bourgeoisie with conniving, depraved hypocrites (nonetheless leaving it to a chambermaid to seduce the young lady of the family).

But the middle class will not concern us much here. While the tribade crosses the literary divide to infiltrate fin-de-siècle fiction, the politics of literature keep her segregated: the lower-class lesbian was unquestionably naturalist, the upper-class one tended to be decadent. Political leanings of individual writers during this polarizing period did not so much determine their subject matter, since so many flocked aboard the sapphic wagon, as it did their manner of harnessing it. While naturalists were apt to agree with the essayist Léo Taxil that "without exception, all prostitutes are tribades," decadent writers were more inclined to concur with the equally prominent opinion of Dr Coffignon, popularizer of medical literature, that "the aristocracy furnishes the greatest number of women practicing tribadism."[36]

To understand the sexual politics in play here will necessitate a brief detour into the "woman question" at a moment when the stakes for masculinity were never higher. As we have seen, feminist activity and tentative gains in women's civil rights were met with suspicion and reaction from all corners. Despite many differences on the right or left, among extremists and moderates, between politicians and men of letters, the French responded in unison to women's demands for civil rights as a threat. They retaliated energetically with protestations that frequently floated the threat of female homosexuality.

The virulent anti-feminism of this period attests to the social and political power of literary as well as political men, power abused most grievously in turbulent times, and to the equal-opportunity misogyny from all sides.[37] Unsettled by issues such as population decline and the threat of divorce, hostile towards the mounting number of women writers in a competitive market, men of letters used their social and professional capital and their literary talents to speak out against feminist demands.[38] Alexandre Dumas *fils*, a successful dramaturge soon to be elected to the powerful and increasingly conservative Académie française (1874), is illustrative. This Catholic and monarchist, "a product of the established order in literature and its social illustration" (Charle, *Crise*, 118), created a stir when he published his goading *L'Homme-femme* (1872). Writing in response to a murder trial in which a husband killed his adulterous wife, Dumas muses, "Must we pardon the adulterous woman or should we kill her?"[39] He addresses men ("useless to add that what I write is not written for women"), dismisses women ("women never surrender to reason [...] only to feeling and to power"), and cavalierly concludes that murder is preferable to pardon (5, 6). He writes of the adulterous woman: "she is not even a woman; she does not belong to divine conception, but is purely animal; she's the monkey from the land of Nod, Cain's wife; kill her" (176). Dumas ultimately recommends supporting divorce legislation before resorting to violence; nonetheless, his provocation garnered the largely positive publicity that he sought, although he was roundly condemned by feminists.[40]

Across the board, feminism was seen as a threat to the family: work took women from the home and desexualized them, while abortion and birth control lowered an already dangerously low birth rate and encouraged promiscuity.

Many antifeminists feared the blurring of gender boundaries and loss of traditional womanhood. A common denominator in this rhetoric was the masculine woman. The pursuit of typically male activities, be they intellectual or physical, stripped women of their femininity, with the result of rendering them physically unattractive, amorously unappealing, sterile, and delinquent in their reproductive and marital duties. Women by nature were modest, passive creatures, a position, Bard has suggested, justified by science and medicine. These fields contrasted a positive vision of the natural Eternal Feminine with pathological femininity, characterized by traits such as hypersexualization, frigidity, ambition, intellectual engagement, physical activity, and desire for independence. Feminists, suffragists, sportswomen, professional women, and working women were conflated and portrayed as manly, which in turn contributed to the designation of the lesbian as scarecrow. A bellwether of normative femininity's perceived vulnerability in the context of seismic social shifts, the tribade provided a target for moralists of all political stripes wishing to defend traditional family structures and deny women access to the workforce, the arts, and public debate. In short, she became a scapegoat for men and sometimes women, regardless of political sentiment or affiliation, invested in protecting spheres and activities whose alteration or decline could be associated with unconventional femininity.

Corruption from Below: Naturalism and the Sapphic Prostitute

> it's the rot from below [...] that surges upward to corrupt the superior classes.
>
> (Zola)[41]

Until the advent of naturalism, the literature of tribadism had been a largely aristocratic affair. Convents and *hôtels particuliers* set the scene for most of the corpus until the first naturalists began to lurk around the slums, which they found teeming with female homosexuals. This new venue opened up untried symbolic possibilities. By locating sapphic activity primarily in the working class, often among prostitutes and their associates (other sex workers, lovers, procurers), naturalists were able to examine the interrelation between class affiliation and sexual expression. The results present some revelatory scenarios to be visited in this section, colourfully gendered terrains peopled by masculine women and feminine men, inflamed by fatal femininity and male brutality, altered by hereditary flaws and the effects of working-class squalor. Prostitution and lesbianism coincided with contemporary stereotypes of brutish, socially illegitimate underclass sexualities (sexual violence, promiscuity, heterosexual concubinage, "grotesque marriages"). Strangers to the social contract, prostitutes and lesbians defied acceptable codes of conduct and inspired female characters that were alluring, abhorrent, or both.

The product of urban degeneracy, condemned for immorality, blamed for the spread of venereal disease, supervised and regulated by the vice police, scrutinized and diagnosed by criminologists and medical doctors, the prostitute was observed from various quarters and roundly vilified.[42] Even as she was considered to be a necessary evil, she symbolized moral decay. Female homosexuality had long been associated with prostitution in scientific texts, going back at least to Alexandre Parent-Duchâtelet's influential study *De la prostitution dans la ville de Paris* (1836). In Alain Corbin's analysis, prostitution was seen to be the lesser threat, a necessary safety valve because it permitted the release of male sexual energy in a way that did not threaten familial and therefore social stability. However, when coupled, female homosexuality and prostitution presented the most dangerous form of undesirable sexuality. Prostitutes seduced into lesbianism were diverted from performing an essential role: "The prostitute runs the risk of one day becoming a lesbian; she therefore represents a terrible threat to sexual order, of which she is otherwise the best safeguard" (*Women for Hire*, 7). If the prostitute was vital to the maintenance of the social order, the female homosexual represented its most insidious menace, and an invisible one: "For Parent-Duchâtelet the danger is all the greater in that female homosexuality is an incurable malady whose external characteristics are difficult to observe objectively." I will spend more time with Parent-Duchâtelet in the following chapter; suffice it for now to note that the enormous influence of his work on prostitution was felt by novelists as well as by medical practitioners.

Nearly all of the original Médan group examined the correlation between female homosexuality and the underclasses. Zola's *Nana* and Paul Alexis's short story "La Fin de Lucie Pellegrin," both published in 1880, placed the figure of the sapphic prostitute in circulation. Other naturalists quickly followed suit, including Maupassant ("La Femme de Paul," 1881), Alphonse Daudet (*Sapho*, 1884), and Paul Adam (*Chair molle, roman naturaliste*, 1885). All paint scenes of class antagonism and rivalry between men and women of different stations. There are numerous common elements in these near-contemporaneous stories and novels, leading one to wonder what their authors discussed around the dining table during their trips to the country.[43]

For all their similarities, the works that will be the focus of this section present sapphic characters who run the gamut of the hierarchy of prostitution. There are legal and illegal *filles*, as prostitutes were typically called: the former, *filles soumises*, were registered with and regulated by the vice police and subject to regular medical examination. The latter, *filles insoumises* or *filles clandestines*, lacked oversight and protection and were subject to arrest. Nana's lover, Satin, works the street despite her "terrible fear of the police" and sleeps with an agent from the vice division in order to avoid registration and police supervision.[44] However Adam's Lucie Thirache, a registered prostitute who works in a brothel, scorns "filthy streetwalkers" and considers it "foolish to want to be free at that price."[45] We see Nana, raised by an alcoholic mother in a dreary working-class neighbourhood, rise from factory work to become first an actress and occasional prostitute, and finally a courtesan of the highest order. Such women were known as *grandes horizontales*, women kept in grand style by wealthy men, potent figures during the Second Empire.[46]

From lowly streetwalkers to regulated brothel workers to the *grandes courtisanes*, these characters all engage in sapphic practices. But there is a special link between the abjection of the streetwalker and that of the lesbian. Naturalists frequently accentuated the association between lesbianism and prostitution by locating female homosexuality not simply among prostitutes, but among prostitutes of the basest type. Zola, who carefully documented his subjects before writing, explicitly associated sapphism with the lowest form of prostitution in his preparatory notes for *Nana*, placing tribades among illegal streetwalkers rather than house prostitutes: "The lowly vice [vice d'en bas] will be represented by two-bit actresses and a whore who works the boulevard."[47] Even the euphemism "vice d'en bas" aligns homosexuality with the *bas-fonds* (slums). While *filles soumises* are sometimes paid to perform homosexual acts for men, real tribades are found outside, in the street: "Few dykes [gougnottes], except in the underworld."[48]

In *Nana*, the title character ascends and descends this ladder several times, but it is after her fall from the privileged position of courtesan that she is initiated into lesbianism. Chased by debts and quarrels among her wealthy and influential lovers, Nana abruptly leaves her sumptuous apartment on the new Boulevard Haussmann for a working-class neighbourhood in Montmartre. She abandons a count and a banker to pursue "the old ideal of her flower-girl days" with a fellow actor, Fontan, "under the influence of the sort of fierce passion which courtesans often feel for a comedian's grimacing ugliness." And yet what begins as a working-class idyll for Nana ("She was in an ecstasy of love, blushing like a schoolgirl") quickly sours.[49] Fontan's native violence emerges; he mistreats her and finally throws her out in exchange for another woman. Penniless, Nana becomes a streetwalker with her old friend Satin. It is under these degrading circumstances, when Nana has fallen to her lowest, that Satin introduces her to same-sex practices. Satin begins by taking Nana to the lesbian *table d'hôte* run by "fat" Laure Piédefer," whose clientele piques Nana's interest: "her curiosity was aroused, and she began questioning [Satin] about obscure vices, astounded to find herself learning things at her time of life and with all her knowledge. She would burst out laughing, and utter cries of surprise, finding what Satin told her terribly funny, and yet she was a little shocked, for she basically disapproved [au fond elle était bourgeoise] of anything outside her own habits."[50]

Satin seduces Nana under the guise of comforting her after a beating by her male lover, an initiation interrupted by the vice police. Although their sexual relations are not illegal, engaging in unregulated prostitution is: the timing of Satin's arrest blurs the lines and accentuates the abject pall cast over such sexual practices in this sordid setting. Nana is nonetheless hooked: "From then on Nana had a passion to occupy her attention. Satin became her vice." No longer a curiosity or amusement, her sapphism is a solemn matter: "One fine evening, however, it took a serious turn, and Nana, who had been so disgusted at Laure's, now understood. She was overwhelmed and excited by this new experience." Having overcome her bourgeois repugnance and stepped over to the other side, Nana lets go of one of the remaining vestiges of social propriety: heterosexuality, however unwholesome its performance. Newly sapphic, she also tries male clothing on for size: "disguised as a man, she would go to infamous houses and watch scenes of debauchery to relieve her boredom."[51]

Alexis's Lucie Pellegrin follows an arc similar to Nana's, from poverty, to the highest level of prostitution as a *grande courtisane*, to ghastly death. Lucie is "born near the end of the avenue in an alleyway full of ragpickers." Unsupervised, "pied nu," sent to gather cast-offs for her parents in a nearby quarry, she is raped at the age of eleven. Her beauty is her ticket out: she "could have bedded the king of Belgium."[52] But like Nana, her success is tenuous owing to her profligacy and the instability of her milieu. These narratives hint at the causation of their characters' sapphism. Social context and genetics battle each other for blame, but they just as frequently join forces to follow Bénédict Morel's model of degeneracy, in which environmental deficits become hereditary traits. Nana's moral and sexual depravity, which she spreads to everyone she encounters, is the product of her squalid upbringing and the genetic weakness that corrupts all descendants of the Rougon and Macquart families: "descended from four or five generations of drunkards, her blood tainted by an accumulated inheritance of poverty and drink, which in her case had taken the form of a nervous derangement of the sexual instinct."[53]

Then there is male brutality – Nana's beatings, Lucie's rape – which medical professionals suggested gave rise to female inversion. In addition to physical violence, coercion by men also plays a role. Daudet's Fanny owes her titular nickname, Sapho, to same-sex encounters promoted by her lover: "I was young, it's Caoudal's fault … I did what he wanted, that crazy fool!"[54] Zola's notes also indicate an interest in such scenes: "I'm going to have the house whores eat each other out. Turn-on."[55] In the proximity of prostitutes, men of all social stations are described as sexualized animals, as *bêtes humaines*. They are "males in heat," "An entire society chasing ass. A pack running after a bitch."[56] Sometimes it is *le peuple* that is bestialized in its sexuality: "The males squatted like toads, some making obscene gestures."[57] Sometimes the wealthy: "the most distinguished-looking men were the most obscene. The varnish cracked, and the beast showed itself, exacting in its monstrous tastes, subtle in its perversions."[58]

Fatal Sapphists

Masculine sexuality corrupts, perverts, and causes physical harm. And yet it pales before the violence of the alluring sapphic prostitute who blossoms into a full-blown femme fatale. She is drawn to women but makes her living through sexual relations with men. Like Belot's Mélinite to the Duke Gontran, she often reaches across class lines to captivate and destroy her well-born victims. Her disdain for men equals if not exceeds that of the heterosexual femme fatale: although she is prodigiously enticing, she betrays no emotional engagement or vulnerability. Instead, she preys on the uncontrolled impulses and moral weakness of men, from innocent boys to men of stature.

In Daudet's *Sapho*, the naive Jean Gaussin, recently arrived in Paris with his Midi accent and "the inexperience of his tender age," is a picture of angelic youth adorned with the glow of the countryside, "his pretty face and blond hair, tanned and golden from the sun."[59] Jean encounters the mysterious Fanny on the novel's first page, and by the end of the first chapter, he is bewitched: "he followed her without hesitating. Why? It wasn't the woman's physical appeal; he had barely looked at her [...] And yet he obeyed a will superior to his own, the impetuous violence of desire."[60] Unable to extricate himself, Jean is debased by his sexually sordid, socially objectionable relationship with an older woman from another world, a world whose wretchedness and corruption he discovers too late. Born "between two rounds at the bar" to a barmaid who dies in childbirth, Fanny is raised by her father, a "hoodlum of the street whose face, in the light of the gas lamp, appears puffy and apoplectic from alcohol."[61] This upbringing is the only explanation given for her capricious and omnivorous sexuality, which engulfs and dirties Jean. For his part, there is a physiological explanation for his submission to Fanny, a questionable inheritance from both parents. In spite of his healthy rustic origins, Jean has acquired "all the nervousness of his mother, of whom he was the picture image." In his father's family an even graver defect threatens, embodied by his paternal uncle, "whose disorders and extravagances nearly ruined their family."[62]

The novel is awash in filth, both literal and figurative. Fanny and Jean walk through "the mud of sunken roads," and Fanny crawls "on her knees through the mud." It covers clothing: Fanny's father's old livery jacket is "dirty with mud," Fanny has "mud on her dress, even in her hair," and Jean's "shoes are covered with mud." It even invades their domestic interior, "a mess of water, soot, and mud."

But most of all, it is metaphorical mud from which Jean tries to pull Fanny, only to succumb himself: "although Jean extracted this woman from the muck, he may well have gotten himself good and dirty while doing so." Filth colours his self-respect ("insulted, dirtied with ridicule"), his sentiments ("under a sky as dingy as his love"), and bonds him inextricably to Fanny: "mud, heavy and thick, his entire past held him still, heavily and indecently" [pesamment et salement].

Fanny's sapphic dalliances, for belonging to a past that precedes the narrative, nonetheless remain present by virtue of her nickname and its titular prominence. While sapphism lacks any relation to plot development, it carries degrading associations and remains a potent symbol of sexual corruption: "And with the five letters of her abominable name, he saw the entire life of this woman pass before him like sewage leaking from a drain."[63] Fanny's sobriquet is indicative of the poet Sappho's fall in stature from mother of lyric poetry to lesbian eponym: "across the centuries, vile legends have dirtied the honour originally associated with the word Sappho; the name of a goddess has become the label for an illness."[64]

Nana, like Fanny, owes her devastating sexuality to her wretched beginnings. Behind Nana's facade of naivety and ignorance lies an erotic power that ensnares the men she encounters: "that hefty wench who slapped her thighs and clucked like a hen, gave off an odour of life, a potent female charm, which intoxicated the audience."[65] We have seen her rise and fall. While among the people, beaten by Fontan, she is submissive and vulnerable, but when she rises she becomes dangerous: "All of a sudden, in the good-natured child the woman stood revealed, a disturbing woman with all the impulsive madness of her sex, opening the gates of the unknown world of desire. Nana was still smiling, but with the deadly smile of a man-eater."[66] Nana feeds on all of Parisian society, reaching into the highest offices of the Second Empire to bring its functionaries to their knees: "her sex rose in a halo of glory and blazed down on her prostrate victims like a rising sun shining down on a field of carnage."[67] It is in her upward mobility ("her sex *rose*") that she becomes menacing. Despite his socialist sympathies, Zola seems to suggest that Nana's departure from her station unleashes the destructive passions that her origins produced: "She had grown up in the slums, in the gutters of Paris; and now, tall and beautiful, and as well made as a plant nurtured on a dungheap, she was avenging the paupers and outcasts of whom she was the product. With her the rottenness that was allowed to ferment among the lower classes was rising to the surface and rotting the aristocracy."[68] Nana wreaks havoc on the male population of Paris, who are helpless before her; ruined physically, financially, morally; and driven to madness and suicide:

> She alone was left standing, amid the accumulated riches of her mansion, while a host of men lay stricken at her feet. [...] She had finished her labour of ruin and

> death. The fly that had come from the dungheap of the slums, carrying the ferment of social decay, had poisoned all these men simply by alighting on them. It was fitting and just. She had avenged the beggars and outcasts of her world.[69]

When it crosses class lines, working-class female sexuality becomes "a force of nature, a ferment of destruction, unwittingly corrupting and disorganizing Paris between [...] snow-white thighs."[70] Zola's novel, a condemnation of the Second Empire, harnesses the sapphic courtesan as a hyperbolic figure of its corruption and social disarray.

Madeleine, the prostitute in Maupassant's "La Femme de Paul" (1881), is less cataclysmically fatal than Nana; like Fanny she leaves only one victim, her upper-class lover, Paul Baron. And like Fanny, Madeleine's appeal is not a physical beauty. And yet her effect on Paul, whose surname underscores his station and reflects his bearing, is nonetheless hypnotic: "that little bit of a woman [...] had taken him prisoner, *possessing* him from head to foot, body and soul. He had submitted to *this feminine witchery*, mysterious and all powerful, [...] arising no one knows whence, but from *the demon of the flesh* – which casts the most sensible man at the feet of some harlot or other without there being anything in her to explain *her fatal and sovereign power*."[71] Described with a vocabulary of the occult, this strangely enthralling, all-powerful, yet unpretentious woman preys on the innocent Paul's weak will and frail masculinity ("The young man, still almost beardless, slender, with a pale countenance").[72] As is typical in Maupassant, this overlay of the fantastic translates the forbidden sexualities in play: Paul's irregular ménage with a woman of a different class, the animality of working-class sexuality that permeates the waterfront setting, and flamboyant lesbianism, which comes floating down the Seine.

"La Femme de Paul" ironically echoes Belot's *Mademoiselle Giraud* in several respects, most obviously in the names of its title character and his lesbian rival, Pauline, which resonate with that of Paule. But while Maupassant parrots, he also mirrors, providing an inverted scenario, whence the irony and, perhaps, a playful inscription of the theme of inversion. His story opposes the impenetrable secret of Paule's sapphic desires with aggressive visibility:

> A canoe covered with an awning and manned by four women came slowly down the current. She who rowed was petite, thin, faded, in a cabin-boy's costume [...] Opposite her, a [fat] blonde, dressed as a man, with a white flannel jacket, lay upon her back at the bottom of the boat, her legs in the air [...] She smoked a cigarette [...] two handsome girls, tall and slender, one dark and the other fair, held each other by the waist as they watched their companions.

> A cry arose from La Grenouillère, "There's Lesbos," and all at once a furious clamour, a terrifying scramble took place; glasses were knocked down; people clambered on to the tables; all in a frenzy of noise bawled: "Lesbos! Lesbos! Lesbos!" [...] the two girls at the back commenced laughing as they saluted the crowd.[73]

Unlike the bawdy working-class crowd celebrating these women ("Their vice was public, recognized, patent to all. People talked of it as a natural thing, which almost excited their sympathy"), the refined Paul finds the spectacle repugnant.[74] When his mistress defends them, Paul declares that "it is the police whom it concerns, and I will have them marched off to [the women's prison] St Lazare."[75] But as in *Mademoiselle Giraud*, the police are helpless to act:

> A neighbour, horrified by these scandalous rumours, notified the police, [...] [who came] to make inquiry. The mission was a delicate one; it was impossible, in short, to accuse these women, who did not abandon themselves to prostitution, of any tangible crime. The inspector, very much puzzled, and, indeed, ignorant of the nature of the offences suspected, had asked questions at random, and made a lofty report conclusive of their innocence.[76]

Like Belot's Adrien, Paul falls victim to both the insufficiency of the law and predatory lesbianism: "If her companion had only been a man. But that! that! He felt as though he were spellbound by the very infamy of it. And he stood there astounded and overwhelmed, as if he had discovered the mutilated corpse of one dear to him, a crime against nature, a monstrous, disgusting profanation."[77] Madeleine's hold on Paul is so intense and her sexuality so powerful that he progresses from love-struck innocence to blind fury when she betrays him with the masculine Pauline. Discovering Madeleine's infidelity, Paul throws himself into the Seine and drowns, recalling Berthe's death at the hands of Paule's husband, but transposing victimhood to the male character.

Class difference comes to the fore in "La Femme de Paul," while it is only hinted at in *Mademoiselle Giraud* (Paule's modest but respectable origins contrast with the wealth and nobility of her husband and her lover). The restaurant on the Seine, Le Grillon, attracts an array of weekend pleasure-seekers, "a gallery consisting of middle-class people dressed in their Sunday clothes, of workmen and soldiers."[78] The son of a senator, Paul stands out in this mixed crowd, his delicacy in sharp contrast with the hypermasculine "huge fellows" [grands gaillards] who have come out for a day of canoeing. Class and gender distinction function in lock step. The author makes a point of exaggerating the physical characteristics of female as well as male working-class characters: "Women and girls with yellow hair and breasts developed beyond all measurement, with exaggerated hips, their complexions plastered with rouge, their eyes daubed with charcoal, their lips blood red, laced up, rigged out in outrageous dresses."[79] Their uninhibited and conspicuous sexuality is likened to the mating of wildlife: "The men [...] moved about vociferating and evidently looking for the quarrels natural to brutes. The women [sought] their prey for the night."[80]

These *bêtes humaines* gathered on the banks of the Seine contrast sharply with Paul's refinement and sensitivity, which is not itself immune from Maupassant's biting cynicism. Their reactions to the boatful of lesbians are equally dissimilar. While the crowd celebrates them ("It was as if these people, this collection of the corrupt, saluted their chiefs"), Paul, on the contrary, reviles them, crying, "They ought to be drowned like [bitches] with a stone about the neck" – the fate that in fact soon awaits him.[81] Despite their disagreement, Paul and the common throng both align the women with the animal world ("like bitches") and the natural ("People talked of it as a natural thing").[82] It is the high-born and well-bred Paul who is out of place among this crowd of workers, prostitutes, and deviants who unapologetically exhibit their sexual drives and proclivities: "Their vice was public, recognised, patent to all." The story's dénouement shows Madeleine leaving the scene of Paul's death as Pauline, who has replaced him, comforts her: "she had found a refuge in a closer and more certain affection, more familiar and more confiding."[83]

Lesbian Genders

"La Femme de Paul" puts lesbianism flamboyantly on display, but it also showcases gender in all its guises, underscored by the ambiguity of the title. In fact, Madeleine tells Paul and the reader quite clearly that "I am not your wife" [ta femme] (212). She is rather his "fille," the woman he keeps and with whom he has had the misfortune of falling in love. Paul's femininity ("La Femme de Paul" = "Paul au féminin") or Pauline's masculinity ("Paul au féminin" = Pauline) provide more apt referents. However one interprets the title, it is obvious from the names of these characters and their opposite and atypical gender presentations that Maupassant is saying something a little different. Men typically do not see lesbians as rivals in this literature. The deeply jealous Count Muffat in fact prefers Satin to Nana's male lovers: "In his jealous anguish the unhappy man got to the point of feeling almost reassured when he left Nana and Satin alone together. He would have gladly encouraged her in this vice, to keep the men away from her."[84] And yet Pauline is threatening to Paul – as much due to her comportment as her sexuality.

Pauline represents a new breed of lesbian, previously represented primarily as a beguiling beauty or member of a complementarily coiffed couple. (This trope, an appeal to male voyeurism, endures in naturalist works and is present in "La Femme de Paul": "two handsome girls, tall and slender, one dark and the other fair, held each other by the waist.")[85] While naturalists offered unconventional sexuality to entice readers, they typically flew unconventional gender expression as a red flag. Female masculinity is perhaps a greater aberration than homosexuality, if one judges by the fulminations lavished on departures from normative femininity. It was illegal at this time for women to wear trousers in public without first obtaining a permit from the police.[86] As was social policy, naturalist portraits of degeneration were buttressed by the scientific community's naturalization of social roles (wife, mother) and validation of sexual difference. Thus female incarnations of the terms clustering around masculinity (active, forceful, intelligent, sexual) were invariably seen as perversions of true femininity (passive, weak, incurious, asexual).

Male attire or bearing was symptomatic of female independence and represented by an emerging type: the physically and morally grotesque masculine lesbian. At a moment when women were increasingly seen as manly and unsexed, naturalism promoted this new image to add to the lesbian canon. No longer merely alluringly androgynous or eccentric, this creature induces disgust in men. Prescient of the medical model soon to follow, she is the *real* tribade, born that way, whose sexual proclivities are visible on her body and in her bearing. She is predictably working class, exclusively homosexual, and frequently the lover of feminine prostitutes. Typically qualified as monstrous and obese, she is dubiously human owing to her indeterminate gender and offensive sexuality. Zola focuses on her corpulence: "This Laure was a lady of fifty whose swelling contours were tightly laced by belts and corsets. [...] There were about a hundred women there, [...] [m]ost of them enormous creatures in their late thirties, with bloated flesh hanging in puffy folds over their flaccid lips."[87] He also spotlights the mouth, metonym for oral sexuality and symbol of their devouring menace.

Paul Alexis amplifies this portrait by placing his character in men's clothing: "that ghastly Chochotte, a little thug in a black smock, very broad across the hips, her cap's visor lowered shiftily."[88] While earlier transvestite characters (Mademoiselle de Maupin, Gabriel) captivated both men and women with their androgyny, these are physically repellent. Chochotte's mouth also appears prominently and is sexually suggestive: "They heard a rasping voice. [...] A thin stream of saliva left her broad, lipless mouth, stippling the shutter of the fireplace with its white spray. [...] She held a cheap cigar between her teeth, hands in pockets, cocky and offensive."[89] Chochotte is masculine in dress and comportment, as well as by virtue of her ejaculatory sexuality ("thin stream of saliva"). An appalling creature with a ridiculous name, she is barely recognizable as a woman: "'What's that over there?' [...] 'Can't you see that it's a woman?'"[90] Like Chochotte, Pauline is overweight and uncouth, a parody of ill-bred underclass masculinity: "a lusty blonde, dressed as a man [...] filling out her white flannel garments with her fat, swelling out her wide trousers with her buttocks and swaying about like a fat goose with enormous legs and yielding knees."[91]

Contagion

Zola wrote in his preparatory notes that "Nana is the rot from below [...] that surges upward to corrupt the superior classes. If you let this ferment germinate, it will then rise up and create chaos."[92] There are several meanings to read into the signifier "Nana" – woman, prostitute, indigent, lesbian. They all threaten to spread outward and upward to the respectable classes. The trope of contagion was widely applied to this nexus of terms due to a confluence of issues. The reality and social significance of prostitution evolved over the course of the century as the number of prostitutes increased. Numerous factors already mentioned – growing industrialization, a changing economy with different demands for labour, shifting demographics, increased urbanization – fed urban poverty, particularly dire for women of the working class, and drove significant numbers of them into prostitution out of financial necessity. Because of its greater prevalence and visibility, prostitution became a prominent social issue and, increasingly, a moral, legal, and medical one. Between the rising incidence of syphilis and Pasteur's discovery of germs, fears of an invisible, deadly menace took hold of the population and were manifested in several ways. The prostitute was identified with contagion, provoking public debate about the regulation of prostitution. The syphilitic prostitute became a stock character in texts of the period. Maupassant's "Le Lit 29" presents a riveting example of a prostitute who wreaks revenge on the Prussian invaders by infecting as many as she can before dying.

The sapphic and diseased prostitute is in fact a redundant symbol of invisible peril since neither syphilis nor female homosexuality can be seen. Microbes escape detection by the eye just as tribades, "whose external characteristics are difficult to observe objectively," at least while presenting as feminine, also elude identification. The former, a physical illness, can be treated and controlled, even if it is difficult to diagnose, but the latter, suggests Corbin, was thought to be incurable. Naturalist representations seem to confirm his thesis of the prostitute as incarnating the fear of contagion. There is perhaps no greater abomination than the diseased lesbian prostitute, nor is there any shortage of them in the literature of the period. In several of the novels and stories in question, their authors punish them with drawn-out, gruesome deaths. Madeleine and Fanny escape this sentence, the first thanks to the author's mordant cynicism and the second attributable to Daudet's more prudish aim of augmenting the pathos of Fanny's victim, Jean.

However the others are not so lucky. Whether of venereal disease or some other infection, they die with bodies in eruption. Lucie Pellegrin succumbs to consumption: "In the blood she was coughing up [...] there must have been small bits of lung [...] The handkerchief she used to wipe her mouth was already soaked with blood like a sponge."[93] Her death is as prolonged, lasting the length of the story bearing her name, and as horrifying as those brought on by syphilis. Lucie Thirache lives in fear of contracting it but does so despite medical intervention. Adam spares no detail in describing its ravages on her body:

> she unwrapped the bandages. They were all stuck together by dry, bloody pus [...] Her wrist had lost its shape and now looked like a reddish, formless swelling under which a pale liquid coursed. A livid fluid, reddened with bloody strands, seeped from narrow fissures [...] There was the sound of a pustule bursting, and a warm liquid flowed from her head, drenching her neck and shoulders.[94]

Satin, having "ruined her health so completely," dies discreetly at the hospital of an unnamed disease. She is seen and mourned only by Nana, who "set off to kiss Satin for the last time, dressed in all her finery."[95] Nana's death from smallpox, the novel's grand finale, is, however, a hideous spectacle witnessed by a troop of acquaintances, their visit to her deathbed moved by curiosity more than pity. The women arrive wearing hats and gloves "as if they were paying a call" and chat about the coming war over Nana's dead body. They leave for fear of catching the disease only when "The corpse was beginning to poison the atmosphere of the room."[96] The novel's last close-up shows Nana's decomposing face, literally effaced by the disease:

> Nana was left alone, her face upturned in the light from the candle. What lay on the pillow was a charnel house, a heap of pus and blood, a shovelful of putrid flesh. The pustules had invaded the whole face, so that one pock touched the next. Withered and sunken, they had taken on the greyish colour of mud, and on that shapeless pulp, in which the features had ceased to be discernible, they already looked like mould from the grave.[97]

Zola explicitly compares Nana's illness to the infectious putrefaction of her underclass roots and sexuality: "It was as if the poison she had picked up in the gutters, from the carcasses left there by the roadside, that ferment with which she had poisoned a whole people, had now risen to her face and rotted it."[98] The novel closes with cries to war against the Prussians, the death knell of the Second Empire.

If political corruption and an ill-conceived war wreak havoc on the Empire, sapphic prostitutes represent a present danger to the Republic as well. Maria

Deraismes engaged in a debate about the country's future in which naturalism and the representation of sapphism played central roles. While the feminist Deraismes applauded Zola's critique of Second Empire corruption among the ruling class, and they were essentially both on the side of a secular, positivist Republic, they were sharply divided by sexual politics. Deraismes flayed Zola's writing as anti-republican pornography, denouncing the "repugnant wantonness" of *Nana*, while Zola considered the naturalist model to be the linchpin of a successful democracy: "The Republic will be naturalistic or it will not be."[99]

Deraismes and other feminists countered rhetoric about the depravity of prostitutes with an analysis based on economic rather than medical and moral reasoning: sexually vulnerable and lacking economic security, working women increasingly relied on the sex trade for survival. They connected prostitution to both women's rights and class issues. When the 1878 International Congress on the Rights of Women called for the end of legal and illegal prostitution and for the authorization of paternity suits (prohibited by the Civil Code), they argued that these problems were linked, since pregnant single women, often the victims of rape or sexual exploitation, became social pariahs and, without support from their child's genitor, sank into poverty and turned to prostitution as their only recourse.[100]

While men saw prostitutes as sexually corrupt, though necessary, feminists countered with calls for the abolition of the "system of corruption" maintained to service men (*Ève dans l'humanité*, 46). Julie Daubié, the first French woman to receive the *baccalauréat* (1861), blamed men (students, soldiers, functionaries) for sexually exploiting women and decried the lack of laws against johns, whom she called "depraved men" (*Femme pauvre*, 255). And yet novelists and medical researchers had little interest in the men who frequented prostitutes, other than in the role of victims, focusing instead on women as a symptom of social decay or medical abnormality.

In addition to promoting family values in the name of progress, the Republic, and women's rights, Deraismes doubled as literary critic to condemn naturalism in general and Zola in particular. Her pamphlet *L'Épidémie naturaliste* (1887) took aim at the "lewd fanaticism" of writers who pushed realism to an unpardonable extreme, who "breached the limits that [Balzac] had respected" (18, 16). She singled out the novel, degraded by its commercialism and focus on depravity: "when the excesses of a dissipated and bestial existence form the basis for literature, decadence is not far off" (92).

Deraismes focused a good part of her critique on sapphic fictions and their authors: "After having depicted the natural passions ad nauseam, our authors in vogue have come to those *against nature*" (42, emphasis added). Of Ernest

Feydeau, the author of *La Comtesse de Chalis* (1868) and *Souvenirs d'une cocodette* (1877), she complained that "his imagination is like that of a delirious prostitute." Naturalism resembled pornography by its imperative to tell all, "the conviction that *everything must be said*," which had the effect of awakening "the most unhealthy kind of curiosity" (27, 41). Deraismes invoked Diderot and enlightenment philosophy, offering the restraint of *La Religieuse* as counterpoint to Zola's unfettered representation of sapphism in *Nana*: "Zola has taken it upon himself to demonstrate how an abnormal, bizarre state, one contrary to universal law, can produce perversion in thought and instinct. This is a delicate, indecent subject, and yet Diderot managed to respect the limits of decency" (52). In attacking naturalist immorality, Deraismes claimed that it resulted from bad science, questionable patriotism, and poor taste. In an essay entitled "Émile Zola et la science" (1880), she maintained that he misunderstood and misapplied the theories of the day: "he features knowledge [science] that he does not master" (68). Positivism, she maintained, is idealistic, since it strives for knowledge and progress – "noble qualities, lofty aspirations, and transcendent faculties distinguish us from inferior species" – rather than the cynical preoccupation with the *bas-fonds* evinced by naturalism (78–9). Deraismes used this same argument, which privileges the higher instincts over "the organic functions" (78), to argue for sexual restraint, which if practised by men would obviate prostitution. Like sexual licence itself, Zola's sexually licentious fiction runs counter to republican ideals: "under the Republic, we are counting on a literary renaissance that results from better and necessarily perfected institutions" (90–1). Deraismes maintained that the Republic in fact depended on the demise of naturalist immorality for its survival. In order for it to flourish, she concluded, in echo of Zola himself, "the Republic will not be naturalist" (93).

Decadence and the Aristocracy of Sapphism

Give me some wine from Lesbos, said Séso to the slave. It's stronger than the other kind.

(Louÿs, *Aphrodite*)

The greater a woman's importance and power in a civilization, the greater the decadence.

(Péladan, "Félicien Rops")[101]

The social critique implicit in the works of many naturalists was countered by decadent disinterest in political debate. While naturalists trained a democratic gaze on the milieus of the popular, lower, and marginal classes, even as they often pathologized them, decadents fled from such banality to focus on restoring the aristocracy's faded glory. As we've seen, naturalism viewed tribadism from the bottom up, placing it in the context of the working class as a symptom of social disease. Now we shall consider the top-down perspective so frequent in decadent novels, which gravitated towards sapphism among the privileged classes. Joséphin Péladan exemplifies decadent interest in the topic. Finding the underclasses offensive, he preferred instead to represent lesbians in their more palatable manifestation as women of the nobility, be they baronesses, countesses, marquises, or duchesses: "If [the tribades] were from a different milieu, transported to the city gates, they would not be worthy of study; the repugnance of the subject must be softened by the elegance of high society."[102]

Out of the great number of decadent sapphic novels, I will focus on two by the fin-de-siècle's most lesbocentric writers: Péladan's *La Gynandre* (1891) and Catulle Mendès's *Méphistophéla* (1890). Both prolific authors, Péladan and Mendès left œuvres preoccupied with aristocratic tribadism. Péladan was an anti-decadent decadent, one who deplored contemporary change and harked to the past, whose lamentations were nonetheless so idiosyncratic and ostentatious that his style can only be qualified as a product of the decadent moment.[103] Mendès's ambiguities were different; his work seems instead to revel in the excesses and atrocities it describes, even while challenging them with contrasting images of bourgeois morality.

Le Sâr Péladan

Periods of decadence display an inversion in sex roles, and degenerate bloodlines are full of women doctors and women artists.

I believe that the end of France is no more than a few years away.[104]

(Péladan)

Joséphin Péladan (1858–1918) was among the most flamboyantly conservative and deeply nostalgic of decadent writers, imbued with regret for the perceived decline of aristocratic values and institutions. A fertile author of a wide-ranging œuvre, he wrote novels, short stories, plays, art criticism, and other non-fictional works on topics that include the occult and metaphysics. Péladan's work is exemplary of the close relationship that conservative ideology and aesthetics shared in the decadent imagination. It bemoans loss in all its forms: the waning influence of religion, the fallen monarchy, changing gender roles, and the emergence of new social categories and economic relationships. The class politics that motivate Péladan's work are well defined. His praise of the elite

("In all matters, the Aristocracy is competence") contrasts sharply with his scorn for the working class: "duty is physical for inferiors [...]; the people, that is to say those who live by working, cannot govern."[105] Péladan blames democratization for social ills and disdains both the women's movement and the ascension of common people, lamenting that "the masses rule and woman becomes emancipated."[106] His views on class thus coincide with his appraisal of gender difference, which maintains women's intellectual inferiority: "woman is not capable of thought."[107] In the novel *La Gynandre*, Péladan sketches in passing an idealized woman, which he would later flesh out in his essay *Comment on devient fée*, whose glorified and hyperbolic femininity approximates the Eternal Feminine: "a woman attracts me because my nature gives me power over her [...] [she is] the princess, the woman who is decorative in her soul as in her body."[108] At the antipodes of this ideal woman we find "the modern woman who has neither passion nor poetry."[109]

For Péladan, naturalism was symptomatic of such decay, a concession to republicanism that pandered to the people: "in naturalism, I see a synchronism with universal suffrage and the anti-aesthetic protagonism of the rabble."[110] Zola, whom Péladan called "the most illiterate of writers" and a "novelist with scientific pretensions," was frequently the recipient of his anti-positivist scorn: "Darwin's scientific materialism corresponds with Zola's literary materialism."[111] As these quotations suggest, for Péladan the stakes are aesthetic as well as political: the representation of common people in literature and the promotion of republican values are tantamount to an anti-aesthetic materialism. Realism could never produce beauty, argues Péladan, given its preoccupation with the present moment and its broad cast of lowly characters: "The representation of contemporaneity, the sailor and the peasant, the worker and the bourgeois, will never appear at our exhibitions."[112]

Péladan's own style is ornate, even ostentatious, and riddled with neologisms and erudite allusions. He calls upon legend; Greek, Roman, and Mesopotamian mythology; various literary and religious traditions; occultism; and, curiously for a writer sceptical of science, botany. In contrast with prosaic and proletarian naturalism, Péladan proffers idealized heroes who undertake noble quests: "There is only one subject in art: a hero struggling with a moral or social enigma."[113] While Péladan is stylistically imaginative and innovative, his idealism looks to the past. The quest for beauty functions as an antidote to the ugliness of the modern, material world, since art carries remedial power: "Art alone can act upon the animistic collective."[114] The gift of creation, however, is limited to an aristocracy of intellectuals and artists, whose duty it is "to impose its own ideal on the public."[115]

Péladan was eccentric in his person, extravagant in his opinions, and esoteric in his writing. His eccentricities were consistent with the decadent ethos, and yet he railed against the idea of it in his writings, in which decadence shares a lexicon with abnormality, perversity, sin, and the modern. He frequently lamented fin-de-siècle dissipation in analogy to the decline of the Roman Empire. But in doing so, he was proclaiming the superiority of southern Europe and the Catholic Church (and the inferiority of all things Germanic) more than decrying the excesses of ancient Rome. Sarah Al-Matary has convincingly argued that "Latin messianism" gave voice to pre-fascism among fin-de-siècle authors. This was certainly the case with Péladan, whose nationalism marched in goose step with his theocratic, aristocratic, and patriarchal beliefs. For him, what was Latin obeyed the laws of tradition ("socialism is not Latin in nature") and represented an idealized norm.[116] Péladan associated "la Norme" with historical convention, rule by the privileged, and normative sexual and gender comportment: "The woman who abandons her attributes and her world defies the norm and will perish."[117] His substantial œuvre can be read as a protracted condemnation of contemporary degeneration and as the promotion of an aesthetic agenda with which his counter-decadent vision is inextricably fused.

Péladan is best known for his ambitious and arrogant novel cycle, *La Décadence latine* (1884–1900). This fourteen-volume *éthopée*, or description of customs, is both idealistic and damning. It is at once idiosyncratic and typical of the decadent marriage of aestheticism and traditionalism. Mario Praz has called *La Décadence latine* "a veritable encyclopaedia of the taste of the Decadents" and, more recently, Birkett has suggested that it "has a symptomatic importance for the understanding of the conservative neuroses of his time."[118] Its dogmatic social critique relies on the assertion that Western culture has arrived at an extreme state of decay. From *Le Vice suprême* (1884) to *La Vertu suprême* (1900), Péladan portrays a dissolute France, corrupted by secularism, egalitarianism, and vulgarity. Irreligion is responsible for aberrant morality; it results in a fall from noble virtues and the loss of artistic vision, closely related qualities in Péladan's vigorously defended world view: "Something is dying in our humanity [...] we are approaching an unforeseen moment in which all that is good, beautiful, and true will be impossible."[119]

While female homosexuality and sapphic characters recur throughout the cycle, it is the particular program of volume 9, entitled *La Gynandre*, to condemn the perceived proliferation of sapphism and call for a return to traditional sexual order. The novel follows one of Péladan's heroes, an idealized androgyne called Tammuz, as he investigates female homosexuality, "that psychopathological innovation" (42). Tammuz, named for the Mesopotamian god likened to Adonis and described as an "ambassador of sexual normalcy," resolves to "discover the law of the abnormal" by spending a year doing fieldwork in the "Parisian theatre of passion."[120] He gains admission into a variety of Parisian circles of gynanders and, over the course of the novel's six sections, succeeds in seducing all those he encounters and ushering them into the heterosexual fold.

The goal of Tammuz's quest is to prove his hypothesis that sapphism does not exist as true desire, at least among women of stature: "I contest Lesbos as love" (25). Same-sex relations are to be found only among the common people: "as for love, such outcomes [...] can only happen among the lower classes."[121] He dismisses "the worthlessness of passionalities from below," since working-class sexuality is by definition animalistic ("animal fibres").[122] In this Péladan and Maupassant appear to agree, although Tammuz's inquiry disregards the rank and file. Those in search of salvation affirm the ideal over the bodily, resisting "physical stupor [...], the lowly instinct for sensual pleasures" that hinder one's fortitude.[123] Even among deviants, this vertical hierarchy holds: "above, Lesbos resides in the imagination; below, in the loins."[124] Sapphism is a *social* problem, both the consequence of a decadent society and the possibility of its ruin. Speaking through Tammuz, Péladan likens the fall of Rome, which he attributes to male homosexuality [l'antiphysisme viril], to the decline of modern Western culture, which he fears will succumb to female homosexuality: "Will female anti-physicism, in all its diversity, destroy our decomposing Latin-Christian civilization?"[125] In *Le Vice suprême*, he uses a vocabulary of homosexuality to describe the Republic, "an *antiphysical* social state," and its democratic motto: "the Republic has judged itself with the three words of its motto, which embody *three propositions that are against nature*: liberty, which is the negation of duty; equality, which is the negation of justice; and fraternity, which is the negation of self-interest."[126] The Republic, in essence, is queer. *La Gynandre* thus does the work of condemning the "unspeakably ugly" contemporary moment by associating it with the tribade (133). Tammuz, himself firmly rooted in the past, damns modern France for having lost its God and its governing principles: "when one banishes the divine, what is normal disappears; sodomitic morals are the lot of an atheistic country."[127] "La sodomie féminine" is a product of the present moment (13).

Tammuz's inquest into female homosexuality is academic, at times clinical, although he employs language borrowed from the jurist, psychologist, artist, dandy, philosopher, ideologue, sociologist, and, especially, doctor and theologian. His reflections about gynandry work the familiar tensions between science and religion, between abnormality and sin. Péladan frequently adopts a scientific vocabulary to describe Tammuz (thinker, psychologist, psychurgist, clinician) and his project to study lesbian Paris: "before this moral illness becomes an epidemic, we must study it and classify it, [and] cure [...] this psychopathological novelty."[128] But the novel is also shot through with the language of moral offence: "it is a sin, not a passion."[129] Péladan claims immodestly that his novel can speak to both: "*La Gynandre* affirms its value, even for the scientist and the confessor, as the only monograph on female sodomy."[130]

Tammuz's first task is to find "a decent word to designate this culprit, one that smells neither of the street nor the clinic."[131] *La Gynandre* differs from previously considered novels for actually using the terminology of female homosexuality. Having tried out several options (*tribade, sodomite, fricarelle, Lesbienne*), Tammuz settles on *gynandre* as his term of choice, one borrowed from botany. From the adjective *gynandrous*, synonymous with hermaphrodite, it has as a primary meaning flowers whose stamens and pistils are united. This field of reference traverses the novel and signals Baudelaire's flowers of evil as intertext. Tammuz defines the gynander as "the woman who aspires to maleness, the woman as sexual usurper [...] all inclinations on the part of a woman to act like a man, and that includes a Mademoiselle de Maupin as well as a bluestocking."[132] This description in fact says much more about gender than sexuality – a gynander is a woman who acts like a man – thus recalling the ambiguous early usage of *lesbienne* to refer to non-normative gender expression as well as same-sex relations. But in Péladan's case, placing the accent on gender rather than sexuality serves both ideological and aesthetic purposes. His gynanders are not really interested in sex because such things only take place among the lower classes, never among the aristocracy that is his focus. That is, worldly gynanders retain the sexual indifference associated with normative, civilized femininity (women of the primitive lower classes are naturally more erotically animated), even in their abnormal masculinity and sentimental attraction to other women. Moreover, the idealism of both Péladan and his protagonist directs the narrative towards the non-sexual; it flees from the material reality of sex just as it shuns realism and the material world.

The book's prologue, a discussion between Tammuz and his friend, the novelist Nergal (named for the Babylonian deity), lingers pedantically on the problem first named *Lesbos* ("an inexact word"), on its historical sources, terminology, and literary precedents (26). In fact, Tammuz seeks to rewrite the Sappho myth ("Let us cleanse Sappho's name from the accusation of sodomy") and refutes the role assigned to female homosexuality in antiquity: "Greek epigraphy is devoted entirely to male sodomy: not a line about sapphism."[133] Nor does Catholic theology shed any light on the psychopathological aspects of this phenomenon, a sin, certainly, but also an abnormality caused by "a depolarized nervous system" having atavistic roots (28).

Tammuz and Nergal banter knowingly about prior literary representations of and historical allusions to female homosexuality and then turn to the nineteenth-century corpus. Tammuz will condemn the work of his contemporaries, "bad novels [...] about feminine sodomy," echoing Péladan himself: "all recent work on this topic has been unseemly and foolish."[134] But first he lavishes praise on the beacons of sapphic literature: Diderot, Balzac, Gautier, and especially Baudelaire. Nergal introduces Tammuz to Baudelaire's "Lesbos," whose "lyrical beauty" astounds him, even as he is "revolted by the subject": "it is due to his distorted thinking that this genius died an aphasiac."[135] Tammuz takes corrective action on two lines from "Lesbos," reworking them into a motto for his program of conversion. In Baudelaire's poem, the watchful speaking subject scans the sea where Sappho died to determine whether its waters will "some evening [...] bring back to forgiving Lesbos the adored body of Sappho, who left" [Un soir ramènera vers Lesbos, qui pardonne, / Le cadavre adoré de Sapho, qui partit]. In Péladan's version, Tammuz becomes the active agent who "will bring back to forgiving Eros Sappho's adored cohort, which left" [*Tammuz* ramènera vers *Éros* qui pardonne / *La cohorte* adorée de Sapho qui partit]. While retaining the mise-en-scène of the Leucadian cliffs from which Sappho, spurned by a man, throws herself into the sea, Tammuz inverts the meaning of Baudelaire's lines. The consoling speaking subject of "Lesbos" keeps watch for the literal and metaphorical return of the heterosexual Sappho's body to the shores of a forgiving Lesbos, with the island standing metonymically for lesbianism. Tammuz's project is instead to return the sapphic flock to the compassionate god of heterosexual love, Eros, as Sappho herself departs in grief.

Tammuz begins his tour of lesbian Paris among the elegant, worldly Orchidées, named for the gynandrous flower and led by the domineering Aril (another botanical reference, to a seed covering), who is surrounded by her flock [pensionnaires]. Tammuz finds them simultaneously circumspect ("these matters were not named") and exhibitionistic: "Lesbos loves the limelight [...] and needs male desire to arouse its pleasure."[136] Given the quantity of contemporary lesbian novels that appeal to male voyeurism, it is a little ironic to hear from one of Péladan's gynanders that "Lesbos's need for male spectators constitutes its inferiority." Despite their exhibitionism, Tammuz concludes that they are asexual: "there is no love among this clan [...]. The Orchids did not seek love among themselves for fear that desire would compromise their friendships."[137] He likens gynandry to "a depraved form of dandyism," suggesting that, without passion, it is nothing more than "a moral transvestism played out in life."[138] By virtue of her power over other women, the architect Aril, who is "masculinized by her activities," incarnates "woman's usurpation of man."[139]

Tammuz's second stop is with the rival to the Orchidées, the Royal Maupin, described as a group of athletic women [d'allure sportive] who spend their time fencing: "These women, who have no desire to be mothers, wives, or lovers, are admirably supple in movement. As a theologian, I will damn them if necessary, but I cannot deny what I see or fail to admire the artistic effect that they achieve."[140] Their name is a transparent reference to Gautier's novel, *Mademoiselle de Maupin*, called "one of the most lesbian of books." Next to the muscled bodies of these women, Tammuz appears effeminate, a label he readily embraces: "You cultivate virile attributes, is it not fitting that some men cultivate feminine characteristics?"[141] And yet gynandry and androgyny are not co-equivalent. While condemning female masculinity, Tammuz defends male femininity. Androgyny in men is superior to the vulgarity of brawny masculinity since "the head makes the man." Male intellectual supremacy cannot be aped; consequently, even the most virile woman remains a "small man," "an atrophied femininity."[142] The women of the Royal Maupin come to appreciate Tammuz's ascendancy: "the gynanders recognized the superiority of his mind and of his sex."[143]

Péladan's linking of gynandry to female inferiority and a consequently illogical quest for equal rights is not unique among writers of his era. What is curious, however, is his assertion that gynandry is inferior to androgyny and even male homosexuality. Tammuz refutes the notion that love between women is appealing to watch, therefore to a certain extent desirable, and its corollary, that male homosexuality is repugnant and therefore evil: "the gynander [...] hides her horrors, presenting only her decorative and sentimental side."[144] He contends, moreover, that androgyny and gynandry have different values, asserting that the former, which "appears in the Bible," has been consecrated by "Graeco-Catholic tradition" (43). Tammuz concludes that gynandry is inferior, a literal travesty (etymologically related to transvestism) of masculinity.

Tammuz's victorious tour of sapphic Paris continues in the third section with a visit to the Pentapolis, a biblical reference to the five sinful cities of the plain, including Sodom and Gomorrah, place names associated with homosexuality.[145] In this artistico-theatrical milieu, Tammuz finds the women "ridiculous rather than erotic [...] a bad joke."[146] A joke, perhaps, and yet full of peril. This pentapolis is peopled by actresses and women artists, writers, and musicians who are compromised by their pursuits, which masculinize them and associate them with lesbianism. Tammuz enumerates a number of hazards to the purity of girls and young women who, out of curiosity, run the risk of slipping down the sapphic slope. Such dangers include serial novels, boarding schools and convents, and "the songs and sayings coming from servants or the street" – dangers from down under, all liable to push an innocent girl towards vice until "she abandons normalcy."[147] Other familiar causes apt to "precipitate women towards sodomy" include lascivious or brutal men, the desire for adventure or drama, masculine temperament, melancholy or lassitude, *faute de mieux*, and so forth. And yet eroticism remains elusive.

The novel's fourth and fifth sections see Tammuz doing his missionary work with individuals rather than groups. He encounters the enigmatic Princess de Simzerla at her château de Leucade, followed by a visit to the reclusive Countess Fantôme on board her yacht, *Sapho*, also called "floating Lesbos." Both present uncommon cases of tragic falls from on high, and both are conquered by Tammuz. To escape a violent mother (herself the product of rape) and a sexually abusive brother, the atavistic Simzerla marries "a lecherous, bankrupt nobleman."[148] She separates from him and turns towards women, although, "at the corporeal moment," she "didn't know what to do" with her lover.[149] Tammuz returns her to the norm: "He was the inescapable male, the man stronger than Lesbos, [...] the living argument against feminine sodomy."[150] The Countess Fantôme describes herself as an "almost barbarian American," who was traumatized by "conjugal reality": "words cannot express what it feels like to be possessed by an imbecile, to begin one's nervous life in terror."[151] She takes a male lover, then takes his mistress "the moment [she] learned that it was possible to do so," and finally goes on to live as a man.[152] But like Simzerla, the countess cannot resist Tammuz, who guides her towards a "renascent femininity [and] return to sexual functioning."[153] Tammuz seduces the countess and celebrates "the defeat of the most resistant of gynanders," a victory he considers to be a moral rather than a sexual one: "I bring as much charity as I can to my passionality; I want to purify with tenderness."[154]

With this final victory, Tammuz is able to claim that "Lesbos is dead: I killed it with a kiss."[155] The novel culminates in a spectacle of conversion, a phallic rite in which fifty gynanders are coupled with fifty men. To the strains of the wedding march from Wagner's *Lohengrin*, Tammuz, "wearing a tunic and cloak, black with gold lamé," recites a "phallic hymn" as he unveils an obelisk (this in echo to the novel's opening scene, in which Tammuz enters Paris and passes by the Luxor Obelisk, "that vertical, rigid witness").[156] His victory is unusual among contemporary novels of female inversion, which typically present sapphism as a danger to masculinity. Instead of succumbing to fatal women, Tammuz is unperturbedly confident and "feels himself become *l'homme fatal* among them."[157]

An effeminate defender of the sexual status quo, this fatal man embodies the antagonism between the conventional and the extraordinary that is inherent in *La Gynandre*, in the Péladanian imagination, and, beyond that, in the idea of decadence itself. Let us recall Nordau's distinction between the ordinary and the unusual: "The ordinary man always seeks to think, to feel, and to do the same as the multitude: the decadent seeks exactly the contrary" (306). Péladan and Tammuz take it upon themselves to stave off chaos and corruption by putting things back in their place and restoring order, be that a sexual, social, religious, political, or artistic order. They concur with Nordau in affirming that decadence implies a departure from the norm: "the decadent seeks spiritualism in what is abnormal and exceptional."[158] And yet what is Tammuz, crusader for normality, if not exceptional? Péladan himself was a defender of Western institutions, above all church and monarchy, from which he strayed in great flights of fancy. A staunch Roman Catholic, he was nonetheless anticlerical, believing the Church to be compromised by modernity. He was also an active member of the Rosicrucian brotherhood, a mystical sect dating to the seventeenth century that claims its adherents possess esoteric wisdom.[159] Moreover, he dabbled in the occult, adopted the Babylonian title "Sâr," and was known for wearing tunics and robes, not unlike Tammuz. Exceptionality is clearly the prerogative of the elite, normality the burden of the masses, the unenlightened, and women. Through Tammuz, Péladan illustrated that there is nothing exceptional about gynanders, that they will never be more than *petits hommes*. In this he differs greatly from Baudelaire, for whom the lesbian, while damned, is an intriguing and grandiose creature, and from Catulle Mendès, whose blighted tribade rises with Péladanian extravagance to the heights of Baudelairean exceptionality.

The Inconstant Catulle Mendès

> A man who wrote gem-like stories and poems, of an eroticism, and of what New England calls immorality, that put him beyond the pale of international appreciation. […] He strewed his way with flowers fully as evil and as beautiful as those of Baudelaire.
>
> (Pollard, "Catulle Mendes")

It is impossible to align Catulle Mendès with any one literary tendency, given the variety and abundance of his output. He began his career as a poet and co-founded Parnassianism, the art-for-art's-sake movement that eschewed political engagement and the material present in favour of the quest for beauty. And yet from the orientalist erudition and neoclassical sobriety of Parnassian poetry, he went on to write decadent-flavoured novels saturated in the scandals and phobias of modern France. Mendès was also the author of innumerable fairy tales, a dramaturge and influential theatre critic, a librettist, and an early champion of Wagner. Never one to be constrained by artistic loyalties, he even published *L'Assommoir* in his review *La République des Lettres* when Zola couldn't find another taker. A voluble and promiscuous writer with an outsized personality, Mendès drew praise from and attracted the contempt of contemporaries who, while divided in their opinions of him, agreed on his versatility. One critic wrote that "because of his love of movement, he has never pledged allegiance to a school," while another complained that "he was distinctly a poseur, a self-advertiser [...] he had an instinct for offering [Parisians] always some new thing."[160] Another detractor called him "grasping," while another still wrote of his "facility in adapting to all topics and all expectations."[161]

Mendès was a visible presence on the Parisian literary scene, well connected and, according to several accounts, beautiful and dandified: "he wore his blond mane brushed back, a tightly buttoned morning coat and a turndown collar whence escaped the bubbling of a white silk tie, decorated with lace and knotted with affected carelessness" (Brisson, 57–8). A ladies' man, according to Léon Daudet he was forever "flanked by a different but constant girlfriend" (161). Mendès married Judith Gautier against the wishes of her father, Théophile, who nicknamed his son-in-law "Crapule Membête," a riff on Mendès's name roughly meaning "the lowlife bothers me" (Talmeyr, 116). He was an eager duellist, ready to take on all comers, typically other writers and critics: "He draws his sword like the late Saint George and engages in duel at the drop of a hat" (Brisson, 58). A *New York Times* article from 1899 relates his fourteenth duel with a fellow drama critic over the staging of Sarah Bernhardt's production of *Hamlet* ("Catulle Mendès in a Duel"). He also crossed swords with writers Octave Mirbeau and Francis Vielé-Griffin. And he defended his honour against aspersions of homosexuality when Jules Huret wrote, during Oscar Wilde's trial for gross indecency, of Mendès's and Wilde's close association.

But where some saw a swashbuckling *tombeur de femmes*, others saw something quite different. He was the "wickedest man in Paris" who "had the morals of an ape. [...] Beneath his winning superficial graces, there lurked such evil as belongs to nothing less than Satanism."[162] An admiring biographer detailed his chameleon qualities more charitably:

> Catulle Mendès possesses a strangely complex and mysterious nature. He is at once naïve and perverse, male and female, robust and supple, pure and unhealthy. He loves in equal parts nature's brutal power, the blue of the sky and that of the water, bawdy houses and feverish boudoirs, these too in azure and gold. With the same passion he loves the songs of birds and those of women, the healthy scent of flowers and the artificial fragrance of perfume; and he worships eternal Art and eternal Passion in equal measure. (Bertrand, 39)

Nor is it easy to get a fix on Mendès's politics. He was one of a handful of writers to remain in Paris during the Commune, which he chronicled in *Les 73 journées de la Commune* (1871). Some have read this text as evidence of his opposition to the Commune (Gullickson, Ireland, Ross), fewer as suggestive of his support (Bertrand). In fact, it shows Mendès's initial sympathies for the rebellion, followed by vacillation, and finally his condemnation of violence from both the Versaillais army and the Communards. Paul Lidsky's admirable study, *Les Écrivains contre la Commune*, demonstrates that few writers supported the uprising, so Mendès's irresolution is perhaps not particularly telling.

However, the considerable uncertainty surrounding his position on the Dreyfus affair is something quite different. Mendès does not fit neatly into Charle's paradigm. As a Jew himself and frequent recipient of anti-Semitic invective, this would have been a loaded topic for him, to say the least. Some have him siding with Dreyfus (Fulcher, 104), while others place him on the other side of the argument. One scholar has called him "a Wagner-worshiping anti-Dreyfusard of Sephardic descent" (Jacobson, 188). Or did he avoid the controversy altogether, "refusing to take sides in the Dreyfus Affair" (Wilson, 708)? As Maurice Samuels has noted, Jewish authors "became more circumspect about their Jewishness" in light of increased anti-Semitism after 1870 (242). Whatever Mendès's position actually was (or however he situated himself publically), he was frequently attacked for his own Judaism. Gide wrote disparagingly of "Jewish literature," naming Mendès in his appraisal that "they all have this in common, that from their work all idea of nobility is excluded. It is a debasing literature" (152). And Jacques de Biez, a member of the Ligue antisémitique de France, questioned Mendès's patriotism based on his religion: "Mr Catulle Mendès's Jewish race reduces the idea of a homeland to the ability to assimilate" (xxi). Historian Pierre Birnbaum has suggested that Mendès engaged in duels on more than one occasion in response to anti-Semitic slander. However, elsewhere we read that Mendès had no reaction to the "unspeakably violent" anti-Semitism of a play by Edmond de Goncourt and was, in fact, one of only two critics to favourably review it.[163]

So what are we to make of all this uncertainty and prevarication? It would be safe to say, for one thing, that Mendès's literary choices were driven more by aesthetics and opportunism than by political conviction or fully formed opinions about public affairs. If some of his works were wilfully provocative, Mendès did not intend to outrage his contemporaries based on any ideological agenda. For all his literary wantonness, art-for-art's-sake is a constant value: whether Parnassian or Baudelairean, lyrical or decadent, Mendès was a stylist, albeit not always an entirely original one. He deployed sapphism in mellifluous tales (*Les Îles de l'amour, Lesbia, La Vie sérieuse*) as well as in portraits of depravity (*Monstres parisiens, Zo'har, Méphistophéla*). Particularly in his novels, which "constitute another *éthopée* of Latin Decadence," abject sapphism amplifies the rhetoric of decay – but in the service of decadent hyperbole and its trope of sexual inversion, rather than out of a coherent political or moral stance (Praz, 343). Praz contended that Mendès "collected succulent morsels from the Baudelairean table" and outstripped with his excessive and unnerving tableaux some of his most audacious contemporary decadents, Barbey d'Aurevilly, Villiers de l'Isle Adam, and Rachilde among them (153).

Embedded in the decadent style, then, sapphism rhymes with hyperbole and excess, as does aristocracy: both are figures of extravagance and prodigality. Mendès's contemporaries frequently accused him of intentionally exploiting the shock value of such portraits ("a mission that is immoral and sometimes even filthy," Talmeyr, 114). Praz asserted, on the contrary, that Mendès sought to sooth his readers and, one could speculate, the censors, with his "pronounced moral pose" (345). More recently, critics have pondered whether Mendès's depraved inverts in fact represent their author's "irreproachable bourgeois sympathies" (Ireland, 173). I would suggest that any attempt to pinhole Mendès is fruitless, that his work is above all morally ambiguous and politically agnostic. Such is the case with *Méphistophéla* (1890), to which I now turn. It summons female homosexuality as a bogeyman for bourgeois anxiety, but also exploits it to rhapsodize about unspeakable desires. In essence, the novel weighs the value of conformity against the grandeur of degeneration, balancing its readers between Nordau's pole of the ordinary and the decadent platform of exceptionality.

Méphistophéla is one of the more fascinating of the late nineteenth-century lesbian novels because of its extravagant main character, Sophor d'Hermelinge, its decadent décor, and its pulpy plot – but also thanks to its ambivalent portrayal of lesbian evil, which the narrator both admires and abhors. It begins with the chaste childhood of Sophie Luberti, who is raised in a privileged and bucolic setting, and chronicles her sexual awakening and initiation. It then follows her to Paris, where, as the Baroness Sophor d'Hermelinge, she rises to social and sexual dominance. In the tragic dénouement, her manifold corruptions lead to her fall.

Sophie's family background and subsequent adventures confirm both the hereditary taint and precipitating social factors that push her towards her unconventional object choice. Her mother, Phédora, a respected widow living comfortably outside of Paris, hides a dark past that, when revealed in a flashback, points to degeneration. The reader learns that Sophie's mother was herself an androgynous, sexually precocious orphan of unknown origins raised in a sordid theatrical milieu by a corrupt aunt ("perverted to the core").[164] The aunt assures her own fortune by compromising the pubescent Phédora with an aging Russian count. Already hypersexual and masculine as a child, she matures into a young woman more conniving than her aunt. In order to secure an inheritance, Phédora rapes the wealthy count's sickly son, Stéphan Tchercélew, who was "infirm from birth [...], a being less than human."[165] He is the last of his line, the "final heir of an opulent and abject race [...],whose ancient sins he bears."[166] His physical infirmities, mental ticks, and even his penchant for reading scientific treatises on atavism all point to degeneration. Sophie is the product of this bizarre, if brief, union.

Such genetic baggage does not bode well for Sophie, whose early years she nonetheless spends in bourgeois tranquillity, marked by nothing more unusual than a particularly exuberant friendship with the young girl next door, Emmeline d'Hermelinge. Sophie begins immediately to transition into a lesbian after her new husband, the Baron d'Hermelinge, Emmeline's military brother, rapes her on their wedding night. Once again, we find male sexual brutality to be one of the precipitating factors in deviant sexual behaviour. Mendès needed go no farther than Baudelaire's "Delphine et Hippolyte" for such a model: "My kisses are light as mayflies at dusk caressing wide transparent lakes, whereas your lover's, like a wagon, will gouge out ruts – or furrows, like a plow; they will ride over you heavily, like yoked horses and oxen, with pitiless hooves."[167] In this entreaty to Hippolyte, Delphine contrasts her tender kisses with the animalistic violence of male sexuality, a trope that Mendès repeats in his description of Sophie's deflowering at the hands of her husband: "This excellent man turned into an animal, becoming nothing more than a male beast. [...] He held her down and crushed her under his weight like a charging bull! [...] He forced the virgin to submit to her husband's triumphal intromission."[168]

This rape, the novel's second, sets Sophie on the road to deviance, whose banner she will later defiantly wave. This road is literal as well as metaphoric, since Sophie flees towards Paris, the "damned city," obsessed with social class and a breeding ground for crime thanks to "its hideous slums" and "rabble scum."[169] In Paris Sophie is initiated by a lesbian prostitute, Magalo, who renames her Sophor, a masculinization that evokes the name Sappho. It is also in Paris that the function of class enters into Mendès's exploration of female homosexuality since Sophor, sired by a count, a baroness by marriage to Emmeline's brother, and wealthy thanks to the inheritance of her mother's ill-gotten fortune, completes her transformation at the expense of Magalo, a meek and powerless *femme du peuple*. *Méphistophéla* is a kind of lesbian novel of education, in which the sexually innocent Sophie, brutalized and frightened, educates herself on the "science" of love and develops into a commanding sexual predator, prominent in the highest social circles of Paris. She reaches the pinnacle of her glory and influence through a series of conquests that eventually turn her into a rebellious pariah heedless of public opinion, one who parades her sexual spoils before Parisian society. She champions the grandeur of the few elected by their difference and condemns "the sweet monotony of honest living."[170]

Sophor's audacity is both sexual and social; indeed, her refusal to conform to expectations of heterosexuality is indistinguishable from her refusal to abide by the social institutions and conventions she abhors: modesty, marriage, domesticity, and maternity. While the narrator clearly admires Sophor's heady and scandalous rise to prominence, two very different voices question her trajectory: those of a doctor and of a prostitute. Dr Glaris, as world-weary as his upper-class female clients, studies the effects of social decay on the idle rich at the opera. This notorious centre of distraction is the meeting place for what Glaris calls "the two conditions of womanhood: prostitution and aristocracy."[171] The opera is where "the Prostitute and the Lady [...] mingle in the same crowd and treat each other as equals."[172] Called the priest's replacement, the doctor has as his task to "cure the modern woman [...], sick women who are not sick and yet suffer infinitely."[173] The fictional Dr Glaris sounds very much like the historical Dr Chevalier (of whom more in the next chapter), who saw the honest labourer as being exempt from the degradation of the modern city: "Not a stone crusher on the main roads, a miner in a narrow tunnel, a farmer sowing or ploughing a field. [...] But the man of the new cities."[174] Excess and indolence, rampant in big cities, breed neurosis and encourage vice among the wealthy; women are particularly prone to succumb and most eager to consume medical advice.

Magalo also questions Sophor's morality by condemning her lesbianism. Abandoned by Sophor, having sunk to the lowest level of streetwalker, delirious and near death, Magalo undergoes a conversion in which she refutes her lesbianism: "there is nothing more filthy [...] it's not true that women can love one another passionately. [...] This pleasure which is not a pleasure is not only dreadful, it's forbidden!"[175] Sophor herself, the most impenitent and defiant of lesbians, contrasts her own despair with bourgeois happiness: "she was not far from thinking that she was wrong, that her life was in error, that only the foolish could be happy."[176]

On her deathbed, Magalo mimics conventional morality and laments her chosen profession: "The bourgeois are right. They live in tranquillity and die in tranquillity [...] Having a husband and children is true and good, because it is permissible."[177] Ultimately, her trespasses against heterosexuality and against the class structure are coextensive: "If I had married a worker or a clerk, I would have been spared so much grief!"[178] The moral of the story, which the dying Magalo relates to a shaken Sophor, is to adhere to one's station, to avoid mixing with other classes, and to seek sexual gratification from men alone: "If you don't extract yourself from this filth, you will suffer even more because you will be the guiltier. A little nobody like me who defiles herself has done no great harm! But you, so great and good, so intelligent, you deserve and will suffer dreadful torture for having debased yourself."[179] Sexual and social transgression are thus indissolubly linked. Sophor, guilty of both, nevertheless retains a certain grandeur in her decadence.

Although unsettled, Sophor rebels against Magalo's "simple-minded prattle and memories of childish religious instruction."[180] She condemns Magalo's interdiction against lesbianism not only as sexual hypocrisy – since indeed "it was odd that the woman who had introduced her to this unique pleasure was the same one denouncing it" – but as class hypocrisy as well: "this opinion was all the more foolish and predictable, coming as it did from such a mediocre and banal creature, one falsely exceptional whose wild bohemian exterior hid the reality of her bourgeois mentality."[181] For Sophor, it is the right and the duty of the exceptional creature to follow her desire: "Doesn't desire, in whatever form it takes, give the man or woman experiencing it the right to follow it? [...] here are women rebelling against their sexual destiny: although exceptional, their inclination is innate and no less legitimate."[182] Lesbianism, finally, is represented as a category of rebellion not only against sexual norms, but against social structures that separate classes, dictate comportment, and limit choices. Chevalier similarly blamed bohemian extravagance for encouraging sapphism: "To forego the permissible pleasures of respectable convention [du bourgeoisisme], disdain the mediocre joys of healthy love, be exceptional, attract. Vice is in style."[183]

Mendès, like Baudelaire, cannot completely denounce this negation of the norm: his repugnance is mixed with a certain admiration. It is curious to note the very similar rhetoric used by Mendès to describe women who fought for the Commune. Their refusal to fulfil their domestic functions, abandoning their homes, husbands, and children, elicits his incomprehension, but also his wonder: "A strange enthusiasm seized the women in turn, and they too began to fall in battle, victims of an execrable heroism. Who are these extraordinary beings who abandon the housewife's broom and the seamstress's needle for a rifle, who leave their children in order to die by the side of their lovers or husbands? Lawless amazons, at once magnificent and abject."[184]

Despite her proud defiance, Sophor falls from grandeur at the novel's end as surely as she rose to it at the beginning. The progressive signs of degeneration appear as a ringing laughter, inherited from her father, which begins to haunt her. This laugh was a sign of the count's own degenerative constitution, "the persistent symptom of an inherited illness," and Sophor hears it ringing in her ears with increased frequency as she travels down the slope of vice: "the laughter rang more distinctly in her ear."[185] A morphine habit alone can quiet it. She prematurely loses her youthful beauty and, as her infamy grows, Parisian society closes its doors to her. Boredom and the need for ever greater sensation send her into the darkest corners of Paris in search of promiscuous encounters. Nothing, finally, seems able to quench her insatiable desire, not the corruption of school girls, not cynical affairs with society ladies, not even the frequentation of lesbian brothels or sexual experimentation ranging from cross-dressing and role playing to sadism. In search of lost innocence, she seeks out Emmeline, her only pure, which is to say non-sexual, love.

This scene both disabuses Sophor of her nostalgic memories of Emmeline and provides another occasion for her to compare her extravagant misery with bourgeois complacency. Sophor finds Emmeline in a small town, far from the corrupting influence of the city, surrounded by husband and children, corsetless and, to Sophor's horror, nursing a male child. The naturalness and mediocrity of the scene equally astound Sophor: "They wallowed happily in familial solitude and righteous idleness [...] It did not trouble them to be merely mediocre."[186] Witnessing Emmeline "happy for having obeyed the banal laws of existence," Sophor flees in disgust.[187]

After this episode, which serves to align heterosexuality with both natural law and bourgeois values, Sophor descends even more rapidly into her self-made hell, as the narration becomes more ornate in its descriptive excess and more gothic in the exploits it recounts. Finally, the narrator seems to wonder with Sophor whether "only the foolish can be happy."[188] Baudelairean to the end, Mendès admires the majesty of his fallen angel, even as he condemns her monstrosity. Sophor's perversion peaks when, in a final attempt to escape her anguish, she follows Dr Glaris's recommendation to solicit the curative effects of maternity. Sophor seeks out the child she conceived when raped on her wedding night, whom she left to be raised in a convent, now a young woman not far from Sophie's age when she fled to Paris. Instead of finding succour in instinctive maternity, Sophor is horrified to realize that she is sexually attracted to her own daughter: "this appalling incest had yet to be imagined!"[189]

Mendès's novel hesitates between claiming the bourgeois social order as the site of authentic happiness and condemning its compliant banality. His narrator draws close to Sophor's point of view through the use of free indirect discourse, all the while condemning her to something like a night of the living dead, as her vampirish, twilight existence protracts her suffering indefinitely. Although she does not die the horrid deaths of Nana, Lucie Thirache, and Lucie Pellegrin, she nonetheless resembles them in living decomposition: "Her face – brow, cheeks, and lips – progresses from pale to pasty, from pasty to ashen; it slackens, lengthens, sags into a doughy, moist, and fleshy flaccidity, as if a putrid cadaver on the verge of liquefaction."[190] Although the novel's end seems nearly supernatural, it finally refuses to choose between an other-worldly and a scientific explanation for Sophor's unique and extravagant monstrosity: "ultimate achievement of an atavistic destiny or triumph of a Demon Temptress? lamentable example of Neurosis or of Possession?"[191]

From the aristocratic to the humble, tribades and the women they attract represent the menace of social instability and sexual contagion. But as *Méphistophéla* makes clear, fin-de-siècle novels do more than observe, control, and punish lesbians: they also provide alluring models of unrestricted passion for avid readers and speak to dark desires of unattainable abandon. Outsider status, signalled by sexual deviance and affiliation with the social margins, attracts as much as it threatens to destabilize. Finally, the social landscape presented in *Méphistophéla* and others of its genre brings into focus the wavering line between the lesbian as socio-economic scarecrow and as emblem of psychosexual alterity.

4 *Scientia Sapphica*

We will study human nature's most shameful defects, its most depraved disorders, its most abject perversions and proceed empirically, in accordance with the prevailing tenets of positivism, by unveiling all the secret and hidden details of this individual and social ill.

(Pierre Garnier, *Onanisme*)

The physician will doubtlessly uncover moral wounds and display shameful depravities, but because he must record everything, he finds himself under the obligation to say everything.

(Tarnowsky, *L'Instinct sexuel*)

British physician Havelock Ellis prefaced his 1897 study *Sexual Inversion* with a vindication of research on human sexuality. He noted the reluctance with which his contemporaries spoke of their intimate lives: "In this particular field the evil of ignorance is magnified by our efforts to suppress that which never can be suppressed. […] It is a mistake, [some] say, to try to uncover these things; leave the sexual instincts alone" (vi). Drawing attention to religion's furtive monopoly on the subject, Ellis contested the Church's authority and disputed its expertise: "the Catholic Church […] took an active and inquiring interest in all the details of normal and abnormal sexuality. […] I deny altogether that [the theologian] is competent to deal with [sexual matters]" (viii–ix). Ellis's determination to wrest sexuality from religion's hold and to expose it to the impartial scrutiny of the medical community was emblematic of a remarkable shift towards secularization during the nineteenth century, a shift promoted in France by the political agenda of the Third Republic. Sexology was a child of positivism, the belief in dispassionate empiricism as gateway to truth: "We want to get into possession of the actual facts, and from the investigation of the facts we want to ascertain what is normal and what is abnormal, from the point of view of physiology and of psychology" (ix).

The roots of sexology took hold during a moment in which the medical field was rapidly undergoing professionalization and diversification, a process that resulted in greater social and political influence for physicians.[1] Developments in the study of human sexuality coincided with the elaboration of the naturalist literary platform; both endeavours were informed by a positivist intellectual environment. Due to similarities in what Bourdieu has called their habitus, naturalists and professionals in emergent medical specialties have perhaps more in common with each other than with practitioners of other literary genres analysed in previous chapters. For both groups, inquiry into female homosexuality served male homosocial and homo-intellectual bonds. Again following Bourdieu, we could say that the intellectual labour associated with this inquiry produced capital that conveyed distinction, a distinction dependent upon symbolic violence against and exclusion of the object of study.

Like novelists, medical researchers were conditioned by the pressures and inducements of their milieus. Like them, they were creatures of their moment who sought out professional contacts to further their careers, they built theories about sexuality that were influenced by various tangentially related socio-political agendas, and they benefited from financial incentives offered through publishing. These networks engaged in factional disputes and defined themselves in contrast to rival schools: French criminologists and those of the Italian school, for example, competed with and identified themselves in opposition to one another as did the naturalists and decadents. Such professional communities, overwhelmingly composed of men during this period, offered mutual aid to their members and support to young initiates.[2]

The products of medical science and those of high literature have always functioned as capital in analogous ways within the elite circles that produce them. Medical texts reference and pay homage to each other explicitly, literature more often implicitly. Although a medical treatise is not an oeuvre, a closed object in the sense of a novel – Krafft-Ebing's ever-expanding *Psychopathia Sexualis*, which went through twelve editions between 1886 and 1902, is exemplary – during the period in question it conferred similar merit through displays of unflinching intellectual rigour grounded in scientific principles and republican ideals. Physicians as well as novelists probed previously unmentionable aspects of illicit sexuality without reserve; in particular, both groups painted a deeply dysphoric picture of female homosexuality.

While the medical pretence of scientific objectivity as cover for regulatory moral discourse is patent from today's perspective, it is instructive to consider the play of language and rhetoric in the elaboration of nineteenth-century theories. Naturalism borrowed its research paradigm from Claude Bernard's *Médecine expérimentale*; conversely, medical writing about sexual deviance tended to be the product of imagination and citation as much as of empirical study – a cross-contamination or epistemic disjuncture that led to disciplinary border wars. Medical writers often borrowed from preceding sources, sometimes liberally and without attribution, sometimes to the detriment of grounding their work in case studies or new knowledge. They nonetheless affirmed their scientific objectivity and steadfast commitment to tell all, resulting in the establishment of a vocabulary – and an ontology – of female homosexuality.

Those who studied sexuality lamented the vilification to which they were subjected. Some adopted pseudonyms in order to protect their reputations; for example, the German sexual reformer Karl Heinrich Ulrichs wrote as Numa Numantius, and French doctor Georges St-Paul used the anagrammatic Dr Laupts. Psychiatrist Richard von Krafft-Ebing deplored such defamation in the first edition of *Psychopathia Sexualis*, which catalogued a variety of sexual aberrations: "He who makes the psychopathology of sexual life the object of scientific study sees himself placed on a dark side of human life and misery" (x–xi). As a result of this condemnation, those writing about sexuality, and about sexual deviance in particular, took pains to establish and defend the legitimacy of their controversial research and to avoid the appearance of prurience. Employing dispassionate tones and clinical precision, they maintained that homosexuality and attendant physical and psychological anomalies were part and parcel of a medical condition that demanded scrutiny. Typically, such works were explicitly addressed to peers, and measures were taken lest their sensitive material fall into the hands of impressionable readers, a concern shared by contemporary novelists.

Krafft-Ebing was one among several who wrote selectively in Latin to shield inappropriate readers (women, children, the uneducated) from their work: "In order that unqualified persons should not become readers, the author found it necessary to choose a title understood only by the learned, and also, where possible, to express himself in technical terms. It also seemed necessary to write certain particularly revolting portions in Latin rather than in German" (xi). In his preface to the twelfth edition, Krafft-Ebing balanced the benefits of his work's success against a renewed effort at linguistic gatekeeping:

> [This book's] commercial success is the best proof that large numbers of unfortunate people find in its pages instruction and relief in the frequently enigmatic manifestations of sexual life. [...] Compassion and sympathy are strongly elicited by the perusal of [readers'] letters, which are written primarily by men of refined

> thought and high social and scientific standing. [...] May it continue to convey solace and social elevation to its readers. The number of technical terms has been increased, and the Latin language is more frequently utilized than in former editions. (xiii)

Similarly, Pierre Garnier carefully monitored his vocabulary in *Onanisme*, his treatise on the explosive topic of masturbation, in order to protect it from charges of immorality: "Technical terms cannot be indecent, only common words, which we have no need to employ" (13). Such was the frequently rehearsed protocol for medical writing about sexuality: scrupulous attention to language and direct address to peer professionals. Regardless of their packaging and intended audience, the success of these works surely depended at least in part upon the prurience of others, both lay and professional.

My aim in the following pages is twofold. First, I will review the context for the medical study of female homosexuality across Europe and in France, noting dissimilarities in the treatment of male and female homosexuality, despite experts' claims of their equivalence. My contention is that the medical discussion of tribadism was initially oblique and quite distinct from the analysis of male homosexuality, which evolved primarily in a legal-medical setting. In contrast, disciplines with significantly different agendas laid the foundation for the construction and oversight of female homosexuality: doctors and moralists concerned with marriage, masturbation, and the regulation of prostitution, all preoccupations linked to the hygiene movement.

The second point to be made here concerns the cross-pollination of literature and medicine in the representation of tribadism. As much as novelists relied on vulgarized medicine in the elaboration of their aesthetic doctrines, their plots and character development, researchers invoked fictional texts. Ellis himself noted that fiction writers avoided representing same-sex relations in men, who provided the overwhelming majority of cases for physicians: "This passion of women for women has, also, formed a favourite subject with the novelist, who has until lately been careful to avoid the same subject as presented in the male" (78). As has already been noted, it was not until the flowering of the decadent movement that male homosexuality was written into literature. Zola famously declined an invitation from an Italian homosexual to use his journal as material for a novel about inversion, instead passing it along to Dr Laupts, a specialist of homosexuality, who published it in a medical review as *Roman d'un inverti*.[3] Novelistic aversion to treating male homosexuality and medical reticence about female homosexuality placed the French sapphic novel in unusual relief. As a consequence, researchers often turned to literature for evidence that it lacked. Dr Louis Martineau affirmed, for example, that "everyone has read Balzac," a transparent allusion to *La Fille aux yeux d'or*. I take the work of Julien Chevalier, a doctor of legal medicine who commented extensively on French literature, as a case study of the exploitation of female homosexuality for symbolic capital in the medical field.

Observations from the Clinic

They are also called "lesbians," because the inhabitants of Lesbos were accused of this depravation.

(Taxil, *Corruption fin-de-siècle*)

While the sapphic literary phenomenon was particular to France, medical interest in sexuality stretched across the continent, to England, and to the United States. Nineteenth-century physicians displayed what might be considered a two-pronged interest in the study of sexual relations, the first prescriptive and the second proscriptive, although each depended on the other as foil. Books that set forth guidelines for healthy marital sexual relations began to appear during the first half of the century, subsequent to which interest in sexual pathology increasingly took over following the mid-century.

Precursors of Sexology

The history of sexology has received an enormous amount of attention since the 1970s.[4] Suffice it here to recall the salient features of its development, which was closely related to the establishment and professionalization of a diversifying scientific community.[5] As the prestige of experimental science grew, particularly in the areas of physiology (Bernard), bacteriology (Pasteur), and pathology, its influence on clinical medicine increased dramatically. Laboratory scientists frequently disdained medical practitioners for their lack of a clear methodology. The *art* of medicine thus aspired to become a *science*, resulting in changes in medical education, professional identity, and technologies of medical practice. International competition, among other forces, accelerated the trend towards specialization. Franco-German rivalry was particularly bitter during this period of scientific ascendency in Germany and perceived decline in France: following France's spectacular defeat by the Prussians in 1871, national honour as well as scientific reputation were at stake. While intent on intellectual achievement, physicians were not above maligning the enemy with nationalistic attacks. Laupts, for example, used Germany's medical prowess as proof of the nation's effeminacy: he claimed that inversion was "extremely rare in France," while German medicine's "wealth of documentation" demonstrated that "inversion abounds in Germany" ("Revue Critique," 740–1).

The new fields that contributed to the study of sexuality were far-ranging, including anthropology, psychiatry, neurology, legal medicine, sociology, and criminology. Research on anomalous sexualities was interdisciplinary or, as Julien Chevalier named it, "polyclinical." These branches of knowledge sprang from the same positivist imperative that would motivate republican secularists to oppose the waning political and moral leverage of the Church. It bears repeating that science, fuelled by ambient anticlericalism, took over from religion in nineteenth-century Europe, replacing a doctrinal moral order with one ostensibly based in empiricism. What was a sin, absolved by confession, became an illness to be treated by doctors or a crime to be judged and punished by legal and penal authorities. As one of Barbey d'Aurevilly's characters declared in *Les Diaboliques*, "The doctor is the confessor of modern times. He has replaced the priest, and is sworn to the secrecy of the confessional, just as the priest."[6]

A preoccupation with taxonomy, evident from the early century in literature (Balzac's comprehensively monumental *Comédie humaine*) as in science, provided a template for this renewed quest for knowledge. The passion for categorization encompassed the normal and, increasingly, the abnormal, from the classification of living organisms to pathological conditions.[7] During the second half of the century, studies in sexuality tended to focus on deviant or, to borrow Foucault's phrase, "peripheral" sexualities, of which homosexuality was a privileged one. Indeed, some historians argue that it was fundamental to the establishment of sexology as a discipline: "modern sex research began in an effort to understand homosexuality and expanded ultimately to include all of sexual behavior" (Bullough, 15). Other aberrant sexual practices subject to scrutiny included fetishism, sadism and masochism, satyriasis and nymphomania, erotomania, rape, exhibitionism, necrophilia, bestiality, and incest. Such anomalies were catalogued with increasingly fine distinctions by specialists intent on establishing a typology of human sexual pathology.

Recent theories of degeneration and evolution informed the analysis of deviant sexuality. Jean-Baptiste de Lamarck posited a theory of the inheritance of acquired traits at the beginning of the century (*Recherches sur l'organisation des corps vivants*, 1802). Although eventually supplanted by Darwinism, Lamarckism continued to inspire scientific thinking in France due to its assertion of environmental causation. Bénédict-Augustin Morel's landmark text, *Traité des dégénérescences* (1857), attributed physical, intellectual, and moral enfeeblement to the cumulative effects of social decay on subsequent generations. Then as now, theories presented in the name of disinterested science were not immune to the biases of their day. Morel, relying on the French naturalist Buffon, saw an analogy between the "inferior races," taken globally and trans-historically, and his contemporaries who suffered from degeneration. This word, propelled into public and professional discourses, derives from the Latin *degeneratus*, meaning "no longer of its kind": degenerates are the maladapted products of adverse environments. Morel points to varieties of the "great and unique family of the human genus" that develop abnormally under harsh climates, such as "the Hottentot nation" and "all the indigenous peoples of the new world," who thus deviate from the "normal type of humanity" (15, 34, 37).

In fact Morel describes the "normal type" in idealized terms. His is a Eurocentric ideal, one both physical ("the most attractive, the whitest, and the strongest men on earth," 12) and intellectual ("the intelligent and energetic inhabitants of European lands," 25). Non-European races find their analogue in contemporary European degenerates. Morel is particularly interested in the adverse conditions affecting the working class: insalubrious housing, rampant alcoholism and ingestion of other intoxicating agents, and unhealthy work environments (factories, mines). But more generally, he groups under the categories of acquired and hereditary degeneracy those who are on the margins of society and the physically or mentally infirm. Following Morel, the label "degenerate" became applicable to people whose appearance diverged from a northern European racial and ethnic profile, and to individuals and groups whose behaviour perturbed social norms, including sexual minorities, criminals, and atypical or rebellious women.

Charles Darwin's theory of evolution supported Morel's claims about the impact of heredity on degeneration. *On the Origin of Species by Means of Natural Selection* (1859) became a foundational text for the study of sexual perversions and criminal behaviours. It also fuelled the racist fire that consumed scientists for decades. These same preoccupations – with natural selection, or the forward-march of mankind, and degeneration, its reversions – gave rise to the field of eugenics, named by Darwin's cousin Francis Galton, in his *Inquiries into Human Faculty and its Development* (1883). The abuses of eugenics, from forced sterilization and institutionalization to genocide, are well known today. As were many of the other new fields of the period, it was driven by the authoritarian impulse to differentiate, appraise, categorize, and control.

Darwinism weighed heavily upon the Italian school of criminology, led by anthropologist Cesare Lombroso. Lombroso's deterministic theory of the born criminal (*Uomo delinquente*, 1876) held that heredity, rather than free will, dictated the actions of criminals. He detailed the physical traits that distinguished the criminal type and posited atavism as a cause of deviance, thus aligning criminality with primitivism. Lombroso's theory held sway until challenged by the French school, which was anchored by Alexandre Lacassagne at the School of Medicine in Lyon. The French bent was more sociological than biological, thus focusing on social milieu as a determining factor in criminal activity.[8] The nature-nurture debate was also central to the discussion of homosexuality among doctors of legal medicine, psychiatrists, and jurists, and it played a considerable role in the typology of inversion: specialists across Europe largely agreed on the distinction between innate and acquired behaviours, the former generally considered an illness, the second a vice or crime.

While French men of letters had already cornered the market on literary representations of lesbians, Germans and Austrians led in the scientific study of inversion and were largely responsible for the emergence of sexology as a discipline at the beginning of the twentieth century.[9] Homosexual jurist Karl Ulrichs, one of the first to write on the topic, elaborated a theory of a third sex, which he referred to as Urnings. Although his intent was to find an innate and therefore natural basis in defence of homosexuality, Ulrichs was marginalized by medical professionals whose theories of innateness ultimately served to pathologize rather than to vindicate homosexuality. The examination of inversion took off following German psychiatrist and neurologist Carl Westphal's 1869 case study of homosexuality in a woman, "Die Konträre Sexualempfindung," an article broadly credited with the introduction of the term, translated in French as *inversion sexuelle*. Although groundbreaking, Westphal's focus on female sexual inversion would quickly be overshadowed by subsequent work devoted overwhelmingly to inversion in men. In addition to Westphal, Krafft-Ebing had a profound effect on the institutionalized study of sexual pathology. One of his protégés, psychiatrist Albert Moll, authored the influential *Perversions de l'instinct génital* (1891, prefaced by Krafft-Ebing). And Sigmund Freud, a student of neurologist Jean-Martin Charcot, contributed *Three Essays on the Theory of Sexuality* (1905), in keeping with a pattern of mentorship around the topic, to be explored more fully below. The discipline was finally named sexology when in 1907 Iwan Bloch called for its establishment as a field, following which Magnus Hirschfeld edited the first *Journal of Sexology* (1908).

It has been argued that France, which decriminalized homosexuality following the 1789 revolution, had a lesser investment in its study than did other European nations where it was proscribed and thus placed under the purview of legal medicine. And yet, as Régis Revenin has masterfully demonstrated, homosexuality in France was by no means overlooked by the legal authorities.[10] The Napoleonic Code fixed a higher age of consent for homosexual acts (eighteen instead of fifteen), and sexual encounters between men were frequently punished under vague provisions against public indecency (*atteinte publique à la pudeur*). Regardless of their legal status, same-sex practices were monitored either by the medical community, the police, or public opinion and subject to various forms of social constraint.

In fact, the study of male homosexuality in France saw some of its most important developments in the field of criminology. Forensic doctors addressed lawful sexual activity between men in the context of studies on sexual crime: Ambroise Tardieu's authoritative *Étude médico-légale sur les attentats aux mœurs* (1857) discussed public indecency by *sodomites* at length and broke new ground in research on sexual criminality in men.[11] Review articles made German research known to the French medical community beginning in the late 1870s, and prominent works were translated into French fairly quickly.[12] France had important players of its own working on homosexuality. The topic drew the attention of leading researchers, including Charcot (remembered today for his work on hysteria, hypnotism, and aging), who co-wrote the 1882 article "Inversion du sens génital" with psychiatrist Valentin Magnan. Psychologist Alfred Binet credited Charcot and Magnan with introducing the idea of inversion in France. And Lacassagne, the pioneering specialist of legal medicine, published the important article "Pederasty" (1886), a term used more frequently "in everyday language" to refer to male homosexuality than to child sexual abuse (239).

In France as across the rest of the Continent, the fields of legal medicine, psychiatry, and criminal anthropology focused primarily on male homosexuality through the turn of the century: "Although just as frequent as pederasty, the vice [of female homosexuality] is rarely the subject of medical evaluation; we will do no more than mention it here" (Lacassagne, *Précis*, 454–5). Tribadism received far less attention for varying ostensible reasons. Some claimed that it was no different than masculine inversion, suggesting implicitly that it sufficed to study the generic male homosexual: "the phenomena are identical in both sexes and develop in the same way" (Charcot and Magnan, 302–3). Others declined to pursue it due to the paucity of data on the subject: "Science in its present stage has but few data to fall back on, so far as the occurrence of homosexual instinct in woman is concerned as compared with man" (Krafft-Ebing, 395). Others still displayed revulsion ("let us draw a veil over a topic that is so unfortunate for the honour of humanity," Moreau de Tours, 178) or simple lack of interest, while some argued that its infrequency obviated the need for its study: "observations relative to women are more rare."[13] Lombroso waited nearly two decades before he complemented his work on male criminals with *La donna delinquente* (1893), in which he associated lesbianism with prostitution and atavism. That same year, Albert Moll acknowledged that "we have much less data on the phenomenon of inversion between women" (220). The research-based domains responsible for the medical and legal pathologizing of minority sexual behaviour – contributors to the creation and imposition of sexual identities – derived their findings first and foremost from male sexual deviance.

Despite assertions of their resemblance, the "male homosexual" and the "female homosexual" in fact followed significantly different trajectories in becoming socially relevant categories that were meaningful to and recognizable by contemporaries, whether lay or specialist. Early scientific information about female homosexuality was instead the by-product of studies on marriage, masturbation, and prostitution that dated back to the early nineteenth century and beyond. All of them relate same-sex practices to social problems and domestic misconduct and, in so doing, posit the suppression of female homosexuality as necessary for the maintenance of social equilibrium. The hypertrophied clitoris attributed to unnaturally sexed women is emblematic of their perceived arrogation of male privilege and sexual prowess.

Marital Hygiene

Hygiene was a word laden with meaning during the nineteenth century, an era increasingly preoccupied with health and cleanliness, and capable of developing technologies and teaching the means to combat the unsanitary conditions spawned by urban and industrial growth.[14] What came to be known as the hygiene movement addressed numerous public issues, including urban planning (it inspired the Haussmannization of Paris), education, and communicable disease; but also private considerations, such as the consumption of food, drink and tobacco, issues of morality, and interpersonal relations.

Hygiene campaigns targeted patent, fetid filth, but also invisible disease. As syphilis spread and Louis Pasteur's contributions to germ theory revealed microorganisms to be a cause of disease, fear of physical contagion grew conspicuously. More insidious than microscopic germs were the impalpable moral and social ills imagined analogically to be afflicting the populace in the form of crime, sexual perversion, and other anti-social behaviours. As water canalization and sewage treatment cleansed the city, pasteurization preserved comestibles, and public health measures protected bodies from disease, social hygiene sought to wipe out crime and immorality. The concept of moral hygiene masked what was actually moral regulation, which governed proper – and increasingly sanctioned improper – conduct in both public and private realms.

Domestic hygiene manuals began to appear early in the century. First addressed to lay audiences, they became progressively more specialized.[15] Such manuals advised married couples in wholesome sexual practices, guided them through fruitful intercourse and healthy pregnancies, and instructed them on the care of newborns. They also broached problems such as sterility, impotence, frigidity, and "conjugal fraud," a term designating a variety of non-reproductive sexual acts. Incidental passages warned of irregular sexual practices in women, while scrupulously avoiding the topic of sexual or gender non-conformity in men. It is in these pages that the tribade makes her appearance in the guise of the unnatural, socially destructive woman.

Whether addressed to a general or specialized audience, these books often enjoyed considerable commercial success. Auguste Debay's *Hygiène et physiologie du mariage* (1848) is illustrative. Debay (1802–90), a physician, was the author of a number of pseudo-scientific studies that rode the wave of the hygiene obsession, among other fashionable topics. He also wrote books about magnetism, occult science, female beauty, perfume and flowers, chocolate and coffee, "vestimentary hygiene," and human monstrosities. While initially published elsewhere, the sales of *Hygiène et physiologie du mariage* – and of its companion volume, *Philosophie du mariage* (1849) – skyrocketed in the late 1850s when they were acquired by voguish editor Édouard Dentu, who also published Adolphe Belot.[16] Debay's two titles were regularly reprinted for over fifty years, going through 178 editions by 1891. There is no doubt about the breadth of Debay's intended audience: the author's advice on sexual hygiene, addressed alternately to men and women, reached a vast public. He taught that conventional behaviour was *natural* and, conversely, unconventional behaviour unnatural and dangerous.

Hygiène et physiologie du mariage universalized and naturalized marriage, calling it "one of the great laws of living nature" (11). Debay considered its "physiologic" role to be strictly procreative: "considered from the point of view of physiology, marriage is simply the union of the sexes with the aim of perpetuating the species" (1). But it also served a *civilizing* function: "marriage is the only way to control the genital instinct while subjecting it to moral aims" (18). According to Debay, moral hygiene dictated proper roles for husbands and wives: "marriage prevents debauchery, moderates sensual passions by facilitating the means of satisfying them, and thus safeguards public decency and the honour of the family" (2). Social historian Peter McPhee has suggested that *order* was the watchword of marriage hygiene manuals: "what were those behaviours which bourgeois men and women should adopt if they were to create domestic harmony and social order? Could the moderate virtues of domesticity create political stability?" (236). The domestic order that Debay sought to consolidate was predictably predicated upon gender conformity. His doctrinaire politics of gender expression reinforced conventionally polarized norms by medicalizing the literary and cultural trope of the Eternal Feminine.

Warning of the dangers of celibacy, Debay extolled the virtues of healthy marriage and detailed the optimal conditions for procuring one. He held that gender polarity was universal in both humans and animals: "the female sex, exceptions aside, is by nature more tranquil and less disposed to amorous combats than is the masculine sex" (237). Male sexual drive is necessarily stronger – "the needs of men are more imperious" – and more violent: "it's true that men are brutal" (136, 138). In contrast, women frequently find intercourse distasteful and are inclined to frigidity. In order to maintain harmony in marriage, Debay counselled wives to submit to their husbands: "cede to the needs of your husband [...] in spite of your momentary aversion for the pleasures he solicits, do your best to satisfy him" (138). He suggested that men be sensitive to their wives' menstrual cycle and moods: "respect the proscribed days. When you are met with indifference or disgust, be prudent enough to wait until later." Rape, moreover, is to be avoided whenever possible: "Never take violently or by force what is refused to you" (139). Instead, Debay advised men to awaken the desire of their wives by employing foreplay and *le langage d'amour*.

Debay contended that dissimilar dispositions between men and women were naturally beneficial to the species, since exceptions to the rule were overwhelmingly sterile. The delicate sexual drive of normal women served as baseline for and counterpoint to oversexed or unnaturally sexed women. Debay's mission to instruct about moral hygiene and salubrious heterosexual relations justified his delving explicitly into human anatomy and sexuality. The promise of a peek at human sexual oddities, implicit in his subtitle ("in their most curious details") and present in many of Debay's other works, undoubtedly contributed to his book's success. Abnormal femininity and tribadism numbered among the curious details that attracted readers, in much the same way that popular fiction drew readers interested in the scabrous subject matter it ostensibly condemned.

Tellingly, Debay broached the topic of tribadism in passages related to hermaphroditism and female genitalia. As would sexologists after him, he associated same-sex practices with unconventional gender expression and genital malformation: "As a general rule, when men and women stray from sexual characteristics specific to them, such as when their genital organs are not adequately developed, the inability to procreate results. *Feminized* men and *virilized* women who unite with one another are usually sterile" (293). Debay saw nonconformist behaviour as coextensive with genital malformation, displaying a greater interest in this phenomenon among women than in men. He named the mystical warrior Jeanne d'Arc and the fiery revolutionary Théroigne de Méricourt – "as well as numerous other bellicose women who are better suited to trousers than to a dress" – as examples of women who "displayed signs of genital imperfections and did not menstruate" (294). But those considered to fall outside the norm included a contradictory bunch: Jeanne d'Arc, called the virgin "maid of Orleans," was placed in the company of highly sexual women, "ardent women affected by uterine passion" (237). What they shared was an association with masculinity, be that atypical gender expression (warrior women), an active sexual drive, or genital deformity in the form of a penis-sized clitoris.[17]

While according to Debay hermaphroditism weakened the sex drive in men and rendered them "indifferent to love," it had the opposite effect on "female hermaphrodites or women with long clitorises" who turned towards other women for sexual fulfilment (298, 297). Incurious about male homosexuality, Debay lingered on the topic of "clitorism," which he associated with "the women of Lesbos who abandoned themselves to voluptuous caresses still known today as *lesbian games*" [jeux lesbiens] (45). This physical abnormality could also lead to moral transgression: "it has been said that the famous Sappho was infected with this vice." In contrast with others writing only a few decades later, Debay found more evidence of "the vice of *tribady*" in ancient times than in the present (289). He argued contradictorily that enlarged clitorises both preceded and developed from sexual activity between women, while contending that amputation "normally returns the woman to natural proclivities" (290–1). By associating tribades (synonymous with the colloquial *titilleuses, frotteuses, gratteuses, ribaudes*, he informs his reader) with masculine attributes, behaviours, and prerogatives, Debay essentially brought the word into service as a catch-all for women who were not conventionally feminine in either behaviour or appearance. Women who enjoyed sex too much or too little, those who looked or acted like men, and those unable to bear children were all painted with the sapphic brush.

Thirty years later, Pierre Garnier published a volume on marital hygiene, *Le Mariage dans ses devoirs* (1879), which in its differences from Debay reveals the increased stakes of gender and sexual conformity under the Third Republic. Also a best-seller, it was reprinted regularly through the turn of the century. Its success inspired him to write extensively about procreative health and, increasingly, sexual abnormality and disease, in a series entitled "Hygiène de la génération."[18] Garnier (1819–1901), a physician by training like Debay, has been called "the most prolific and undoubtedly the most widely read author of popular medicine during his time."[19] And yet he had seemingly closer ties to the medical community than did Debay, and in presenting his material to the public he took greater pains than did his predecessor to "use the uncompromising language of science, history, ethics, and reason [...] without offending common decency" (xi).[20] Garnier's marriage volume was not, in fact, his own work, but translated "freely" from a book written twenty years before by Spanish physician Pedro Felipe Monlau.

Garnier significantly altered Monlau's work in order to make it relevant to a contemporary French audience. He updated the original with "recent discoveries," naming pioneers in evolutionary, cell, and germ theories, thus buttressing his scientific authority. He also rejected Monlau's clericalism, while maintaining the "moral principles, elevated thought, and hygienic precepts" of the original (xi, xx). It is here that one also finds articulated significant differences between the mid- and later century, differences attributable to changes in sexual and national politics, to the advances of secularism and the influence of positivism, and to the evolving face of medicine. Garnier exhibited a much greater interest in social issues than did Debay, Monlau's contemporary, writing with urgency about the nation's need for healthy, reproductive marriages. Garnier's deployment of the female invert must be understood in this context, which melds national politics and dogmatic moralizing with the imperative to procreate. His work is based on an explicitly republican agenda and dominated by concern for increased natalism at a critical moment of population decrease: "The social question of marriage is so pressing in France today because of the decline of legitimate unions, increased illegitimacy, falling birth rate, proliferation of infanticides, considerable infant mortality, and because of the deplorable depopulation resulting from these factors. [...] This study thus arrives at a propitious moment to remind us of the duty of marriage and procreation" (ii). Garnier's major concern in *Mariage* was to encourage reproduction and, in so doing, to condemn non-reproductive sex in all its forms. Stable, happy marriages provided optimal conditions for maximal procreation, which, he argued, was essential for the health of the nation. Contending that unhappy marriages were unproductive, Garnier supported divorce as ultimately favouring population growth. It became legal five years after his book was published.

Garnier named liberty, property, and family as the three "conditions essential to human society," an interesting variation on the republican trilogy of *Liberté, Égalité, Fraternité* (12). Garnier's values were also unarguably republican: he positioned himself against socialists on the left by invoking property rights, and against legitimists and Catholics on the right by advancing the family as the cornerstone of the Republic. Both sides presented a threat to bourgeois stability. Garnier pointed to Fourierism, the utopian socialist movement that championed free love and communal living, as "a frontal attack on the family" (14). Although Fourierism, which flourished during the first half of the century, was no longer a compelling force, the Church remained a potent rival. In a curious rhetorical gesture, Garnier equated the two by comparing monastic life to a phalanstery, the term designating self-sufficient, collective communities that Fourier himself coined *in opposition to* the idea of monasticism, or solitary living. Garnier wrote that religious orders constituted "a veritable communism without the mixing of the sexes" and that cloisters defied "the principal duties and charges of the State": marriage and reproduction (17). In calling for the marriage of priests and condemning celibacy in all its forms, "both civil *and* religious," Garnier was challenging core Church precepts still under fire today (373, emphasis added). He concluded that "voluntary celibacy is often nothing more than egotism and laziness" (372).

In addition to celibacy, Garnier denounced "medical Malthusianism" (birth control), abortion, masturbation, conjugal fraud (or "artificial copulation"), sodomy (anal sex), and any other sexual practice that privileged pleasure over conception: "those infamous artifices, shameful stratagems, frauds, all the abominable obstacles currently used against procreation [will lead] to the extinction of the family" (370). Garnier's positions on issues of concern to women were in keeping with the anticlerical, natalist republican agenda outlined above. An advocate of divorce in view of enhanced procreation rather than of women's rights, he opposed birth control and designated narrow limits of acceptable sexual behaviour for the same reason. Similarly, he both supported education for girls and opposed the vote for women, again in the name of the family. Garnier claimed to favour emancipation, but in the private sphere alone: "It is important to ask what the *Emancipation of women*, currently under experiment in the United States, entails. Does it concern the right to vote and eligibility for public employment? But women clearly already exercise their legitimate influence in the family by their conduct, their actions, and their counsel" (18). Garnier argued that woman already had the vote ("she is unquestionably a voter in the second degree") and should content herself with influence in the domestic sphere: "Woman's place is in the home and not in the public square" (18, 19). He encouraged "the development of her instruction" in order to optimize the intelligence of her administration and influence at home (19).

Garnier's ideological stance on women's issues underlies his treatment of female sexuality, which he harnessed to reproduction at the expense of independence. His descriptions of male and female genitalia betray little interest in sexual gratification. Garnier focused on the vagina as the sole external "copulatory apparatus" necessary for reproduction, with all else being superfluous, mere add-ons: "various accessories are attached to this singular organ [the vagina]" (183). Garnier passed quickly over the ornamental clitoris, "a small elongated protuberance that is erectile and can expand unduly" (184). He offered no word about its capacity for pleasure – although admittedly he remained elusive about the role of pleasure in readying the penis for intercourse: "soft and hanging, it grows, hardens, and becomes erect under various physical and mental influences, which do not always have to do with love" (179).

Men were nonetheless widely assumed to need outlets for their robust sexual drive, whereas adulterous or sexually autonomous women endangered not only the family, as we saw in Debay, but the very social fabric. Garnier raised the spectre of the unnatural masculine woman, and, while Debay looked to ancient Greece for examples, Garnier saw a menace in contemporary France, and especially in the capital city, locus of female independence and emancipation. He described intelligent, ambitious women – exemplified by female doctors, perhaps the most immediate threat to his own livelihood – as unfeminine deviants, calling them "women-men [femmes-hommes] incapable of fulfilling the role that is naturally assigned to them" (20). Physically masculine women blend secondary male sex characteristics with virile gender expression and moral perversion: "there are mannish women [femmes hommasses] with masculine builds, low voices, and hair above their lips, who have all the audacity and easy manners of men; such physical perversions often lead to moral perversions" (190–1). Like Debay, Garnier equated atypical femininity with hermaphroditism, making the leap from a psychosocial trait such as self-sufficiency to the physical aberrations thought to be symptomatic of inversion: "instead of a man, it was a bearded woman without breasts and having an overdeveloped clitoris" (193). In Garnier's model, the slippage from female doctors to physical and sexual deviance in women betrays the heightened stakes for pathologizing minority sexualities, which threaten the male birthright, be that economic, sexual, or intellectual.

By detailing and reinforcing the norms against which pathology was defined, works such as those of Debay and Garnier provided necessary points of reference for the diagnosis of sexual abnormality, which soon became a more compelling preoccupation than marital harmony, although both served to enforce gender and sexual conformity. Foucault refers to the "centrifugal movement with respect to heterosexual monogamy," which was "spoken of less and less," although maintained as an "internal standard" (*History*, 38). Hygiene treatises provided the first foray into, as well as a foil for, the work on marginal sexualities that would follow. Masturbation and prostitution were at the top of the list of non-reproductive practices that attracted the scrutiny of the medical community.

While marriage manuals offered a rich and varied vocabulary of sapphism, a more precise lexicon of male and female homosexuality emerged from the treatises on sexual pathology that followed. Different fields regulated female sexuality in diverse ways (studies on hygiene to remedy abnormality, on masturbation to condemn sexual pleasure, and on prostitution to police sexual independence), and yet all were inclined to present the figure of the tribade as the embodiment of deviant femininity. As was the case with hygiene manuals, changes over time in the representation of masturbation show to what extent thinking about illegitimate sexuality was tied to the politics of the day.

Masturbation

Like marriage manuals, works about masturbation associated same-sex practices with social disorder: authorities weighed in on private matters out of concern for public hygiene.[21] During the nineteenth century, masturbation in women was to a certain extent synonymous with sapphism and tribadism. In cataloguing different kinds of solitary and mutual masturbation (e.g., clitoral, vaginal), those who studied it consistently invoked Sappho of Lesbos to characterize sex between women, although they frequently disagreed about which specific act was determinant of female homosexuality.

Swiss physician Samuel-Auguste Tissot provided the text of reference with his pivotal treatise, *Onanisme*, which went through sixty-three editions between its initial publication in 1760 and 1905. It had an uncontested influence on nineteenth-century physicians. The word *onanism* derives from the biblical character Onan, who avoided impregnating his brother's widow during intercourse by withdrawing before ejaculation (an act that would later be characterized as conjugal fraud). For Tissot, onanism was primarily a *male* concern characterized by the loss of seminal fluids, a loss undoubtedly regretted all the more following the discovery of spermatozoa in the seventeenth century. Onanism became synonymous with masturbation insofar as premature withdrawal and self-stimulation expend semen in a fashion that is not conducive to impregnation, regardless of the number of participants involved. Tissot held "unnatural means" responsible for "a considerable quantity of lost semen" (16, 15). The value assigned to semen, which Garnier called "one of the most precious fluids in the animal economy," was seemingly symbolic as well as utilitarian: at issue was the abuse of a substance having intrinsic worth as well as the misuse of reproductive material (*Mariage*, 178). Tissot maintained that the onanistic expense of sperm was also a quite dangerous expenditure, an "act of suicide": "Masturbation leads to problems more terrible even than the excesses of natural copulation" (8).

Although he focused on onanism as a problem in men, Tissot devoted a brief chapter to women masturbators in which he claimed, contradictorily, that "the illness appears to present *more activity among women than among men*" (63, emphasis added). (Others would later contest this conclusion based on the inherent delicacy of female sexuality: "onanism is more widespread among men than among women" [Christian, 365].) With respect to women, Tissot's concern is not the loss of reproductive matter, but rather sybaritic indulgence and excess liable to produce fits of hysteria, vapours, genital deformations, and "uterine furores that deprive women of both modesty and reason, placing them on the level of the most lascivious of brutes until such time as death delivers them from their pain and infamy" (63). Tissot was particularly anxious about the possibility of masturbation leaving women indifferent to "legitimate means of deadening the urges of the flesh"; in other words, women risked opting for masturbation over procreative sex with their husbands (66). While the problem of onanism lay in the divorce of sexual activity and procreation for both sexes, secondary ills diverged as a *loss* of semen in men and a *gain* in pleasure for women.

Tissot did not refer to female ejaculate, although the concept was not unknown at the time.[22] What Thomas Laqueur has called the "one-sex model," dating back to Galen in the second century BCE, imagined male and female reproductive organs as identical but inverted. Galen believed that women ejaculated a semen-laden fluid during orgasm, and thus that female sexual pleasure was necessary for conception. The discovery of sperm and ova set the conditions for a two-sex or differential model of male and female anatomy and, by extension, comportment, which diminished the importance of female pleasure and allowed for the construction of a more passive vision of female sexuality.

Tissot lingered on one activity particular to women: "Aside from masturbation, or manual pollution, there is another defilement that can be called *clitoral*, whose origin dates back to *Sappho*" (68, italics in original). This practice depends on an enlarged clitoris, "the unnatural size of a body part that is normally very small," with which women "have taken possession of the virile functions." These outsized organs obscure sexual difference, allowing women to disregard "the arbitrary differences of birth" (69). According to Tissot, they enable same-sex relations ("women who love girls with as much fervour as the most passionate of men," 70), but above all pose a danger to traditional gender comportment and sexual reproduction.

Tissot's taxonomy of masturbatory practices does not differentiate between solitary acts and those involving a partner: what they all have in common is their uncoupling of sexuality and procreation. Across the nineteenth century, physicians equated same-sex acts with masturbation, particularly in women, seen as the pursuit of pleasure at the expense of reproduction. Numerous subsequent studies refined and codified the terminology of sex acts between women and, in so doing, eventually settled on a consensus of what a female homosexual was and what she did. I will take three as representative of how concern for women masturbators developed during the second half of the century: Thésée Pouillet, *De l'onanisme chez la femme* (1876); Julien Christian, "Onanisme" (1881); and Pierre Garnier, *Onanisme, seul et à deux* (1888). Pouillet and Christian were both published by distinguished medical publishers (Delahay and Masson, respectively), while Garnier's book (part of his series, "Hygiène de la génération") came out with Garnier Frères, a house that did not specialize in medicine.[23]

All these contributions took Tissot's work as a point of departure, although they distanced themselves from his moralizing tone and used what they claimed to be the more dispassionate language of science. They also corrected what they considered to be an overly narrow definition of onanism. According to Pouillet, it pertained equally to women and referred to *any* non-reproductive sexual act: "Onanism in women is an unnatural act accomplished with the aid of a living organ (hand, tongue, etc.), any phallic substitute, or by means of movements intended to provoke the venereal spasm, whether the act is carried out alone or with another" (22). Christian similarly defined onanism in terms of the refusal or the avoidance of procreation, moving away from its original sense of loss of seminal fluids. In contrast with conjugal sexual intercourse, it encompassed "a variety of practices employed by both sexes with the aim of achieving venereal orgasm *artificially,* outside of the conditions of normal coitus" (362).

Christian used onanism as an umbrella term to refer to a number of anomalous sexual behaviours, including homosexuality: "[onanism] encompasses not only masturbation, but also all genital aberrations such as pederasty, sodomy, bestiality, etc., and is derived, to my mind, from the same source" (362). Once admitted to be a pressing problem, female masturbation became a forum for the discussion of sapphism. Pouillet wrote that "I consider Tribady or Tribadism to be a form of masturbation" (xiii). While masturbation and same-sex acts between women were increasingly co-articulated, male homosexuality shifted to other rubrics.

The organization of Amédée Dechambre's vast and authoritative *Dictionnaire encyclopédique des sciences médicales,* in which Christian's article appeared, is instructive in this regard. Although Christian attributed "sodomy" and "pederasty" to the same source as other sexual aberrations, including female inversion, he respected the editorial decision to treat them separately: "to conform with standard practice, I will pass over *pederasty*, which will have its own article in this dictionary" (362). Medical convention generally placed pederasty under the auspices of legal medicine; fittingly, it was the forensic specialist Lacassagne who contributed the essay on "Pédérastie" to the dictionary. While Lacassagne's and Christian's articles are detailed and well documented, the unattributed entry on "Saphisme" contains only the following short paragraph and refers the reader to Christian's article on onanism: "Sapphism is a depraved practice, *attributed to Lesbians and particularly to Sappho*. It consists of the rubbing or sucking of the genital organs, and in particular of the clitoris, causing localized deformations of interest to the medical specialist. These are produced by the actions of manual masturbation and are complicated by the special lesions that sucking produces."[24]

The descriptions of specific masturbatory practices show the nomenclature of sapphism still to be in flux. Garnier identified "three kinds of female onanism" (425), which he enumerated as *tribady, clitoridism*, and *sapphism*, while Christian noted "*tribadism, clitoridism, lesbianism*" (362). They agreed more or less on a tripartite division and on the definitions of these terms (frottage, penetration, cunnilingus). Penetrative sex between women relied on an enlarged clitoris: "Clitorism is the simulation of the virile sex act that certain women, endowed with a clitoris developed in the manner of penis, are able to carry out; teratologists have assigned the term Clitorismy to such development" (Pouillet, xiiin1). For Garnier, this "imperfect coitus" or "clitoridian exuberance" constituted "the most shameful and ignominious vice of women" (431). Tissot held that penetrative sex ("clitoridian defilement" [souillure]) enabled by a hypertrophied clitoris *defined* sapphism.

While they differed on which act was constitutive of female homosexuality, they all associated it with a practice surmised to have begun with Sappho and the women of ancient Lesbos. Sappho was thus established as a kind of proto-identity or archetype. Pouillet disagreed with the prevalence of enlarged genitals, questioning whether one should "believe that Clitorismy was strangely endemic among the women of Lesbos" (26). He maintained instead that frottage was the act *par excellence* of female same-sex eroticism: "Among the Greeks, the erotic Sappho and the young Lesbians had a reputation for disdaining men and of offering themselves to Venus without men; they have been called 'Tribades.' Tribadism or Tribady (to rub) was then as mutual masturbation is now" (26). Garnier called this "reciprocal rubbing": "*Tribady* [...] was none other than a vulval onanism between women. This is the shameful vice in which they seek out their own kind to rub themselves together lustfully. Whence the name *fricatrices* or *frotteuses*" (428).

But for Garnier, oral sex was the activity most closely associated with Sappho. He insisted that "the technique and influence of true sapphism distinguish it completely from manual stimulation, tribady, and clitoridism" (457). Christian concurred, adding that "Sappho is accused of being the first to introduce the practice of buccal onanism and to spread it among the girls of Lesbos, whence the name of *lesbianism*" (370). This association would eventually carry the day: *sapphism* became a technical synonym for cunnilingus and, like *tribadism*, was also generalized to refer to lesbianism.

Pouillet details the many reasons that girls and women succumb to these activities. The physical, social, and moral hazards he enumerates are striking for their underlying ideological tenor. Based in social stereotyping, they point to the political allegiances and moral agenda of the author and, insofar as he is representative, of the medical profession. The habits of the rich (idleness) and the poor (promiscuity) promote female masturbation, as do traits and environments associated with other objectified populations, real or imagined. These include women from the orientalized south (warm climates, spicy foods) and those exhibiting moral or physical anomalies (genital deformities, imbecility, disease, poor hygiene, indecent conversation, consumption of alcohol). Pouillet also polices art with his prescription to limit girls' access to culture: they should be shielded from artwork depicting nudes, from theatre, and from inappropriate novels, all which invite them to masturbate. He cautions women against inappropriate activities (dance and equitation), professions (use of the sewing machine: "the pedal, in its to-and-fro motion," 64), milieus (boarding schools are "veritable seats of infection," 69), and associations (servants and nursemaids initiate the young). Middle-class women must avoid excessive activity in general and sports in particular, remain under the watchful eye of men, and shun contact with other classes.

Pouillet also suggests that impediments to "acceptable" sexual fulfilment, "anything that causes a woman to be frustrated by the rightful pleasures nature has given her," can lead women to masturbate (76). Potential contributors to such frustration include a husband's impotence; a woman's frigidity, advancing age, widowhood, ugliness, or physical infirmity; and "the lack of harmony between the copulatory organs of the two sexes or the slowness with which some women conclude the venereal act." In essence, the female masturbator and the maritally procreating woman are at antipodes: "the masturbating girl detests marriage" (170).

Masturbation leaves traces that are physical (languor, rapid weight loss, trembling, night sweats, encephalitis, paralysis, deafness, blindness, epilepsy, changes to the genitalia) and moral or intellectual (loss of concentration, depression, neurosis, impaired mental faculties, idiocy, hypochondria, criminality, madness, suicide). The danger is grave: "I am convinced that the consequences of habitual masturbation are sometimes deadly, often terrible, and always detrimental" (109).

Pouillet offers several suggestions for curing girls and women having already taken up the habit. Appropriate physical exercise, recitation of the negative effects of masturbation, the threat to "make their shameful practices known," and an appeal to the maternal instinct number among what he calls the "gentle means" of dissuading such activity (188). He even counsels a limited sexual education "in keeping with propriety and morality." If these methods are not successful, parents should not hesitate with a wilful daughter "to marry her as quickly as possible," regardless of the aversion Pouillet claims masturbators have for marriage. As a last resort, admissible "means of repression" include corporal punishment, use of a straight jacket or chastity belt, and, if all else fails, amputation of the clitoris.[25] Pouillet addresses the ethics of clitoridectomy ("does one have the right to sever at their source the joys that could have been life's delight?"), concluding that it is justifiable: "one must not hesitate to undertake this operation in order to save a life" (210). He also proposes cauterization of the vulva and clitoris, a remedy he practises successfully on masturbating children and women, which creates "an unpleasant feeling that becomes a sharp pain when in contact with an object – and especially when rubbed with fingers" (213). Pouillet advises re-cauterization until the patient is broken of the habit of masturbating.

Homosexuality and masturbation in men would seem to be an even greater threat to reproduction, due to loss of seminal fluid, in contrast with tribadism, which involves no equivalent expense. It is instead the experience of gratification outside of marital sex that appears most to trouble the experts. Pouillet notes, and Christian concurs, that for both sexes masturbatory orgasm leads to a "loss of energy" and, when practised excessively, to nervous exhaustion. While generally orgasm is the culminating event of masturbation for both sexes, Pouillet reminds his reader that it is required only of men in reproductive intercourse: "Woman is passive in the venereal act; when it pleases her [quand il lui plait], she can free herself [s'affranchir] from all bodily and moral participation in sexual congress" (82). Pouillet's word choice in this sentence is extraordinary enough to merit a closer look. Beyond suggesting that a woman can detach herself from the physical and emotional experience of sexual intercourse (and today such dissociation is recognized as a psychic reaction to the trauma of rape), his language proposes that to do so would be a *liberatory* gesture ("free herself") that she can make *when it pleases her*. While the goal of masturbation "is to seek sensual pleasure," according to Pouillet marital sexuality is antithetical to it (82). If wasted seed differentiates masturbation from procreative sex in men, in women the defining difference is *pleasure*, which can be taken in masturbation but, during heterosexual intercourse, found only in psychic flight.

Onanism (conjugal fraud, male and female masturbation, and female homosexuality) thus threatens the family and, by extension, the nation insofar as it is non-reproductive. Female masturbation and female homosexuality present the more abstract problem of usurping male control of "the copulating organs": where there is female sexuality for the sake of pleasure alone, there is a menace to male authority.

Prostitution

When intentions as noble as the public good drive our research, we must not neglect anything that might have a bearing on our topic, even in the observation of the most abject of subjects.

(Parent-Duchâtelet, *De la prostitution*)

This topic is indeed repellent to people, who are revolted by coarse details. And yet they fail to recognize the moralizing aim that is the true objective of such an analysis.

(Martineau, *La Prostitution clandestine*)

Prostitution consumed public interest in France throughout the nineteenth century, and with growing frequency the lesbian prostitute appeared as a hyperbolic symbol of unbridled sexuality, represented in medical literature and fiction as a danger to society.[26] This figure was central to the debate about regulating prostitution, which dates to 1802, when Napoléon ordered that prostitutes be registered with the state and regularly examined for venereal disease. Following these new directives, legal brothels (*maisons de tolérance* or *maisons closes*) quickly spread in the capital. During the first half of the century, growing preoccupation with delinquency and dangerous classes drew attention to this already suspect sexuality and contributed to its vilification.[27]

In the year of his death, Dr Alexandre Parent-Duchâtelet (1790–1836) published his foundational treatise, *De la prostitution dans la ville de Paris, considérée sous le rapport de l'hygiène publique, de la morale et de l'administration*, which would link prostitution with female homosexuality and have an enormous impact on writers in numerous domains through the turn of the century.[28] Parent-Duchâtelet's far-reaching influence was equivalent to that of Tissot on masturbation.[29] Based on his experience with incarcerated and hospitalized prostitutes, Parent-Duchâtelet examined their morals, habits, and physiology in the contexts of both legal and illegal prostitution. An early medical hygienist, he had previously published important work on the sewers of Paris. Turning his attention to prostitution, he claimed that "in order to study [prostitutes], I needed even greater strength of will than that which motivated me when I visited sewers filled with sludge and foul air" (1:17). Despite his repugnance, Parent-Duchâtelet concluded that prostitution was both universal and necessary. Extending his sewer analogy, he claimed that "wherever men collect in great numbers, prostitutes are as inevitable as sewers, public works, and the garbage dump" (2:338). Consequently, he supported continued government supervision of prostitutes, which involved their regular screening for syphilis at state-run health clinics.

Parent-Duchâtelet's analysis combined moral disdain with sociological insight. On the one hand, he numbered laziness and vanity among the prime causes of prostitution: "it is the desire to gratify oneself without working, [...] to dazzle with sumptuous dresses, [...] for the love of clothing" (1:99, 1:100). On the other hand, Parent-Duchâtelet acknowledged the role played by poverty, abandonment, and single motherhood in obliging women to turn to prostitution in order to survive. But he was less equivocal in his feelings about female homosexuality, which he frequently encountered among prostitutes. In no uncertain terms, he condemned tribades ("this is what those known for their unnatural tastes are called") who entered into "disgusting and monstrous *marriages*" (1:160, 1:159). Parent-Duchâtelet contended that female homosexuality was found primarily among unregistered prostitutes and those imprisoned for lengthy periods of time. He supported the *régime cellulaire* and enhanced scrutiny by prison directors as a precaution against such promiscuity.[30] But he also considered government supervision of prostitutes to be an effective weapon against tribadism. Indeed, one of Parent-Duchâtelet's central rationales for continued legalization and regulation was the need for oversight of the significant number of tribades he found among the prostitutes he studied: "they demand a particular supervision from those who are charged with overseeing call girls" [filles publiques] (1: 167).

The prostitute rhymed perfectly with the tribade. Both attracted increasing attention as the century progressed, triggering and representing sexual fears, obsessions, and fantasies. Rolled into one figure, the lesbian prostitute stood for the deepest form of depravity imaginable. Parent-Duchâtelet affirmed that "We can consider lesbian prostitutes to be vicious creatures having reached the final degradation possible." Above all, society must be protected from this vice, which constituted a "direct attack on the morality of female sexual behavior" (Corbin, *Women for Hire*, 4–5).

Even though Parent-Duchâtelet's support of regulation later came into question by abolitionists who sought to ban government-sanctioned prostitution, his portrait of the lesbian prostitute endured, was propagated in a number of venues, and entered the popular culture. Subsequent writers drew liberally from *De la prostitution*, some quoting its author at length, others paraphrasing with or without attribution, in keeping with the lax citation standards of the period. Corbin surmised that "Parent-Duchâtelet's portrait of the prostitute was repeated so often in the literature on prostitution and inspired so many novelists that [...] *it probably determined to some extent the behavior of the prostitutes themselves.*"[31] Corbin's hypothesis goes to the heart of this study, which conjectures that the abject portrait of the lesbian, developed and repeated so often in medical literature and in fiction, contributed if not to the behaviour, at least to the sense of self of women erotically and emotionally drawn to other women.

Corbin has documented the rise of the abolitionist movement in reaction to a number of factors, including increasing numbers of prostitutes, especially undocumented ones, the diversification of prostitution, and the abuses of the vice police and their illegal collaboration with the sex trade. He illustrates that the debate between abolitionists and regulationists was at its sharpest between 1876 and 1884, a period whose changing political climate created odd bedfellows among abolitionists. Those affiliated with "moral order" on the right and those pursuing individual liberties on the left united in opposition to governmental involvement in prostitution. Both sides agreed on the infamy of lesbian prostitutes. Regulationists wanted, like Parent-Duchâtelet, to control prostitution and, with it, tribadism. Abolitionists sought to do away with prostitution and, with it, the tribadism they believed it bred.

Government officials feared that female homosexuality was growing as rapidly as the population of prostitutes. They painted sapphism with the brush of prostitution and sought to regulate them in a similar manner, despite the fact that female homosexuality was not legally proscribed. Regulationists were typically physicians affiliated with the police. Julien Jeannel, a doctor for the hygiene department in Bordeaux, authored several treatises on which the imprint of Parent-Duchâtelet's work is patent.[32] In *De la prostitution dans les grandes villes* (1874), he treats tribadism as a contagious disease and describes lesbian rages born of jealousy similar to those described by Parent-Duchâtelet. Jeannel also borrows Parent-Duchâtelet's vocabulary of surveillance in support of regulation: "We know what degree of moral perversion these degraded creatures reach when, tired of satisfying the pleasures and vices of others, they do violence to nature and abandon themselves to monstrous passions. We see *to what extent the lack of surveillance encourages these excesses.*"[33]

A decade later, Louis Martineau, doctor at the Lourcine hospital (devoted to treating women with venereal disease), published *La Prostitution clandestine* (1885). While acknowledging Parent-Duchâtelet's work, Martineau dismissed previous authors, both those in favour of regulation and those opposed, calling them inconclusive.[34] He promised, beginning with fresh research, to articulate a precise plan for regulating prostitution to the greatest benefit of society. Martineau's scrupulously scientific method for doing so was "to forget all that has been said and written on this topic and take into account only those facts derived from direct observation, and to introduce nothing other than the 'human document,' to quote a modern author" (3). This expression is, of course, an allusion to naturalism and another indication of the interdependence of literature and science in the analysis of female sexual deviance. Let us recall that Bernard's *Médecine expérimentale* (1865) provided the model for Zola's *Roman expérimental* (1880), whose language Martineau subsequently referenced in *La Prostitution clandestine*. Was he suggesting that literature provided a more apt model for a rigorous scientific method than medicine?

Of the word *sapphism*, Martineau declared: "while the word could appear new, the act that it defines is old" (89). Although he could have cited any number of medical texts going back to the eighteenth century, Martineau reached instead for a familiar literary precedent to illustrate what he claimed as his neologism: "in [*La Fille aux yeux d'or*], the great novelist recounted the habits of tribades, those women in love with their own sex who abandon themselves to *the act that I have named sapphism*" (90, emphasis added).

Martineau described the practice of clandestine prostitution and enumerated the reasons for its regulation. Whereas his central interest in the question was, as a physician, the detection and treatment of syphilis, he also wrote as a moralist whose project was the "study of moral pathology" (3). Finally, like Parent-Duchâtelet, he referred to sapphic prostitutes as a further reason for continued regulation. Not only did the profession encourage tribadism, Martineau asserted that a growing female clientele frequented brothels in search of sapphic sex. He also gave talks entitled "Sapphic and Sodomitic Prostitution" and "Vulval Deformations Produced by Sapphism" in a series of lectures about the physical signs of sexual deviance, delivered at the Clinique Ginécologique et Syphiliographique of the Lourcine hospital. Graphic illustrations of the damaging effects of such practices on female genitalia accompany the published lectures (see figs. 4.1 and 4.2).

Prostitution and declining morals increasingly pose problems, but so does sapphism. Martineau asserted that "In only a few years, sapphism has developed considerably; its adherents have become legion" (*Prostitution*, 100). Regulationists and abolitionists agreed that the spread of tribadism posed a danger to society at all its levels. Martineau decries "The moral illness that is slowly invading all classes of society. It is not only in the prostitute that I observe deformities produced by sapphism or by sodomy; I also find them among married women" (*Déformations*, 10).

The republican journalist Léo Taxil wrote two books on prostitution available to a wide public, in which he called for the abolition of prostitution and described the growth of tribadism: "the number of women in Paris who are drawn to other women is incalculable" (*Corruption*, 258). The turpitude had originated in houses of prostitution: "Sapphism makes its home in the official brothel [...] it is understandable that the prostitute working in these establishments – a woman who is no longer even female – ends up feeling profound disgust for men" (258). It subsequently spilled out from the *maisons closes*,

MARTINEAU.—Déformations.
Pl. II.
Fig. 1.
A
D
B
C
E
F
Fig. 1bis
A
B
G
H
D
E
C
A. Karmanski del. et lith.
Imp. Becquet fr. Paris.

PLANCHE II

MASTURBATION DE L'ENFANCE — SAPHISME

(Fig. 1)

A **Clitoris.**
B **Capuchon clitoridien hypertrophié.**
C **Petites lèvres.**
D **Grandes lèvres.**
E **Orifice vulvo-vaginal.**
F **Anus.**

(Fig. 1 *bis*)

A **Clitoris.**
B **Capuchon clitoridien hypertrophié relevé en casque.**
C **Petites lèvres.**
D **Grandes lèvres.**
E **Orifice vulvaire.**
G **Gland clitoridien.**
H **Freins du clitoris hypertrophiés.**

Figure 4.1. Louis Martineau, *Déformations*, plate II, Figures 1 and 1bis

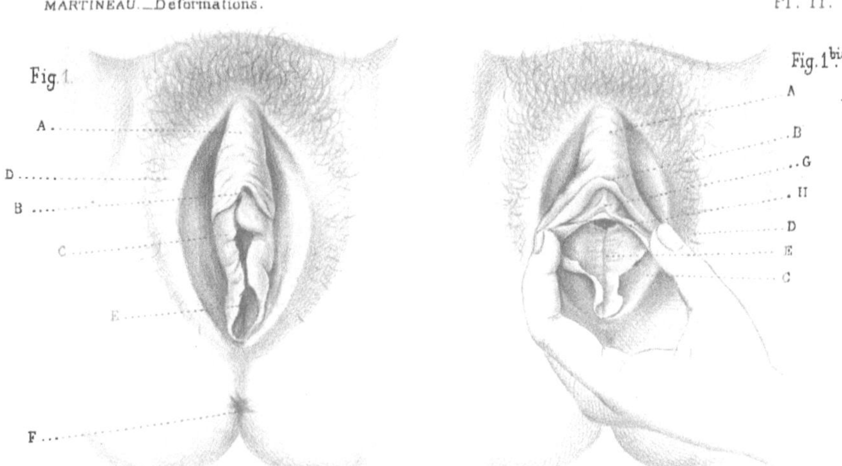

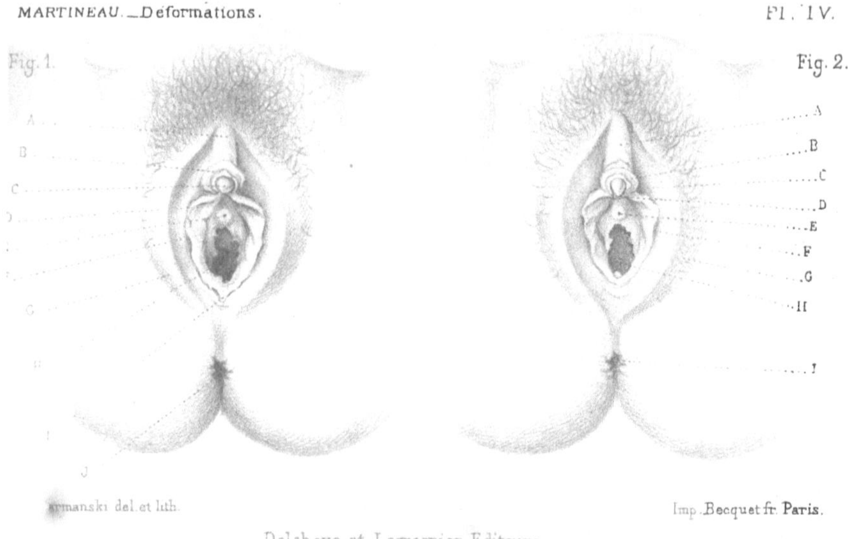

PLANCHE IV

SAPHISME

(Fig. 1)

A **Clitoris.**
B **Capuchon clitoridien relevé.**
C **Gland clitoridien.**
D **Freins du clitoris.**
E **Méat urinaire.**
F **Petites lèvres.**
G **Grandes lèvres.**
H **Orifice vulvo-vaginal.**
I **Fourchette.**
J **Anus.**

(Fig. 2)

A **Clitoris.**
B **Capuchon clitoridien.**
C **Gland clitoridien.**
D **Freins du clitoris.**
E **Méat urinaire.**
F **Petites lèvres.**
G **Grandes lèvres.**
H **Orifice vulvo-vaginal.**
I **Anus.**

Figure 4.2. Louis Martineau, *Déformations*, plate IV, Figures 1 and 2

now frequented by aristocratic women with sapphic tendencies, and affected all classes of society: "little by little, the lesbian vice has spread its devastation, even among married women." Taxil went on to detail the contagion: "there are ladies who hire a Sapphist to be their chambermaid. [There are] actual lesbian academies, where [groups of tribades] abandon themselves to indescribable orgies."[35] State oversight is thus responsible for the diffusion of deviant sexuality: "Official prostitution, which resides in establishments instituted by the State and protected by the so-called vice police, propagates all the horrors of debauchery." He opposed Parent-Duchâtelet's plea for tolerance and called for the criminalization of prostitution – as did many feminists, but for very different reasons.

The legacy of these discussions of female inversion in the context of studies on masturbation and prostitution is evident in later works devoted specifically to female homosexuality. Parent-Duchâtelet is broadly referenced, as is the literature on masturbation. The lexicon of female homosexuality, which describes a variety of practices, came out of these works and was adopted and refined by the early sexologists. Just when the debate around regulation raged during the 1870s and 80s, some fifty years after Parent-Duchâtelet's study, the experimental novel rallied to the challenge of observing the tribade, contributing to her typology, and cementing the figure of the dissolute lesbian prostitute. It is open to debate as to whether literature or science provided the aptest model for the sapphic prostitute. I would propose, however, that literary representation ultimately surpassed medical discourse in securing this identification for posterity. While Dr Martineau is rarely read today, as he himself wrote, "everyone has read Balzac."

The Medical Student and the Female Invert: The Case of Julien Chevalier

> we must have the courage to declare loudly that [the contemporary novel] is the most active of the agents of contamination and propagation of evil.
>
> (Chevalier, *L'Inversion sexuelle*)

Scientists and fiction writers were codependent in their attempts to name and define same-sex female eroticism and determine its causes, and they frequently quoted each other. In some instances, novelists made forays into the medical domain. For example, Zola wrote the preface to Dr Laupts's *Tares et poisons; perversions et perversité sexuelle* (1896). Conversely, Havelock Ellis translated Zola's *Germinal*, prefaced the English-language edition of *Nana*, and wrote critical essays on Zola and Huysmans (*Affirmations*). Doctors – "modern priests," according to Catulle Mendès – played an increasingly important role in lesbian novels, in which medical language replaced moralistic and psychological explanations for lesbian activity.

Jean-Louis Dubut de Laforest wrote, in clinical prose, an exemplary novel called *Mademoiselle Tantale* (1884), which he dedicated to Charcot. The title character, Mary Folkestone, the illegitimate daughter of a dancer and a senile aristocrat – a "victim of heredity" – suffers from "sexual impotence," the impossibility of experiencing "the spasm of love" (49). She consults doctors, undergoes various treatments (hydrotherapy, electroshock), but nonetheless succumbs to erotomania. At one point she surrenders to the seduction of her friend Camille, whom she met – where else – at boarding school. The author supplies a lengthy footnote to explain Camille's sexual dysfunction, citing Chevalier's *Inversion sexuelle* and Martineau's *Leçons sur les déformations vulvaires.* Dubut de Laforest insists in his preface that "Art and Science must remain separate, but they do not have the right to ignore one another" (5). In fact, art and science are hardly separate at all in his novel, which he published in his collection entitled *Pathologie sociale.*[36]

For their part, nearly all of those in the medical field who worked on homosexuality, regardless of nationality, referred to French literary precedents. According to Krafft-Ebing, "It is a remarkable fact that in fiction, lesbic love is frequently used as the leading theme, *viz.* Diderot, ... Balzac, ... Feydeau, *La Comtesse de Chalis*; ... Belot, *Mlle Giraud*; Rachilde, *Monsieur Vénus*" (396n3). Moll echoed him: "We find numerous novels of the French naturalist school treating of this subject. Diderot had already developed the theme in his *Religieuse*" (223). The Italian criminologist Scipio Sighele added that "The broad diffusion of sapphism is proven by novelists, who do not content themselves with merely alluding to it in their books, but make it the principal subject of certain works" (183n1).

French physicians were equally, if not more, inclined to invoke their national literature, regularly naming Diderot, Balzac, Gautier, Baudelaire, Verlaine, as well as decadent and, particularly, naturalist novelists. Jeannel referenced "immoral literature," and psychiatrist Paul Moreau de Tours insisted that "It is impossible for us to avoid mentioning [...] those insane passions that modern authors of great renown fearlessly describe and even glorify with all the talent they possess. They offer these depressing and fatal lessons to people with ardent imaginations who don't delay in putting them to practice!" (*Les Aberrations du sens génésique*, 175). Such references do more than supply images to readers in the medical profession; they suggest that literary representations have the power to incite lay readers to act upon the models offered to them. Perhaps more than any other, it was Julien Chevalier who explored the role of literature in creating female homosexuals: "Because I consider the modern novel to be a cause rather than a consequence, I have numbered literature among the factors contributing to the vice" (2–3). Indeed, "lesbosism" could be contracted in a number of ways, not least among them by a literary virus, "sapphism by literature" (251).

Julien Chevalier (1860–1943) specialized in the study of sexual inversion at the end of the century. He is both remarkable for having written the first comprehensive study of homosexuality in France and undistinguished by the mixed reception he received from his contemporaries. Although he is cited broadly by his peers, Havelock Ellis, for one, wrote that Chevalier's work "contain[s] little that is original [and] is lacking in critical perception." Chevalier subsequently faded into obscurity, becoming a military doctor in Algeria and abandoning research and publishing for the remaining fifty years of his life. I disinter him to consider the function of his scholarship within an emergent profession while focusing, in particular, on his theories about acquired female homosexuality. Chevalier's work can be read both as a highly personal story about male discipleship in the context of a developing field of study and, at the same time, as a window onto ideologies about female sexuality and gender difference in late nineteenth-century France.

It was in 1885 that Julien Chevalier, then a young student of medicine, submitted his dissertation, "De l'inversion de l'instinct sexuel au point de vue médico-légal," the first extensive treatment of homosexuality in France. Its ranking suggests that it was judged an average dissertation, the only one of three submitted to the Prix Moreau de Tours not to receive mention, although Chevalier was granted honourable mention by the faculty of the medical school of Lyon. His dissertation was published a year before Krafft-Ebing's landmark *Psychopathia Sexualis* appeared in Germany and ten years before its French translation. Chevalier studied under the direction of Lacassagne, who, in addition to his work as a researcher and consultant, mentored hundreds of medical students during a thirty-year career as professor of legal medicine at the University of Lyon.[37] The apparently close relationship between Lacassagne and Chevalier revolved around the acquisition of knowledge about sexual inversion and the advance of the younger man's career. This unexamined homosocial bond between professor and student depended upon the scrutiny of homosexuality.

Beyond his article on pederasty (in which he cited Chevalier extensively), Lacassagne did not pursue inversion as the primary focus of his work (he became known, among other things, for bloodstain pattern analysis and the study of bullet striations).[38] However, the revue he founded, *Archives d'anthropologie criminelle*, was an important forum for the discussion of homosexuality (including for his student Laupts's work), and the book series he directed, "Bibliothèque scientifique judiciaire," included several titles of primary importance on the subject.[39]

Chevalier's emulation of his professor is apparent in the language of his work, which both explicitly and implicitly references Lacassagne. Chevalier credits his "savant maître" with inspiring him to write his thesis on inversion when he was a floundering student in search of a dissertation topic: "Imagine my dilemma: no thesis topic in view, and yet the deadline for submitting one was fast approaching" ("De l'inversion," 314). Chevalier tells the story of how Lacassagne "offered" the subject to him and vanquished his "scruples and hesitations" about treating such an awkward problem.

An important linguistic lesson accompanied Lacassagne's gift of a thesis topic. The professor emphasized the need for a precise, scientific terminology and methodology in order to validate sexual perversion as a viable object of study: "It's time to finally abandon the old prejudice against studying subjects of this nature; it is urgent to replace this sentimental and timorous baggage with the calm and lofty study of sexual aberrations, especially of their causes and origins" (315). Accordingly, Chevalier reassured his reader that "I have made my best effort to be neither common nor coarse" in his 1893 book, *L'inversion sexuelle: Une maladie de la personnalité*. I will focus on this re-edited and significantly expanded version of Chevalier's thesis. It is an ambitious treatise that studied the psychology and physiology of the invert from historical, clinical, anthropological, and forensic perspectives. It was both prefaced by Lacassagne and published in his book series. Under Lacassagne's continued tutelage, Chevalier took pains to establish the scientific legitimacy of his new and potentially scandalous field of research: "I propose to determine all the causes of the perversion, to locate the characteristics of its diverse forms, and to submit [...] a rational medical-legal solution" (158).

Chevalier's methodical analysis of the causation of inversion fell in step with a number of contemporary works, which held that homosexuality, like so much other deviant behaviour, had two primary attributions: it was either hereditary [l'inversion congénitale] or acquired [acquise], or some combination of the two [l'inversion secondaire]. This distinction represented the difference between an irrepressible illness and a guilty vice, between "a pathological perversion or a moral perversity," as Krafft-Ebing wrote. Chevalier concurred with other specialists that occasional inverts enjoyed dissolute pleasures, while born homosexuals suffered the psychic and physical discomforts of their condition. He contended that the legal code alone should control acquired homosexuality, a vice and therefore a sexual crime worthy of punishment, agreeing with Krafft-Ebing that it was the duty of the courts to suppress pleasure, although psychiatry should reward pain with compassion: "Law [...] is constantly in danger of passing judgment on individuals who, in the light of science, are not responsible for their acts [...] the state cannot be too careful as a protector of morality in the struggle against sensuality" (Krafft-Ebing, 419). Chevalier concluded that congenital inversion was "an instinctive anomaly that goes beyond any perverted instruction. [...] their interior anarchy and distress make them truly sick people who should receive psychiatric treatment rather than be subject to the law" (397–8). Chevalier thus placed congenital inversion under the auspices of psychiatry: insofar as it derived from a hereditary flaw, it merited compassion and medical attention.

At the heart of Chevalier's analysis of inversion lies a substantial discussion of the sociological factors leading to acquired inversion. Because it has no congenital basis, he writes, acquired inversion merits containment: "nothing pathological: we must therefore prevent, we can therefore *repress*" (269, emphasis added). While Chevalier finds environmental factors to be determining in the acquisition of both male and female homosexuality, his discussion of acquired inversion in women amounts to a sweeping condemnation of contemporary social decay and the breakdown of traditional roles for women. Factors that encourage homosexuality in both men and women include depravity, sex segregation (in convents, prisons, schools, the military), *syphilophobie*, and fear of pregnancy (216). Prostitution is also an incentive to homosexuality in men. But while he contends that male and female homosexuality are equivalent, "two modalities of a single deviation," he enumerates what he briskly calls "a few particularities" of acquired female homosexuality (217). Ellis's appraisal of his lack of originality notwithstanding, Chevalier's writing on acquired lesbianism, and in particular on the role played by literature in its propagation, constitutes the most creative aspect of his work. Indeed, his account of the specific category of female inversion acquired by reading and the application of literary exegesis to medical diagnosis are uniquely his. Moreover, when discussing the aetiology of what he also calls *artificial* female inversion, his style deviates notably from the scientific rationality and neutrality he promised; instead, he becomes urgent, hyperbolic, and indignant. Following this change in tone, Chevalier sounds more patently like a social critic than a man of medicine; as such, this section is particularly revelatory about French cultural attitudes on sex and gender at the fin de siècle.

Chevalier's ostensibly scientific conclusions rely on identifying condemnable social factors. He blames feminism and equal rights for women for creating the conditions that encourage the proliferation of lesbianism: "This social revolution entails nothing less than placing both sexes on absolutely equal footing" (218). Education for girls, careers for women, women who abandon their homes for the public sphere: these are some of the primary factors that masculinize women. Independent of men, they accumulate vices and lose their feminine modesty: "Girls behave like tomboys to their hearts' content. Under the pretext of pursuing a male education, they persevere in escaping from their sex and lose their most enviable and precious qualities: their loveliness, their ignorance, their carefree nature. They lose everything that constitutes their femininity: they become desexualized" (224–5). Liberty, equality, and the refusal of conventional values thus lead to lesbianism: "The sudden explosion of the lesbian vice is to such an extent contemporary with the evolution in morals that it is hard not to see a relation of cause and effect. They abandon the legitimate pleasures of bourgeoisism and disdain the mediocre joys of healthy love. [...] Vice is in fashion" (227, 231).

Within this framework of sweeping social change, Chevalier identifies another, related factor, namely, the effect of literature on morality and behaviour, *saphisme par littérature*: "In this purely scientific work, we must now turn to purely literary works."[40] He designates literature as a sociological contributor to the epidemic of acquired inversion and attests to the broad range of contemporary literary texts that grappled with the topic, which he deplores as a "veritable torrent of literature that is pornographic, and, in particular, lesbian" (256). Chevalier's analysis of the social production of female inversion is intriguing if sometimes incoherent. He both praises writers for their expertise and blames them for contributing to the sexual corruption of women. While asserting that the contemporary novel is the greatest source of contagion, he also maintains that it is important to "know the opinion of writers and novelists" (251). Chevalier offers a lengthy review of literary representations from Diderot's *La Religieuse* to contemporary works, covering the gamut of genres from poetry to naturalist and decadent literature.

What emerges is a hierarchy of taste, in which Chevalier *commends* time-tested classics but *condemns* what he calls "the reigning literary school." In so doing, he privileges poetic language while deriding the scientific pretences of fiction writers. Moreover, he rebukes authors with a propensity to "scrutinize everything" and "lay it bare" (260) – code words for naturalism – but admires those who show restraint and use euphemistic language. In fact, the more closely a literary doctrine resembles the tenets of the medical profession, the greater Chevalier's disapproval: unlike Martineau, he clearly has no patience for naturalism. The use of a precise, clinical language, the casting of an unflinching eye on subjects considered taboo, the need for careful documentation: these are elements that Chevalier enumerates as critical for the *medical* study of homosexuality. However, when found in the novel, he deems them inappropriate, essentially policing the borders between literature and medical science and condemning "the troublesome invasion of medicine in the novel."

More to Chevalier's taste are "the poets who have sung of Lesbos's sterile intoxication." He praises Baudelaire, whose "superb apostrophe, mixing pity and condemnation, renders the excesses of horror and remorse with such intensity" (254–5). Affect and pathos are at a premium here, both in Baudelaire's poetry and in Chevalier's prose. Similarly, Chevalier applauds Gautier's artistry: "in his fine book, *Mademoiselle de Maupin*, he deals with the case as an artist and poet." Chevalier's own language becomes more colourful as he reviews decadent representations of female same-sex eroticism: "Mendès, obsessed by androgyny; Péladan, the sorcerer and Sâr haunted by hermaphrodites; Verlaine, the acrobatic bard of *Amies*."

Chevalier praises authorial restraint, appreciating the "timidity" employed by Ernest Feydeau and Adolphe Belot in their representations of lesbian couples. He singles out Belot's *Mademoiselle Giraud, ma femme*, calling it "the classic literary treatise on the subject" and extolling its moderation (254). Moreover, he prefers intuitive accuracy to realist precision, commending, for example, Gautier's visionary anticipation of contemporary pathologies: "Gautier predicts today's androgyne, he envisages the born intervert" [l'interverti-né]. And he admires Diderot's astute perceptions: "I commend his grasp of the causes and mechanisms of anti-physical tastes; his book shows clearly that laziness, mysticism, celibacy, and communal living lead to disorders" (252). Chevalier likewise appreciates Balzac moral correctness: "the dénouement of [*La Fille aux yeux d'or*] energetically notes the tragedy of such loves."

Chevalier's flowery and often blithe survey establishes him as an avid reader of contemporary literature and as a writer in his own right having a certain stylistic flair. Indeed, even Ellis, who questioned the usefulness of Chevalier's work, allowed that it is "written with much facility and considerable exuberance." Chevalier's prose becomes particularly extravagant when he turns his attention to works he deems blameworthy rather than laudable: "Everyone who reads is familiar with those scrawny pen-pushers who prattle on about neuroses and mental disturbances and equate scandal with success" (256). While he does not name the authors of whom he disapproves, he is vituperative in his discussion of their "mediocre and salacious productions."

Chevalier contends that popular writers, whom he calls *érotographes*, rely on the public's unhealthy curiosity and exploit readers' "depraved taste [...] for ugliness of all kinds" (256). Their primary interests are notoriety and sales; consequently, the broad distribution of their novels assures the dissemination of the vice that they hypocritically condemn. Without naming naturalism, he suggests that contemporary novelists hide their own prurient interest behind the cloak of scientific detachment: "they imagine that their preoccupation with observation, passion for 'the natural,' cult of the document, and penetrating analysis legitimate these rhapsodies" (257).

Chevalier's unscientific foray into literature invites a stylistic comparison as much as it treads a disciplinary divide. Although seeming to suggest that literature and science are worlds apart, Chevalier demonstrates his own writerly flamboyance while deriding novelists' metaphoric use of the microscope and the scalpel. It is hard not to see a double standard at work here, especially when Chevalier displays outrage at literary outspokenness, after having reiterated the lesson that any topic, no matter how depraved, is worthy of scientific inquiry. But he is consistent on this point: the need to limit the audience of books about homosexuality. Indeed, Chevalier is as concerned with readers of medical texts as he is with readers of literature. Just as "sapphism by literature" results from exposure of suggestible women to novelistic excess, Chevalier insists that his own work must be reserved for an elite, male audience of medical and legal specialists: "I forbid all women from reading this, [...] however domestic and maternal they might be" (xxiv). He claims to strive for "limited publicity and circumscribed success."

Chevalier's work underscores the power of the word, be that the influence of literature in seducing and corrupting women, or the persuasive force of Professor Lacassagne's language. He recalls the "attraction" of anticipating a lesson by Lacassagne about "cases of morbid psychology barely imagined by the broader medical public." He emerges "charmed and instructed" from the lecture, which inspires him to study homosexuality ("De l'inversion sexuelle," 314). Chevalier believed that discussion of homosexuality should be restricted to the closed environment of the amphitheatre rather than be aired in best-selling novels. In this way, impressionable young women are protected from the contaminating influence of sensationalistic writers. At the same time, the powerful sway of a professor's lecture remains free to inspire a young man's emulation and his scholarly treatise on homosexuality, which could be considered a labour of love.

5 Intertexts and Afterlives: From the French Canon to U.S. Lesbian Pulps[1]

Where does the public obtain its image of the lesbian? From a rare newspaper story, a not-too-infrequent joke, a disparaging rumor, an occasional occurrence in a school or office, and from a large and growing body of literature.

(Donald Webster Cory, *The Lesbian in America*)

As this tour of male-authored sapphic literature has aimed to show, nineteenth-century French fictional works of all genres factored predominantly in the construction of female homosexuality, with scientific studies playing a significant, but secondary, role. From novels destined for canonicity to now-forgotten best-sellers, from the poetic to the pornographic, and in naturalist as well as decadent fiction, the texts composing this considerable body of literature responded to each other and left traces of themselves in subsequent works. Creative writers referred to, borrowed from, embellished, and sometimes satirized existing portraits, including clinical studies, thereby linking their work to predecessors and contemporaries and creating an intertextual chain of sapphic fictions.

Fiction and non-fictional texts, produced largely by men jostling for dominance in their given fields, provided pretexts for each other and, in so doing, constituted a primarily literary rhetoric of female homosexuality that eventually seeped into the broader culture. As I have argued, this collaborative web was to a considerable extent unmotivated, the result of a confluence of discourses and representations impelled by disparate factors and having potentially divergent ideological stakes, with unadulterated misogyny and antifeminism a frequent common denominator. The authors considered here were lured to sapphism by such inducements as professional ambition, the quest for prominence or notoriety, prurient curiosity, and desire for profit. They laid claims to the *saphiste* by aesthetic appropriation and metaphorical deployment, and they charged her with the weight of cultural and political contention. All told, nineteenth-century male authors invested the tribade with meaning having very little to do with the lives of the kind of women they ventured to portray.

Despite the varying and often arbitrary provenance of these representations, it is fair to suggest that, taken together, they furnished overwhelmingly dysphoric images of female sexual minorities and that their accumulated force established a coherent network of controlling and exclusionary discourses. Even the gauzy, sometimes utopian, and predominantly poetic literature, which was set in antiquity and relied on the Sappho myth, tended towards symbolically violent representation.

Regardless of their motivation or context, the moment in which these texts first appeared fades to the images that endure. As Bourdieu has noted, "texts circulate without their context, they don't carry with them the field of production that gave rise to them" ("Conditions sociales," 3). Divorced from their origins, these works bequeath to their readers physical portraits and psychological profiles; incarnations as seductress or object of desire, victim or monster; figures imbued with moral and social value (or lack thereof) – all accruing literary cachet and provoking scientific interest. Novels serve as signifiers, literary characters become iconic figures, types jell, attributes become predictable. The aggregate of these images and characterizations contributed to the creation of an imaginary sapphic world, a lesbian architext.

The power of an image for proscribed and covert populations is difficult to fathom. To see oneself finally as a product of and thus belonging to a collective imagination is liberating because it places one in culture. But insofar as an image is abject, it can have a crippling effect on subjects looking to it for self-recognition. Such objectifying portraits filled a representational void, providing a questionable but entrenched backdrop for the understanding of same-sex desire between and by women. Although this patriarchal, intertextual world gave no voice to historical subjects nor faithfully reflected their realities, it was inevitably present when women began to write (of) themselves, when literature *about* same-sex desire came to be written *by* writers with a personal knowledge of same-sex desire. Paternal fictions also intervened in non-literary contexts, undoubtedly serving as a composite mirror that contributed to the framing of self-portraits, thus playing a role in identity formation among women on the sexual margins.

In passing from objectifying constructs to instances of subjective expression and speculation about identification, I hope to sidestep the sometimes internecine academic debates about sexual identity. The word "lesbian," as we have seen, has a specific history, although its usage is now generalized. It also has many synonyms from an assortment of registers (euphemistic, pejorative, erotic, medical ...), all of which are signifiers capable of bearing an infinite variety of content. Let us take as common denominator the idea of sexual and/or emotional relations between women. The expression "lesbian writer," applied to the object of scrutiny, could then encompass anyone who for any reason chooses to consider with printed words any sort of sexual or emotional ties between women: Sappho, Baudelaire, Chevalier, Colette, Monique Wittig, Lynne Cheney.[2] I would consider a *subjective* "lesbian writer" to be a self-identifying female subject, a biological or transgendered woman personally implicated (exclusively or otherwise) in sexual and/or emotional relations with other women, and one who chooses to write about it. Such subjective lesbian expression has been performed by Sappho, Colette, and Wittig. But these kinds of attributions can be unknown or ambiguous: I would not, for example, presume to know whether Cheney *mère* belongs on this list. (Parenthetically, it is pertinent for our purposes to note that that she, too, reached for French literature when discoursing on sapphism in her potboiler *Sisters*, 1981: "This was a fantasy, wasn't it? […] A woman pleading with another woman to go off with her – one might suppose it the plot of a French novel!")

The argument that the identity or experiences of an author are of no import has long held sway. And yet if we claim that the author is dead à la Barthes, we desexualize her and obscure the pertinence of her historical context, of the realm of possibilities in which she writes. All the more so when her position is fraught due to social and sometimes legal constraints. I would agree with Stephanie Foote's contention that "Authorship's relationship to the lived identity of the writer has a special intensity for almost all writing by minority subjects who recognize themselves in a marginal relationship to major literary traditions" (174). Monique Wittig has suggested that for minority writers, "literary experimentation is a favoured way to bring a subject to light," and that a particular viewpoint can ascend to the universal, thus functioning as a kind of war machine.[3] Wittig's privileging of high literary tradition and her (very French) attachment to the universal are worthy of discussion. And yet what is pertinent here is Wittig's validation of the particular as a credible viewpoint from which to write.

Philosopher William Wilkerson has written compellingly of identity as "a kind of emergence" that results from what he calls the mutually constitutive fusion of a number of factors, including "the experience of desire, our biological constitution, the social roles and norms of society, and our individual choices" (*Ambiguity*, 8, 4). While (as Wilkerson acknowledges) one could argue with some of his terms, his discussion of the social element in relation to desire and identity is particularly resonant for the present discussion. Using his framework, I would suggest that, in direct proportion to its cultural prominence (measured by prestige and/or dissemination), a text (or body of texts) takes part in the social, interacts with a subject's experience of desire, and contributes to emergent identities.

In order to convey the enduring power of French sapphic fictions, this concluding chapter will consider their import for the negotiation of sexual identities in subsequent texts and, in a more speculative fashion, for the extra-textual reality of the reader. French sapphic fiction constitutes, for better or worse, an unavoidable legacy, more specifically a *patrimony*, placed into representation by and passed down from literary fathers to lesbian writers and subjects near and far. I will first look at contacts between the works studied here and their immediate entourage and aftermath, and then travel a greater distance to find their traces in popular lesbian literature of mid-twentieth-century America.

Paris-Lesbos

The first evidence of this legacy's impact on lesbian self-expression involves the fairly sudden apparition of subjective homoerotic literature at the turn of the century. With the twentieth century came Colette's *Claudine à l'école* (1900), Liane de Pougy's *Idylle saphique* (1901), Natalie Clifford Barney's *Cinq petits dialogues grecs* (1902), Renée Vivien's *Une femme m'apparut* (1904), and more than a dozen collections of poetry by Vivien published between 1901 and 1910. These women belonged to a Parisian community of writers, a fertile terrain of study that surpasses the scope of this project, but which is necessarily related to it. I will therefore briefly give a few examples of the relationship between their emancipated lesbian literature and the work of the sapphic fathers.

Belle Époque Paris became a kind of welcoming centre for French and expatriate women writers, artists, and performers, the "women of the left bank," as Shari Benstock calls this group in her seminal work bearing this title.[4] This environment favoured the establishment of an independent lesbian culture and gave rise to unprecedented visibility both in the social sphere and in creative works. Since collectively labelled Paris-Lesbos (Bonnet) and Sappho 1900 (Billy), these women were drawn together in large part by the salon of the American Natalie Clifford Barney. In addition to those named above, the habitués of Barney's salon included Lucie Delarue-Mardrus, Djuna Barnes, Janet Flanner, Remy de Gourmont, Pierre Louÿs, Edith Sitwell, and Gertrude Stein, among many other women and (less frequently) men of the cultural avant-garde.

Elaine Marks has suggested that "A major thematic transformation takes place when women begin to write about women loving women" (361). In her pioneering article "Lesbian Intertextuality," she analysed viewpoint in lesbian-authored texts that relate the "experience of awakening, the revelation of an unknown, unsuspected world […] a momentous discovery" (361–2). Marks noted the difference between objectifying representations such as those of the sapphic fathers and the "female voyeurism" she finds in Colette: "In 1900, for the first time since Sappho, the narrator Claudine in *Claudine à l'école* looks at another woman as an object of pleasure" (363). However, this voyeurism is "in contrast to what transpires in male novels, is neither secret nor cerebral. It is a public activity." It is above all an *intersubjective* activity not reliant on a male intermediary (be that inter- or extra-diegetic) for its telling.

These women wrote in close geographic and chronological proximity to the male literary and medical traditions preoccupied with sapphism. This proximity alone assured an often self-conscious and explicit intertextuality, in which lesbian authors expressed opinions about, responded to, took issue with, or fell into the mould of existing images. Their nearness to the sapphic fathers was frequently social and professional as well: they belonged to the same circles, read the same books, lived in the same city, and sometimes collaborated with those who wrote the works considered in the preceding chapters.

The literary and social relations between Natalie Barney and Pierre Louÿs present one such instance. In addition to his signed sapphic works (*Chansons de Bilitis*, *Aphrodite*), Louÿs, like Belot, wrote lesbian erotica on the side, much of it appearing after his death. Notable examples of this large body of work include his *Chansons secrètes de Bilitis* (1898), the posthumous *Manuel de civilité pour les petites filles à l'usage des maisons d'éducation* (1926), and the unfinished novel *L'Île aux dames*. As a young woman, Barney solicited the older Louÿs's help in publishing some of her early writing because of his association with sapphic literature. He and Barney became lifelong friends; they left an abundant correspondence and an indelible mark on each other's work. Not unlike the founding members of the Daughters of Bilitis, although with a greater willingness to engage his portrait of lesbian sexuality, Barney admired Louÿs's representation of Bilitis: "Bilitis gave me rapture wilder and tenderness more tender than any other mistress."[5] In response to Louÿs's dedication of his *Chansons* to "young girls of the future," Barney dedicated her *Cinq petits dialogues grecs* to him "from a girl of the future." She invoked women "who appreciate what you have done for them and who want to thank you, however incoherently and awkwardly."[6]

Jean-Paul Goujon, who has written extensively on these circles, has dubiously suggested that lesbianism united Louÿs and Barney as if by a mutually sympathetic bond: "He was interested in lesbians and was able to understand them. Natalie Barney therefore felt intuitively that she would find him to be a precious advisor and a prestigious defender."[7] And yet Louÿs's erotica presents a libidinally objectifying, rather than an identificatory, investment in lesbianism. With greater complexity, Tama Lea Engelking has explored Barney's indebtedness to

Louÿs, concluding that "far from endorsing Louÿs's lesbian 'translations,' [Barney] was actually putting the author and his book to use in the service of her own Sapphic vision" (63). Neither an unquestioning disciple nor unimpressed by his work and stature, Barney took from Louÿs and gave to him, doubtlessly more attuned than he to how the "young girls of the future" might respond to their work. This response to Louÿs has been ambivalent: while women from the era of the DOB sometimes appeared indiscriminate in their eagerness to read books acknowledging their existence, others have, more recently, bristled at Louÿs's objectifications. As Engelking has pointed out, Lillian Faderman reviled Louÿs's work. Others have sought to downplay male involvement in Barney's circle. Writing in *Amazon Expedition: a lesbianfeminist anthology* (1973), Bertha Harris lamented that "Barney felt it necessary to admit men as well as lesbians into her house," while claiming that she "outdid even the French in the great tradition of the intellectual salon" (81, 82).[8]

The poetry of Renée Vivien is equally equivocal. Its relation to precedent demonstrates both indebtedness and re-creation, leaving it open to varying interpretations. Like Barney's, her work illustrates the changing reception of lesbian-authored literature. Vivien's poetry has long been read in light of Baudelaire's, and some of her early critics saw her work as derivative. In his 1905 essay on "Le Romantisme féminin," Charles Maurras argued that Vivien was driven by "feminine imitation," and he went so far as to accuse her of plagiarism: "we have noticed time and again Renée Vivien's petty larcenies [...] from *Les Fleurs du Mal*" (159, 236). Maurras considered Vivien to be more indebted to Baudelaire than to Sappho, whose poetry she translated: "our Baudelairean has completely fallen short of what I'll call *the sapphic truth*" [la vérité saphique] (169, emphasis added). Harris counters accusations of plagiarism and asserts that "Vivian wrote some of the most outspoken poetry concerning lesbian passion since Sappho" (85). She avoids mention of all the male-authored lesbian poetry written in between, with the exception of asking why Baudelaire's name "is as much a household word in literary circles as a detergent's is in daytime tv," while Vivien's name remains relatively unknown to the reading public (86).

More recent (and less impassioned) critics have looked at Vivien's work as a self-making, even while presuming that her poetry is in some way indebted to Baudelaire.[9] Historian Florence Tamagne, for example, suggests that "[the literary] myth of the decadent lesbian was [...] maintained [entretenu] by lesbians such as Renée Vivien and Liane de Pougy, who embraced this imagery as the basis for their triumphant marginality" [une marginalité revendiquée comme une gloire] ("Identité"). And as I have argued elsewhere, Vivien reshaped the lesbian images she grew up with and made them her own by reinvesting a broad range of cultural and literary myths.[10] Neither immaculately conceived nor simply derivative, the lesbian's lesbian of the Belle Époque was the product of her time and her culture. Vivien and, indeed, all sexually non-normative subjects faced with a wasteland of objectifying images necessarily begin with what Foucault has called the "shifts and reutilizations of identical formulas for contrary objectives" (*History*, 100).

The changing critical attitudes toward such author-identified representations is noteworthy, as is the growing body of scholarly work devoted to these women who wrote as both descendants and forbears. Responses to their ambiguous relationship with the sapphic fathers have run the ideological gamut. During the first half of the twentieth century, bastions of ultraconservatism, fearful of usurpation and their own obsolescence, belittled the work of Barney and Vivien as derivative. During the heyday of lesbian feminism, cultural feminists repudiated the sapphic fathers and sought to cleanse lesbian writers of suggestions of indebtedness, with the arguably understandable goal of reversing past invisibility and celebrating underappreciated works. More recently, the relationship between Sappho 1900 and nineteenth-century sapphic literature has been mined for more tempered analyses.

The contrary is true of the topic to which I now turn: French literature as intertext in mid-century America. Not only is this virgin territory, but the questions raised by such a comparative confrontation are also quite different from what is at stake for Parisian writers of the Belle Époque. Authors such as Barney and Vivien interacted with the work of sapphic fathers in the rarefied literary circles of turn-of-the-century Paris. This context as well as their privilege and wealth permitted them the freedom of flamboyant visibility and self-creation. And yet they can tell us little about the impact of such texts on common readers. In the remainder of this chapter, we pass from socially advantaged authors to anonymous readers, from high literature to low, from a proximate relationship to a much more remote one. But first there is an ocean to cross.

Transnationalism, Mass Culture, and Sexual Identity

The discursive constructs of the sapphic fathers left tangible traces outside the confines of French literature and European science. Many of them continued to circulate beyond the disciplines that produced them, beyond the nineteenth century, beyond France, and often beyond attribution to enter the amorphous realm of the collective imagination. While today many of these imagined figures appear ludicrous or offensive and thus, perhaps, are easily dismissed, a great deal remains of them, their painted milieus, and the plots they inhabit. And as they circulated among and between literary and scientific spheres, they provided models and foils for readers as well as writers. The search for a cause-and-effect relationship between such discourses, on one hand, and lives lived, on the other, admittedly springs from dubious intent and bears fraught results. While there is no way of determining exactly when, how, or to what extent these representations made their way into public consciousness, there is clear evidence that they did.

The connection between the lesbian literature of nineteenth-century France and the readers of mass-market paperbacks in twentieth-century America is perhaps a less self-evident point of attack, but it is a no less fruitful one. It is, moreover, farther-ranging as it shows the transatlantic reach of French paternal fictions, their presence not only in high literature, but also in popular fiction and, most pointedly, their extra-textual involvement with lesbian identifications during the dark ages of the homophile movement.

The thread of sapphic literature as it appeared first in France and spread across Europe finally arrived in the American popular press. As this crossing participated in an international flow of traffic, globalization studies provides a useful frame for its discussion. Since the early 1990s, globalization studies has given rise to a fascinating debate about the impact of international exchange on minority sexual cultures. What Dennis Altman has called the "global gay" of the twenty-first century derives from, among other elements, increased travel and tourism, the Internet, new communication networks, and virtual communities. Such new or enhanced modes of interaction have altered the processes of self-identification for many sexual minority subjects across the globe. Some critics have praised these changes as evidence that non-normative cultures are coming of age on the world stage. But others have condemned the "gay international" as the product of capitalist, orientalist assimilation to Western gay cultural norms.[11]

While the stakes were quite different before the information age, one finds in looking to the past that the dissemination of homosexual constructs played a role in the articulation of identities even then. A number of theorists have rejected the notion that globalization is a strictly contemporary phenomenon, positing a proto-globalization beginning as far back as the sixteenth century and achieving the status of modern globalization during the period of colonial expansion and industrialization that stretched from around 1800 until the Second World War.[12] Jean-François Bayart, author of *Global Subjects*, describes the nineteenth century as "foundational" to the establishment of what he calls "postcolonial globalization." The nineteenth century, for the very reasons it is foundational to contemporary globalization, also offers a crucial, and underexplored, prelude to the study of the worldwide, rapid-fire communication networks that shape the global gay today.

Arts and ideas pertaining to sexuality were increasingly exported and imported thanks to new modes of travel and communication, which were beginning to make possible the international dispersal of national literatures and scientific research. As Bayart has noted, "From the nineteenth century onward, the construction of national, continental, and sometimes intercontinental railways, the establishment of worldwide telegraph systems [...] the appearance of mass publishing and a mass press [...] ensured that there was an unprecedented circulation, right across the planet, of information, ideas, goods, and people" (16). These are the very elements constitutive of what Walter Benjamin has called the age of mechanical reproduction, to which Baudelaire's *Fleurs du Mal*, he contends, fell victim. And yet it is thanks to these elements that Baudelaire's poetry in fact *participated* in the international dissemination of lesbian images. Alongside Baudelaire, sapphic poetry and fiction more broadly, and still other, blatantly commercial sapphic texts, which were the most visible by-products of these new technologies, found readers in foreign countries. Indeed, regardless of their degree of prestige, nineteenth-century French literary works both high and low contributed to the transmission and apprehension of lesbian identities across time and space.

The portrait of the lesbian, developed and repeated so often in nineteenth-century France and bequeathed to twentieth-century America, contributed if not to the behaviour, then at least to the sense of self of women erotically and emotionally drawn to other women. The sustained and far-reaching reverberations of French sapphic fictions indicate to what extent France came to signify "lesbian" in the United States.[13] Soon after their appearance in France, works by sapphic fathers began to inform the discussion and perception of female homosexuality in the United States. Translated, referenced, anthologized, plagiarized, alluded to, modelled upon: they infiltrated fiction and non-fiction, erudite and sensationalist writing, lofty and lurid prose.

Beginning in the nineteenth century, often shortly after their publication in France, a number of the French authors who contributed to this corpus were translated into English. Adolphe Belot was enormously successful in the United States during his lifetime, as he was in France, and widely translated. *Mademoiselle Giraud, ma femme* (1870) first appeared in English in 1891 (*Mélinite*, 1888, in 1892). As historian Lisa Duggan has shown, this translation played a significant role in an 1892 American murder trial featuring lesbian lovers. One newspaper article from the period states that "In the Criminal Court of Memphis, Shelby County, Adolphe Belot's *Mlle. [Giraud] Ma Femme* will be the only textbook at hand" (Duggan, 24). Another paper headlined its copy as "A Tragedy Equal to the Most Morbid Imaginings of Modern French Fiction" (181). Duggan has demonstrated more broadly that "The mass circulation press in the United States, and the Anglo-American medical journals, turned to French novels for reference in assembling the lesbian love murder story, noting repeatedly that no American authors produced any similar literature" (182). French titles had become a kind of shorthand for lesbianism in the United States by the end of the century, as they had for the European medical community. They would continue to do so into the twentieth century: the impact of these works, and of France more generally, on lesbian representations and identifications became particularly pronounced in mid-century America. Here, too, mass culture, in this instance mass-produced fiction, played an important role.

In 1939 the company Pocket Books appeared and began to manufacture inexpensive, mass-market paperbacks, an event that would have a profound impact on the publishing industry. Often called pulps for the cheap paper (first used in magazines) that permitted inexpensive production and broad circulation, they responded to an expanding readership and increased demand. Pulp novels were characterized by lurid covers and sensational copy designed to attract readers, and they were easily accessible, sold in dime stores, drugstores, and bus stations. Mid-century America echoed, to a certain extent, France's nineteenth-century revolution in publishing, which lowered the price of print matter and enabled the broad distribution of best-sellers, sapphic and otherwise, at kiosks and in train stations across France. The first mass-produced paperbacks would help create a market for and facilitate the dissemination of lesbian-themed works. As Susan Stryker has noted, in the early years of the paperback, publishers re-released classics with provocative packaging: "Most publishers of these earlier lesbian titles had coyly justified their attention to the potentially sensationalistic topic by presenting it in the form of reprinted historical fiction" (51). Stryker cites several French titles, pointing to Zola's *Nana* (Pocket Books, 1941) as "a particular favorite" that "created a stir" with a cover showing "the brazen heroine in a revealing, diaphanous white gown." Stryker also names Gautier's *Mademoiselle de Maupin* (Quick Reader, 1945) and Daudet's *Sappho* (Avon, 1951), to which one could add Balzac's *Girl with the Golden Eyes* (Avon, 1931) and Louÿs's *Aphrodite* (Avon, 1946). As Stryker remarks, "By situating homosexuality 'over there' in decadent Europe, and by safely relegating it to an earlier historical period, American paperback publishers apparently hoped to make the topic palatable enough for domestic consumption [and] cash in on the public's anxious fascination with queer stories" (51–2). These earlier reissues amounted to a fraction of the number of lesbian-themed books that were to appear in North America beginning around 1950. Lesbian pulp fiction was spawned by the meeting of a new profit-driven publishing vehicle and a newly visible (but certainly not new) fascination with female homosexuality.

Homophobia and Lesbophilia during the Cold War

This resurgent interest in homosexuality followed the Second World War, during a contradictory period when new urban networks for gay men and lesbians coincided with renewed oppression. Social intolerance and a focus on domestic conformity were amplified during the cold war. Government policy targeted homosexuals with purges in the military and government, where "sex perverts" were determined to pose a security risk.[14] McCarthyism linked homosexuality with communism, and it thus became grounds for deportation and discrimination in hiring.

Despite this context of persecution, the homophile movement was established and a new generation of research on sexuality attracted the attention of general readers. Gay groups sprang up nearly at the same time in Europe and in the United State, participating in what David Churchill has called "homophile internationalism," based upon dialogue among and between Europeans and Americans: "American-based homophiles were aware of their European counterparts and sought to familiarize their readers with what was happening across the Atlantic" (36). The International Committee for Sex Equality (ICSE), which Churchill describes as "an umbrella group for European homophiles," was founded shortly after the war, in the wake of Nazi persecution and extermination of homosexuals, and of recriminalization in France under the Vichy regime.[15] In France, André Baudry established Arcadie (1954–82), a non-political group that created discreet social networks for (predominantly male) homosexuals and sought acceptance through educational outreach.[16] Nonetheless prosecuted for offending morals, Baudry shunned expressions of difference and spurned any association with gay ostentation. U.S. groups, including the Mattachine Society (1950–61) and the Daughters of Bilitis (1955–70), generally sought greater visibility and had political goals, although similarly encouraged conservative, gender-typical appearance.[17]

In order to reach sometimes deeply closeted and isolated members, these groups disseminated newsletters and periodicals such as, in the United States, the DOB's *Ladder*, the *Mattachine Review*, and *ONE Magazine*. The French *Arcadie* was one of several European titles. These publications also created a forum for European and American homophiles to communicate with each other. To different degrees, homophile groups preached respectability and coveted acceptance. They also followed a similar historical arc. With the coming of gay liberation and the founding of radical groups such as the Front homosexuel d'action révolutionnaire (FHAR) in 1971, Arcadie came to be associated with the conciliatory posture of an older generation and retired into obsolescence.[18] Similarly, in the United

States, the conciliatory voices of the homophile movement would be questioned by radicals after the Stonewall riots (1969) and the beginnings of the gay liberation movement.

As these groups were forming, American biologist Alfred Kinsey's pioneering work on sexual behaviour was attracting a great deal of attention for its methods and conclusions. His *Sexual Behavior in the Human Male* (1948), followed shortly by *Sexual Behavior in the Human Female* (1953), was based on in-depth interviews with a large number of subjects. The author studied all manner of sexual expression and demonstrated the prevalence of same-sex practices in the American population. Kinsey concluded that upwards of 28% of women had participated in some form of homosexual activity and 13% had experienced "overt contacts to the point of orgasm" (474–5). He found that the sexual lives of 3 to 8% of women could be qualified as "mostly" or "exclusively homosexual," compared to 7–26% for men (488). Perhaps more important than these statistics was the dispassionate manner of their presentation. Homophiles referred to Kinsey's scale of sexual expression as proof of their normalcy, while psychoanalysts cited his work as indication of a prevalent and growing pathology based in psychology, not genetics. *Sexual Behavior in the Human Female* was widely read, remarkably so for a university press publication, and eventually appeared in paperback (Pocket Books, 1965).[19]

A number of other specialized works soon followed, including Frank Caprio's influential *Female Homosexuality: A Psychodynamic Study of Lesbianism* (1954), which was inspired by Kinsey and dedicated to him. A psychiatrist and psychoanalyst, Caprio's credentials are listed at length on the cover flap, describing him as an international authority whose books "have been widely acclaimed both in the general press and in scientific journals." We learn that he studied in Austria "where he was psychoanalyzed by the world-famous Dr. William Stekel," an early disciple of Freud and author of books on homosexuality and female frigidity. In his introduction, Caprio points to the relative paucity of "readily accessible authoritative information" devoted to female homosexuality, stating his intent to shed light upon what he calls a "hidden disease" (vii). He considers lesbianism to be an urgent topic, since it is "capable of influencing the stability of our social structure," particularly with regard to marriage and an increasing divorce rate (viii). Using rhetoric similar to that of European doctors at the end of the previous century, he stresses the need for a "scientific attitude about sexual aberrations." However Caprio insisted that the knowledge gained must be shared in order to better educate the public, thus differing from such predecessors as Krafft-Ebing and Chevalier, who cautioned that such sensitive material should be limited to a small circle of medical researchers.

The subject of lesbianism inevitably brings Caprio's focus to France. He writes that he "circled the globe with the specific purpose of accumulating scientific information dealing with the prevalence and practices of lesbianism in various parts of the world" (ix). In tracing the "historical evolution" of lesbianism, he finds it to be widespread in eighteenth- and nineteenth-century France, and he cites both a sexologist (Bloch) and a writer of fiction (Pidansat de Mairobert) as proof. While Caprio's chapter entitled "The Lesbian Theme in Literature" focuses primarily on English-language works, such as Radclyffe Hall's *The Well of Loneliness* (1928) and the anonymous, purportedly autobiographical *Diana* (1939), he opens it by noting that "we find lesbianism dealt with by some of the greatest writers of the nineteenth century [...] in France" (32). He names Balzac and quotes Daudet at length.

Subsequent to Kinsey's pioneering work during this period of underground organization and tentative activism, a number of voices emerged in other domains to address the "question" of homosexuality. While non-specialized, their works carried all the marks of seriousness: reputable publishers, sober style, extensive bibliographies, forwards by professionals. As did Kinsey and his team, writers such as journalist Jess Stearn and sociologist Donald Webster Cory wrote volumes on male homosexuality before turning to lesbianism. The investigative reporter Stearn (whose accomplishments would later include serving as associate editor of *Newsweek*) published *The Grapevine: A Report on the Secret World of the Lesbian* (1964) following upon the best-selling success of his study of male homosexuality, *The Sixth Man* (1961). Stearn's relatively dispassionate account focused on unveiling the enigma of lesbianism, seen as "far more secretive" that male homosexuality, employing a rhetoric of invisibility similar to Caprio's.

Donald Webster Cory contributed a volume on lesbianism from an inside perspective entitled *The Lesbian in America* (1964), which he published subsequent to *The Homosexual in America: A Subjective Approach* (1951) and dedicated "to the courageous women of the Daughters of Bilitis." A self-declared homosexual, Cory is described on the back flap as being "widely acknowledged as spokesman for the homosexual community in the United States." Cory was the pseudonym (which nods to André Gide's novel *Corydon*) of Edward Sagarin, a CUNY professor of criminology and sociology who was an early and influential participant in the homophile movement.[20] His *Lesbian in America* was published in hardback by Citadel Press, Caprio's publisher, and prefaced by the notable psychologist Albert Ellis, PhD (also Cory's co-writer for *The Homosexual in America*). All these marks of prestige, as we shall see, would be absent in the non-fiction paperbacks that later capitalized on these titles.

While psychoanalysts relied on Kinsey to gauge the breadth of sexual pathology in American society, Cory used his data to make a case for minority rights. From Kinsey he extrapolated the number of women engaging in homosexual activity in America, estimating upwards of 2.5 million, and argued that the country could not afford to marginalize so sizable a group. Cory's work shares a number of commonalities with his contemporaries, including the shift to a psychodynamic, rather than genetic, explanation for homosexuality. Like Caprio, Cory even held out the possibility of a therapeutic "cure" for homosexuality.

More importantly for the purposes of this study, both authors forefront the visibility of female homosexuality in literature. As does Caprio, Cory devotes a chapter to the question of literary representation, entitled "The Mirror of Literature." The difference here is in the value they attribute to fictional portraiture. Caprio analyses lesbianism as a literary "theme" bearing a plausible resemblance to lesbian psychopathology. For instance, he reads Hall's *Well of Loneliness* as a "contribution" to psychiatry and an "opportunity" for the lay reader to "gain insight into the psychological mechanisms that operate in the development of sexual inversion among women" (38). But Cory considers fiction to be a "mirror" not of reality, but of *perception*: "For the lesbian, [literature] can offer a view of how she is seen by society, and hence influence how she sees herself" (147). He considers French literature to be of primary importance in calling attention to female homosexuality, placing it on par with Freud's work and the birth of psychoanalysis: "two forces were making themselves felt: on the one hand, the French romanticists and symbolists; on the other, the new interest in all psychological and psychosexual subjects that would arise with the turn of the century when a doctor in Vienna initiated the sexual revolution" (139). A hyperbolic claim to be sure, but one that indicates the degree to which, even in twentieth-century America, the sapphic fathers were felt to have made a fundamental contribution to lesbian self-perception. Cory names the usual suspects: "many of their most prominent nineteenth-century authors, including Baudelaire, Balzac, and de Maupassant, did much to make the female homosexual an important literary figure." He also adds some "minor French authors, such as Latouche, Belot, and Mendès" (140), but his most interesting addition to the list is Musset's violently pornographic *Gamiani*, which serves for Cory as an example of how abject some of these representations really were. Baudelaire emerges as a benevolent figure, to whose poetry "one turns to find human sympathy for all that is socially condemned, beauty in all that the world finds evil" (139–40).

Cory repeats the trope of lesbians as a hidden or obscure group: "The lesbian is among the most difficult of people to identify" (89). But he finds a new, if condemnable, visibility in contemporary popular fiction: "today, a vast literature has grown, and a curious aspect of that literature is the new American paperback pulp, […] obsessed with sex and particularly with women, sometimes with one woman but often with two or even more" (146). Cory's contention that "lesbians seldom buy these books [whose] readers are almost exclusively male" has been countered by the many women readers who avidly consumed them (149). However, it is difficult to disagree with his appraisal that most pulps "in no way reflect [their] life" and deliver "so distorted a picture" of it (150). It is to the lesbian paperbacks that I now turn, distorting mirrors that frequently reveal shadows of nineteenth-century French precedents.

The Golden Age of the Lesbian Paperback Original

Perhaps the most intriguing aspect of mid-century American lesbophilia lies in the representations found in mass-produced paperbacks. Branching out from translations and reprinted classics, publishing houses began to commission homegrown books targeted to satisfy proven reading tastes. With such titles, publishers bypassed hardcover and went directly to inexpensive, widely available paperback editions, which became known as paperback originals (PBOs). In 1950, the lesbian PBO emerged as a popular, visible, and highly profitable subgenre. What has been called the "golden age" of lesbian pulps spanned around fifteen years, until the mid- to late 1960s and the beginnings of sexual liberation movements.[21] The true paperback originals – novels of frequently questionable literary value published in inexpensive format – were written overwhelmingly by men. Racy fiction and spurious non-fiction alike commonly issued from the same publishing houses: Midwood, Fawcett Gold Medal, and Avon were among the imprints specializing in lesbian pulps. As the illustrations reproduced below suggest, cover art played an important role in the marketing strategy of PBOs.[22] This artwork did not discriminate on the nature of the books it adorned. Whether French classics in translation, fraudulent medical research, contemporary fiction, personal confession, or poorly written potboilers, lesbian-themed paperbacks had covers that showed a woman or women in some state of undress; facial expressions depicting fear, longing, or lust; or some other graphic promise of a lesbian plot.

Although pulps are primarily associated with lowbrow fiction, a good number of non-fictional titles that treated lesbianism appeared in this format as well. Inauthentic research into both male and female homosexuality capitalized on the success of studies written by professionals and academics. Coinciding with the peak of lesbian pulp fiction, such ostensibly accredited, but in fact misleadingly marketed books muddied the line between scholarship and fiction. The Kinsey Institute library is said to include a "shelf full of" fraudulent studies that rode the coat-tails of Kinsey's work (Pomeroy, 340).

W.D. Sprague, PhD, author of *The Lesbian in Our Society: A Problem that Must be Faced* (Midwood, 1962; see fig. 5.1), provides one such example. The

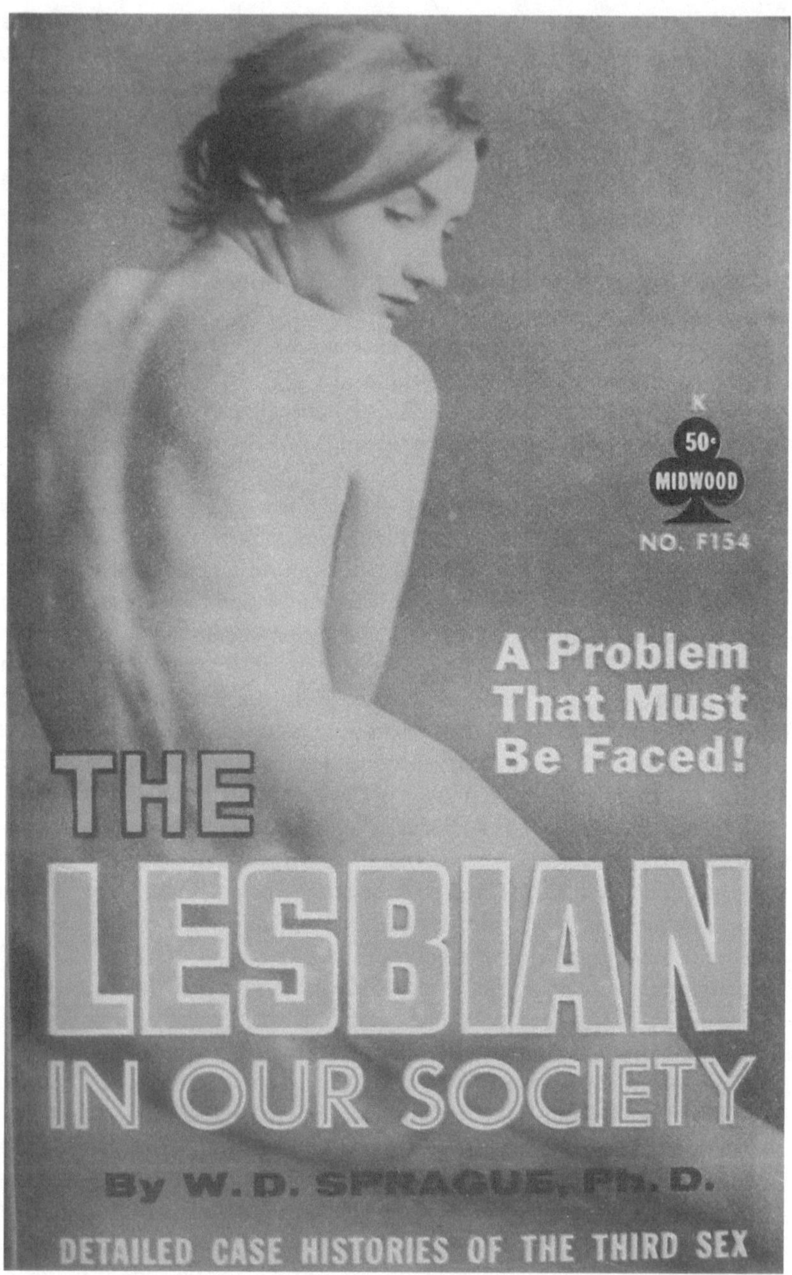

Figure 5.1. W.D. Sprague, PhD, *The Lesbian in Our Society*

author is identified as the associate director of the Psychoanalytical Assistance Foundation and aligns himself with the work of Kinsey, whom he names as a "trailblazer." Sprague's book purports to relate the findings of the Psychoanalytical Assistance Foundation's 1960 "Survey of the Sexual Habits of American Lesbians," involving in-depth case histories taken from 4620 women. This report is preceded by a "Short History of Lesbianism," in which Sprague credits the French Revolution with the masculinization and perversion of women: "Innumerable Frenchwomen, fired by their newly-discovered sense of equality with men, consciously divested themselves of their femininity." According to Sprague, this was but a short step from "overt and aggressive homosexuality" (24–5).

As it turns out, W.D. Sprague was one of a dozen pseudonyms of Bela von Block, who as Sprague wrote a series of paperback originals examining the sexual habits of various female populations, including *Sex Behavior of the American Housewife* (1961), *Sexual Behavior of American Nurses* (1963), and *Sex and the Secretary* (1964). The Psychoanalytical Assistance Foundation was a hoax, the author was without credentials, and no such broad-based scientific survey of the sexual habits of lesbians had ever been undertaken. Although a Kinsey expert describes it as "a compilation of old material gathered from here and there and simply thrown together," this book nonetheless sold widely and was accepted by many as legitimate (Pomeroy, 341).

Lucius B. Steiner's *Sex Behavior of the Lesbian* (Viceroy, 1964; see fig. 5.2) is another candidate for the Kinsey Institute's collection of bogus sexological studies. Its cover copy similarly boasted that its author was a "leading authority" whose "report" was based on "actual case histories." Among other claims made, Steiner asserted that "The Normans indulged themselves freely" in female homosexuality, and that "France had an irrepressible group of lesbians in the eighteenth century who called themselves Vestals of Venus [...] Branches of the cult grew and spread over the entire country" (9, 10). Lucius B. Steiner was in fact one of several pseudonyms of Doug Warren "Fatty" Rosencrans, a would-be actor turned writer. A field reporter for UPI during the Vietnam war, he later wrote books on Hollywood stars (among whom was Betty Grable) and several "self-proclaimed potboilers," including *Sex Behavior of the Homosexual* (Jewell, 2).

R. Leighton Hasselrodt, MA, maintained, in *Lesbianism around the World* (Midwood, 1963; see fig. 0.1, p. xiv), that present-day France, and Paris in particular, harboured an unusual quantity of female homosexuals:

> Paris has a very high population of confirmed, "fixed" Lesbians. Large colonies of them can be found living on the Rive Gauche, in St. Denis, Montmartre, and other quarters of the city. Paris has innumerable "Temples of Sappho," elaborate establishments devoted to providing Lesbians with entertainment – and with paid partners if they are lonely and desire homosexual relations. (107–8)

Figure 5.2. Lucius B. Steiner, *Sex Behavior of the Lesbian*

He characterized Paris in much the same way as did fin-de-siècle literature, as being populated by lesbians on both extremes of the social spectrum. From prostitutes and showgirls to lesbians of "the jaded, decadent upper classes," these women met no legal restrictions or social opprobrium, but instead were protected thanks to an abundance of influential homosexuals.[23] To these groups Hasselrodt adds "exponents of neo-existentialist philosophies" for whom bisexuality "is considered the ultimate expression of sophistication" and who affirm "post-Sartre doctrines of complete sexual promiscuity and amorality" (110). He finally asserts that bisexuality "is so commonplace in Paris that it has become a virtual cliché" and presents as unexceptional a scenario in which "two or more young women sharing an apartment [will] bring home male – or female – lovers who are passed around or who share in pluralistic orgies." Hasselrodt identifies Paris as "the Lesbos of modern-day Europe, in truth the 'Mecca' for female homosexuals of the Western World" (111). He invokes Ulrichs, Hirschfeld, and Ellis to authorize his sweeping findings. W.D. Sprague's endorsement appears on the book's cover, calling it "An enlightening study which [...] does much to dispel the prevalent ignorance of the subject."

France and the French literary tradition were of great interest to fiction and non-fiction writers alike at the mid-century. Self-identified American lesbian authors themselves contributed to the French mystique. Marijane Meaker, writing as Ann Aldrich (and who also wrote pulp novels under the pseudonym Vin Packer), devoted a chapter to "Gay Paris" in *We Walk Alone* (Fawcett Gold Medal, 1955; see fig. 5.3).[24] Billed as a native informant – the first lesbian to write of her underworld – she maintained that "Paris, perhaps more than any other city in the world, has accustomed itself to the existence of the homosexual in its midst with relatively little furor" (59). The emphasis placed on Paris in these works is noteworthy, mirroring scientific findings of the previous century and confirming Altman's claim that "cities play a special role in the ways we imagine the history of sex" (10). Aldrich went on to name a newer canon of what she called France's "leading literary lights" – Gide, Proust, and Colette – as evidence of the country's insouciance in "dwell[ing] upon this abnormality."

The prolific Aldrich also edited an anthology of lesbian literature, one of several from the period that helped keep French titles in the American public eye. In her introduction to *Carol in a Thousand Cities* (Fawcett Gold Medal, 1960), Aldrich states that "most of the lesbian literature was in French in [the nineteenth] century (for in France, then as now, there was a more receptive disposition on matters of sex)" (13).[25] Aldrich's anthology and others like it reflect the addition of more recent French works alongside nineteenth-century

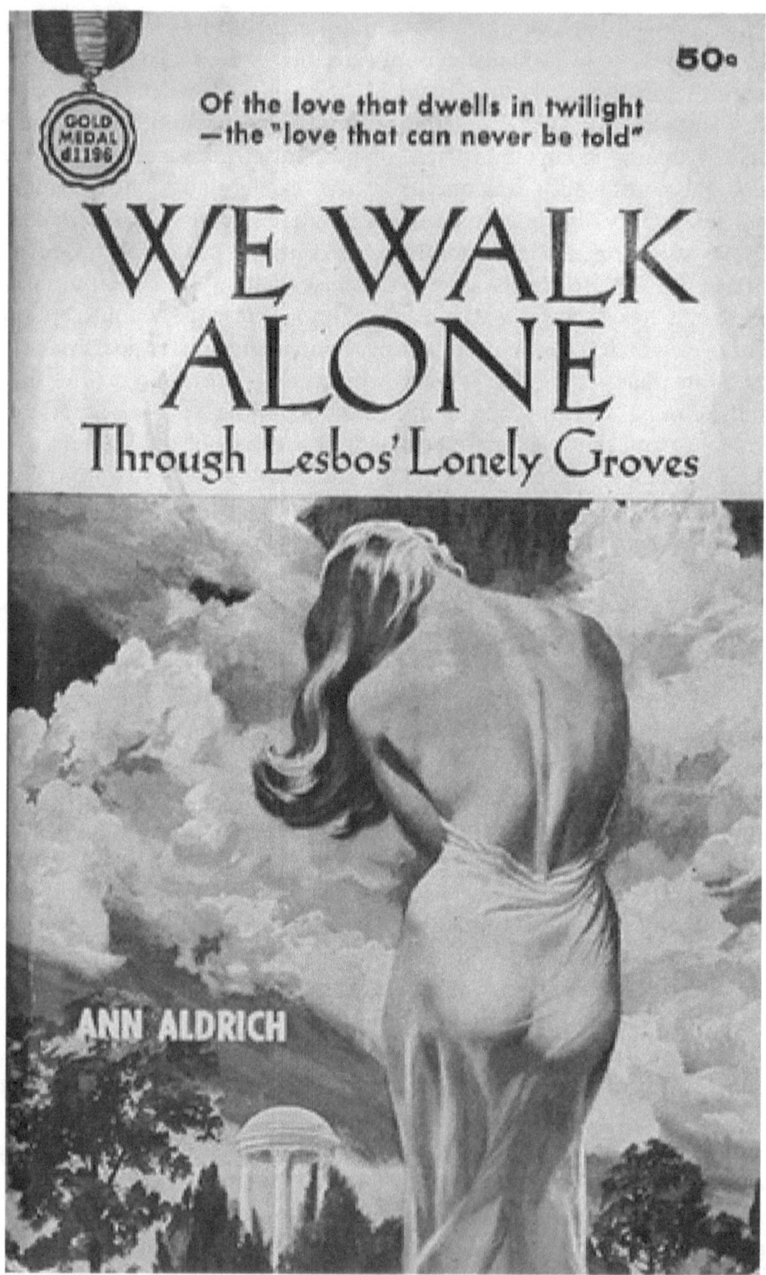

Figure 5.3. Ann Aldrich, *We Walk Alone*

authors. Aldrich includes excerpts from Françoise Mallet-Joris's novel *Le Rempart des béguines*, first published in France in 1951 and translated as *The Loving and the Daring* (Popular Library, 1957; see fig. 5.4). Lucie Marchal's *The Mesh* (Bantam Books, 1951; see fig. 5.5) and Guy des Cars's *The Damned One* (Pyramid Books, 1956; see fig. 5.6), also newly issued translations of contemporary novels, provide further evidence of France's distinct association with lesbianism.

Women's Barracks

The rush to market contemporary French novels in pulp format in the United States is undoubtedly a reflection of the success of Frenchwoman Tereska Torres's *Women's Barracks* (Fawcett Gold Medal, 1950; see fig. 5.7), which is frequently credited with being the first of the lesbian pulp genre. Torres's novel sold so well, several million copies in the five years following its first printing, that it created a market for lesbian paperback titles and has been called "the book that launched the tidal wave of lesbian fiction" (Forrest, xii). It also undoubtedly contributed to the prevalence of references to France in subsequent lesbian pulps. The discussion surrounding the writing, packaging, publication history, and reception of *Women's Barracks* is noteworthy on many accounts, both for its conformity to and departure from preceding rhetoric.

Women's Barracks relates the lives of a group of young women working in London for the French Resistance during the Second World War. And where there are same-sex living quarters there are, of course, lesbians. The story it recounts was told in published form several times, although the way this story presented itself varied enormously: was it American pulp or French literature, a novel or private journal, an account of sexual intrigue or of wartime courage, a lesbian tale or pansexual coming-of-age story?

Women's Barracks was first marketed and received as a lesbian pulp novel. Its cover shows several women in what appears to be a locker room. With cigarettes dangling from lips, exchanging meaningful glances, and in various states of undress, they entice the reader with the promise of homoerotic intrigue. Between its covers, the novel's unnamed narrator, although identified as a member of this group, acts primarily as observer of her female cohort, some very young and far from home during the chaos of war. She recounts stories of homesickness, camaraderie, frivolous and deadly adventures, but above all of hormone-addled women coming into all manner of sexual awakening. These awakenings are predominantly heterosexual, although the novel takes a keen interest in the tender Ursula's seduction by

Figure 5.4. Françoise Mallet-Joris, *The Loving and the Daring*

Figure 5.5. Lucie Marchal, *The Mesh*

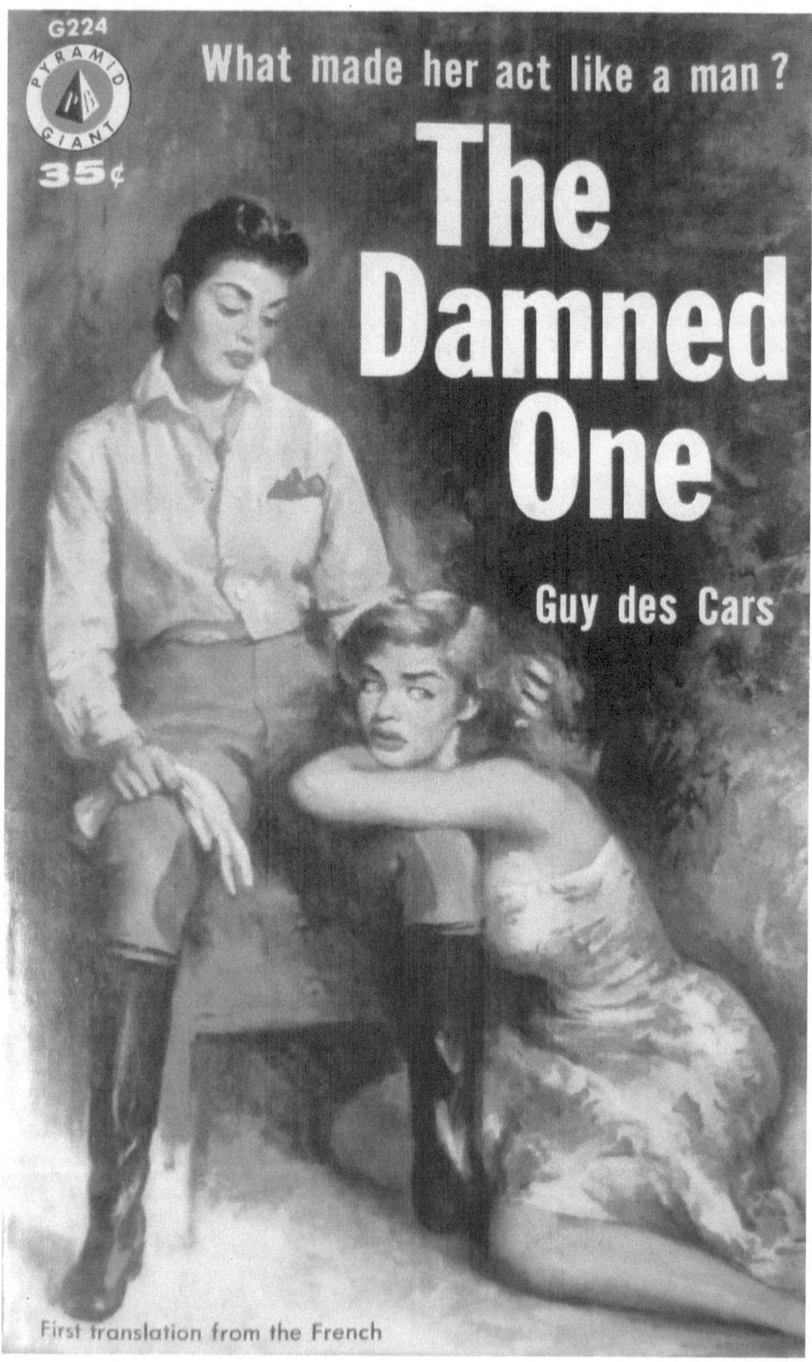

Figure 5.6. Guy des Cars, *The Damned One*

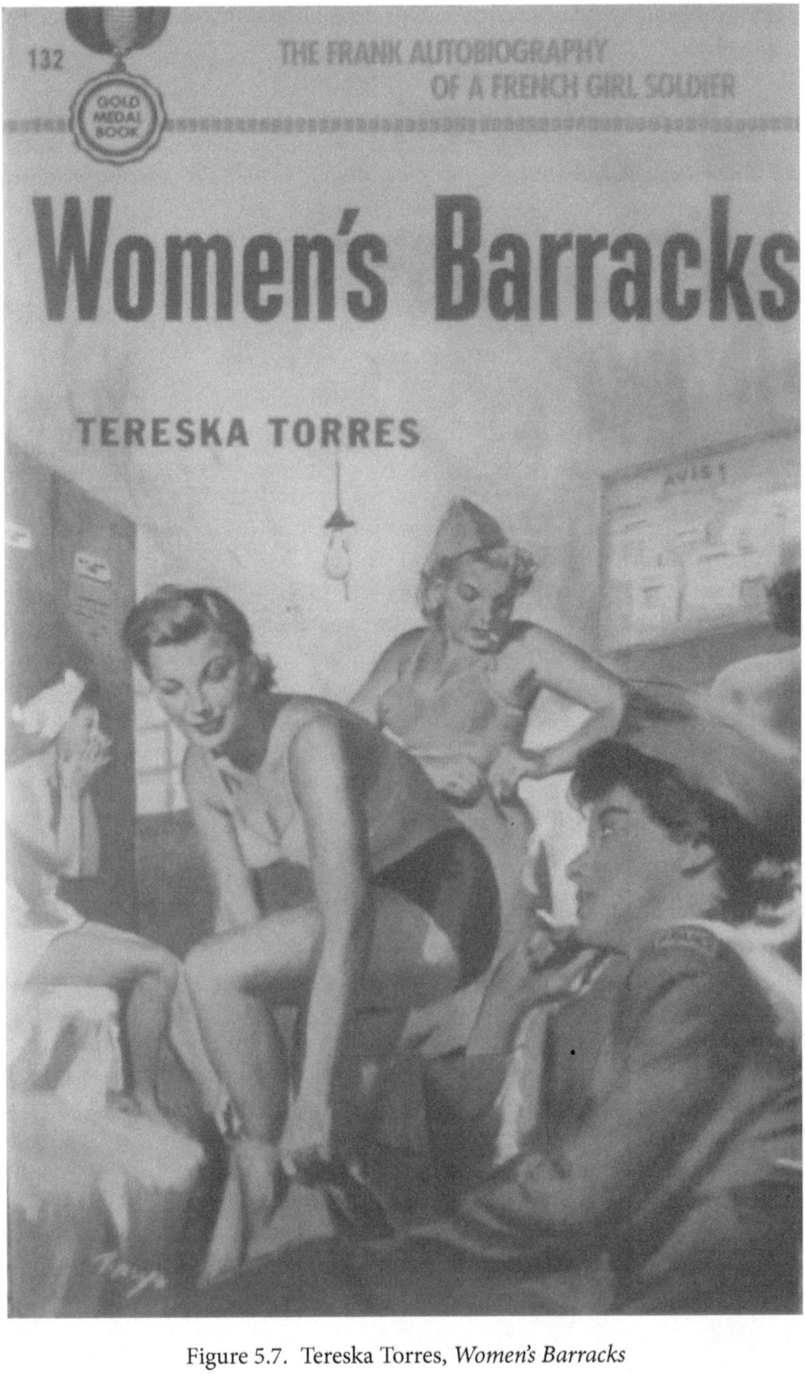

Figure 5.7. Tereska Torres, *Women's Barracks*

an older, bisexual femme fatale, Claude. Its sexual content is more suggestive than explicit:

> Ursula felt Claude's lips burning hers. She didn't know what was happening to her. She was lost, invaded, inflamed. [...] She placed her cheek on Claude's breast. Her heart beat violently, but she didn't feel afraid. She didn't understand what was happening to her. Claude was not a man; then what was she doing to her? What strange movements! What could they mean? Claude unbuttoned the jacket of her pajamas, and enclosed one of Ursula's little breasts in her hand, and then gently, very gently, her hand began to caress all of Ursula's body, her throat, her shoulders, and her belly. (49)

In this paragraph we find the familiar trope of the innocent young girl seduced by an older woman, with free indirect discourse capturing Ursula's naive viewpoint.

The narrator presents a typology of the "various grades [of] Lesbianism," which situates Claude's and Ursula's mobile sexualities in relation to the true-blue homosexuals. We meet the masculine Ann, "one of those people who seem entirely explained by their very appearance" (85), the ethereal Englishwoman Lee, and the starchy warrant officer Petit. Lesbianism is equated with drama, since "the taste for intrigue was the one feminine trait that seemed to remain with them, and it was developed to the maximum" (89). By the novel's end, Ursula has escaped from Claude's clutches and fallen in love with a young soldier. When he dies in combat before they are able to marry, the pregnant Ursula takes her own life. Is Ursula punished for having succumbed to Claude, or in order to save her from the ignominy of mothering an illegitimate child, or both? Her death was doubtless a publisher's requirement for a respectable resolution, to which authors were often obliged to adhere in order to avoid censorship and maintain a veneer of morality.

Nonetheless, *Women's Barracks* did not escape official condemnation. It was censured in the 1953 report by the U.S. House Select Committee on Current Pornographic Materials, which was formed to consider the negative impact of the paperback industry.[26] The novel was also tried and found guilty on charges of obscenity in Canada in a 1952 court case that unfolded like a replay of Baudelaire's trial. The prosecutor highlighted all passages involving lesbian characters (and disregarded depictions of unbecoming heterosexual behaviour), while "the basis of defense arguments was that Torres's novel served the public good by warning its readers, especially young women, about the dangers of lesbianism" (M. Adams, 111).

Although *Women's Barracks* is plainly framed as a lesbian novel, its author would later declare herself astounded that anyone could read it as such. As does its cover, the translator's preface directs the reader's attention to the novel's lesbian subplots, which in fact contribute only a few stars to its constellation of sexual intrigue. The pseudonymous translator describes "the story of women in war" as being a cautionary tale about "the effect of living together in military barracks upon a group of young girls, many of them utterly innocent when they entered the service, where they were to encounter jaded women who had lived through every type of experience" (1). The novel's intent is to "bring understanding of these special problems [...] that must be recognized wherever women have to live together without normal emotional outlets." This sounds remarkably like the front matter of Belot's *Mademoiselle Giraud*, which stands on moral high ground and alerts its readers to the vulnerability of young women in sex-segregated spaces, be that a convent school or an army barracks.

Torres's own foreword follows, in which the author tells a slightly different story about the book's provenance, and one that acknowledges its voyeuristic appeal. The author describes the work as a fiction based on her wartime diary, a novel that she wrote reluctantly upon the prodding of her husband, to whom she assigns responsibility for the idea of the book. "My husband," the American writer Meyer Levin and her uncredited translator, "tells me laughingly it will make a sensational book" and "insists that the story will be interesting to Americans because we were a barracksful of French women in exile, and it seems that Frenchwomen have a great deal of allure abroad" (3). Much later Torres confessed candidly to an interviewer that "One wet summer in Brittany, when [we] were short of money, [I] began to write *Women's Barracks*" (Lichfield, "Reluctant Queen"). This was indeed a lucrative undertaking for the couple: "Gold Medal Books of Fawcett specialized in paperback 'originals' and paid authors a minimum of $2,000. *Women's Barracks* by Tereska Torres [...] received a minimum contract of $40,000 for her first book" (Schick, 97). And yet Torres was less candid about the importance of the novel's lesbian content, her appraisal of the book's shock value, and her reasons for publishing it in the United States and not in France.

While the novel is packaged as a lesbian potboiler, Torres's foreword distances her from the lesbian intrigue by asserting her heterosexuality. She describes herself as a storyteller more interested in relating the experiences of others than her own. Her authorial "I" of the foreword (already a fiction) slips into the first-person narrator who stands at a distance from the events she recounts. And yet the experiences attributed to Ursula in *Women's Barracks* are revealed in Torres's subsequently published wartime journal to be those of the author, who describes freeing herself from a manipulative older woman, then falling in love with a soldier, but surviving his death to bear his child. This equivocal relationship to the lesbian content is a persistent theme, with the author repudiating for herself what the published material places front and centre. In interviews conducted late in her life, the elderly Torres (1920–2012) claimed to have been surprised upon hearing of the notoriety of *Women's Barracks* among lesbian readers: "I look on the internet and I learn that I am the literary queen of the lesbians, the person who wrote the first lesbian, erotic pulp novel. I hate it. I hate it" (Lichfield, "Reluctant Queen"). In fact, Torres wrote at least two subsequent pulps for an American audience that featured female homoeroticism: *The Dangerous Games* (Dial Press, 1957, translated into French as *Le Labyrinthe*, 1959) and *By Cécile* (1963).

Over the years, Torres refused to release the novel in France: "Even now [in 2005], they say, maybe we should publish *Women's Barracks*. And I always say, no, I don't want it to be published in France."[27] Torres has given contradictory explanations for this. She claimed to have wanted to publish the diaries rather than the fictionalized version in France because "truth was more interesting than fiction. And the diary, which appeared in France as *Free French*, had the same stories about the same girls, but not written as fiction, written as my life in the army." In 1981 she did indeed publish her wartime journal, *Les Années anglaises: Journal intime de guerre, 1939–1945*. While it is true that the content is quite similar, the packaging is not in the least. The distinguished publishing house Seuil released *Les Années anglaises* with no cover image. The cover photo of a subsequent edition, which appeared in 2000 from the primarily literary press, Phébus Editions, under the title *Une Française libre: Journal, 1939–1945*, portrays the author as a young woman in cravatted uniform, holding her hands in her lap and demurely smiling for the camera.

On one hand, Torres delivers a "fiction" about "a barracksful of French women in exile" as a lark to an American audience since "Frenchwomen have a great deal of allure abroad." On the other, a wartime diary from a resistant, perhaps the noblest mark of patriotism in contemporary France, is soberly marketed to the French. Here, a trivial appeal to American sensationalism; there, the gravitas of French history and a "concern for historical veracity." The division the author maintains between her two audiences and these two genres relies in part on the platitude opposing American prudishness to French sexual freedom. Torres contends she was surprised by the success of *Women's Barracks* and the scandal that it caused in North America: "I thought I had written a very innocent book. I thought, these Americans, they are easily shocked [...] what [they] accept today was accepted in France in the 1950s" (Smallwood). Such claims would turn up regularly in the lesbian pulps that followed: "This is France, and people here are not as quick to condemn as in your country" (Spain, *Who Calls it Sin?* 11). Torres points to literary tradition as proof of this difference: "French literature is full of sexual description – Flaubert and Proust and everything. I felt I was extremely tame!" (Smallwood).

And yet in 2011, sixty years following the publication of *Women's Barracks*, the author did an about-face, finally permitting the novel to be published in France as *Jeunes femmes en uniforme*, also from Phébus. The cover reads "littérature française," and its candid photo captures three young uniformed women, smiling broadly but innocently, as they walk in a London street carrying duffel bags. This novel displays neither the solemnity of *Française libre* nor the come-hither allure of *Women's Barracks*. And yet it remains equivocal about its sapphic content. The back cover of *Jeunes femmes* explains the long delay in its French publication by stating, in contrast to Torres's earlier claim of having written a "very innocent book," that "At the time, the author had opposed a French publication for fear of shocking her compatriots." While less lurid in its presentation than *Women's Barracks*, *Jeunes femmes* signals its lesbian content with its title, which echoes the French title of the German film, *Mädchen in Uniform* (Leontine Sagan, 1931), a lesbian cult classic. This film, which has its own history of international success and censorship, deals with blooming lesbian ardour and adult cruelty in an authoritarian Prussian boarding school on the eve of the First World War.

In her parallel writing career in France, Torres published numerous highly regarded works, both fiction and autobiography, several that feature her own search for identity: raised Catholic, she later discovered that her parents were Polish Jews who chose to convert. It is perhaps understandable that Torres preferred to be remembered for her high-minded publications while distancing herself from commercial and sensational successes. And yet, being no stranger to identity struggles herself, she might have been less dismissive of her lesbian readers. The contradictions that emerge here suggest that national differences in sexual matters go beyond a simple opposition between French sexual freedom and American prudishness.

The Warped Vices of Paris

Although she had an enormous effect on those that followed, Torres was not typical of lesbian PBO writers. The vast majority of these books were voyeuristic fictions written by men, frequently under (sometimes female) pseudonyms. There was also a small core of women writers with a personal investment in their subject matter who rode the wave of public interest, taking advantage of the opportunity to create characters who resembled themselves. Stryker estimates that two thousand lesbian pulps were published during this period, and that among them "at least fifteen lesbian authors [...] produced over a hundred paperbacks in which lesbianism was presented in as favorable a light as publishers would allow" (61).

Most of these women were deeply closeted, many wrote under pseudonyms, some made homes for themselves in gay and bohemian enclaves in large cities, and others led conventional lives with husbands and children. While a number remain obscure, some later emerged from behind their pen names to become public figures celebrated by their readers. Valerie Taylor (pseudonym of Velma Nacella Young, 1913–97) wrote several well-known lesbian novels, including *Whisper Their Love* (1957), *The Girls in 3–B* (1959), *Stranger on Lesbos* (1960), *A World Without Men* (1963), *Return to Lesbos* (1963), and *Journey to Fulfilment* (1964). She was involved in the homophile movement and an activist for other progressive causes. Ann Bannon (pseudonym of Ann Weldy, born 1932), author of the five-novel *Beebo Brinker Chronicles*, has been quite visible in her later years, writing and speaking on her experience of authoring lesbian pulps in the late 1950s and early 60s. Some have had parallel careers as writers of other genres. Patricia Highsmith (1921–95), author of *Strangers on a Train* (1950, adapted for film by Hitchcock) and *The Talented Mr Ripley* (1955) and its sequels, wrote the 1952 lesbian classic *The Price of Salt* as Claire Morgan. Marion Zimmer Bradley (1930–99) was a fantasy novelist (*Mists of Avalon*) who wrote lesbian fiction as Miriam Gardner and Lee Chapman. The prolific Marijane Meaker (born 1927, lesbian titles as Ann Aldrich and Vin Packer) is also acclaimed as a writer of young adult fiction (M.E. Kerr).[28]

Meaker authored *Spring Fire* (1952, writing as Packer), which was Fawcett's "first lesbian paperback designed to capitalize on the success of *Women's Barracks*" (Stryker, 57). *Spring Fire* was enormously successful, and the lesbian PBO was off and running. Meaker has described being held to the same conventions as glaringly exploitive pulps, unpalatable guidelines imposed by editors who feared public disapproval and government censorship. Above all, writers were obliged to doom their lesbian characters or to return them to the heterosexual fold by novel's end. Meaker recounts her editor advising her that "it couldn't have a happy ending [...] or the Post Office might seize the books as obscene."

The imprint of France as an emblem for sex – and in particular for lesbianism – is clearly marked in many of the subsequent pulps. With titles like *Appointment in Paris* (Fay Adams, Fawcett Gold Medal, 1952; see fig. 5.8), *Mademoiselle Lesbian* (Renee Coquelin, Brandon House, 1964; see fig. 5.9), and *The French Way* (Monique Monet, All Star Books, 1965; see fig. 5.10), they frequently invoke Paris as a privileged setting for sapphic adventures. The front cover of Vicki Spain's *Who Calls It Sin?* (Domino Books, 1965) proclaims that "Paris was the ideal place for Sharon to search for her special kind of love!" (this despite the novel's Riviera setting). Paris often becomes a character in its own right, a kind of sexual inferno in which nothing is taboo. The cover copy of Don Morro's *The Virgin* screams: "All the warped vices of Paris lay in wait to trap her!" (Beacon,

Figure 5.8. Fay Adams, *Appointment in Paris*

Figure 5.9. Renee Coquelin, *Mademoiselle Lesbian*

Figure 5.10. Monique Monet, *The French Way*

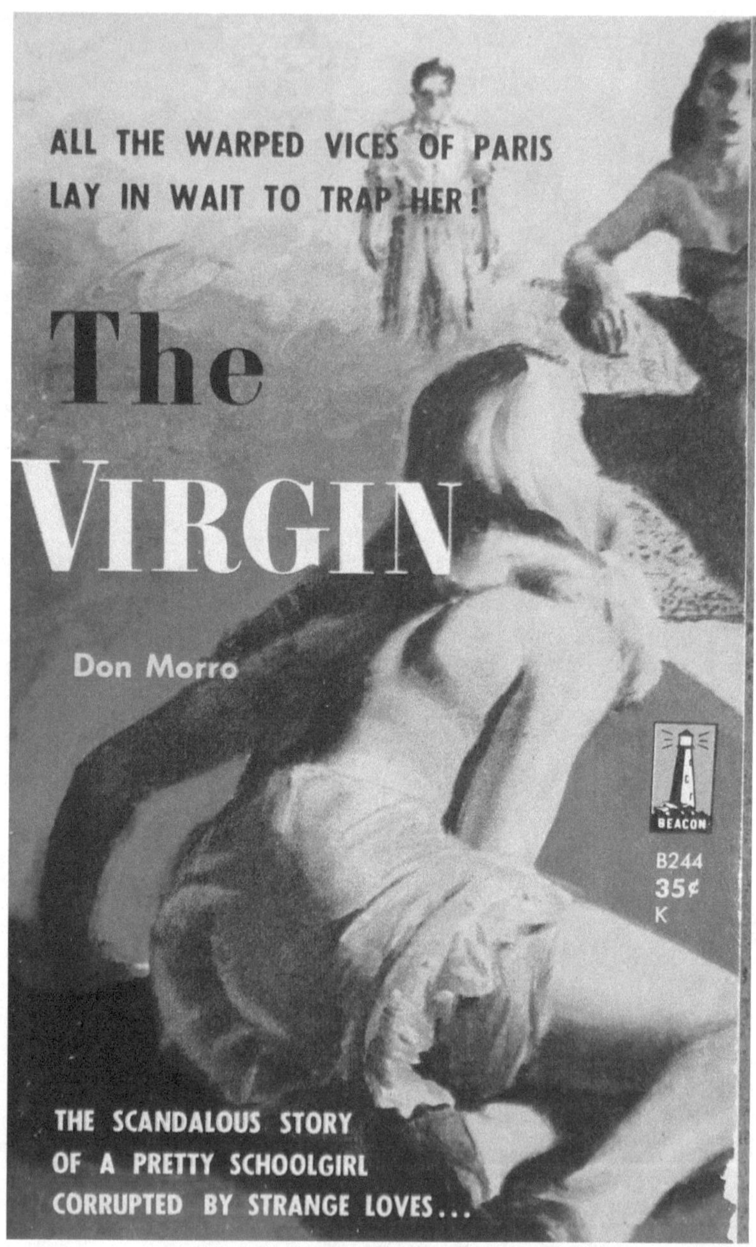

Figure 5.11. Don Morro, *The Virgin*

1955; see fig. 5.11). This novel features Diana, a headstrong but naive American, who flees her domineering father, arrives in France, and is taken in by her sexually experienced cousin, aptly named Frances. The omnisexual Frances has a hint of the invert to her: "She was not unlike certain women teachers Diana had known. Domineering, selfish, and with a far from normal interest in the prettier girls" (44). Frances takes Diana under her wing, buys her a new wardrobe, and then one evening takes her unawares to a lesbian sex show in Pigalle. When Diana is unappreciative ("You're filthy!" 52), Frances throws her out on the street. Diana ends up with Frances's former lover, Tamar, an exotic dancer who soothes her and will later seduce her: "Don't be afraid, little one. Everything happens in the Latin Quarter" (42). There are many twists and turns to the melodramatic plot, which involves such elements as an art theft ring, a bacchanalian "Beaux Arts Ball," Tamar's death, Diana's deflowering by a "foppish" French art student, and a bloody riot pitting the police against "Paris Communists" (a not atypical cold-war conflation of communism and sexual deviance). But by the novel's end, all falls back into orderly place. Diana goes off with a manly American, and they leave the depravity of Paris for the sedate south of France. The plot has come full circle: from rejecting her father (the paternal law, his sexual order, the fatherland) she has, if only narrowly, survived by returning to the safe harbour of American manhood and the cleansing, calming beaches of the Mediterranean.

As with *The Virgin*, many of these plots were in fact not exclusively lesbian, although the cover art and copy highlighted the same-sex intrigue. A number revolve around a triangle in which an innocent girl is seduced by an older woman, only to be reintegrated into sexual normalcy by novel's end. In an international version of this plot, it is an older Frenchwoman who seduces a young American ("Americans are so naïve about love," Morro, 32). One finds permutations of this template in Adams's *Appointment in Paris*, in which a fifteen-year-old American girl called Havoc is seduced by a French courtesan, Madame Marcelle, but ends up marrying an American boy from her hometown. As in *The Virgin*, a relationship with an unsuitable Frenchman weans her from her attachment to the maternal Marcelle and acts as a mediator between sapphic attachments and the return to her American and heterosexual origins. Like *Women's Barracks*, *Appointment* is set during the Second World War. And like both novels, it is self-conscious about national differences. Pierre, Havoc's sexually brutal lover, will not marry her because she is not French: "In my country we believe in a pure race, an aristocracy of the French" (125). Johnny, her American fiancé, will not sleep with her because they are not yet married. Attitudes towards same-sex encounters are also determined by nationality: "The Anglo-Saxons always consider this the worst of sins. [...] The French are more reasonable" (85).

Torres's *The Dangerous Games*, set in Paris, is told from the point of view of the "boyish" young wife, Juliette, of a philandering husband. It relates her introduction to extramarital sex, which occurs when the affair between her husband and her best friend turns into a threesome. While Juliette's subsequent affair with another man takes up much more plot space, the book's cover (also reproduced as the cover of the present volume) shows two women eying each other and an endorsement by Ann Aldrich that promises a peek at "The unorthodox love experiences of a young French woman." Like the others, Juliette has strayed, but finds refuge and security when she returns to her husband's embrace.

Books within Books

Capitalizing on the power of France as a signifier for lesbian sex, one Californian publishing company went so far as to name itself France Books. It specialized in lesbian novels with titles such as *Lesbian Torment, Hollywood Lesbian, Prisoners of Lesbos, Strange Harem,* and *Man Hater* (see fig. 5.12). As an online cataloguer has commented, these books were "Hardly 'French,' but the suggestion of [their] being imported from France ["First American Printing"] implied that [they] might prove to be racier than [the] home-grown variety" ("Strange Harem"). The creation of France Books and its focus on lesbianism indicates the centrality of female homoeroticism to a marketing strategy intended to lure readers, above all male readers. The cover art's visual punch was essential to this strategy: it was determined by production teams without author input, and sometimes, as we've seen, it reflected inaccurately on the book's content. These covers revealed no distinction between what Barbara Grier has called "nearly pornographic tripe," on one hand, and "highly sympathetic novels," on the other (D'Emilio, 135).

Barbara Grier was an early member of the Daughters of Bilitis and wrote the book column for the group's monthly newsletter, *The Ladder*. The books she featured included a considerable number of French titles. She was always careful to comment on both the quality of the writing and the nature of the lesbian portraits they contained, from exploitive and demeaning to positive or favourable. Grier eventually compiled a bibliography called *The Lesbian in Literature* (first edition 1967) in which she used a code system to categorize books by two standards, the first being the amount of lesbian content they contained (noted as A, B, C). To this she added a scale reflecting how lesbianism was represented in each book, based on the attribution of one to three asterisks (with three being most positive). This system "has nothing to do with the 'literary' quality of the material, only with the quality of the Lesbian material." Grier's ranking contained a final, dismissive qualifier: "The 'T' is for 'trash'" (xx). In

Figure 5.12. R.C. Gold, *Man Hater*

contrast, the highest grade possible was A***. Changes in the second edition of 1975 reflect what Grier called "the changing consciousness of the world," which permitted the editors to delete most "T" titles (xix). This was presumably because of relaxed censorship leading to their proliferation and, at the same time, the explosion of self-identified lesbian literature, allowing lesbian readers a broader choice and the luxury of being more demanding.

Today's critics would consider Grier's quantitative ranking of fiction to be an unsophisticated method by which to evaluate literary texts. However, her bibliography was of undeniable value to women in the sixties and early seventies who, lacking any sense of collectivity, had no way to identify and access such titles, and were in want of what radical feminist Kate Millet, in reference to her own youthful reading experience, has called "books where one woman kissed another" (D'Emilio, 136). The welcome reception that bibliographic works, including Grier's *The Lesbian in Literature* and Jeannette Foster's *Sex Variant Women in Literature* (1956) before it, received from their targeted audience offers evidence that women readers thirsted for literary representations of female homoeroticism – the less damning the better, but in the vast desert of the pre-Stonewall years, they often took what they could get.

This premium placed on literary representation is reflected in a number of the pulp novels themselves, which frequently posit books as a source of sexual knowledge. Torres's novels are shot through with references to literature. For Ursula, fiction frames her experience of lesbian sexuality: "Ursula remembered a novel that she had read that said of a woman who was making love, 'Her body vibrated like a violin.' Ursula had been highly pleased by this phrase, and now her body recalled the expression and it too began to vibrate" (*Women's Barracks*, 46). In Torres's *By Cécile*, a fictional account of Colette's marriage and birth as a writer, French lesbian literature is the name of the game. Torres has compared her own marriage with Levin to Colette's with Willy, both of them older men who encouraged their wives' sapphic writing. *By Cécile* contains a passage strikingly similar to the story Torres recounts, in her foreword to *Women's Barracks*, of Levin's coaxing her to write the book. Maurice persuades his wife Cécile to write about same-sex intimacy by saying that "Lesbianism is in fashion right now. I want some suggestive scenes, that's what sells the best – something scabrous, plenty of sex, some amusing lines, a little perversity" (*By Cécile*, 126). Moreover, Louÿs's *Chansons* functions as implicit recognition of the attraction between Cécile and her teacher. Cécile begins to recite from the collection: "She entered and, with her eyes half-closed, she passionately brought her lips to mine; our tongues met … Never have I shared a kiss such as that one." The novel then describes Mademoiselle's aroused response: "'Oh Cécile, not so loud! Someone might hear you! You have no idea what you're reciting!' But her arm presses Cécile a little more strongly against herself and Cécile, forgetting the game, feels herself strangely moved" (72).

Such self-referentiality is particularly notable in what Grier has called the "good Lesbian paperbacks," predominantly lesbian-authored pulps offering, if not always a happy ending, at least the possibility of some measure of identification with its characters ("Lesbian Paperback," 313). As Stephanie Foote has argued compellingly, metafictional references serve as "recognition of the seriousness with which pulps were read by [...] lesbian readers" ("Deviant Classics: Pulps and the Making of Lesbian Print Culture" 169). Such novels name French literature as authoritative references and cultural currency between lesbians. In Kay Martin's *The Whispered Sex* (see fig. 5.13), one character shares "a wonderful book about our kind of love" with her lover (84). And Valerie Taylor's *Return to Lesbos*, which features a relationship between a suburban housewife and a bookstore clerk, depicts book-lined shelves as hypnotic keys to another world: when Erica comes upon Baudelaire's *The Flowers of Evil* in a bookstore, "the fascination of print took over" (44).

Shirley Verel's *The Dark Side of Venus* (1962) sets the sexual initiation of two British women in France. After timidly flirting with each other for months in London, they vacation in the Dordogne, where they become intimate and share their limited knowledge of lesbianism: "I'd read things in books, of course, something in a French girl's novel once about some horrible club where a lot of women in leather jerkins danced with a lot of other women and everyone was more or less drunk on gin. There was something in a war book I read, too, about sinister sisterhoods, and obscenity" (136–7). Such abject associations (with seedy bars, alcoholism, and vulgarity) were typical of American lesbian paperbacks, just as they were of fin-de-siècle French novels. Let us recall Mendès's *Méphistophéla*, in which the main character holds black masses and is addicted to morphine, or Zola's *Nana*, featuring a lesbian restaurant peopled by grotesque women who intermingle irrespective of social standing.

Just as pulp characters rely upon books for knowledge about and representations of their own sexuality, so did their readers. For lesbian pulps had a double audience. Targeted to male consumers, their vivid covers and suggestive titles also beckoned to unintended readers, women in search of images and a vocabulary with which to identify their sexual attractions. Although the pulps presented an overwhelmingly abject view that associated same-sex love with social marginality, betrayal, suicide, and substance abuse, there is significant evidence to show that women in search of mirrors for their difference consumed them avidly. Novelist Katherine Forrest reminisced that "A lesbian pulp fiction paperback first appeared before my disbelieving eyes in Detroit, Michigan, in 1957 [...] the cover leaped out at me from the

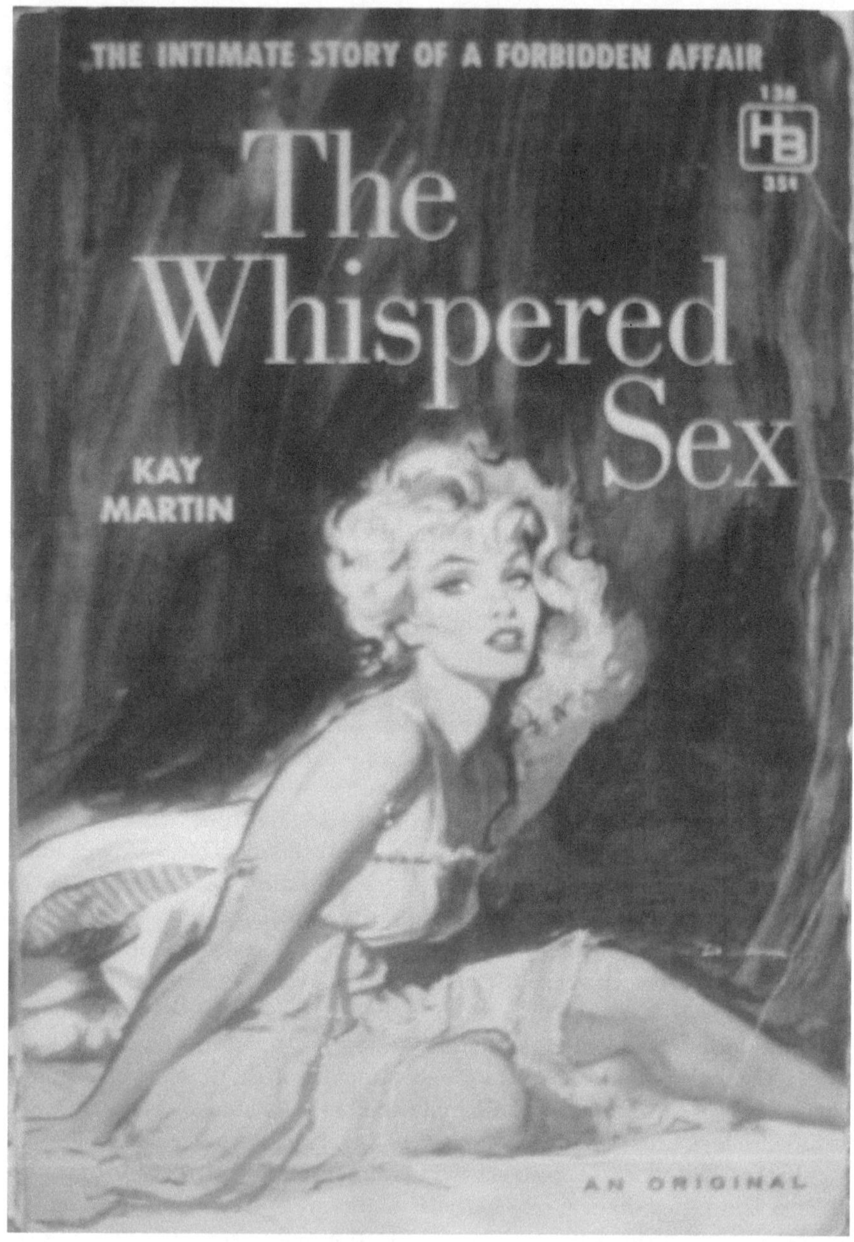

Figure 5.13. Kay Martin, *The Whispered Sex*

drugstore rack [...]. I found [the book] when I was eighteen years old. It opened the door to my soul and told me who I was. It led me to other books that told me who some of us were, and how some of us lived" (ix).

Such recollections about pulps by women coming of age and into their sexuality in the 1950s and 60s are not unusual. Indeed, their language reveals how dire and barren their environment was and how important these novels, the "good" ones and the bad, were to their sense of self. Forrest writes that the novels of Ann Bannon "saved my life," and Bertha Harris similarly employed a rhetoric of survival to explain her eager consumption of exploitive lesbian pulps: "when you are starving, a soda cracker will do."[29]

There are remarkable resemblances between late nineteenth-century France and mid-twentieth-century America: the widespread interest in homosexuality, the increased activity and visibility of sexologists and psychiatrists delving into reviled sexual practices, the broad dissemination of lesbian-themed novels thanks to new print technologies. We might surmise that another commonality lies in analogous groups of unintended readers, solitary women who could purchase suggestive titles anonymously, be that in a drugstore on Main Street or at a train station in provincial France. There is no information to tell us how many Frenchwomen of the late nineteenth century read books like Péladan's *La Gynandre*, and no testimony remains from readers claiming to have seen themselves for the first time in *Mademoiselle Giraud*. One wonders whether women would have had access to racier titles such as the pseudo-scientific *Scènes d'amour morbide* by the medical popularizer Dr Caufeynon (see fig. 5.14) or even anonymous erotic literature sold under the counter. The impact of Baudelaire's *Fleurs du Mal* (see fig. 5.15), arguably the most important collection of poetry published in France during the nineteenth century, on subsequent sapphic literature and readers also remains to be fully explored. Given the ambivalent reception by American women of books that both degraded them with portrayals of disquieting and disturbed lesbians and elated them with scenes of same-sex tenderness, I would conjecture that nineteenth-century Frenchwomen consumed lesbian literature in an analogous manner, as mirrors of representation.

Literary and non-fictional explorations of nonconformist sexuality say more about the context in which they were undertaken than about the historical realities of sexual minorities, individuals living largely in social isolation until quite recently. Although representations of female homosexuality could be called both arbitrary and ideological products, targeted specifically to an audience of men, they contributed to the growing portfolio of portraits that would amount to a heritage for sexually unconventional women excluded from society and collective memory, in search of identities, and drawn to images of and explanations for their difference.

Figure 5.14. Dr Caufeynon, *Scènes d'amour morbide*

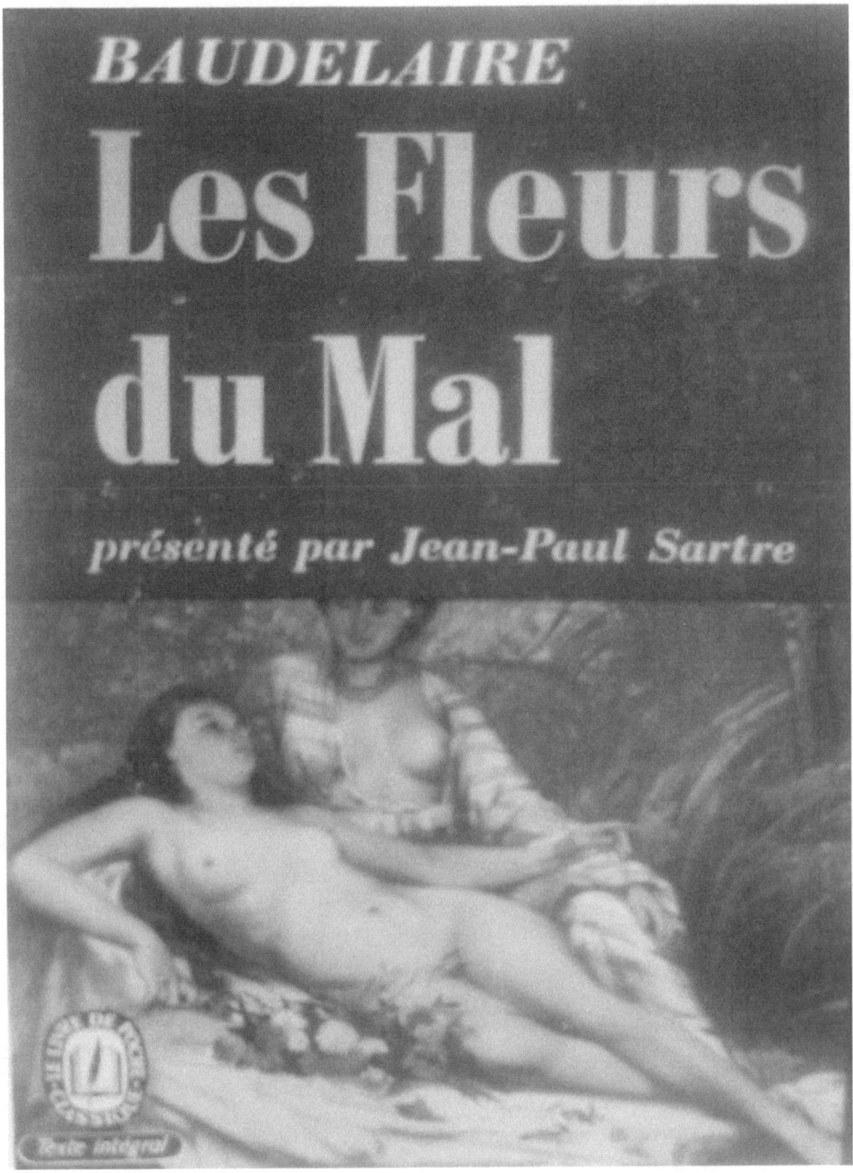

Figure 5.15. Charles Baudelaire, *Les Fleurs du Mal*

Reading American lesbian pulps through the lens of nineteenth-century French literature provides evidence that international exchanges of LGBTQ representations and cultures take many forms and were fully operative well before the information age. Moreover, it reveals the impact of nineteenth-century sapphic texts on distant identity formation and their importance for a population of readers that their authors could never have imagined. French male authors, and the pulp culture that drew from them, contributed significantly to the public recognition of the female homosexual. By inventing and diffusing her, they played a part in the construction of her identity, her values, her norms, and her myths.[30]

Notes

Introduction: Backstories

1 "Les pères saphistes [...] les frères prêcheurs de l'amour factice et de l'extase artificielle" (Lorrain, *Dans l'oratoire*, 48). Except where indicated otherwise, all translations are my own.
2 The name Bilitis was felt to be more discreet than a reference to Sappho of Lesbos, who was already broadly associated with lesbianism. See Faderman on lesbian culture in the twentieth-century United States; Gallo on the history of the DOB; Schultz ("Daughters") on the name's genealogy.
3 DeJean, 278; *The Ladder* 1 (1956): 2–3.
4 Also including titles by Barbey d'Aurevilly, Baudelaire, Belot, Diderot, Dumas *père*, Flaubert, Gautier, Louÿs, Maupassant, Mendès, Rachilde, Sand, and Verlaine. See Grier, *The Lesbian in Literature*.
5 *Dans l'oratoire*, 47, 50.
6 In fact, Castle's *Literature of Lesbianism* shows much more female-authored work published in English than what one finds in France during the nineteenth century (Rossetti, *Goblin Market*; poems by Dickinson and Michael Field, among others). English sapphic fathers include, most notably, Coleridge (*Cristabel*), Swinburne ("Anactoria," *Lesbia Brandon*), Hardy (*Desperate Remedies*), and Henry James (*The Bostonians*).
7 I borrow from categories proposed by philosopher Martha Nussbaum, who delineates seven types of objectification, as follows:
   - Instrumentality: The objectifier treats the object as a tool of his or her purposes.
   - Denial of autonomy: The objectifier treats the object as lacking in autonomy and self-determination.
   - Inertness: The objectifier treats the object as lacking in agency, and perhaps also in activity.

- Fungibility: The objectifier treats the object as interchangeable (a) with other objects of the same type, and/or (b) with objects of other types.
- Violability: The objectifier treats the object as lacking in boundary-integrity, as something that it is permissible to break up, smash, break into.
- Ownership: The objectifier treats the object as something that is owned by another, can be bought or sold, etc.
- Denial of subjectivity: The objectifier treats the object as something whose experience and feeling (if any) need not be taken into account (257).

8 "Je ne changerai plus de culte" (Belot, *Mélinite*, 257).

9 Donoghue takes this as the title for her impressive study of desire between women in literature. While *Inseparable* is primarily devoted to English-language texts, it also touches upon a number of French sapphic fictions from the twelfth through the twentieth centuries.

10 Choux, 344; Martineau, *Prostitution clandestine*, 89.

11 Halperin, 51; Delvau, *Dictionnaire de la langue verte*, 276, original emphasis.

12 Parent-Duchâtelet, 69n1; Sue, 363; Banville, *Parisiennes*, 169; Christian, 362; Dubut de Laforest, 80; Taxil, *Corruption*, 246.

13 Moll, 225; Chevalier, *L'Inversion sexuelle*, 250.

14 Moll, 225.

15 Chevalier, *L'Inversion sexuelle*, 250.

16 On the vocabulary of sapphism, see Brécourt-Villars, *Petit Glossaire raisonné de l'érotisme saphique*. See also DeJean, *Fictions of Sappho*.

17 See histories of homosexuality by, among others, Bonnet, Gunther, Halperin, Tamagne, Vicinus.

18 "They Wonder," 470. See also Marcus, "Quelques problèmes," on the difficulties posed by the project of determining a history of lesbianism.

19 Judith Bennett has noted that gay and lesbian history is "relatively poor in scholarship about the ordinary lives of average people" (1). She explains that "Women wrote less; their writings survived less often (Sappho's works are the classic example); and they were less likely than men to come to the attention of civic or religious authorities" (2). Existing scholarship relies heavily on prominent figures, such as Vicinus's authoritative *Intimate Friends* or Lillian Faderman's *Surpassing the Love of Men*.

20 On non-elite lesbian populations in Paris, see in particular Albert, "De la topographie invisible"; Choquette, "Homosexuals in the City"; Sautman, "Invisible Women."

21 There is a small but growing body of scholarship on lesbian representations in France during the nineteenth and early twentieth centuries. I would like in particular to point to Nicole Albert's rich and authoritative *Saphisme et décadence* and Melanie Hawthorne's research on Natalie Clifford Barney, both invaluable to my study. See also Waelti-Walters, *Lesbians in French Novels*, and Latimer, *Women Together/Women Apart*, which treats visual representations.

22 See Ladenson's volume, *Men and Lesbianism*, which includes Schor's "Male Lesbianism," and Ladenson's insightful reading of *Proust's Lesbianism*.

23 See extensive bibliographies in Bonnet and Foster. Castle (*Literature*) and Donoghue also provide broad panoramas of lesbianism in literature. See also Albert's comprehensive bibliography of nineteenth-century French texts (*Saphisme*).

24 On the medieval period, see Amer, *Crossing Borders*. On the early modern period, see Crawford, *European Sexualities, 1400–1800*.

25 140. On the eighteenth century, see also Wahl, *Invisible Relations*; Lanser, "Au sein de vos pareilles"; Rivers, "Safe Sex"; Corbin, *Harmonie des plaisirs*, esp. 416–21.

26 See Colwill, "Marie-Antoinette as Tribade."

27 See Richardot, "La Secte des anandrynes."

28 See Merrick, "The Marquis de Villette and Mlle de Raucourt"; Vial, *La Raucourt & ses amies*.

29 See Jacques, 31–2.

30 See Monneyron, *L'Androgyne romantique*, V. Thompson, and Weil.

31 See Lucey, *Misfit*, on Balzac.

32 Balzac's other forays into sexual otherness include the homosexual criminal Vautrin (modelled after his contemporary, the notorious crook-turned-chief-of-police, Eugène Vidocq), a recurring character who appears in several novels of the *Comédie humaine*, and the sexualized relationship between a soldier and a panther described his short story "Passion dans le désert."

33 Dans les chemins foulés par la chasse maudite,
Un doux gazon fleuri caresse Hermaphrodite.
Tandis que, ralliant les meutes de la voix,
Artémis court auprès de ses guerrières, vois,
Le bel Être est assis auprès d'une fontaine.
Il tressaille à demi dans sa pose incertaine,
En écoutant au loin mourir le son du cor
D'ivoire. Quand le bruit cesse, il écoute encor.
Il songe tristement aux Nymphes et soupire,
Et, retenant un cri qui sur sa lèvre expire,
Se penche vers la source où dans un clair bassin
Son torse de jeune homme héroïque, et son sein
De vierge pâlissante au flot pur se reflète,
Et des pleurs font briller ses yeux de violette.

34 Torres, *Les Années anglaises*, 99; *Jeunes femmes*, 143.

35 See Leclerc, *Crimes écrits*. On books prosecuted for lesbian content in particular, see Albert, "Books on Trial."

36 See Maugue, *L'Identité masculine en crise* (1987); Nye, *Masculinity and Male Codes of Honor* (1993); Dijkstra, *Evil Sisters* (1996); Forth, *The Dreyfus Affair and the Crisis of French Manhood* (2004); Surkis, *Sexing the Citizen* (2006).

37 Offen, 659, emphasis added. In her groundbreaking article "Depopulation, Nationalism, and Feminism," Offen demonstrated the interrelatedness of depopulation and the "woman question."

38 Social historian Christophe Charle has noted the "irreversible tendency to multiply repressive measures against categories regarded as irremediably deviant and liable to disturb the social order" during this period (*Social History*, 257).

39 This law nonetheless continued the injunction against immoral acts (*attentat aux mœurs*) and a number of sapphic novels were prosecuted, including Adam's *Chair molle* and Maizeroy's *Deux amies*.

40 See Lyons, *Readers and Society*, on new reading populations.

41 Quoted in Angenot, "Des romans pour les femmes," 328.

42 Angenot, "Des romans pour les femmes," 318.

43 Angenot, *Le Cru*, 130.

44 *Experimental Novel*, 124–5.

45 See Clark, *Schooling the Daughters of Marianne.*

46 See Accampo et al., *Gender and the Politics of Social Reform in France, 1870–1914*, in particular chapter 3. See also Copley, *Sexual Moralities in France.*

47 *Ève dans l'humanité,* 46.

48 *Ève dans l'humanité,* 85, 92, 82.

49 61. Deraismes adamantly disagreed with the utopian socialist feminists who, although sharing some of her political agenda (marriage reform, divorce), sought to abolish the family as the primary social unit and championed sexual freedom in the couple. Utopian feminists "proclaimed free love in the name of the absolute equality of the two sexes" (Deraismes, *Ève dans l'humanité*, 58). In *Ma loi d'avenir* (written sixty years earlier, in 1833), Claire Démar affirmed that "the basis of the new moral will be freedom without rules or limits" (32) and championed free love, "bodies essaying bodies" [l'essai de la chair par la chair] (36). Deraismes refuted the Saint-Simonians and Fourierists, considering their stance to be amoral and counterproductive insofar as it scandalized the public. The gulf between socialist utopians and first-wave feminists has been characterized as the opposition between difference and equality feminism by Goldberg Moses. Deraismes portrayed women as strong, while Démar valorized femininity even in its weakness. The strategies of each conformed to the possibilities and obstacles offered by their cultural and political climates: the celebration of a passive but free femininity for utopian feminism and that of an active, maternal femininity for republicans. Démar's idealism and support of workers were politically more radical, while Deraismes's bourgeois pragmatism gave more credence to women's capabilities in the public sphere.

50 Demands for sexual freedom, such as those uttered a generation later by Madeleine Pelletier in *L'Émancipation sexuelle de la femme* (1911), were met with withering ridicule, even from the left. While calling for erotic freedom, Pelletier herself sacrificed an intimate life in exchange for becoming France's first woman doctor, among other accomplishments.
51 On women and the Commune, see Eichner, Gullickson.
52 Lidsky, 112.
53 See Bard, "Antiféminismes de la première vague."
54 *La Pornocratie, ou Les Femmes dans les temps modernes*, 59.
55 Historian Jules Michelet contributed another stridently misogynist voice from the left. Author of *L'Amour* (1858), *La Femme* (1859), and *La Sorcière* (1862), Michelet wrote notoriously that "15 to 20 days a month (that is, nearly always), woman is not merely ill, she is wounded. She ceaselessly endures the eternal wound of love" (*L'Amour*, 8–9). Feminist responses to Proudhon and Michelet included Juliette Lamber, *Idées antiproudhoniennes sur l'amour, la femme et le mariage* (1858); Héricourt, *La femme affranchie: Réponse à Michelet, Proudhon, Girardin, Comte* (1860); Léo, *La Femme et les mœurs: Monarchie ou liberté* (1869).
56 Margueritte, 755, emphasis added.
57 Renooz, 185, emphasis added.
58 Laloë, 410, emphasis added.
59 Belot, *Mélinite*, 60; Mendès, *Méphistophéla*, 490.

1. The Poetics of Lesbian Identification

1 Portions of this chapter were previously published in different form as "Gender, Sexuality and Poetic Identification" in *Nottingham French Studies*.
2 "The virile Sappho, [woman] lover and poet." All translations from *Les Fleurs du Mal* are by Keith Waldrop, unless otherwise noted. Modifications of Waldrop's translations are indicated with brackets.
3 Régnier, 61. My translation.
4 An exception: "objective" poetry, such as Parnassian poetry, privileges description and has very little to say about interior lives.
5 "Homme, il est doux comme une femme" (Hugo, 1:424); "Moi, j'emprunte une voix de femme / … / Mes soupirs, passant par ton âme, / Ont plus de pleurs et plus d'encens!" (Lamartine, 290).
6 Leconte de Lisle, 170.
7 As I am focusing here on male-authored poetry, I will have little to say about poetry by women. However, female poets had greater liberty to let their speaking subjects slip into either gender position: the feminine, which agreed with the author's sex, or the masculine, which agreed with the historically male poet. See my *Gendered Lyric*.

8 Translations from *Journaux intimes* by Christopher Isherwood (*Intimate Journals*, 71, 14, 37, 40). "la seule chose qui vaille la peine de tourner un sonnet" ("Maximes consolantes sur l'amour," *Œuvres*, 1:552); "Il y a dans l'acte de l'amour une grande ressemblance avec la torture, ou avec une opération chirurgicale"; "Ce qu'il y a d'ennuyeux dans l'amour, c'est que c'est un crime où l'on ne peut pas se passer de complice"; "tout amour est [...] prostitution" (*Journaux intimes*, in *Œuvres*, 1:659, 689, 692).

9 *Intimate Journals*, 31–2, translation modified. "Il y a dans tout homme, à toute heure, deux postulations simultanées, l'une vers Dieu, l'autre vers Satan. L'invocation à Dieu, ou spiritualité, est un désir de monter en grade; celle de Satan, ou animalité, est une joie de descendre. C'est à cette dernière que doivent être rapportés les amours pour les femmes et les conversations intimes avec les animaux, chiens, chats, etc. Les joies qui dérivent de ces deux amours sont adaptées à la nature de ces deux amours" (*Œuvres*, 1:682–3).

10 *Intimate Journals*, 40. "Le besoin de sortir de soi" (1:692).

11 *Intimate Journals*, 65. "la jouissance de la laideur provient d'un sentiment encore plus mystérieux, qui est la soif de l'inconnu, et le goût de l'horrible" (1:548–9).

12 "la grossièreté belge"; "bassesse et domesticité"; "férocité, stupidité, avarice, bestialité réunies"; "impiété belge" (*Œuvres*, 2:839, 840, 844, 886). Translations from *Pauvre Belgique!* are mine.

13 "Il est difficile d'assigner une place au Belge dans l'échelle des êtres"; (*Œuvres*, 2:845) "le Belge [...] est un ver qu'on a oublié d'écraser. Il est complètement bête, mais il est résistant comme les mollusques"; "Il flotte depuis le mollusque jusqu'au singe"; "Les Belges sont des *Ruminants* qui ne digèrent rien"; "Peuples grenouilles voulant faire les bœufs"; "curiosité bestiale, semblable à celle des canards qui viennent en troupe" (*Œuvres*, 2:954, 845, 853, 956, 868).

14 "L'animal lui-même fuit ces contrées maudites" (2:944).

15 *Intimate Journals*, 25 ("la femme est *naturelle*, c'est-à-dire abominable," 1:677). "De la tyrannie des faibles. Les femmes et les animaux"; "Type général de physionomie, analogue à celui du mouton et du bélier"; "des jambes d'éléphant [...] et le rengorgement d'un pigeon [...] Poules, pimbêches, pies-grièches" (2:919, 836, 837).

16 "Comme Joubert remerciait Dieu de l'avoir fait homme et non femme, vous le remercierez de vous avoir fait, non pas Belge, mais Français" (2:819).

17 "Pas de *femmes*, pas *d'amour*. [...] Ici, il y a des *femelles*"; "Ce qu'on appelle amour ici est une pure gymnastique animale que je n'ai pas à vous décrire"; "Les Belges croient que la galanterie veut dire bestialité" (2:836, 839, 840).

18 *Intimate Journals*, 35; "nous ne pouvons faire l'amour qu'avec des organes excrémentiels" (1:688).

19 "Amour prodigieux des excréments qu'on retrouve dans les anciens tableaux"; "plaisanteries excrémentielles"; "Il faut voir les quartiers pauvres, et les enfants

nus se rouler dans les excréments. Cependant je ne crois pas qu'ils les mangent"; "La Belgique est un *bâton merdeux*" (2:839, 860, 870, 919); "La mère Belge, sur ses latrines (porte ouverte), joue avec son enfant"; "Pisseries et chieries des dames belges. [...] Dans une petite rue, six dames belges pissant, barrent le passage, les unes debout, les autres accroupies" (2:839).

20 "Manière dont s'exprime le deuil belge. – Ivrognerie, pisseries, vomissements" (2:929). Cf. Carpenter, "Effigies et contrefaçons nationales: *Pauvre Belgique!*"

21 "Penser en bande, pisser en bande"; "Rien de mystérieux, de profond [...] comme le Néant"; "L'ivresse belge [...] bestial[e]: père ivre châtre son fils" (2:858, 867, 842).

22 "Haine de la Beauté"; "L'homme dégradé s'admirerait et appellerait la beauté laideur. Voyez les déplorables Belges" (2:868, 831).

23 "Pas d'artistes, excepté Rops"; "Goût national de l'ignoble"; "L'amateur des beaux-arts en Belgique"; "Pas de composition, ou composition ridicule. Sujets ignobles, pisseurs, chieurs et vomisseurs. Plaisanteries dégoûtantes et monotones" (2:931–2).

24 "Beauté de la sculpture coloriée. [...] Mon attendrissement. [...] [Église] Sainte-Catherine. Parfum exotique. [...] Vierges peintes, fardées et parées" (2:942). "chez la femme, pas de coquetterie"; "Coquetterie religieuse. Le culte de Marie, très beau" (2:838, 944). "Pas de toilette"; "Costumes: hideuse animalité"; "toilette de communiante" (2:832, 872, 949).

25 Translations of *Peintre* by Jonathan Mayne (*Painter of Modern Life*, 32). "Éloge du maquillage": "Tout ce qui est beau et noble est le résultat de la raison et du calcul. Le crime, dont l'animal humain a puisé le goût dans le ventre de sa mère, est originellement naturel. La vertu, au contraire, est *artificielle*" (2:715).

26 *Painter*, 30; "la source des plus vives [...] des plus durables jouissances"; "une divinité, un astre, qui préside à toutes les conceptions du cerveau mâle"; "pour qui, mais surtout *par qui* les artistes et les poètes composent leurs plus délicats bijoux" (2:713).

27 *Painter*, 30; "Tout ce qui orne la femme, tout ce qui sert à illustrer sa beauté, fait partie d'elle-même [...] elle est surtout une harmonie générale, non seulement dans son allure et le mouvement de ses membres, mais aussi dans les mousselines, les gazes, les vastes et chatoyantes nuées d'étoffes dont elle s'enveloppe" (2:714).

28 *Painter*, 31. "quel poète oserait [...] séparer la femme de son costume"; "l'homme [... fait] ainsi des deux, de la femme et de la robe, une totalité indivisible" (2:714).

29 *Painter*, 33. "idole, [la femme] doit se dorer pour être adorée" (2:717).

30 *Painter*, 32. "Le mal se fait sans effort, naturellement, par fatalité; le bien est toujours le produit d'un art" (2:715).

31 *Painter*, 32, translation modified, emphasis added. "c'est cette infaillible nature qui a créé le parricide et l'anthropophagie, et mille autres abominations que *la pudeur et la délicatesse nous empêchent de nommer*" (2:715).

32 *Painter*, 34, 33. "a pour but et pour résultat de faire disparaître du teint toutes les taches que la nature y a outrageusement semées"; "qui oserait assigner à l'art la fonction stérile d'imiter la nature?" (2:717).

33 *Painter*, 32, 31. "la fausse conception du XVIIIe siècle"; "Je suis ainsi conduit à regarder la parure comme un des signes de la noblesse primitive de l'âme humaine" (2:716, 715).
34 *Flowers*, 54. "de l'abîme profond / Jusqu'au plus haut du ciel" (1:41). *Painter*, 38. "nous sommes descendus [...] jusqu'à la fœmina simplex" (2:721).
35 *Painter*, 35. "grande drôlesse à qui il ne manque presque rien (ce presque rien, c'est presque tout, c'est la distinction) pour ressembler à une grande dame" (2:719). While similarly identifying the social implications of taste, Baudelaire undeniably lacked Bourdieu's critique of power in relation to judgments of taste.
36 *Flowers*, 33. "tu rends [. . .] l'univers moins hideux et les instants moins lourds."
37 *Intimate Journals*, 49; *Œuvres*, 1:702.
38 *Painter*, 28. "cette doctrine de l'élégance et de l'originalité" (2:711). "la coquetterie militaire" (2:707).
39 "Baudelaire's Lesbian Connections."
40 See Castle's groundbreaking *The Apparitional Lesbian* for a discussion of the "ghosting" effect in lesbian representations.
41 For example: Lucie Delarue-Mardrus, *Nos secrètes amours* (1951); Violette Leduc, *Thérèse et Isabelle* (1966); Françoise Mallet-Joris, *Le Rempart des béguines* (1951).
42 Baudelaire, *Fleurs*, 413n5.
43 *Filles*, 490–6. All citations, unless otherwise noted, from *Œuvres*. My translation.
44 *Hombres*, 32–3. My translations.
45 Nineteenth-century lexicographer Émile Littré once referred to the convention of rhyme gender as "grammatical childishness" (1:334–5).
46 *Les Amies* in *Œuvres*, 486–9. Translations by Norma Cole and Erin Mouré in Castle, *Literature*, 478–81.
47 Huret, 103.
48 *Selected Poems*, 71 (translated by Martin Sorrell); *Œuvres*, 193. My translations, below, from "Ballade Sappho" (*Œuvres*, 528).
49 Cazals, 441. See also Schultz, "Sexualités de Verlaine."
50 On the hendecasyllable and the poetic bond it represented between Verlaine and Rimbaud, see Schultz, *Gendered Lyric*.

2. Tribades for Sale: Popular Fiction and Backroom Books

1 On mass print culture, see Kalifa, *La Culture de masse*. See also Allen, *In the Public Eye: A History of Reading in Modern France*.
2 See Dumasy, *La Querelle du roman-feuilleton*.
3 See Lyons, *Readers and Society in Nineteenth-Century France*.
4 Queffélec-Dumasy, chapter 2, III. And Charle has argued that "Complaints about commercial literature voiced repeatedly in literary circles came not from disillusioned moralists, but rather reflected competition for the limited space in daily newspapers" (*Crise littéraire*, 48).

5 Compère, 5.

6 Other sapphic potboilers of the period include René Maizeroy, *Deux amies* (1885); Paul Margueritte, *Tous quatre* (1885); Maurice de Souillac, *Zé'Boïm: Étude de mœurs* (1887); Jean Lombard, *L'Agonie* (1888); Henri d'Argis, *Gomorrhe* (1889); Albert Cim, *Les Bas-bleus: Adolphine la lesbienne* (1891); Paul Adam, *Les Cœurs utiles* (1892); Jane de la Vaudère, *Les Demi-sexes* (1896); Armand Dubarry, *Les Invertis: Vice allemand* (1896); Luis d'Herdy, *Monsieur Antinoüs et Madame Sapho* (1899).

7 See Rivers's analysis of the novel as commercial literature ("Introduction").

8 Audouard, *Silhouettes,* 313.

9 Alante-Lima.

10 Peck, "Emile Zola," 233.

11 Vol. 3: 475. 1 August 1885. Belot's divorce is said to have inspired Alphonse Daudet's *Rose et Ninette*. See White, "Paternal Perspectives on Divorce."

12 Crime fiction was a very young genre indebted to such writers as Émile Gaboriau (1832–73), whose detective Lecoq debuted in *L'Affaire Lerouge* (1866), and Fortuné du Boisgobey (1824–91), author of *Le Forçat colonel* (1872) and *La Main froide* (1889). Belot's own detective novels include *La Vénus de Gordes* (1866), *Le Drame de la Rue de la Paix* (1867), *L'Article* 47 (1873), *Les Mystères mondains* (1875), *Les Étrangleurs de Paris* (1879), *Fleur-de-crime* (1882), and *Une femme du monde à Saint-Lazare* (1891).

13 Belot's thematic scope corresponds with his generic breadth. While I focus here on his representation of sexuality, his work notably touches as well on issues of race, reflecting contemporary preoccupation with colonial expansion, such as in *Vénus noire, voyage dans l'Afrique centrale*. See Seillan, "De la scène du vaudeville au théâtre du fantasme: L'Afrique d'Adolphe Belot dans *La Vénus noire*." He also wrote travel literature, drawing on his extensive foreign travel as source material.

14 Similarly, *Deux femmes* (1873) is not, in fact, the story of a couple of women, but rather the repackaging of two separate novellas previously published under separate covers. *Les Baigneuses de Trouville* (1875) and *Madame Vitel et Mademoiselle Lelièvre* (1875) also rely on heterosexual plots.

15 Some contemporary critics gave Belot bad press for recycling his work: "Our literary customs too readily indulge the habit of pulling two or more works from a single idea" (Vapereau, 6:139).

16 The journal goes on to note that "when Belot died, his wife told her friends, 'they owe him his trimester at Monte Carlo,' where he earned 6,000 francs per year" (Goncourt, *Journal*, 4:40).

17 See Marquardt's extensive "Bio-Bibliography of Adolphe Belot" (1973). Although it contains some errors and omissions, it is the most comprehensive to date. It enumerates translations from twelve countries, an indication of Belot's international renown.

18 Belot "was several times a member of the Société des Gens de Lettres. He is honorary vice president of the Association littéraire internationale and Chevalier de la Légion d'honneur since 1867" (Lermina, 134).
19 Cf. the Goncourt journal: "Sunday 5 January 1873. Flaubert wrote to me: 'it's not right, not right at all!' It's absolutely true, and it's killing this man of great talent: his rage in witnessing Droz and Belot's commercial success, his jealousy of big money, the lowly craving for the big publicity of lowly literature" (2:925).
20 *Journal*, 3:399.
21 "L'immonde mystère" (Feydeau, *Comtesse*, 321).
22 See Rivers on Zola's and Belot's mutually profitable professional relationship ("Introduction") and Seillan on their rivalry ("*Mademoiselle Giraud*").
23 Niees, 115.
24 Goncourt, *Journal*, 3:612.
25 Goncourt, *Journal*, 3:516.
26 "Littérature(s) populaire(s)," 98. See also Frigerio.
27 Thiesse, *Roman du quotidien*; Angenot, "Des romans pour les femmes." See also Lyons (*Readers and Society*) and Allen.
28 "Des romans," 329.
29 9. Translation of *Mademoiselle Giraud* by C. Rivers.
30 See Alexis, *Émile Zola*, 74–5.
31 Zola's short text, "Au couvent" (1870), names Belot and sings the same theme of "monstrous passions that are formed in the intimacy of a convent" (368). See also *Zola et les historiens*, especially contributions by Boutry on Zola's anticlericalism and Cadier-Rey on education for girls in his work.
32 Seillan has analysed incoherence of narrative viewpoint in "*Mademoiselle Giraud*."
33 See Todorov, "Typologie du roman policier," in which he discerned three kinds of detective novels: the classic *roman à énigme* or whodunit, the hard-boiled *roman noir*, and the *roman à suspense* or thriller.
34 Taxil, *Corruption*, 258.
35 Debay, *Hygiène*, 290.
36 On sexual curiosity in women, see Corbin, *Harmonie*, 356 ff.
37 Its inventor was wrongly accused of selling it to the enemy, thus drawing even more attention to the explosive. "La Mélinite," a popular song composed by Jules Jouy in 1887, celebrates it ironically. The song begins:

> I' faut le r'connaître, un' jolie invention
> C'est celle de la mélinite.
> Ça fait honneur à la civilisation,
> D' produir' des matièr's de c' mérite.

C'est joli, ça r'ssemble à du miel;
Mais ça fait sauter vingt maisons jusqu'au ciel.
Un simple choc et patatras!
Ça vous coup' la gueule à quinz' pas! (42)

[You have to admit that melinite is a nice invention. Producing materials of this merit does justice to civilization. It's pretty, it looks like honey, but it can blow twenty houses up to the sky. A little bump and crash! You'll smell it a mile away!]

The reputedly lesbian cabaret dancer Jane Avril, immortalized in Toulouse-Lautrec's posters, was also known as La Mélinite.

38 Other, less flamboyant tribades blend in: "Cette femme était habillée sans aucune excentricité" (Prille, 173).

39 Joseph Sheridan Le Fanu wrote "Carmilla" (1871), the classic lesbian vampire tale, a genre that has since recently received a good deal of attention. See, for example, Keesey, *Daughters of Darkness: Lesbian Vampire Tales.*

40 273. On the supposed perils of sexual privation for men, see Corbin, *Harmonie*, 117 ff.

41 *Gamiani* has been attributed to Alfred de Musset, *Sélect luxure* more dubiously so to Belot.

42 See Binet's analysis of this character's "fétichisme de la bouche" in *Étude de psychologie expérimentale* (78–82).

43 Works subject to prosecution included "Une fille" (Maupassant, 1880), *Autour d'un clocher* (Desprez, 1884), *Charlot s'amuse* (Bonnetain, 1884), *Monsieur Vénus* (Rachilde, 1884), *Deux amies* (Maizeroy, 1885), *Chair molle* (Adam, 1885), *Gaga* (Dubut de Laforest, 1886), *L'Enfant du crapaud* (Lemonnier, 1888). Cf. Leclerc, *Crimes écrits.*

44 Audouard authored a number of feminist books, including *Guerre aux hommes* (1866), *La Femme dans le mariage, la séparation et le divorce* (1870), and *Gynécologie, la femme depuis six mille ans* (1873). She also shared a publisher, Dentu, with Belot.

45 145. See also Lanser, "*Au sein de vos pareilles*: Sapphic Separatism in Late Eighteenth-Century France"; Merrick, "Sexual Politics and Public Order in Late Eighteenth-Century France." See also Cryle's "Lesbos" chapter in his study of eighteenth- and nineteenth-century erotica.

46 And a very few women writers of erotica, including the Countess de Choiseul-Meuse and the Marquise de Mannoury d'Ectot. On women-authored French erotica of the period, see Frappier-Mazur, "Marginal Canons: Rewriting the Erotic." On Choiseul-Meuse, see Glessner.

47 See Alexandrian, *L'Érotisme au XIX*[e] *siècle.*

48 See Perceau, *Bibliographie du roman érotique au 19e siècle*; Pia, *Dictionnaire des œuvres érotiques*; Dutel, *Bibliographie des ouvrages érotiques*.

49 Original editions, with full titles and Dutel's descriptive notes: *L'Éducation d'une demi-vierge* (Paris, 1883), "The story of a demi-mondaine pending divorce who initiates her daughter into the secrets of brothels"; *La Maison à plaisirs, ou La Passion de Gilberte* (Amsterdam: A. Brancart, 1888), "La Maison à Plaisirs is one of those mysterious refuges known only to a hand-picked clientele, a place of aristocratic debauchery where one has to state one's credentials in order to gain entry"; *Les Heures érotiques modernes, comprenant "La Petite bourgeoise," "Le Rat," "Bouillie de maïs," Trois nouvelles inédites par l'auteur de La Maison à Plaisirs* (Amsterdam, 1890); *Les Péchés de Minette* (Brussels: Kistemaeckers, c. 1890), "A young woman newly married to the husband of her dreams, a husband who is also truly a lover and who introduces his better half to all the practices of libertinage"; *La Canonisation de Jeanne d'Arc, Histoire amoureuse d'une soirée fin de siècle précédée de L'Art de payer sa couturière, pièce érotique en un acte* (Amsterdam: A. Brancart, 1890), "*La Canonisation de Jeanne d'Arc* is merely a pretext for socialites, elegant and aristocratic Parisiennes, to get together with their lovers. The author appears to be perfectly well acquainted with those mysterious Parisian orgies of which some have heard tell, but in which only a small number of initiates can boast of participating"; and *Stations de l'amour: Lettres de l'Inde et de Paris* (Brussels: Kistemaeckers, 1896), "the love story of a married couple temporarily separated from one another."

50 Particularly the final three, published as sequels to the earlier *L'Éducation d'une demi-vierge*: *Toute la lyre! Manœuvres de Lucienne, Suite et fin de l'Éducation d'une demi-vierge* (1911); *Sélect luxure ou Variations sur Toute la lyre* (1911); and *La Luxure en ménage* (1912). The language of degeneration and vice in these contrasts patently with the celebratory sexuality of the earlier erotic novels, pointing to a different author. Dutel also notes that *Une aventure photographique ou la Chandelle de Sixte-Quinte* (1893) is attributed to "the author of *la Maison à plaisir* [*sic*]" (86–7).

51 Unattributed source cited in Alexandrian. Original source: "Préface" to A. Belot, *L'Éducation d'une demi-vierge*, 9, original italics.

3. Dystopian Sapphism: Anti-Feminism, Class Warfare, and the Elite Novel at the Fin de Siècle

1 "ces deux états de la femme: la prostitution et l'aristocratie, la Fille et la Grande Dame" (Mendès, *Méphistophéla*, 254).

2 "étant donné un homme puissant et une femme inassouvie, chercher en eux

la bête, ne voir même que la bête, les jeter dans un drame violent, et noter scrupuleusement les sensations et les actes de ces êtres" (preface).

3 "mon but a été un but scientifique avant tout [...] J'ai simplement fait sur deux corps vivants le travail analytique que les chirurgiens font sur des cadavres." Although beside the point of this study, it is curious to note that the *fait divers* itself provided the pulpiest plot of all. It occurred on Christmas Eve, 1861, when the victim was shot by his rival just before midnight mass. Its dénouement involved such elements as a penal colony, a prison escape, a self-sacrificing second lover, death from yellow fever, and a virtuous bastard child (see Brotte).

4 *Experimental Novel*, 87.

5 "vérifier par des expériences en laboratoire l'existence des lois qu'on a cru discerner dans la nature"; "on donne aujourd'hui une prépondérance exagérée à la forme [...] Nous sommes actuellement pourris de lyrisme" (84).

6 *Roman naturaliste*, 3.

7 "une crise de pudibonderie ridicule" (*Roman*).

8 See Sacquin, "Entre positivisme et laïcité."

9 "la littérature est au sommet avec la science"; "spéculateurs de la vertu"; "ceux qui prennent la spécialité de ne pas faire rougir les femmes et ceux qui mettent leur gain à les faire rougir [...] les véritables artistes [...] n'écrivent pas pour une classe, ils ont l'ambition d'écrire pour les siècles [...] sans s'inquiéter du scandale de leurs audaces" (*Roman*, 328, 335, 336).

10 Bourdieu, *Rules*, 116. Substantial commercial success, a sign of mass appeal, in fact worked against positive critical recognition. Naturalists therefore maintained a symbolically inferior position, "close to commercial literature" (Charle, *Paris fin-de-siècle*, 78).

11 On the evolution of literary value with respect to the novel, see Charle, who notes that "the hierarchy of literary values evolves, and the novel achieves academic approval as early as the Empire, but particularly under the Third Republic with the urbane psychological novel, intended for the dominant class in reaction to the 'vulgar' naturalist novel" (*Crise littéraire*, 33).

12 See Marquèze-Pouey on decadent poetry.

13 Huret, 100.

14 See Stephen, *Paul Verlaine and the Decadence.*

15 See Ponton on the *roman psychologique*.

16 More recently, scholars such as Hawthorne have noted that Rachilde's *Monsieur Vénus*, published the same year, deserves similar credit.

17 "[l'école naturaliste] n'admettait guère, en théorie du moins, l'exception; elle se confinait donc dans la peinture de l'existence commune, s'efforçait, sous prétexte de faire vivant, de créer des êtres qui fussent aussi semblables que possible à la bonne moyenne des gens"; "Nous autres, moins râblés et préoccupés d'un art plus

subtil et plus vrai, nous devions nous demander si le naturalisme n'aboutissait pas à une impasse" (19, 22).

18 Besnard-Coursodon, 119. Besnard-Coursodon offers an excellent analysis of the political implications of Péladan's œuvre. One sees an analogous divide among some contemporary critics of decadent literature. Birkett focuses on the ambiguity of the decadent aesthetic, pointing to the liberating potential of decadent literature. She affirms its power to "facilitate [...] the potential for social change" and "imagine new relationships" (31). In contrast, Constable has studied reactionary aspects of decadence, seeing in Barrès, for example, a link between his fascism and his aestheticism.

19 On the importance of positivist philosophy for the period, see *Les Positivismes.*

20 Charles, *Paris*, 178.

21 Ziegler, *Beauty*, 36.

22 "Que Dreyfus ait trahi, je le conclus de sa race."

23 See Angenot, "'Un juif trahira': La Préfiguration de l'Affaire Dreyfus."

24 Bourdieu, *Rules*; Charle, *Crise*. See also Datta and Silverman, *Intellectuals and the Dreyfus Affair*.

25 Charle's analysis is fascinating and goes well beyond the naturalist/decadent split. He shows that those associated with the dominant literary pole of the period, which is to say those with a stake in literary traditionalism or institutional approval (members of the Académie française, psychological novelists, Parnassian poets), were overwhelmingly against Dreyfus, while those on the "dominated" pole were largely supportive of him: the avant-garde of poetry and theatre. Charle places the naturalists in the middle of the "secteur de grande production" (*Crise*, 162).

26 The naturalist project has been deconstructed many times over. It was, of course, neither scientific nor objectively neutral. Rather, its pretension of neutrality cloaked sometimes acerbic social commentary (this is particularly so of Maupassant).

27 Because associated with Puritanism, which Zola blamed for much of the criticism his novels received.

28 Ziegler interprets the ascension of decadent writers following 1884 as indicative of a "rupture with their naturalist predecessors" and details the points of contrast between them (27). Other critics have focused on their commonalities. For example, Bernheimer asserts with reason that "Most naturalist texts include, or [...] produce decadent moments, whereas the sense of natural process that subtends most decadent texts is entirely naturalistic in character" (*Decadent Subjects*, 58). While I would take issue with Bernheimer's hyperbolic "most," it is true that the lines of demarcation can scramble. Other critics who have elaborated upon their

proximity include Thorel-Cailleteau ("le naturalisme aigu et la décadence se rejoignent," 413).

29 Henri d'Argis, Dubut de Laforest, Camille Lemonnier, Octave Mirbeau, to name a few writers who draw from both literary tendencies.

30 Ziegler has argued that decadence rejected naturalism's "infatuation with science and so disavowed the principle of environmental and hereditary determinism" (*Beauty*, 29).

31 The most notable exception is Balzac's Vautrin cycle. The few realist treatments of the subject were predictably abject (e.g., Joseph Méry, *Monsieur Auguste*, 1859). Homosexuality also made its way into military novels, such as Lucien Descaves's *Sous-offs, roman militaire* (1889) and Georges Darien's *Biribi* (1890). Pierre Loti's work exceptionally provides subjective, if veiled portraits of male homoeroticism, as in *Mon frère Yves* (1883).

32 "l'âme d'une femme réside dans les nerfs" (Péladan, *Gynandre*, 53).

33 Verlaine famously composed "Le Sonnet du trou du cul" with Rimbaud and later published some homoerotic poems in *Parallèlement* (1889) and the erotic collection *Hombres* (1904). While Lorrain's work dealt with gender and sexual nonconformity more tentatively in men than in women, his novels *Le Vice errant* (1900) and, most notably, *Monsieur de Phocas* (1901) were groundbreaking, and his poetry more candid still. Belgian writer and militant Eekhoud was tried but not convicted for his pioneering novel, *Escal-Vigor* (1899).

On this emergent literature, see, for example, Cardon (*Discours littéraires*), Carter (*Proust in Love*), Dubuis (*Émergence de l'homosexualité*), Ladenson (*Proust's Lesbianism*), Lucey (*Never Say I, Gide's Bent*), Lucien (*Akademos, Georges Eekhoud*), Revenin (*Hommes et masculinités*), Schehr (*French Gay Modernism*), Sedgwick (*Epistemology*), Winn (*Sexualités décadentes chez Jean Lorrain*).

34 See, for example, Sinfield, *The Wilde Century*, and Hanson, *Decadence and Catholicism*.

35 "les démocrates, [...] goujats faits pour obéir"; "races faites pour commander" (Barbey d'Aurevilly, preface to Péladan's *Vice suprême*, xi–xii.)

36 Taxil, *Corruption*, 248; Coffignon quoted in Moll, 225.

37 Bard's *Un Siècle d'antiféminisme* spectacularly demonstrates the breadth and depth of nineteenth-century misogyny.

38 See Mesch, *The Hysteric's Revenge: French Women Writers at the Fin de Siècle*.

39 1. See Ronsin, *Les Divorciaires*, 168–74.

40 Including Deraismes (*Ève contre Dumas fils*, 1872) and the author of the unsigned pamphlet, *La Femme-Homme: Mariage – adultère – divorce* (1872), which has been attributed to Audouard. Goldstein has argued that anonymity was a common strategy used to avoid the censor's punishment in the early Third Republic. Only two years before, at the end of the liberal Empire, Audouard

openly published *Réponse à Barbey d'Aurevilly contre les bas-bleus*. Incongruously, Dumas gained the support of Julie-Victoire Daubié, who hailed him as a supporter of divorce in *La Question de la femme par A. Dumas fils* (1872).

41 "c'est la pourriture d'en bas [...] se redressant et pourrissant les classes d'en haut" (*Nana*, 549).

42 On representations of prostitution in nineteenth-century literature, see Bernheimer and Matlock. On its convergence with homosexuality, see Choquette, "Degenerate or Degendered? Images of Prostitution and Homosexuality in the French Third Republic."

43 The frame story of Maupassant's collection, *Contes de la bécasse* (1881), describes a ritual in which a group of men exchanges stories over dinner after a day of hunting.

44 *Nana*, 273. Translations from *Nana* by George Holden.

45 "sales filles qui font le trottoir"; "une bêtise à vouloir être libre à ce prix-là" (*Chair molle*, 42, 43; my translation). Like *Chair molle*, Lorrain's *La Maison Philibert* details the sapphic activities of registered prostitutes working in controlled brothels.

46 Descending the social spectrum, a *lorette* depends on several men to support her financially, and a *grisette* refers to a working woman obliged to supplement her income by moving in with a lover. On the vocabulary of prostitution, see Dumas *père*, *Filles, Lorettes, et courtisanes*, and Matlock, 67.

47 "Le vice d'en bas me sera donné par deux figurantes et par une fille qui roulera le boulevard" (*Nana*, 559).

48 "Peu de gougnottes – dans le monde inférieur oui" (*Carnets*, 310).

49 "son ancien idéal de fleuriste"; "Prise de la toquade enragée des filles pour la laideur grimacière des comiques"; "dans un ravissement d'amour; toute rose comme une vierge" (242, 240, 246).

50 270. "la curiosité mise en éveil, elle la questionnait [Satin] sur des coins de vice, stupéfiée d'en apprendre encore à son âge, après tout ce qu'elle savait; et elle riait, elle s'exclamait, trouvant ça drôle, un peu répugnée cependant, car au fond elle était bourgeoise pour ce qui n'entrait pas dans ses habitudes."

51 326, 327, 433. "Dès lors, Nana eut une passion, qui l'occupa. Satin fut son vice"; "un beau soir, ça devint sérieux. Nana, si dégoûtée chez Laure, comprenait maintenant. Elle en fut bouleversée, enragée"; "Puis, sous un déguisement d'homme, c'étaient des parties dans des maisons infâmes, des spectacles de débauche dont elle amusait son ennui."

52 "née vers le bas de l'avenue [...] dans une ruelle de chiffonniers"; "aurait couché le roi des Belges" (13, 15).

53 221. "née de quatre ou cinq générations d'ivrognes, le sang gâté par une longue hérédité de misère et de boisson, qui se transformait chez elle en un détraquement nerveux de son sexe de femme."

54 Daudet, 43. "J'étais jeune, c'est Caoudal... ce grand fou... Je faisais ce qu'il voulait."
55 "On va faire gougnotter les putains du bordel. Allumage" (*Carnets*, 310).
56 "mâles en rut" (P. Adam, 19). "Toute une société se ruant sur le cul. Une meute derrière une chienne" (Zola, *Carnets*, 312).
57 Maupassant, 221. "Les mâles s'accroupissaient comme des crapauds avec des gestes obscènes."
58 *Nana*, 272. "les plus comme il faut étaient les plus sales. Tout le vernis craquait, la bête se montrait, exigeante dans ses goûts monstrueux, raffinant sa perversion."
59 "l'ingénuité de son âge tender [...] sa jolie figure de blond hale et doré par le soleil" (7). Translations from Daudet's *Sapho* are mine.
60 "il la suivit sans hésiter. Pourquoi? Ce n'était pas l'attrait de cette femme; il l'avait à peine regardée [...]. Mais il obéissait à une volonté supérieure à la sienne, à la violence impétueuse d'un désir" (12).
61 "entre deux tournées de comptoir"; "maraudeur [...] montrant sous le gaz du trottoir une face bouffie, apoplectisée d'alcool" (59, 58).
62 "toutes les nervosités de sa mère à laquelle il ressemblait comme un portrait [...] dont les désordres, les folies avaient à demi ruiné leur famille" (24).
63 "Et avec les cinq lettres de son nom abominable, toute la vie de cette femme lui passait en fuite d'égout sous les yeux."
64 "ce mot de Sapho qui à force de rouler les siècles s'est encrassé de légendes immondes sur sa grâce première, et d'un nom de déesse est devenu l'étiquette d'une maladie."
65 *Nana*, 38. "cette grosse fille qui se tapait sur les cuisses, qui gloussait comme une poule, dégageait autour d'elle une odeur de vie, une toute-puissance de femme, dont le public se grisait."
66 44–5. "Tout d'un coup, dans la bonne enfant la femme se dressait, inquiétante, apportant le coup de folie de son sexe, ouvrant l'inconnu du désir. Nana souriait toujours, mais d'un sourire aigu de mangeuse d'hommes."
67 453. "son sexe montait et rayonnait sur ses victimes étendues, pareil à un soleil levant qui éclaire un champ de carnage."
68 221. "Elle avait poussé dans un faubourg, sur le pavé parisien; et, grande, belle, de chair superbe ainsi qu'une plante de plein fumier, elle vengeait les gueux et les abandonnés dont elle était le produit. Avec elle, la pourriture qu'on laissait fermenter dans le peuple, remontait et pourrissait l'aristocratie."
69 452–3. "Elle demeurait seule debout, au milieu des richesses entassées de son hôtel, avec un peuple d'hommes abattus à ses pieds. [...] Son œuvre de ruine et de mort était faite, la mouche envolée de l'ordure des faubourgs, apportant le ferment des pourritures sociales, avait empoisonné ces hommes, rien qu'à se poser sur eux. C'était bien, c'était juste, elle avait vengé son monde, les gueux et les abandonnés."

70 *Nana*, 221. "une force de la nature, un ferment de destruction, [...] corrompant et désorganisant Paris entre ses cuisses de neige."

71 "Femme de Paul," 214–15, emphasis added. "ce petit criquet de femme [...] l'avait pris, captivé, possédé des pieds à la tête, corps et âme. Il subissait cet ensorcellement féminin, mystérieux et tout-puissant, [...] venue on ne sait d'où, du démon de la chair, et qui jette l'homme le plus sensé aux pieds d'une fille quelconque sans que rien en elle explique son pouvoir fatal" (117). Translation by Ernest Boyd.

72 203. "Le jeune homme, presque imberbe encore, mince, le visage pale."

73 210. "Un canot couvert d'une tente et monté par quatre femmes descendait lentement le courant. Celle qui ramait était petite, maigre, fanée, vêtue d'un costume de mousse [...] En face d'elle, une grosse blondasse habillée en homme, avec un veston de flanelle blanche, se tenait couchée sur le dos au fond du bateau, les jambes en l'air sur le banc des deux côtés de la rameuse, et elle fumait une cigarette, tandis qu'à chaque effort des avirons sa poitrine et son ventre frémissaient, ballottés par la secousse. Tout à l'arrière, sous la tente, deux belles filles grandes et minces, l'une brune et l'autre blonde, se tenaient par la taille en regardant sans cesse leurs compagnes.

"Un cri partit de la Grenouillère: 'V'là Lesbos!' et, tout à coup, ce fut une clameur furieuse; une bousculade effrayante eut lieu; les verres tombaient; on montait sur les tables; tous, dans un délire de bruit, vociféraient: 'Lesbos! Lesbos! Lesbos!' [...]

"La rameuse, devant cette ovation, s'état arrêtée tranquillement. La grosse blonde étendue au fond du canot tourna la tête d'un air nonchalant, se soulevant sur les coudes; et les deux belles filles, à l'arrière, se mirent à rire en saluant la foule."

74 212. "Leur vice était public, officiel, patent. On en parlait comme d'une chose naturelle, qui les rendait presque sympathiques."

75 212. "C'est la police que ça regarde, et je les ferai flanquer à Saint-Lazare, moi!"

76 213. "Un voisin, révolté de ces bruits scandaleux, avait prévenu la gendarmerie, et le brigadier, suivi d'un homme, était venu faire une enquête. La mission était délicate; on ne pouvait, en somme, rien reprocher à ces femmes, qui ne se livraient point à la prostitution. Le brigadier, fort perplexe, ignorant même à peu près la nature des délits soupçonnés, avait interrogé à l'aventure, et fait un rapport monumental concluant à l'innocence."

77 225. "Oh! si c'eût été un homme, l'autre! mais cela! cela! Il se sentait enchaîné par leur infamie même. Et il restait là, anéanti, bouleversé comme s'il eût découvert tout à coup un cadavre cher et mutilé, un crime contre nature, monstrueux, une immonde profanation."

78 203. "une galerie composée de bourgeois endimanchés, d'ouvriers et de soldats" (291).

79 206–7. "Des femmes, des filles aux cheveux jaunes, aux seins démesurément

rebondis, à la croupe exagérée, au teint plâtré de fard, aux yeux charbonnés, aux lèvres sanguinolentes, lacées, sanglées en des robes extravagantes."

80 207, emphasis added. "les hommes [...] s'agitaient en vociférant par un besoin de *tapage naturel aux brutes.* Les femmes cherch[aient] *une proie* pour le soir" (emphasis added).

81 211. "on eût dit que ce peuple, ce ramassis de corrompus, saluait un chef"; "On devrait les noyer comme des chiennes."

82 212. "On en parlait comme d'une chose naturelle."

83 211, 228. "leur vice était public, officiel, patent"; "comme réfugiée dans une tendresse plus intime et plus sûre, plus familière et plus confiante" (127).

84 433. "dans l'angoisse de sa jalousie, le malheureux en arrivait à être tranquille, lorsqu'il laissait Nana et Satin ensemble. Il l'aurait poussée à ce vice, pour écarter les flammes."

85 209. "deux belles filles grandes et minces, l'une brune et l'autre blonde, se tenaient par la taille" (114).

86 See Bard, *Histoire politique du pantalon.*

87 *Nana,* 257. "ce monstre [...] cette Laure, était une dame de cinquante ans, aux formes débordantes, sanglées dans des ceintures et des corsets; une centaine de clientes, [...] la plupart touchant à la quarantaine, énormes, avec des empâtements de chair, des bouffissures de vice noyant les bouches molles" (270–1).

88 "cette horreur de Chochotte [...] un petit voyou en blouse noire, très large de hanches, la visière de la casquette baissée sournoisement" (Alexis, 47).

89 "On entendit une voix éraillée. [...] Et un jet mince de salive partit de sa large bouche sans lèvres, alla moucheter d'écume blanche le tablier de la cheminée. [...] Un cigare d'un sou entre les dents, les mains dans les poches, gouailleuse et provocatrice" (47).

90 "'Qu'est-ce c'est que celui-là?' ... 'Vous voyez bien que c'est une femme'" (47).

91 Maupassant, 210, 212. "une grosse blondasse habillée en homme [...] emplissant de sa graisse ses vêtements de flanelle blanche, bombant de sa croupe le large pantalon, se balançant comme une oie grasse, ayant les cuisses énormes et les genoux rentrés" (114, 116).

92 "Nana, c'est la pourriture d'en bas [...] se redressant et pourrissant les classes d'en haut. Vous laissez naître ce ferment, il remonte et vous désorganise ensuite" (*Nana,* 549).

93 "Dans ce sang qu'elle crachait [...] il devait y avoir de petits morceaux de poumon [...] Le mouchoir dont elle se tamponnait la bouche, était déjà imbibé de sang comme une éponge" (31, 45).

94 "elle défit les bandes enroulées. L'une à l'autre, elles étaient unies par un pus sanglant, desséché [...] Le poignet avait perdu ses formes et présentait seulement une bouffissure rougeâtre, pâteuse, indécise de contours, sous laquelle un liquide pâle fluctuait. D'étroites fentes une liqueur livide sourdait, rubéfiée de fils

sanglants [...] Il y eut le bruit d'une vessie qui s'écrase; un liquide chaud coula de son crane, lui inonda le cou et les épaules" (*Chair molle*, 243).

95 453. "en grande toilette pour embrasser Satin une dernière fois."

96 469. "le cadavre commençait à empoisonner la chambre."

97 470. "Nana restait seule [...] C'était un charnier, un tas d'humeur et de sang, une pelletée de chair corrompue, jetée là, sur un coussin. Les pustules avaient envahi la figure entière, un bouton touchant l'autre; et, flétries, affaissées, d'un aspect grisâtre de boue, elles semblaient déjà une moisissure de la terre, sur cette bouillie informe, ou l'on ne retrouvait plus les traits."

98 470. "Il semblait que le virus pris par elle dans les ruisseaux, sur les charognes tolérées, ce ferment dont elle avait empoisonné un peuple, venait de lui remonter au visage et l'avait pourri."

99 Deraismes, *Épidémie*, 21; Zola, *Experimental Novel*, 375. "la République sera naturaliste ou elle ne sera pas" (*Roman*, 341).

100 *La recherche de la paternité* was not granted until 1912 as one among several measures intended to reverse the long-declining birth rate.

101 "Donne-moi du vin de Lesbos, dit Séso à l'esclave. Il est plus fort que l'autre," Louÿs, *Aphrodite*, 142.

"Plus la femme a d'importance et de pouvoir dans une civilisation, plus la décadence est grande," Péladan, "Félicien Rops," quoted in Palacio (1994, 187n20).

102 "Changées de milieu, transportées aux barrières, elles [les tribades] ne vaudraient pas l'étude; il faut que la répugnance du sujet s'attenue de l'élégance du grand monde et d'une perversité long voilée qui dupe l'opinion" (*Femmes honnêtes*, 17).

103 See Guillerm's thoughtful article on the internal contradictions of Péladan's aesthetics, "un délire où le néo-classicisme lui-même est porté à l'incandescence du baroque" (75).

104 "Les décadences montrent une inversion des rôles sexuels et les fins de race s'emplissent de femmes docteurs et de femmes artistes" (*Comment on devient fée*, 106); "je juge que la fin de la France n'est plus qu'une question d'années" (Péladan in Huret, 86).

105 "L'Aristocratie, en toute matière, c'est la compétence"; "le devoir est physique pour les inférieurs [...] le peuple, c'est-à-dire ceux qui vivent du travail, ne peuvent gouverner" (*Sceptre*, 163, 66, 175).

106 "la foule règne et la femme s'émancipe" (*Gynandre*, 5).

107 "il n'y a pas de pensée chez la femme" (146).

108 "la femme qui m'attire parce que ma nature me fait puissant sur elle [...] la princesse, la femme décorative de l'âme comme du corps" (*Comment on devient fée*, 24, 351)

109 "la jeune fille moderne, sans élan ni poésie" (23).

110 Huret, 82–3.

111 "le plus illettré des écrivains" (*Rapport*, 55); "le romancier à prétentions

scientifiques" (*Initiation*, 9); "Au matérialisme scientifique de Darwin correspond le matérialisme littéraire de M. Zola" (*L'Art ochlocratique*, 15).

112 "La représentation de la contemporanéité, le marin et le paysan, l'ouvrier et le bourgeois ne paraîtront jamais à nos expositions" (*Gynandre*, 351).

113 Huret, 84.

114 "L'Art seul peut agir sur le collectif animique" (*Gynandre*, 349).

115 Huret, 83.

116 "le socialisme n'est pas de nature latine" (*Sceptre*, 162).

117 "La femme qui sort de ses attributs et de son mode contrarie la norme et périra" (*Comment on devient fée*, 121).

118 Praz, 339; Birkett, "Masochistic Inscriptions," 843.

119 "Quelque chose meurt dans l'humanité [...] nous touchons à ces temps imprévus où le bien, le beau, le vrai seront impossibles" (*Gynandre*, 319).

120 "ambassadeur de la sexualité normale," "découvrir la loi de l'anormal," "théâtre passionnel de Paris" (22).

121 "je nie Lesbos comme amour"; "quant à l'amour, [c]es dénouements [...] peuvent arriver [...] seulement dans les basses classes" (25).

122 "la non-valeur des passionalités d'en bas," "les cordes animales" (298).

123 "l'hébétude physique [...], le bas instinct de volupté"; "[la] force d'âme" (279, 298).

124 "en haut, Lesbos est dans l'imagination, en bas, dans les reins" (301).

125 "La civilisation latino-chrétienne décomposée va-t-elle pourrir sous les espèces de l'antiphysisme féminin?" (41).

126 "un état social antiphysique," "La République s'est jugée par les mots de sa devise qui renferment trois propositions contre nature: la liberté, c'est la négation du devoir; l'égalité, c'est la négation de la justice; la fraternité, c'est la négation de l'égoïsme" (390, emphasis added).

127 "on proscrit le divin et le normal disparaît; à pays athée, mœurs sodomiques" (319).

128 "avant que cette maladie morale s'épidémise, il faut l'étudier, la classer, [...] guérir [...] cette nouveauté de la psychopathie" (41).

129 "[c'est] un pêché, non pas une passion" (15).

130 "*La Gynandre* prétend valoir même devant le savant et le confesseur, comme la seule monographie de la sodomie féminine" (xi).

131 "un mot décent pour désigner cette coupable [...] qui ne sen[t] ni la rue, ni la clinique" (43).

132 "la femme prétendant à la mâleté, l'usurpatrice sexuelle [...] toute tendance de femme à faire l'homme: et cela s'entend d'une mademoiselle de Maupin comme d'un bas bleu" (43).

133 "Le nom de Sapho se désinfecte de l'accusation de sodomie"; "L'épigraphie grecque se consacre toute à la sodomie masculine: pas un vers sur le saphisme" (32, 28).

134 “les mauvais romans [...] où la sodomie féminine fait la trame”; “les auteurs récents ont tous touché à cette matière en malpropres et en niais” (96, 58, xxi).
135 “c’est pour avoir ainsi faussé les notions que ce génie mourut aphasique” (37).
136 “les choses ne se nommaient point”; “Lesbos aime le lieu public [...] et veut qu’un désir masculin fouette son plaisir” (51, 83).
137 “L’infériorité de Lesbos, c’est son besoin de galerie male” (83); “en ce clan connu de tout Paris, pas d’amour [...]. Les Orchidées ne se recherchaient pas entre elles, craintives de compromettre leur bonne amitié en l’érotisant” (96).
138 “une forme dépravée du dandysme”; “un travesti porté au moral et joué dans la vie” (97–8).
139 “hommassée par ses occupations”; “l’usurpation de la femme sur l’homme” (95).
140 “un des livres les plus lesbiens”; “Ces femmes qui ne veulent être ni mères, ni épouses, ni amantes, ces femmes sont d’admirables plastiques en mouvement. Théologien, je les damnerai s’il le faut, mais puis-je dénier mes yeux et ne pas admirer l’impression d’art qu’elles réalisent” (94, 36, 102).
141 “Vous cultivez les attributs viriles, ne serait-ce pas un juste retour que quelques hommes cultivassent les féminines manières d’être” (104).
142 “ce qui fait l’homme c’est la tête”; “petit homme [...], une féminité atrophiée” (104; 144, 145).
143 “Alors la supériorité de son cerveau et de son sexe apparut aux yeux des gynandres” (135).
144 “la gynandre [...] cache ses horreurs, présentant son côté décoratif et sentimental” (171).
145 Cf. Alfred de Vigny’s “La Colère de Samson”:

Bientôt, se retirant dans un hideux royaume,
La Femme aura Gomorrhe et l'Homme aura Sodome,
Et, se jetant, de loin, un regard irrité,
Les deux sexes mourront chacun de son côté.

146 “ridicules au lieu d’érotiques [...] une mauvaise blague” (168, 170).
147 “les chants ou dires de la rue ou des domestiques”; “elle renonce au normal” (194).
148 “un gentilhomme ruiné et vicieux” (213).
149 “au moment physique [...] ne savai[t] que lui faire” (215).
150 “Il était le mâle qu’on n’élude pas, l’homme plus fort que Lesbos, [...] le vivant argument contre la sodomie féminine” (242).
151 “Américaine, presque une barbare [...] la réalité conjugale [...] aucun mot ne rendra l’impression d’être possédée par un imbécile, et de commencer la vie nerveuse par l’effroi” (263).
152 “le jour que j’ai su que cela se faisait.”
153 “féminité renaissante [et] son retour à l’agissement sexuel” (261–2).

154 "la défaite de la plus résistante des gynandres"; "je mêle à ma passionnalité le plus de charité que je peux: je voudrais purifier par ma tendresse" (267, 269).
155 "Lesbos est morte, je l'ai tué d'un baiser" (328).
156 "en tunique et manteau noir, lamé d'or" (324); "cette verticale, rigide témoin" (4).
157 "se sentit devenir dans ce milieu l'homme fatal" (53, emphasis added).
158 "Le décadent cherche son spiritualisme dans l'anormal et l'exceptionnalité" (32).
159 With Stanislas de Guaita he cofounded the Ordre Kabbalistique de la Rose-Croix in 1888, from which he broke to found the syncretic Ordre de la Rose-Croix Catholique et esthétique du Temple et du Graal in 1891. The following year he organized the first Salon de la Rose-Croix to great success. See Ziegler, "The Elitist Metaphysic of Joséphin Péladan," and Birkett, "Masochistic Inscriptions."
160 Jourdain, 75; Peck, 176.
161 Brisson, 58; Lazare, 55.
162 Pollard; Peck, "One of the Parnassians," 175.
163 Meyer-Plantureux, 24–5. Nor did Mendès directly denounce Wagner's anti-Semitism, but allowed a stand-in to do so. He instead took the composer to task for maligning France ("Wagner a écrit contre la France, contre Paris assiégé et vaincu") and for mocking Hugo ("il a essayé de bafouer Victor Hugo, le plus grand des poètes"). Mendès reconciles his esteem for Wagner's music with the latter's unpalatable opinions by taking a lesson from an acquaintance who "haïssait Wagner, à cause d'un livre sur les juifs": "Il faut penser comme ce juif hongrois; il faut détester et admirer l'auteur de Lohengrin" (Richard Wagner, v).
164 "pervertie jusqu'à la moelle" (85).
165 "infirme dès sa naissance…[un] être moins qu'humain" (95, 96).
166 "suprême héritier d'une opulente et abjecte race […] la race abominable de qui [il] porte […] les antiques péchés" (98, 103).
167 *Flowers*, trans. Waldrop, 189.

Mes baisers sont légers comme ces éphémères
Qui caressent le soir les grands lacs transparents,
Et ceux de ton amant creuseront leurs ornières
Comme des chariots ou des socs déchirants;

Ils passeront sur toi comme un lourd attelage
De chevaux et de bœufs aux sabots sans pitié ...

168 "il s'animalisa. Tout ce brave homme n'était plus qu'un mâle. […] Il l'opprima, l'écrasa sous une pesanteur de bœuf qui se rue! […] il obligea la vierge à subir l'intromission triomphale de l'époux" (137, 138).
169 "ville damnée," "ses bas-fonds hideux," "la crapule populacière" (31, 32, 33).
170 "La douce monotonie de la vie honnête" (484).

171 "les deux états de la femme: la prostitution et l'aristocratie."
172 "la Fille et la Grande Dame [...] ne [font] qu'une foule [et] se trait[ent] en égales" (254).
173 "soigner la femme moderne [...] des malades qui ne sont point malades et souffrent infiniment" (248, 251).
174 "Pas [...] un casseur de pierres sur les grandes routes, un mineur dans l'étroite galerie, un paysan qui sème ou laboure. [...] Mais l'homme des cités nouvelles" (240).
175 "il n'y a rien de plus sale [...] ce n'est pas vrai que les femmes peuvent s'aimer d'amour. [...] Ce n'est pas seulement vilain, ce plaisir qui n'est pas un plaisir, c'est défendu!" (388).
176 "elle n'était pas éloignée de penser qu'elle avait tort, que sa vie s'était trompée, qu'il faut être comme les sots pour être comme les heureux" (487).
177 "Ce sont les bourgeois qui ont raison. Ils vivent tranquilles, ils meurent tranquilles [...] ce qui est vrai, ce qui est bon, parce que c'est permis, c'est d'avoir un mari et des enfants" (387, 389).
178 "Si j'avais épousé un ouvrier, ou un employé, je m'en serais épargné, des chagrins!" (389).
179 "Toi, si tu ne sors pas de cette ordure, tu souffriras plus encore parce que tu seras plus coupable. En souillant une petite rien du tout comme moi, je n'ai pas fait grand mal! mais, pour t'être avilie, toi, si grande, si bonne, qui as tant d'esprit, tu mériterais des supplices effrayants et tu les subirais" (389).
180 "ce qu'il y avait de niais bavardage et de souvenirs de puéril catéchisme dans les paroles de Magalo" (391).
181 "il était bizarre [...] que la malédiction sur l'unique plaisir eût été prononcée par celle à qui elle devait de le connaître"; "Pensée plus stupide encore, bien digne d'une médiocre et banale créature, faussement extraordinaire, bourgeoise en réalité malgré ses apparences de bohème affolée" (393, 396).
182 "Est-ce que le désir, quel qu'il soit, n'entraîne pas, chez celui ou celle qui l'éprouve, le droit d'y obéir? [...] voici que des femmes se révoltent contre la fatalité sexuelle, et, pour être exceptionnelle, leur vocation, innée, n'est pas moins légitime" (396, 397).
183 "Sortir du bourgeoisisme des jouissances permises, dédaigner les joies médiocres de l'amour sain, être une exception, attire. Le vice est à la mode" (231).
184 "Un étrange enthousiasme saisit les femmes à leur tour, et voici qu'elles tombent aussi sur le champ de bataille, victimes d'un exécrable héroïsme. Quels sont ces êtres extraordinaires, qui abandonnent pour le chassepot le balai de la ménagère et l'aiguille de l'ouvrière; qui quittent leurs enfants pour se faire tuer à côté de leurs amants ou de leurs maris? Amazones-voyous, magnifiques et abjectes" (*Les 73 jours*, 134).
185 "symptôme persistant d'un mal familial" (96); "le rire sonnait plus distinctement dans son oreille" (544).

186 "Ils se complaisaient en leur familiale solitude, en leur honnête oisiveté; [...] Cela leur était bien égal de n'être que médiocres" (478).
187 "heureuse pour avoir obéi aux lois banales de l'existence" (483).
188 "il faut être comme les sots pour être comme les heureux" (487).
189 "quel effroyable inceste encore inimaginé!" (547).
190 "Sa face, – le front, la joue et les lèvres, – devenue, de pâle, livide, de livide, terreuse, se détend, s'allonge, défaille en une lâcheté comme pâteuse et grassement fluide; on dirait d'une momie qui va couler en putréfaction" (554).
191 "parfait accomplissement d'une atavique fatalité ou triomphe de la Démone tentatrice [...], exemple lamentable de la Névrose ou de la Possession?" (558).

4. *Scientia Sapphica*

1 See J. Ellis, *The Physician-Legislators of France.*
2 On masculine cohesion in the medical field, see Nye, "Medicine and Science as Masculine 'Fields of Honor.'"
3 See Laupts, Grojnowski.
4 On the history of sexuality in medicine, see Foucault's foundational *History of Sexuality*. Other important contributions include Laqueur, *Making Sex*; Chaperon, *Origines de la sexologie*; Corbin, *Harmonie des plaisirs*. On homosexuality in nineteenth-century France, see Hahn, *Nos ancêtres les pervers*; Copley, *Sexual Moralities in France*; Rosario, *Science and Homosexualities* and *Erotic Imagination*; Merrick and Sibalis, *Homosexuality in French History and Culture*; Peniston, *Pederasts and Others*; Murat, *La Loi du genre*. Béjin has edited a special issue of *Sexologies* entitled *Histoire de la sexologie française.*
5 On disciplinary developments and changes, professionalization and specialization, see Geison, *Professions and the French State*; Paul, *From Knowledge to Power*; Bonner, *Becoming a Physician*; Bynum, *Science and the Practice of Medicine*; Warner, "The History of Science and the Sciences of Medicine"; Weisz, *Divide and Conquer.*
6 "Le Bonheur dans le crime" (151).
7 See Canguilhem, *The Normal and the Pathological.*
8 See Mucchielli, *Histoire de la criminologie française*; Nye, "Heredity or Milieu"; Shichor, "The French-Italian Controversy."
9 See Oosterhuis, *Stepchildren of Nature*; Amidon, "Sex on the Brain."
10 See Revenin, *Homosexualité et prostitution masculines à Paris: 1870–1918.*
11 See Revenin, "Conceptions et théories savantes de l'homosexualité masculine en France."
12 See review articles by Ritti (1878) and Hildenbrand (1883). Krafft-Ebing's *Psychopathia Sexualis* was first translated into French in 1895, Moll's *Perversions de l'instinct génital* in 1893.

13 Charcot and Magnan, 303. And as Lacassagne noted, "Tardieu cites only four examples [...] of attacks committed by women on people of their own sex" (*Précis*, 455). Basing these few observations primarily on child sexual abuse committed by women, Tardieu concluded that, due to their rarity, "the law has not frequently had to penetrate into these disgraceful mysteries" (Tardieu, 56).

14 On the hygiene movement, see Corbin, *The Foul*; Csergo, *Liberté, égalité, propreté.*

15 See Corbin (*Harmonie*) on conjugal pleasure. Mainardi traces marriage conduct manuals to the Restoration, a time in which "conjugal literature" (including fictions such as Balzac's *Physiologie du mariage*, 1829) flourished in response to changes in the Civil Code.

16 Let's recall that Dentu also published Olympe Audouard, the Goncourt brothers, Catulle Mendès, among many other prominent novelists and essayists. He has been described as "the attention-grabbing king of the latest thing in print, the fashionable pamphlet, the ephemeral publication" (Chartier, 579). On Dentu, see also Mollier, *L'Argent et les Lettres*, 299–318.

17 Interest in this physical abnormality, attested since the renaissance, remained common in later works on female homosexuality. See Park, "The Rediscovery of the Clitoris."

18 "Our expectations have been surpassed! [...] success obliges us to follow this work with a series of several others related to the same subject" (*Mariage*, xxi). Garnier was so prolific that Foucault named him (along with Thésée Pouillet) one of France's "inglorious scribes" of science (*History*, 54). The other titles in Garnier's series are *La Génération universelle: Lois, secrets, et mystères chez l'homme et chez la femme* (1881); *Impuissance physique et morale chez l'homme et la femme* (1882); *La Stérilité humaine et l'hermaphrodisme* (1883); *Célibat et célibataires: Caractères, dangers et hygiène chez les deux sexes* (1887); *Anomalies sexuelles, apparentes et cachées, par aberration physique ou morale* (1889); *Le Mal d'amour: Contagion, préservatifs et remèdes* (1891); *Onanisme seul et à deux* (1888); *Épuisement nerveux génital (neurasthénie sexuelle)* (1895); *Hygiène de la génération: Fausses maladies vénériennes* (1898).

19 Chaperon, "De l'anaphrodisie," 192.

20 In fact, Garnier takes a shot at an unnamed author of a popular marriage manual, reminiscent of Debay, when he compares Monlau's volume to "another *Hygiène du mariage* in French, hugely popular" that lacks the erudition, refined style, moral principles found in Monlau (i).

21 See Stengers, *Masturbation*; Laqueur, *Solitary Sex*; Singy, "Friction of the Genitals"; Brenot, "Les Médecins français et la masturbation."

22 "the phenomenon of female ejaculation has been discovered, described and forgotten in eastern and western culture repeatedly over the last 2,000 years" (Korda et al., "The History of Female Ejaculation").

23 Chaperon suggests that Garnier Frères's collaboration with Pierre Garnier was entrepreneurial rather than scholarly (*Origines*, 22).
24 *Dictionnaire*, 3rd series, 15:78, my emphasis.
25 On this last point, Pouillet's opinion seems to have rapidly evolved in subsequent enlarged editions. In his first edition (1876), he writes "these surgical procedures are repugnant and, in my opinion, only to be used as a final measure [...] when all other means have failed and a life is in jeopardy" (50). By his third edition (1880), Pouillet had added eight pages of commentary and case studies to demonstrate its efficacy.
26 On the history of prostitution in nineteenth-century France, see Corbin, *Women for Hire*.
27 In his seminal *Laboring Classes and Dangerous Classes*, historian Louis Chevalier documented the association between the working classes and the dangerous classes that took hold during the Restoration, an association whose corollary identified the sexual menace of the underclass as the prostitute.
28 Published by the distinguished medical publisher, Baillière, as were the second (1837) and third (1857) editions, posthumously corrected and updated by François Leuret (1837) and A. Trebuchet and Poirat-Duval (1857). I refer to the third edition.
29 In fact Pouillet defends them in the same sentence against charges of immorality (3).
30 On cellular prisons, see Foucault, *Discipline and Punish*.
31 *Women for Hire*, 7, emphasis added.
32 Jeannel's affiliations included "Member of the Army Health Service Council, former chief medical officer for the Health Clinic of Bordeaux, and member of the Health and Sanitation Council for the Gironde department."
33 *De la prostitution*, 561. Here Jeannel is quoting an 1872 report by the "commission named by the Society of Medicine and Surgery of Bordeaux."
34 Charles Lecour, head of the Parisian police division in charge of overseeing prostitutes, was another prominent regulationist and the author of *La Prostitution à Paris et à Londres, 1789–1870*. Yves Guyot, author of *Études de physiologie sociale: La Prostitution*, is exemplary of the abolitionists.
35 *Corruption*, 259.
36 Including essays on "Fécondation artificielle," "Tératologie," and "Les Rayons X et le Fluoroscope."
37 The "225 dissertations of his students": can be found at http://www.bm-lyon.fr/decouvrir/collections/fonds-lacassagne.htm.
38 On Lacassagne, see Salle, "L'Avers d'une Belle Époque. Genre et altérité dans les pratiques et les discours d'Alexandre Lacassagne."
39 In addition to Laupts, "Roman d'un inverti-né," see articles by Chevalier and Raffalovich, "Chronique de l'unisexualité." See also Artières, "A. Lacassagne."

40 251. One wonders if this is not an homage to Lacassagne, a broadly read bibliophile whose own article on pederasty includes references to literary works. Cf. Artières, *Livre des vies coupables*, 26–35. In addition to scores of dissertations, Lacassagne directed the writing of prison autobiographies, included in Artières's volume.

5. Intertexts and Afterlives: From the French Canon to U.S. Lesbian Pulps

1 Parts of this chapter were published as "Transnationalism and Sexual Identity in Literature: From the French Canon to US Pulp Fiction" in *Contemporary French Civilization*.

2 Cheney did her homework in preparation for writing her novel *Sisters* (1981), which involves a same-sex romance: "I would also like to acknowledge Carroll Smith-Rosenberg. Her article 'The Female World of Love and Ritual,' in *Signs* (1975), helped guide my thinking."

3 61. Feminist and queer critics have disagreed on Wittig's politics of identification: Fuss finds her guilty of essentialism (*Essentially Speaking*), while Bourcier defends her refusal of naturalized or homogenized identities and sees in her writing a strategy of disidentification.

4 *Women of the Left Bank: Paris, 1900–1940* (1986). Recent work on Parisian lesbian circles and their literary and artistic productions include Hawthorne, ed., *Natalie Barney and Her Circle* (2005); Latimer, *Women Together/Women Apart: Portraits of Lesbian Paris* (2005); Rodriguez, *Wild Heart: Natalie Clifford Barney and the Decadence of Literary Paris* (2002); Souhami, *Wild Girls: Paris, Sappho, and Art: The Lives and Loves of Natalie Barney and Romaine Brooks* (2005). See also Billy, *L'Époque 1900*; Jay, *The Amazon and the Page: Barney and Vivien*; Lorenz, *Sapho 1900: Renée Vivien*; Marks, "Sapho 1900"; Van Casselaer, *Lot's Wife: Lesbian Paris*; Weiss, *Paris was a Woman*.

5 Goujon, *Correspondances croisées*, 53. Vivien echoed these words: "For a long time, *The Songs of Bilitis* have captured the passionate tenderness that I reserve for a few books that are inseparable from my thinking and my existence" (*Correspondances*, 87).

6 Goujon, *Correspondances*, 53.

7 *Correspondances croisées*, 19.

8 Regardless of their gender and sexuality, other writers have also taken offence with Louÿs's *Bilitis*: Robb has labelled it "cliché-ridden sleaze" (232).

9 On Vivien, see Gubar, "Sapphistries"; Perrin, *Renée Vivien, Le Corps exsangue*; Albert and Rollet, *Renée Vivien, une femme de lettres entre deux siècles*; Murat, *Loi du genre*; Engelking, "Translating the Lesbian Writer."

10 "Terms of Estrangement: Renée Vivien's Construction of the Lesbian Subject."

11 See, for example, Massad.

12 See Gills and Thompson.

13 Among many other things in varying contexts, including the not unrelated terms of sex, indulgence, cowardice.

14 See D'Emilio, *Sexual Politics, Sexual Communities: The Making of a Homosexual Minority in the United States*; D. Johnson, *The Lavender Scare: The Cold War Persecution of Gays and Lesbians in the Federal Government*; Meeker, *Contacts Desired: Gay and Lesbian Communications and Community.*

15 See Sibalis, "Homophobia, Vichy France, and the 'Crime of Homosexuality.'"

16 See Jackson, *Living in Arcadia.*

17 Curiously, the men who formed the Mattachine Society drew on French antecedents as did the DOB, in this case the Société Mattachine, referring to mask-wearers.

18 See Gunther, *The Elastic Closet.*

19 See Terry on the impact of Kinsey's research, *An American Obsession: Science, Medicine, and Homosexuality in Modern Society.*

20 See Summers on Cory.

21 On lesbian pulps, see Forrest, Keller, Villarejo.

22 See Stryker, Zimet on pulp fiction cover art.

23 See, in the same vein, Bellaugh, *The Hollow Venus: A Study of the Female Sexual Deviate.*

24 Meeker ("A Queer and Contested Medium") and Mitchell ("'Who Is She?'") have both written thoughtful articles on Aldrich's non-fiction in relation to representational politics and lesbian identity.

25 Stella Fox's anthology, *Lesbian Love in Literature* (Avon, 1962), also features several French authors.

26 See Speer, "Paperback Pornography."

27 Smallwood. The same year the Feminist Press reissued *Women's Barracks.* A number of other presses, particularly Cleis Press, have reissued classic lesbian pulps in recent years. And online: Digital Vintage Pulps.

28 Katherine Forrest's anthology, *Lesbian Pulp Fiction*, contains biographical information on several lesbian writers of pulps. In addition to Forrest, see Server, *Encyclopedia of Pulp Fiction Writers*, for biographical details. There is little to no biographical information available for many of the authors named in this chapter (doubtlessly all pseudonyms). Fay Adams (pseudonym of Velma Clark) also wrote *Lili of Paris* (1952) and *To Love, to Hate* (1953). The name Renee Coquelin appears on no book other than *Mademoiselle Lesbian.* Kay Martin (pseudonym of Adela Maritano) wrote a number of potboilers in the 1960s (*Suburban Wife, The Divorcees, Payment in Sin, Cry Shame!*). Don Morro published one additional pulp title, and Vicki Spain a handful of pulps in the mid-1960s.

29 Forrest, xix. Harris quoted by Keller, "Ab/normal looking" (188).

30 To paraphrase Bourdieu's description of literature's ability to create public recognition of what he calls "new social entities" (*Rules*, 99).

Bibliography

Accampo, Elinor, et al., eds. *Gender and the Politics of Social Reform in France, 1870–1914*. Baltimore: Johns Hopkins UP, 1995.

Adam, Paul. *Chair molle: Roman naturaliste*. Brussels: Brancart, 1885.

Adams, Fay. *Appointment in Paris*. Greenwich, CT: Fawcett Publications, Gold Medal Series, 1952.

Adams, Mary Louise. "Youth, Corruptibility, and English-Canadian Postwar Campaigns against Indecency, 1948–1955." *Journal of the History of Sexuality* 6, no. 1 (1995): 89–117.

Alante-Lima, Willy. "Adolphe BELOT, Romancier, Dramaturge et Éropraticien, 1829–1890." *G.H.C. Bulletin* 98 (1997): 2100. *Généalogie et Histoire de la Caraïbe*. http://www.ghcaraibe.org/bul/ghc098/p2100.html. Accessed 19 February 2014.

Albert, Nicole G. "Books on Trial: Prosecutions for Representing Sapphism." In *Disorder in the Court: Trials and Sexual Conflict at the Turn of the Century*. Edited by George Robb and Nancy Erber. New York: NYU P, 1999. 119–39.

– "De la topographie invisible à l'espace public et littéraire: Les lieux de plaisir lesbien dans le Paris de la Belle Époque." *Revue d'histoire moderne et contemporaine* 4, nos. 53–4 (2006): 87–105.

– *Saphisme et Décadence dans Paris fin-de-siècle*. Paris: Éditions de La Martinière, 2005.

Albert, Nicole G., and Brigitte Rollet, eds. *Renée Vivien, une femme de lettres entre deux siècles (1877–1909)*. Paris: Champion, 2012.

Aldrich, Ann. *Carol in a Thousand Cities*. Greenwich, CT: Fawcett Publications, Gold Medal Series, 1960.

– *We Walk Alone*. Greenwich, CT: Fawcett Publications, Gold Medal Series, 1955.

Alexandrian, Sarane, ed. *L'Érotisme au XIX*[e] *siècle: Œuvres choisies*. Paris: Jean-Claude Lattès, 1993.

Alexis, Paul. *Émile Zola, Notes d'un ami*. Paris: Charpentier, 1882.

– "La Fin de Lucie Pellegrin." 1880. *La Fin de Lucie Pellegrin*. Geneva: Slatkine Reprints, 1979. 1–49.

Allen, James Smith. *In the Public Eye: A History of Reading in Modern France, 1800–1940*. Princeton, NJ: Princeton UP, 1991.

Al-Matary, Sarah. "Du caractère national à l'identité supranationale: Le Messianisme latin, une voie inexplorée du préfascisme français." *Les Cahiers de psychologie politique* 11 (2007). http://lodel.irevues.inist.fr/cahierspsychologiepolitique/index.php?id=675. Accessed 19 February 2014.

Altman, Dennis. *Global Sex*. Chicago: U of Chicago P, 2002.

Amer, Sahar. *Crossing Borders: Love Between Women in Medieval French and Arabic Literatures*. Philadelphia: U of Pennsylvania P, 2008.

Amidon, Kevin. "Sex on the Brain: The Rise and Fall of German Sexual Science." *Endeavour* 32, no. 2 (2008): 64–9.

Angenot, Marc. *Le Cru et le faisandé: Sexe, discours social et littérature à la Belle Époque*. Brussels: Éditions Labor, 1986.

– "Des romans pour les femmes: Un secteur du discours social en 1889." *Études littéraires* 16, no. 3 (1983): 317–50.

– *Le Roman populaire: Recherches en paralittérature*. Montreal: Presses de l'Université du Québec, 1975.

– "'Un juif trahira': La Préfiguration de l'Affaire Dreyfus (1886–1894)." *Romantisme* 87 (1995): 87–114.

Anon. "Catulle Mendes in a Duel." *New York Times*. 24 May 1899. http://query.nytimes.com/gst/abstract.html?res=F00814FC3F5414728DDDAD0A94DD405B8985F0D3. Accessed 19 February 2014.

Argis, Henri d'. *Gomorrhe*. Paris: Charles, 1889.

Artières, Philippe. "A. Lacassagne: De l'archive mineure aux *Archives d'anthropologie criminelle*." *Criminocorpus, revue hypermédia*. 1 January 2005. http://criminocorpus.revues.org/110?lang=fr. Accessed 19 February 2014.

– *Livre des vies coupables*. Paris: Albin Michel, 2000.

Ashley, Katherine. *Edmond de Goncourt and the Novel: Naturalism and Decadence*. Amsterdam: Rodopi, 2005.

Audouard, Olympe. *Silhouettes parisiennes*. Paris: C. Marpon et E. Flammarion, 1883.

Baguley, David. *Naturalist Fiction: The Entropic Vision*. Cambridge: Cambridge UP, 1990.

Balzac, Honoré de. *La Fille aux yeux d'or*. 1835. *The Girl with the Golden Eyes*. New York: Avon Books, 1931.

Banville, Théodore. *Les Exilés*. 1867. Paris: La Différence, 1991.

– *Les Parisiennes de Paris*. Paris: Michel Lévy Frères, 1866.

Barbey d'Aurevilly, Jules. 1874. *Les Diaboliques*. Paris: Lemerre, 1882.

– *Le Théâtre contemporain* (1869–1870). Vol. 3. Paris: Stock, 1909.

Bard, Christine. "Les Antiféminismes de la première vague." Bard, *Siècle*, 41–65.

– *Une histoire politique du pantalon*. Paris: Seuil, 2010.

– "Pour une histoire des antiféminismes." Bard, *Siècle*, 21–36.
– ed. *Un siècle d'antiféminisme*. Paris: Fayard, 1999.
Barthes, Roland. "The Death of the Author." *Image Music Text*. New York: Hill and Wang, 1977. 142–8.
– "L'Effet de réel." In *Littérature et réalité*. Edited by T. Todorov. Paris: Seuil, 1982. 81–90.
– *S/Z*. Paris: Seuil, 1976.
Baudelaire, Charles. *Les Fleurs du Mal*. Edited by Antoine Adam. Paris: Garnier frères, 1961.
– *The Flowers of Evil*. Trans. Keith Waldrop. Middletown, CT: Wesleyan UP, 2007.
– *Intimate Journals*. Trans. Christopher Isherwood. New York: Howard Fertig, 1930, 1977.
– *Œuvres complètes*. Edited by Claude Pichois. 2 vols. Paris: Gallimard Pléiade, 1975–6.
– *The Painter of Modern Life*. Trans. Jonathan Mayne. London: Phaidon Press, 1995.
Bayart, Jean-François. *Global Subjects: A Political Critique of Globalization*. Cambridge: Polity Press, 2007.
Béjin, André, ed. *Une histoire de la sexologie française/A History of French Sexology*. Special issue of *Sexologies* 16, no. 3 (2007): 169–262.
Bellaugh, James. *The Hollow Venus: A Study of the Female Sexual Deviate*. Hollywood, CA: Brandon House, 1965.
Belot, Adolphe. "L'Art de payer sa couturière." 1890. Alexandrian 609–28.
– *La Bouche de Madame X*. Paris: Dentu, 1885.
– *La Canonisation de Jeanne d'Arc*. 1890. Alexandrian 629–92.
– *L'Éducation d'une demi-vierge*. 1883. s.l.: Le Musée secret, s.d.
– *Les Heures érotiques modernes*. Amsterdam, 1890.
– *Mademoiselle Giraud, ma femme*. 1870. Translated and edited by Christopher Rivers. New York: MLA, 2002.
– *La Maison à plaisirs, ou La Passion de Gilberte*. 1888. Paris: Chez la petite Lolotte, Galeries du Palais Royal, 1890.
– *Mélinite*. Paris: Dentu, 1888.
– *Les Péchés de Minette*. 1890. Paris: Maison "Mystère," 1900.
– *Sélect Luxure ou Variations sur toute la lyre*. Paris: n.p., 1911.
– *Les Stations de l'amour*. 1896. Paris: La Musardine, 1999.
Belot, Adolphe, and Ernest Daudet. *La Vénus de Gordes*. Paris: Lasseray, 1875.
Benjamin, Walter. *The Writer of Modern Life: Essays on Charles Baudelaire*. Cambridge, MA: Harvard UP, 2006.
– *The Arcades Project*. Cambridge, MA: Harvard UP, 1999.
Bennett, Judith. "'Lesbian-Like' and the Social History of Lesbianisms." *Journal of the History of Sexuality* 9, no. 1–2 (2000): 1–24.
Benstock, Shari. *Women of the Left Bank: Paris, 1900–1940*. Austin: U of Texas P, 1986.

Bernard, Claude. *Introduction à la médecine expérimentale*. 1865. Charleston, SC: Bibliobazaar, 2007.

Bernheimer, Charles. *Figures of Ill Repute: Representing Prostitution in Nineteenth-Century France*. Durham, NC: Duke UP, 1997.

Bernheimer, Charles, T. Jefferson Kline, and Naomi Schor. *Decadent Subjects: The Idea of Decadence in Art, Literature, Philosophy, and Culture of the Fin de Siècle in Europe*. Baltimore: Johns Hopkins UP, 2002.

Bersani, Leo. *Baudelaire and Freud*. Berkeley: U of California P, 1977.

Bertrand, Adrien. *Catulle Mendès*. Paris: E. Sansot, 1908.

Besnard-Coursodon, Michèle. "Nimroud ou Orphée: Péladan et la société décadente." *Romantisme* 13, no. 42 (1983): 119–36.

Biez, Jacques de. *Un maître imagier, E. Frémeit*. Paris: Aux bureaux de *l'Artiste*, 1896.

Billy, André. *L'Époque 1900*. Paris: Tallandier, 1951.

Binet, Alfred. *Étude de psychologie expérimentale*. Paris: Octave Doin, 1888.

Birkett, Jennifer. "Masochistic Inscriptions: Politics, Fetishism, and Form in the Work of Joséphin Péladan." Hustvedt 842–51.

– *The Sins of the Father*. London: Quartet Books, 1986.

Birnbaum, Pierre. *Un mythe politique: La « République juive »*. Paris: Fayard, 1988.

Bonner, Thomas Neville. *Becoming a Physician: Medical Education in Great Britain, France, German, and the United States, 1750–1945*. New York: Oxford UP, 1995.

Bonnet, Marie-Jo. *Les Relations amoureuses entre les femmes*. 1981. Paris: Odile Jacob, 1995.

Bonnetain, Paul, et al. "*La Terre*: à Émile Zola." *Le Figaro*. 18 August 1887. http://gallica.bnf.fr/ark:/12148/bpt6k2801256. Accessed 19 February 2014.

Bordas, Éric, ed. *Sodome et Gomorrhe*. Special issue of *Romantisme* no. 159 (2013).

Bordas, Éric. "Bibliographie chronologique générale." Bordas 99–107.

Bourcier, Marie-Hélène. *Sexpolitiques: Queer Zones 2*. Paris: La Fabrique éditions, 2005.

Bourdieu, Pierre. "Les Conditions sociales de la circulation internationale des idées." *Actes de la recherche en sciences sociales* 5, no. 145 (2002): 3–8.

– *La Distinction: Critique sociale du jugement*. Paris: Minuit, 1979.

– "Le Fonctionnement du champ intellectuel." *Regards sociologiques* 17–18 (1999): 5–27.

– *Les Règles de l'art: Genèse et structure du champ littéraire*. Paris: Seuil, 1992. *The Rules of Art: Genesis and Structure of the Literary Field*. Stanford, CA: Stanford UP, 1996.

– *Les Usages sociaux de la science: Pour une sociologie clinique du champ*. Paris: INRA, 1994.

Bourget, Paul. *Essais de psychologie contemporaine*. 1883. Paris: Gallimard, 1993.

Boutry, Philippe. "Zola, l'anticléricalisme et l'antichristianisme." Sacquin 45–64.

Brantôme, Pierre de Bourdeille, seigneur de. *Vies des dames galantes*. 1666. Paris: Adolphe Delahays, 1857.

Brécourt-Villars, Claudine. *Petit Glossaire raisonné de l'érotisme saphique, 1880–1930.* Paris: Pauvert, 1980.
Brenot, Philippe. "Les Médecins français et la masturbation avant 1945." *Sexologies* 16, no. 3 (2007): 212–18.
Brisson, Adolphe. *Portraits intimes, deuxième série*. Paris: Armand Colin, 1904.
Brotte, Jacqueline. *Gordes, un rêve de pierre*. Le Pontet: Éditions Alain Barthélemy, 2006.
Brunetière, Ferdinand. *Le Roman naturaliste*. Paris: Calmann Lévy, 1896.
Bullough, Vern L. "The History of the Science of Sexual Orientation, 1880–1980." *Journal of Psychology and Human Sexuality* 9, no. 2 (1997): 1–16.
Butler, Judith. *Bodies that Matter.* New York: Routledge, 1993.
– *Gender Trouble: Feminism and the Subversion of Identity*. New York: Routledge, 1990.
Bynum, W.F. *Science and the Practice of Medicine in the Nineteenth Century*. Cambridge: Cambridge UP, 1994.
Cadier-Rey, Gabrielle. "Zola et l'éducation des filles." Sacquin 88–92.
Canguilhem, Georges. *The Normal and the Pathological*. 1966. New York: Zone Books, 1991.
Caprio, Frank. *Female Homosexuality: A Psychodynamic Study of Lesbianism*. New York: Citadel Press, 1954.
Cardon, Patrick. *Discours littéraires et scientifiques fin-de-siècle: Autour de Marc-André Raffalovich*. Paris: Orizons, 2008.
Cardonne-Arlyck, Elisabeth. "Women Poets: The Speaking *E*." In *Reconceptions: Reading Modern French Poetry*. Edited by Russell King and Bernard McGuirk. Nottingham: U of Nottingham P, 1996. 167–82.
Carpenter, Scott. "Effigies et contrefaçons nationales: *Pauvre Belgique!* de Baudelaire." In *L'œuvre d'identité: Essais sur le romantisme de Nodier à Baudelaire*. Edited by D. Maleuvre and C. Nesci. Quebec: Bibliothèque Nationale du Québec, 1996. 75–86.
Carter, William C. *Proust in Love*. New Haven, CT: Yale UP, 2006.
Castle, Terry. *The Literature of Lesbianism: A Historical Anthology from Ariosto to Stonewall*. New York: Columbia UP, 2003.
– *The Apparitional Lesbian: Female Homosexuality and Modern Culture*. New York: Columbia UP, 1993.
Caufeynon, Dr [Jean Fauconney]. 1903. *Scènes d'amour morbide*. Paris: Librairie artistique, [1930].
Cazals, F.-A., ed. *Paul Verlaine: Ses portraits*. Paris: Bibliothèque de l'association, 1896.
Chaperon, Sylvie. "De l'anaphrodisie à la frigidité." *Sexologies* 16, no. 3 (2007): 189–94.
– *Les Origines de la sexologie, 1850–1900*. Paris: Audibert, 2007.
Charcot, Jean-Martin. *Contribution à l'étude de l'hypnotisme chez les hystériques*. Paris: Progrès médical, 1881.
Charcot, Jean-Martin, and Valentin Magnan. "Inversion du sens génital." *Archives de neurologie* 3 (1882): 53–60, 296–322.

Charle, Christophe. "Champ littéraire et champ du pouvoir: Les Écrivains et l'Affaire Dreyfus." *Annales. Économies, Sociétés, Civilisations* 32, no. 2 (1977): 240–64.

– *La Crise littéraire à l'époque du naturalisme*. Paris: Presses de l'École normale supérieure, 1979.

– *Histoire sociale de la France au XIXe siècle*. Paris: Seuil, 1991. *A Social History of France in the 19th Century*. Oxford: Berg, 1994.

– *Paris fin de siècle: culture et politique*. Paris: Seuil, 1998.

Chartier, Roger, and Henri-Jean Martin, eds. *Histoire de l'édition française*. Vol. 3. Paris: Fayard, 1990.

Cheney, Lynne. *Sisters*. New York: New American Library, 1981. whitehouse.georgebush.org. Accessed 21 June 2012.

Chevalier, Julien. *De l'inversion de l'instinct sexuel au point de vue médico-légal*. Paris: Doin, 1885.

– "De l'inversion sexuelle aux points de vue clinique, anthropologique, et médico-légal." *Archives d'anthropologie criminelle* 5 (1890): 314–36 and 6 (1891): 500–19.

– *L'Inversion sexuelle: Une maladie de la personnalité. Psycho-physiologie, sociologie, tératologie, aliénation mentale, psychologie morbide, anthropologie, médecine judiciaire*. Lyon: A. Storck, 1893.

Chevalier, Louis. *Classes laborieuses et classes dangereuses à Paris pendant la première moitié du 19e siècle*. Paris: Plon, 1958. *Laboring Classes and Dangerous Classes in Paris During the First Half of the Nineteenth Century*. New York: Howard Fertig, 1973.

Choquette, Leslie. "Degenerate or Degendered? Images of Prostitution and Homosexuality in the French Third Republic." *Historical Reflections/Réflexions historiques* 23 (1997): 205–28.

– "Homosexuals in the City: Representations of Lesbian and Gay Space in Nineteenth-Century Paris." Merrick and Sibalis 149–67.

Choux, Jules. *Le Petit Citateur: Notes érotiques et pornographiques*. N.p.: 1881.

Christian, Julien. "Onanisme." *Dictionnaire encyclopédique des sciences médicales*. Edited by Amédée Dechambre. Paris: Masson, 1864–89. 2nd series, vol XV (1881): 359–85.

Churchill, David. "Transnationalism and Homophile Political Culture in the Postwar Decades." *GLQ* 15, no. 1 (2008): 31–66.

Cim, Albert. *Les Bas-bleus: Adolphine la lesbienne*. Paris: Savine, 1891.

Clark, Linda L. *Schooling the Daughters of Marianne: Textbooks and the Socialization of Girls in Modern French Primary Schools*. Albany: SUNY P, 1984.

Code civil des Français: Édition originale et seule officielle. Paris: Imprimerie de la République, 1804.

Coffignon, Ali. *La Corruption à Paris*. Paris: Librairie illustrée, 1888.

Colwill, Elizabeth. "Pass as a Woman, Act Like a Man: Marie-Antoinette as Tribade in the Pornography of the French Revolution." Merrick and Ragan 54–79.

Compère, Daniel. *Dictionnaire du roman populaire français*. Paris: Nouveau monde, 2007.

Constable, Liz, et al., eds. *Perennial Decay: On the Aesthetics and Politics of Decadence*. Philadelphia: U of Pennsylvania P, 1999.

Copley, Antony. *Sexual Moralities in France, 1780–1980*. New York: Routledge, 1989.

Coquelin, Renee. *Mademoiselle Lesbian*. New York: Brandon House, 1964.

Corbin, Alain. *L'Harmonie des plaisirs: Les Manières de jouir du siècle des Lumières à l'avènement de la sexologie*. Paris: Perrin, 2008.

– *The Foul and the Fragrant: Odor and the French Social Imagination*. Cambridge, MA: Harvard UP, 1988.

– *Women for Hire: Prostitution and Sexuality in France after 1850*. Cambridge, MA: Harvard UP, 1996.

Cory, Donald Webster. *The Lesbian in America*. New York: Citadel Press, 1964.

Crawford, Katherine. *European Sexualities, 1400–1800*. Cambridge: Cambridge UP, 2007.

Cryle, Peter. *The Telling of the Act: Sexuality as Narrative in 18th- and 19th-Century France*. Newark: U of Delaware P, 2001.

Csergo, Julia. *Liberté, égalité, propreté: La Morale de l'hygiène au XIXe siècle*. Paris: Albin Michel, 1988.

Darwin, Charles. *On the Origin of Species by Means of Natural Selection, or The Preservation of Favoured Races in the Struggle for Life*. London: John Murray, 1859.

Datta, Venita, and Willa Silverman, eds. *Intellectuals and the Dreyfus Affair*. Special issue of *Historical Reflections/Réflexions historiques* 24, no. 1 (1998).

Daubié, Julie-Victoire. *La Femme pauvre au XIXe siècle*. Paris: Guillaumin, 1866.

– "Avant-propos." *La Question de la femme par A. Dumas fils*. Paris: Association pour l'émancipation progressive de la femme, 1872.

Daudet, Alphonse. *Sapho*. 1884. Paris: Flammarion, 1995.

Daudet, Léon. *Devant la douleur: Souvenirs des milieux littéraires, politiques, artistiques et médicaux de 1880 à 1905*. Paris: Nouvelle librairie nationale, 1915.

Daughters of Bilitis. *The Ladder* 1 (1956).

Debay, Auguste. *Hygiène et physiologie du mariage: Histoire naturelle et médicale de l'homme et de la femme mariés dans ses plus curieux détails*. 1848. Paris: Dentu, 1862.

– *Philosophie du mariage: Études sur l'amour, le bonheur, la fidélité, les sympathies et les antipathies conjugales*. Paris: Moquet, 1849.

DeJean, Joan. *Fictions of Sappho, 1546–1937*. Chicago: U of Chicago P, 1989.

Delvau, Alfred. *Dictionnaire érotique moderne*. Bâle: Imprimerie de Karl Schmidt, n.d.

– *Dictionnaire de la langue verte. Argots parisiens comparés*. Paris: Dentu, 1866.

Démar, Claire. *Ma loi d'avenir*. Paris: Bureau de la tribune des femmes, 1834.

D'Emilio, John. *Sexual Politics, Sexual Communities: The Making of a Homosexual Minority in the United States, 1940–1970*. Chicago: U of Chicago P, 1983.

Deraismes, Maria. *L'Épidémie naturaliste*. Paris: Dentu, [1887].
- *Ève contre Dumas fils*. Paris: Dentu, 1872.
- *Ève dans l'humanité*. 1891. Paris: Éditions Côté-femmes, 1990.

des Cars, Guy. *La Maudite*. 1954. Trans. *The Damned One*. New York: Pyramid Books, 1956.

Diderot, Denis. *La Religieuse*. 1796. *Contes et Romans*. Paris: Gallimard Pléiade, 2004.

Diderot, Denis, ed. *Encyclopédie ou Dictionnaire raisonné des sciences, des arts et des métiers*. 1751–72. ARTFL. http://encyclopedie.uchicago.edu. Accessed 8 March 2014.
- "Lesbian." *The Encyclopedia of Diderot & d'Alembert Collaborative Translation Project*. Translated by Bryant T. Ragan, Jr. Ann Arbor: MPublishing, University of Michigan Library, 2003. http://quod.lib.umich.edu/d/did/. Accessed 8 March 2014. Trans. of "Tribade," *Encyclopédie*. Vol. 16. Paris, 1765.

Dijkstra, Bram. *Evil Sisters: The Threat of Female Sexuality and the Cult of Manhood*. New York: Alfred A. Knopf, 1996.
- *Idols of Perversity: Fantasies of Feminine Evil in Fin-de-Siècle Culture*. Oxford: Oxford UP, 1986.

Doan, Laura. *Fashioning Sapphism*. New York: Columbia UP, 2001.

Donoghue, Emma. *Inseparable: Desire Between Women in Literature*. New York: Knopf, 2010.

Drumont, Édouard. *La Fin d'un monde*. Paris: Savine, 1889.

Dubuis, Patrick. *Émergence de l'homosexualité dans la littérature française, d'André Gide à Jean Genet*. Paris: L'Harmattan, 2011.

Dubut de Laforest, Jean-Louis. *Mademoiselle Tantale*. Paris: Dentu, 1884.

Duggan, Lisa. *Sapphic Slashers: Sex, Violence, and American Modernity*. Durham, NC: Duke UP, 2000.

Dumas, Alexandre, *fils*. *L'Homme-femme*. 1872. Paris: Calmann-Lévy, 1884.

Dumas, Alexandre, *père*. *Filles, lorettes, et courtisanes*. 1843. Paris: Flammarion, 2000.

Dumasy, Lise, ed. *La Querelle du roman-feuilleton: Littérature, presse et politique, 1836–1848*. Grenoble: ELLUG, 1999.

Duchesne, Alphonse. "Livres bons et mauvais." *Le Figaro*. 18 January 1870. 3. http://gallica.bnf.fr. Accessed 5 August 2012.

Dutel, Jean-Pierre. *Bibliographie des ouvrages érotiques publiés clandestinement en français entre 1880 et 1920*. Paris: Dutel, 2002.

Duverger, Alexandre. *De la condition politique et civile des femmes*. Paris: A. Marescq ainé, 1872.

Eichner, Carolyn Jeanne. *Surmounting the Barricades: Women in the Paris Commune*. Bloomington: Indiana UP, 2004.

Ellis, Havelock. *Affirmations*. 1898. Boston: Houghton Mifflin, 1926.

Ellis, Havelock, and John Addington Symonds. *Sexual Inversion*. 1897. New York: Arno Press, 1975.

Ellis, Jack D. *The Physician-Legislators of France: Medicine and Politics in the Early Third Republic, 1870–1914*. Cambridge: Cambridge UP, 1990.

Engelking, Tama Lea. "Translating the Lesbian Writer: Pierre Louÿs, Natalie Barney, and 'Girls of the Future Society.'" Hawthorne, *Natalie Barney and Her Circle*, 62–77.

Faderman, Lillian. *Odd Girls and Twilight Lovers: A History of Lesbian Life in Twentieth-Century America*. New York: Columbia UP, 1991.

– *Surpassing the Love of Men: Romantic Friendship and Love between Women from the Renaissance to the Present*. New York: Quill, 1981.

Ferragus [Louis Ulbach]. "La Littérature putride." *Le Figaro*. 23 January 1868. http://gallica.bnf.fr. Accessed 11 August 2012.

Feydeau, Ernest. *La Comtesse de Chalis, ou Les Mœurs du jour*. Paris: Michel Lévy, 1868.

– *Souvenirs d'une cocodette*. 1877. n.p.: Le Pré aux clercs, 1997.

Foote, Stephanie. "Deviant Classics: Pulps and the Making of Lesbian Print Culture." *Signs: Journal of Women in Culture and Society* 31, no. 1 (2005): 169–90.

Forrest, Katherine, ed. *Lesbian Pulp Fiction*. San Francisco: Cleis Press, 2005.

Forth, Christopher. *The Dreyfus Affair and the Crisis of French Manhood*. Baltimore: Johns Hopkins UP, 2004.

Foster, Jeannette. *Sex Variant Women in Literature*. New York: Vantage Press, 1956.

Fox, Stella, ed. *Lesbian Love in Literature*. New York: Avon, 1962.

Foucault, Michel. *Discipline & Punish: The Birth of the Prison*. New York: Vintage, 1995.

– *Language, Counter-Memory, Practice*. Ithaca, NY: Cornell UP, 1977.

– *The History of Sexuality*. New York: Vintage, 1980.

Frappier-Mazur, Lucienne. "Marginal Canons: Rewriting the Erotic." *Yale French Studies* 75 (1988): 112–28.

Freud, Sigmund. "On Narcissism: An Introduction." 1914. *The Standard Edition of the Complete Psychological Works*. Vol. 14. London: Hogarth, 1957. 67–102.

– *Three Essays on the Theory of Sexuality*. 1905. *The Standard Edition of the Complete Psychological Works*. Vol. 7. London: Hogarth, 1953. 125–245.

Frigerio, Vittorio. "Cui Prodest? Réflexions sur l'utilité et l'utilisation de la théorie des genres dans la culture de masse." *Belphégor: Littérature Populaire et Culture Médiatique* 3, no. 1 (2003): n. pag. http://etc.dal.ca/belphegor/. Accessed 25 March 2014.

Fulcher, Jane F. *French Cultural Politics and Music: From the Dreyfus Affair to the First World War*. New York: Oxford UP, 1999.

Fuss, Diana. *Essentially Speaking*. New York: Routledge, 1989.

– *Identification Papers*. New York: Routledge, 1995.

Gallo, Marcia. *Different Daughters: A History of the Daughters of Bilitis and the Rise of the Lesbian Rights Movement*. New York: Seal Press, 2006.

Garnier, Pierre. *Le Mariage dans ses devoirs*. Paris: Garnier frères, 1879.

– *Onanisme, seul et à deux, sous toutes ses formes et leurs conséquences*. Paris: Garnier frères, 1888.

Gautier, Théophile. *Émaux et Camées*. 1852. Paris: Gallimard Poésie, 1981.

– *Enamels and Cameos*. Trans. Agnes Lee. Project Gutenberg. http://www.gutenberg.org. Accessed 13 March. 2014.

– *Mademoiselle de Maupin*. 1835. *Romans, contes et nouvelles*. Vol. 1. Paris: Gallimard Pléiade, 2002.

Geison, Gerald, ed. *Professions and the French State, 1700–1900*. Philadelphia: U of Pennsylvania P, 1984.

Gide, André. *Journals*. Vol 3: 1928-39. Translated by Justin O'Brien. Urbana: U of Illinois P, 2000.

Gills, Barry, and William Thompson. *Globalization and Global History*. New York: Routledge, 2006.

Glessner, Beth A. "The Censored Erotic Works of Félicité de Choiseul-Meuse." *Tulsa Studies in Women's Literature* 16, no. 1 (1997): 131–43.

Gold, R. C. *Man Hater*. Hollywood, CA: France Book, 1963.

Goldberg Moses, Claire. *French Feminism in the 19th Century*. Albany, NY: SUNY, 1984.

Goldstein, Robert Justin. "Fighting French Censorship, 1815–1881." *The French Review* 71, no. 5 (1998): 785–96.

Goncourt, Edmond and Jules de. 1862. *La Femme au XVIIIe siècle*. Paris: Flammarion, 1982.

– *Journal: mémoires de la vie littéraire*. 4 vols. Paris: Flammarion, 1959. ARTFL. artfl-project.uchicago.edu. Accessed 25 March 2014.

Goujon, Jean-Paul, ed. *Correspondances croisées: Pierre Louÿs – Natalie Clifford-Barney – Renée Vivien*. Muizon: À l'écart, 1983.

Grier, Barbara. *The Lesbian in Literature*. Tallahassee, FL: Naiad Press, 1981.

– "The Lesbian Paperback." Grier and Reid 313–26.

Grier, Barbara, and Coletta Reid, eds. *The Lesbians [sic] Home Journal: Stories from the Ladder*. Baltimore: Diana Press, 1976.

Grojnowski, Daniel, ed. *Confessions d'un inverti-né*. Paris: Corti, 2007.

Gubar, Susan. "Sapphistries." *Signs* 10, no. 1 (1984): 43–62.

Gueslin, André, and Dominique Kalifa, eds. *Les Exclus en Europe, 1830–1930*. Paris: Éditions de l'Atelier, 1999.

Guillerm, Jean-Pierre. "De l'Artiste à l'Ariste: Joséphin Péladan contre les décadences." *Romantisme* 20 (1990): 59–75.

Gullickson, Gay L. *Unruly Women of Paris: Images of the Commune*. Ithaca, NY: Cornell UP, 1996.

Gunther, Scott. *The Elastic Closet: A History of Homosexuality in France*. New York: Palgrave Macmillan, 2009.

Guyot, Yves. *Études de physiologie sociale: La Prostitution*. Paris: Charpentier, 1882.

Hahn, Pierre. *Nos ancêtres les pervers: La Vie des homosexuels sous le Second Empire*. Paris: Olivier Orban, 1979.

Halperin, David. *How to do the History of Homosexuality*. Chicago: U of Chicago P, 2002.

Hamon, Philippe, and Alexandrine Viboud, eds. *Dictionnaire thématique du roman de mœurs et de la nouvelle réaliste et naturaliste (1850–1914)*. Paris: Presses Sorbonne nouvelle, 2003.

Hanson, Ellis. *Decadence and Catholicism*. Cambridge, MA: Harvard UP, 1997.

Harris, Bertha. "Lesbian Society in Paris in the 1920s." In *Amazon Expedition: a lesbianfeminist anthology*. Edited by Phyllis Birkby et al. Washington, NJ: Times Change Press, 1973. 77–88.

Harris, Ruth. *Murders and Madness: Medicine, Law, and Society in the Fin de Siècle*. Oxford: Oxford UP, 1989.

Hasselrodt, R. Leighton. *Lesbianism around the World*. New York: Midwood Books, 1963.

Hawthorne, Melanie. *Rachilde and French Women's Authorship: From Decadence to Modernism*. Lincoln: U of Nebraska P, 2002.

Hawthorne, Melanie, ed. *Natalie Barney and Her Circle*. Special issue of *South Central Review* 22, no. 3 (2005).

Héricourt, Jenny d'. *La Femme affranchie: Réponse à MM. Michelet, Proudhon, E. de Girardin, A. Comte et aux autres novateurs modernes*. Paris: A. Bohn, 1860.

Hildenbrand, Charles. "De la sexualité contraire." *Annales Médico-psychologiques* 9 (1883): 160–2.

Holmes, Diana, and Carrie Tarr, eds. *A Belle Époque? Women in French Society and Culture, 1890–1914*. New York, Oxford: Berghahn Books, 2006.

Hugo, Victor. *Poésie*. Paris: Seuil, 1972. 3 vols.

Huret, Jules. *Enquête sur l'évolution littéraire*. 1891. Paris: Corti, 1999.

Hustvedt, Asti. *The Decadent Reader: Fiction, Fantasy, and Perversion from Fin-de-Siècle France*. New York: Zone Books, 1998.

Huysmans, Joris-Karl. *À rebours*. 1884. Paris: Pocket, 1999.

Ireland, Craig. *The Subaltern Appeal to Experience: Self-Identity, Late Modernity, and the Politics of Immediacy*. Montreal: McGill-Queen's UP, 2004.

Irigaray, Luce. *Quand nos lèvres se parlent*. Paris: Minuit, 1977.

Jackson, Julian. *Living in Arcadia: Homosexuality, Politics, and Morality in France from the Liberation to AIDS*. Chicago: U of Chicago P, 2009.

Jacobson, David J. "Jews for Genius: The Unholy Disorders of Maurice Sachs." *Yale French Studies* 85 (1994): 181–200.

Jacques, Jean-Pierre. *Les Malheurs de Sapho*. Paris: Grasset, 1981.

Jay, Karla. *The Amazon and the Page: Barney and Vivien*. Bloomington: Indiana UP, 1988.

Jeannel, Julien. *De la prostitution dans les grandes villes au dix-neuvième siècle et de l'extinction des maladies vénériennes: questions générales d'hygiène, de moralité publique et de légalité*. Paris: Baillière, 1874.

– *Mémoire sur la prostitution publique*. Paris: Baillière, 1862.

Jewell, Shannon. "Hollywood Changed 'Fatty' Rosencrans!" *Elyria Chronicle Telegram* 8 January 1982. Magazine 2, 11. http://chronicletelegram.newspaperarchive.com/elyria-chronicle-telegram/1982-01-08. Accessed 26 March 2014.

Johnson, Barbara. "Gender and Poetry: Charles Baudelaire and Marceline Desbordes-Valmore." In *Displacements: Women, Tradition, Literatures in French*. Edited by Nancy K. Miller and Joan DeJean. Baltimore: Johns Hopkins UP, 1991. 163–81.

Johnson, David K. *The Lavender Scare: The Cold War Persecution of Gays and Lesbians in the Federal Government*. Chicago: U of Chicago P, 2004.

Jourdain, Frantz. *Les Décorés: Ceux qui ne le sont pas*. Paris: H. Simonis Empis, éditeur, 1895.

Jouy, Jules. *Les Chansons de l'année 1887*. Paris: Bourbier et Lamoureux, 1888.

Kalifa, Dominique. *La Culture de masse en France (1860–1930)*. Paris: La Découverte, 2001.

Keesey, Pam, ed. *Daughters of Darkness: Lesbian Vampire Tales*. San Francisco: Cleis Press, 2006.

Keller, Yvonne. "Ab/normal Looking: Voyeurism and Surveillance in Lesbian Pulp Novels and US Cold War Culture." *Feminist Media Studies* 5, no. 2 (2005): 177–95.

– "'Was It Right to Love Her Brother's Wife So Passionately?': Lesbian Pulp Novels and U.S. Lesbian Identity, 1950–1965." *American Quarterly* 57, no. 2 (2005): 385–410.

Kinsey, Alfred. *Sexual Behavior in the Human Female*. Bloomington: Indiana UP, 1953. New York: Pocket Books, 1965.

Koehler, Peter. "About Medicine and the Arts: Charcot and French Literature at the Fin-de-Siecle." *Journal of the History of the Neurosciences* 10, no. 1 (2001): 27–40.

Korda, Joanna, Sue Goldstein, and Frank Sommer. "The History of Female Ejaculation." *Journal of Sexual Medicine* 7, no. 5 (2010): 1965–75.

Krafft-Ebing, Richard von. *Psychopathia Sexualis*. First German edition 1886. First French translation 1895. Burbank, CA: Bloat Books, 1999.

Lacassagne, Alexandre. "Pédérastie." *Dictionnaire encyclopédique des sciences médicales*. Edited by Amédée Dechambre. Paris: Masson, 1864–89. 2nd series, vol. XXII (1886): 239–59.

– *Précis de médecine judiciaire*. Paris: Masson, 1878.

Ladenson, Elisabeth, ed. *Men and Lesbianism*. Special issue of *GLQ* 7, no. 3 (2001).

– *Proust's Lesbianism*. Ithaca, NY: Cornell, 2007.

Laloë, Jeanne. "Les Deux féminismes." *La Nouvelle Revue* (1908): 405–10.

Lamartine, Alphonse de. *Recueillements poétiques*. 1839. Paris: Garnier, 1966.
Lamber, Juliette. *Idées antiproudhoniennes sur l'amour, la femme et le mariage*. Paris: Taride, 1858.
Lanser, Susan. "*Au sein de vos pareilles*: Sapphic Separatism in Late Eighteenth-Century France." Merrick and Sibalis 105–16.
Laqueur, Thomas. *Making Sex: Body and Gender from the Greeks to Freud*. Cambridge, MA: Harvard UP, 1990.
– *Solitary Sex: A Cultural History of Masturbation*. New York: Zone Books, 2003.
Latimer, Tirza True. *Women Together/Women Apart: Portraits of Lesbian Paris*. New Brunswick, NJ: Rutgers UP, 2005.
Laupts, Dr [Georges Saint-Paul]. "Revue critique: Dégénérescence ou pléthore?" *Archives d'anthropologie criminelle* 23 (1908): 731–49.
– ed. "Roman d'un inverti." *Archives d'anthropologie criminelle* 9 (1894): 212–21; 10 (1895): 228–44, 320–36.
– *Tares et poisons; Perversions et perversité sexuelle*. Paris: Masson, 1896.
La Vaudère, Jane de [Jeanne Scrive]. *Les Demi-sexes*. Paris: Ollendorff, 1897.
Leclerc, Yvan. *Crimes écrits: La Littérature en procès au 19e siècle*. Paris: Plon, 1991.
Leconte de Lisle, Charles. *Articles, préfaces, discours*. Paris: Les Belles Lettres, 1971.
Lecour, Charles. *La Prostitution à Paris et à Londres 1789–1870*. 3rd ed. Paris: Asselin & Cie, 1882.
Léo, André. *Aline-Ali*. Paris: Librairie internationale, 1869.
Lermina, Jules, ed. "Belot, Adolphe." *Dictionnaire universel illustré de la vie française contemporaine*. Paris: Boulanger, 1885.
Lichfield, John. "Amours féminines sous les bombes." *Courrier international*. 15 April 2011. http://www.courrierinternational.com/article/2011/04/15/amours-feminines-sous-les-bombes. Accessed 26 March 2014.
– "Tereska Torres: The Reluctant Queen of Lesbian Literature." *The Independent*. 5 February 2010. http://www.independent.co.uk/arts-entertainment/books/features/tereska-torres-the-reluctant-queen-of-lesbian-literature-1889957.html. Accessed 26 March 2014.
Lidsky, Paul. *Les Écrivains contre la Commune*. 1970. Paris: la Découverte, 1999.
Lister, Anne. *No Priest But Love: The Journals of Anne Lister, 1824–1826*. Edited by Helena Whitbread. New York: New York UP, 1992.
– *The Secret Diaries of Miss Anne Lister*. Edited by Helena Whitbread. London: Virago Press, 2012.
Littré, Émile. *Histoire de la langue française*. Paris: Didier et Cie, 1863. 2 vols.
Lombard, Jean. *L'Agonie*. Paris: Savine, 1888.
Lombroso, Cesare, and G. Ferrero. *La Donna delinquente: la prostituta e la donna normale*. 1893. *La Femme criminelle et la prostituée*. Paris: Alcan, 1896.
Lorenz, Paul. *Sapho 1900: Renée Vivien*. Paris: Julliard, 1977.

Lorrain, Jean [Paul Duval]. *Dans l'oratoire*. Paris: Dalou, 1888.
- *La Maison Philibert*. Paris: Librairie universelle, 1904.
Louÿs, Pierre. *Aphrodite*. 1896. Trans. New York: Avon Books, 1946.
- *Chansons de Bilitis*. 1894. Paris: Gallimard, 1990.
- *Manuel de Gomorrhe suivi de L'Île aux dames*. Paris: La Musardine, 2004.
Lucey, Michael. *Gide's Bent: Sexuality, Politics, Writing*. New York: Oxford UP, 1995.
- *The Misfit of the Family: Balzac and the Social Forms of Sexuality*. Durham, NC: Duke UP, 2003.
- *Never Say I: Sexuality and the First Person in Colette, Gide, and Proust*. Durham, NC: Duke UP, 2006.
Lucien, Mirande. *Akademos: Jacques d'Adelswärd-Fersen et « la cause homosexuelle »*. Lille: QuestionDeGenre/GKC, 2000.
Lucien, Mirande, and Patrick Cardon. *Georges Eekhoud, un illustre uraniste*. Montpellier: QuestionDeGenre/GKC, 2012.
Lyons, Martyn. *Readers and Society in Nineteenth-Century France: Workers, Women, Peasants*. New York: Palgrave Macmillan, 2001.
- *Reading Culture & Writing Practices in Nineteenth-Century France*. Toronto: U of Toronto P, 2008.
Mainardi, Patricia. *Husbands, Wives, and Lovers: Marriage and its Discontents in Nineteenth-Century France*. New Haven, CT: Yale UP, 2003.
Maizeroy, René [René-Jean Toussaint]. *Deux amies*. Paris: Victor-Havard, 1885.
Mallarmé, Stéphane. *Correspondance*. Vol. 2: 1871–85. Paris: Gallimard, 1965.
Mallet-Joris, Françoise. *Le Rempart des béguines*. 1951. Trans. *The Loving and the Daring*. New York: Popular Library, 1957.
Marchal, Lucie. *La Mèche*. 1948. Trans. *The Mesh*. New York: Bantam Books, 1951.
Marcus, Sharon. "Comparative Sapphism." In *The Literary Channel*. Edited by Margaret Cohen and Carolyn Dever. Princeton, NJ: Princeton UP, 2002. 251–85.
- "Quelques problèmes de l'histoire lesbienne." In *Les Études gay et lesbiennes*. Paris: Éditions du Centre Pompidou, 1998. 35–43.
Margueritte, Paul and Victor. *Femmes nouvelles* (première partie). *Revue des deux mondes* 152 (1899): 721–66.
Marks, Elaine. "Lesbian Intertextuality." Stambolian 353–77.
- "'Sapho 1900': Imaginary Renée Viviens and the Rear of the Belle Époque." *Yale French Studies* 75 (1988): 175–89.
Marquardt, Steve R. "A Bio-Bibliography of Adolphe Belot." MA thesis, University of Minnesota, 1973.
Marquèze-Pouey, Louis. *Le Mouvement décadent en France*. Paris: PUF, 1986.
Martin, Kay. *The Whispered Sex*. New York: Hillman Books, 1960.
Martineau, Louis. *Les Déformations vulvaires et anales produites par la masturbation, le saphisme, la défloration et la sodomie*. Paris: Delahaye et Lecrosnier, 1886.

– *La Prostitution clandestine*. Paris: Delahaye et Lecrosnier, 1885.
Massad, Joseph. "Re-Orienting Desire: The Gay International and the Arab World." *Public Culture* 14, no. 2 (Spring 2002): 361–85.
Matlock, Jann. *Scenes of Seduction: Prostitution, Hysteria, and Reading Difference in Nineteenth-Century France*. New York: Columbia UP, 1994.
Maugue, Annelise. *L'Identité masculine en crise au tournant du siècle*. Paris: Rivages, 1987.
– "Littérature antiféministe et angoisse masculine au tournant du siècle." Bard, *Siècle*, 69–83.
Maupassant, Guy de. "La Femme de Paul." 1881. *Contes et Nouvelles*. 2 vols. Paris: Gallimard Pléiade, 2001. Translated by Ernest Boyd as "Paul's Mistress." In *The Collected Novels and Short Stories of Guy de Maupassant*. New York: Knopf, 1922. 203–28.
Maurras, Charles. *L'Avenir de l'intelligence*. Paris: Albert Fontemoing, 1905.
McPhee, Peter. *Social History of France, 1789–1914*. New York: Palgrave Macmillan, 2004.
Meeker, Martin. *Contacts Desired: Gay and Lesbian Communications and Community, 1940–1970s*. Chicago: U of Chicago P, 2006.
– "A Queer and Contested Medium: The Emergence of Representational Politics in the 'Golden Age' of Lesbian Paperbacks, 1955–1963." *Journal of Women's History* 17, no. 1 (2005): 165–88.
Mendès, Catulle. *La Légende du Parnasse contemporain*. Brussels: A. Brancart, 1884.
– *Méphistophéla*. 1890. Paris: Séguier, 1993.
– *Richard Wagner*. Paris: Charpentier, 1886.
– *Les 73 Journées de la Commune*. Paris: E. Lachaud, 1871.
Mendès-Leite, R. and P-O de Busscher, eds. *Gay Studies from the French Cultures*. Binghamton, NY: Haworth Press, 1993.
Merrick, Jeffrey. "The Marquis de Villette and Mademoiselle de Raucourt." Merrick and Ragan 30–53.
– "Sexual Politics and Public Order in Late Eighteenth-Century France: The *Mémoires secrets* and the *Correspondance secrète*." *Journal of the History of Sexuality* 1, no. 1 (1990): 68–84.
Merrick, Jeffrey, and Bryant T. Ragan. *Homosexuality in Modern France: Studies in the History of Sexuality*. New York: Oxford UP, 1996.
Merrick, Jeffrey, and Michael Sibalis, eds. *Homosexuality in French History and Culture*. Binghamton, New York: Haworth Press, 2001.
Mesch, Rachel. *The Hysteric's Revenge: French Women Writers at the Fin de Siècle*. Nashville: Vanderbilt UP, 2006.
Meyer-Plantureux, Chantal. *Les Enfants de Shylock ou l'antisémitisme sur scène*. Paris: Éditions complexe, 2005.
Meyers, Diana. *Gender in the Mirror: Cultural Imagery and Women's Agency*. New York: Oxford UP, 2002.

Michelet, Jules. *L'Amour*. Paris: Hachette 1859.

Migozzi, Jacques. *Boulevards du populaire*. Limoges: PULIM, 2005.

– "Littérature(s) populaire(s): Un objet protéiforme." *Hermès* 42 (2005): 95–100.

Millaud, Albert. "M. Émile Zola." *Le Figaro*. 1 Sept 1876. http://gallica.bnf.fr. Accessed 11 August 2012.

Mirbeau, Octave. *L'Amour de la femme vénale*. 1922. Paris: Éditions Côté-femmes, 1997.

Mitchell, Kaye. "'Who Is She?' Identities, Intertextuality and Authority in Non-Fiction Lesbian Pulp of the 1950s." In *Queer 1950s: Rethinking Sexuality in the Postwar Years*. Edited by Heike Bauer and Matt Cook. New York: Palgrave Macmillan, 2012. 150–66.

Moll, Albert. *Perversions of the Sex Instinct*. 1891. Newark, NJ: Julian Press, 1931.

Mollier, Jean-Yves. *L'Argent et les Lettres: Histoire du capitalisme d'édition*. Paris: Fayard, 1988.

Monet, Monique. *The French Way*. North Hollywood, CA: All Star Books, 1965.

Monneyron, Frédéric. *L'Androgyne décadent: Mythe, figure, fantasmes*. Grenoble: ELLUG, 1996.

– *L'Androgyne romantique du mythe au mythe littéraire*. Grenoble: ELLUG, 1994.

Moreau de Tours, Paul. *Les Aberrations du sens génésique*. Paris: A. Helm, 1880.

Morel, Bénédict-Augustin. *Traité des dégénérescences physiques, intellectuelles et morales de l'espèce humaine*. Paris: Baillière, 1857.

Morro, Don. *The Virgin*. New York: Beacon Books, 1955.

Mucchielli, Laurent, ed. *Histoire de la criminologie française*. Paris: L'Harmattan, 1994.

Murat, Laure. *La Loi du genre: Une histoire culturelle du troisième genre*. Paris: Fayart, 2006.

Musset, Alfred de. *Gamiani, ou deux nuits d'excès*. 1833. *Gamiani, or Two Nights of Excess*. Trans. John Baxter. New York: Harper, 2007.

Newman, Sally. "Archival Traces of Desire." *Journal of the History of Sexuality* 14, no. 1–2 (2005): 51–75.

Niees, Robert J. "An Early Zola Letter." *Modern Language Notes* 69, no. 2 (1954): 114–16.

Nordau, Max. *Degeneration*. 1892. First French translation 1896. Lincoln: U of Nebraska P, 1993.

Numa Numantius [Karl Heinrich Ulrichs]. *Vindex. Sozial-juristische Studien über mann-männliche Geschlechtsliebe*. Leipzig: Matthes, 1864.

Nussbaum, Martha C. "Objectification." *Philosophy and Public Affairs* 24, no. 4 (1995): 249–91.

Nye, Robert. "Heredity or Milieu: The Foundations of Modern European Criminological Theory." *Isis* 67, no. 3 (1976): 334–55.

– *Masculinity and Male Codes of Honor in Modern France*. New York: Oxford UP, 1993.

– "Medicine and Science as Masculine 'Fields of Honor.'" *OSIRIS* 12 (1997): 60–79.

Offen, Karen. "Depopulation, Nationalism, and Feminism in Fin-de-Siecle France." *The American Historical Review* 89, no. 3 (1984): 648–76.

Olivier-Martin, Yves. *Histoire du roman populaire en France de 1840 à 1980*. Paris: A. Michel, 1980.

Oosterhuis, Harry. *Stepchildren of Nature: Krafft-Ebing, Psychiatry, and the Making of Sexual Identity*. Chicago: U of Chicago P, 2000.

Palacio, Jean de. *Figures et formes de la décadence*. Paris: Éditions Séguier, 1994.

– *Figures et formes de la décadence*. Deuxième série. Paris: Éditions Séguier, 2000.

Parent-Duchâtelet, Alexandre. *De la prostitution dans la ville de Paris, considérée sous le rapport de l'hygiène publique, de la morale et de l'administration*. 1836. 3rd ed. Paris: Baillière, 1857.

Park, Katharine. "The Rediscovery of the Clitoris: French Medicine and the Tribade." In *The Body in Parts: Fantasies of Corporeality in Early Modern Europe*. Edited by David Hillman and Carla Mazzio. New York: Routledge, 1997. 171–93.

Paul, Harry W. *From Knowledge to Power: The Rise of the Science Empire in France, 1860–1939*. Cambridge: Cambridge UP, 1985.

Peck, Harry Thurston. "Emile Zola." *The Bookman* 16 (November 1903): 233–40.

– "One of the Parnassians." *The Bookman* 29 (April 1909): 174–8.

Péladan, Joséphin. *L'Art ochlocratique: Salons de 1882 & 1883*. Paris: Camille Dalou, 1888.

– *Comment on devient fée*. Paris: Chamuel, 1893.

– *Les Femmes honnêtes*. 1885. n.p.: Adamant Media, 2005.

– *La Gynandre*. 1891. n.p.: Adamant Media, 2005.

– *Initiation sentimentale*. Paris: Edinger, 1888.

– *Le Livre du sceptre*. Paris: Chamuel, 1895.

– *Rapport au public sur les beaux-arts*. Paris: Sansot, 1908.

– *La Science de l'amour*. Paris: Mosseic, 1911.

– *Le Vice suprême*. 1884. Geneva: Slatkine, 1979.

Pelletier, Madeleine. *L'Émancipation sexuelle de la femme*. Paris: M. Giard et E. Brière, 1911.

Peniston, William. *Pederasts and Others: Urban Culture and Sexual Identity in 19th-Century Paris*. Binghamton, NY: Haworth Press, 2004.

Perceau, Louis, ed. *Bibliographie du roman érotique au 19e siècle*. Paris: Georges Fourdrinier, 1930.

Perrin, Marie. *Renée Vivien: Le Corps exsangue, de l'anorexie mentale à la création littéraire*. Paris: L'Harmattan, 2003.

Perrot, Michelle. "Zola antiféministe? Une lecture de *Fécondité* (1899)." Bard, *Siècle*, 85–102.

Pia, Pascal, ed. *Dictionnaire des œuvres érotiques*. Paris: Laffont, 2001.

Pick, Daniel. *Faces of Degeneration: A European Disorder, 1848–1918*. Cambridge: Cambridge UP, 1989.

Pidansat de Mairobert, Mathieu-François. *Confession d'une jeune fille*. 1784. *Romanciers libertines du XVIIIe siècle*. Vol 2. Paris: Gallimard Pléiade, 2005.

Pierrot, Jean. *L'Imaginaire décadent, 1880–1900*. Paris: PUF, 1977.
Planté, Christine. "Voilà ce qui fait que votre *e* est muette." *Clio* 11 (2000): no pag. http://clio.revues.org/215. Accessed 26 March 2014.
Pollard, Percival. "Catulle Mendes, Boulevardier, 'Wickedest Man in Paris.'" *New York Times*. 14 February 1909. 40.
Pomeroy, Wardell Baxter. *Dr. Kinsey and the Institute for Sex Research*. New Haven, CT: Yale UP, 1982.
Les Positivismes. Special issue of *Romantisme* 21–2 (1978).
Pouillet, Thésée. *De l'onanisme chez la femme*. 1876. Paris: Delahaye, 1880.
Praz, Mario. *The Romantic Agony*. 1933. Oxford: Oxford UP, 1970.
Prille, Pol. *Bois de Boulogne, bois d'amour*. Paris: Éditions Montaigne, 1925.
Proudhon, Pierre. *La Pornocratie, ou Les Femmes dans les temps modernes*. Paris: Lacroix, 1875.
Queffélec-Dumasy, Lise. *Le Roman-feuilleton français au XIXe siècle*. 1989. Special issue of *Belphégor: Littérature Populaire et Culture Médiatique* 7, no. 1 (2007). http://etc.dal.ca/belphegor/. Accessed 15 June 2012.
Raffalovich, Marc-André. "Chronique de l'unisexualité." *Archives d'anthropologie criminelle* 24 (1909): 353–91.
– *Uranisme et unisexualité: Étude sur différentes manifestations de l'instinct sexuel*. Lyon: Storck, 1896.
Régnier, Henri de. *Médailles d'argile*. Paris: Mercure de France, 1900.
Renooz, Céline. *Psychologie comparée de l'homme et de la femme*. Paris: Chez l'auteur, 1897.
Revenin, Régis. "Conceptions et théories savantes de l'homosexualité masculine en France, de la Monarchie de Juillet à la Première Guerre mondiale." *Revue d'histoire des sciences humaines* 17 (2007): 23–45.
– *Homosexualité et prostitution masculines à Paris: 1870–1918*. Paris: L'Harmattan, 2005.
Revenin, Régis, ed. *Hommes et masculinités de 1789 à nos jours. Contributions à l'histoire du genre et de la sexualité en France*. Paris: Éditions Autrement, 2007.
Richardot, Anne. "La Secte des anandrynes: Un difficile embarquement pour Lesbos." *Tangence* 57 (1998): 40–52.
Ridpath, John Clark, ed. "Belot, Adolphe." *The Ridpath Library of Universal Literature*. Philadelphia: Avil Printing Company, 1903. 149–52.
Rimbaud, Arthur. *Œuvres complètes*. Paris: Gallimard Pléiade, 1972.
Ritti, Antoine. "De l'attraction des sexes semblables (Perversion de l'instinct sexuel)." *Gazette hebdomadaire de médecine et de chirurgie* 15, no. 1 (1878): 1–3.
Rivers, Christopher. Introduction. *Mademoiselle Giraud*. By Adolphe Belot. ix–xxxiv.
– "Safe Sex: The Prophylactic Walls of the Cloister in the French Libertine Convent Novel of the Eighteenth Century." *Journal of the History of Sexuality* 5, no. 3 (1995): 381–402.

Robb, Graham. *Strangers: Homosexual Love in the Nineteenth Century*. New York: Norton, 2004.
Robic, Myriam. *"Femmes damnées": Saphisme et poésie (1846–1889)*. Paris: Classiques Garnier, 2012.
Rodriguez, Suzanne. *Wild Heart: Natalie Clifford Barney and the Decadence of Literary Paris*. New York: Harper Collins, 2002.
Ronsin, Francis. *Les Divorciaires: Affrontements politiques et conceptions du mariage dans la France du XIX*[e] *siècle*. Paris: Aubier, 1992.
Rosario, Vernon. *The Erotic Imagination: French Histories of Perversity*. New York: Oxford UP, 1997.
– ed. *Science and Homosexualities*. New York: Routledge, 1997.
Ross, Kristin. "Commune Culture." *A New History of French Literature*. Edited by Denis Hollier. Cambridge, MA: Harvard UP, 1989. 751–7.
Sacquin, Michèle. "Entre positivisme et laïcité: Zola et la 'non-religion' de l'avenir." Sacquin 65–75.
– ed. *Zola et les historiens*. Paris: Bibliothèque nationale de France, 2004.
Sainte-Beuve, Charles-Augustin. "De la littérature industrielle." *Revue des deux mondes* series 4, vol. 19 (1839): 675–91.
Salle, Muriel. "L'Avers d'une Belle Époque: Genre et altérité dans les pratiques et les discours d'Alexandre Lacassagne, médecin lyonnais (1843–1924)." Diss. Lyon 2, 2009. http://theses.univ-lyon2.fr/documents/lyon2/2009/salle_m#p=0&a=top. Accessed 26 March 2014.
Samuels, Maurice. *Inventing the Israelite: Jewish Fiction in Nineteenth-Century France*. Stanford, CA: Stanford UP, 2010.
Sapiro, Gisèle. "De l'usage des catégories de 'droite' et de 'gauche' dans le champ littéraire." *Sociétés et Représentations* 11 (2001): 19–53.
Sautman, Francesca Canadé. "Invisible Women: Lesbian Working-Class Culture in France, 1880–1930." Merrick and Ragan 177–201.
Schaffner, Anna Katharina. "Fiction as Evidence: On the Uses of Literature in Nineteenth-Century Sexological Discourse." *Comparative Literature Studies* 48, no. 2 (2011): 165–99.
Schehr, Lawrence R. *Figures of Alterity: French Realism and its Others*. Stanford, CA: Stanford UP, 2003.
– *French Gay Modernism*. Urbana: U of Illinois P, 2004.
Schick, Frank L. "Paperback Publishing." *Library Trends* 7, no. 1 (1958): 93–104. *IDEALS*. https://www.ideals.illinois.edu/bitstream/handle/2142/5794/librarytrendsv7i1k_opt.pdf?sequence=1. Accessed 19 June 2012.
Schor, Naomi. "Male Lesbianism." Ladenson, *Men and Lesbianism*, 391–9.
Schultz, Gretchen. "Baudelaire's Lesbian Connections." In *Approaches to Teaching Baudelaire's* Fleurs du Mal. Edited by Laurence Porter. New York: Modern Language Association, 2000. 130–8.

– "Daughters of Bilitis: Literary Genealogy and Lesbian Authenticity." Ladenson, *Men and Lesbianism*, 377–89.
– *The Gendered Lyric: Subjectivity and Difference in 19th-Century French Poetry*. West Lafayette, IN: Purdue UP, 1999.
– "Gender, Sexuality and Poetic Identification." *Nottingham French Studies* 47, no. 3 (2008): 91–102.
– "Sexualités de Verlaine." *Revue Verlaine* 5 (1997): 46–59.
– "Terms of Estrangement: Renée Vivien's Construction of the Lesbian Subject." In *The Rhetoric of the Other: Lesbian and Gay Strategies of Resistance in French and Francophone Contexts*. Edited by M. Antle and D. Fisher. New Orleans: UP of the South, 2002. 79–100.
– "Transnationalism and Sexual Identity in Literature: From the French Canon to US Pulp Fiction." *Contemporary French Civilization* 37, no. 2–3 (2012): 193–215.
Sedgwick, Eve Kosofsky. *Epistemology of the Closet*. Berkeley: U California P, 1990.
Seillan, Jean-Marie. "De la scène du vaudeville au théâtre du fantasme: L'Afrique d'Adolphe Belot dans *La Vénus Noire* (1877)." In *Regards sur les littératures coloniales*, vol. 2. Edited by Jean-François Durand and Jean Sévry. Paris: L'Harmattan, 1999. 313–42.
– *Huysmans, politique et religion*. Paris: Éditions Classiques Garnier, 2009.
– "*Mademoiselle Giraud, ma femme* d'Adolphe Belot (1870) ou Les Mésaventures d'un sot narratologique." In *Marginalité et Littérature*. Edited by M. Accarie, J.-G. Gouttebroze, and E. Kotler. Nice: Université de Nice-Sophia Antipolis, 2001. 523–42.
Server, Lee. *Encyclopedia of Pulp Fiction Writers*. New York: Facts on File, Inc., 2002.
Shapiro, Ann-Louise. "Criminelles à Paris à la fin du XIXe siècle." Gueslin and Kalifa 436–46.
Shichor, David. "The French-Italian Controversy: A Neglected Historical Topic in Criminological Literacy." *Journal of Criminal Justice Education* 21, no. 3 (2010): 211–28. http://www.tandfonline.com/doi/abs/10.1080/10511253.2010.488109#.UzMRsNzhrgI. Accessed 26 March 2014.
Sibalis, Michael. "Homophobia, Vichy France, and the 'Crime of Homosexuality': The Origins of the Ordinance of 6 August 1942." *GLQ* 8 (2002): 301–4.
Sighele, Scipio. *Le Crime à deux: Essai de psycho-pathologie sociale*. Lyon: Storck; Paris: Masson, 1893.
Sinfield, Alan. *The Wilde Century*. London: Cassell, 1994.
Singy, Patrick. "Friction of the Genitals and Secularization of Morality." *Journal of the History of Sexuality* 12 (2003): 345–64.
Smallwood, Christine. "Sapphic Soldiers." *Salon.com*. 9 August 2005. http://www.salon.com/2005/08/09/torres_3/. Accessed 26 March 2014.
Souhami, Diana. *Wild Girls: Paris, Sappho, and Art: The Lives and Loves of Natalie Barney and Romaine Brooks*. New York: St Martin's Press, 2005.

Spain, Vicki. *Who Calls it Sin?* New York: Domino Books, 1965.

Speer, Lisa. "Paperback Pornography: Mass Market Novels and Censorship in Post-War America." *Journal of American & Comparative Cultures* 24, nos. 3–4 (2001): 153–60.

Sprague, W. D. *The Lesbian in Our Society.* New York: Midwood Books, 1962.

Stambolian, George, and Elaine Marks, eds. *Homosexualities and French Literature.* Ithaca, NY: Cornell UP, 1979.

Stearn, Jess. *The Grapevine: A Report on the Secret World of the Lesbian.* New York: Doubleday, 1964.

Steiner, Lucius B. *Sex Behavior of the Lesbian.* Hollywood: Viceroy, 1964.

Stengers, Jean, and Anne van Neck. *Masturbation: The History of a Great Terror.* New York: Palgrave Macmillan, 2001.

Stephan, Philip. *Paul Verlaine and the Decadence, 1882–90.* Manchester: U of Manchester P, 1974.

"Strange Harem by Hudson, Jan." *alibris.com.* http://www.biblio.com/books/376783022.html. Accessed 26 March 2014.

Stryker, Susan. *Queer Pulp: Perverted Passions from the Golden Age of the Paperback.* San Francisco: Chronicle Books, 2001.

Sue, Eugène. *Jean Bart et Louis XIV: Drames maritimes du XVIIe siècle.* Paris: Marescq et Cie, 1851.

Summers, Claude, ed. *Gay and Lesbian Literary Heritage.* New York: Henry Holt Publishers, 1994.

Surkis, Judith. *Sexing the Citizen: Morality and Masculinity in France.* Ithaca, NY: Cornell UP, 2006.

Talmeyr, Maurice. *Souvenirs d'avant le déluge. 1870–1914.* Paris: Perrin, 1927.

Tamagne, Florence. *Histoire de l'homosexualité en Europe.* Paris: Seuil, 2000.

– "L'Identité lesbienne: Une construction différée et différenciée?" *Cahiers d'histoire. Revue d'histoire critique* 84 (2001): n. pag. http://chrhc.revues.org/1871. Accessed 26 March 2014.

Tardieu, Ambroise. *Étude médico-légale sur les attentats aux mœurs.* Paris: Baillière, 1857.

Tarnowsky, Benjamin. *L'Instinct sexuel et ses manifestations morbides, du double point de vue de la jurisprudence et de la psychiatrie.* Paris: Carrington, 1898.

Taxil, Léo. *La Corruption fin-de-siècle.* Paris: Noirot, 1891.

– *La Prostitution contemporaine; Étude d'une question sociale.* Paris: Librairie populaire, 1884.

Taylor, Valerie. *Return to Lesbos.* New York: Midwood Books, 1963. Tallahassee, FL: Naiad Press, 1982.

Terry, Jennifer. *An American Obsession: Science, Medicine, and Homosexuality in Modern Society.* Chicago: U of Chicago P, 1999.

Texier, Edmond. *Les Femmes et la fin du monde*. [Paris]: C. Lévy, 1877.

Thiesse, Anne-Marie. *Le Roman du quotidien: Lecteurs et lectures populaires à la Belle Époque*. Paris: Seuil, 2000.

Thompson, Victoria. "Creating Boundaries: Homosexuality and the Changing Social Order in France, 1830–1870." Merrick and Ragan 102–27.

Thorel-Cailleteau, Sylvie. *La Tentation du livre sur rien: Naturalisme et Décadence*. Mont-de-Marsan: Éditions interuniversitaires, 1994.

Tissot, Samuel-Auguste. *L'Onanisme: Dissertation sur les maladies produites par la masturbation*. Nouvelle édition considérablement augmentée. Lausanne: Chez l'écrivain, 1822.

Todorov, Tzvetan. "Typologie du roman policier." *Poétique de la prose*. Paris: Seuil, 1971. 55–65.

Torres, Tereska. *Les Années anglaises: Journal intime de guerre (1939–1945)*. Paris: Seuil, 1981.

– *By Cécile*. New York: Simon & Schuster, 1963.

– *The Dangerous Games*. Greenwich, CT: Fawcett Publications, 1957.

– *Jeunes femmes en uniforme: roman*. Paris: Éditions Phébus, 2011.

– *Women's Barracks*. Greenwich, CT: Fawcett Publications, 1950. New York: Feminist Press, 2005.

Traub, Valerie. *The Renaissance of Lesbianism in Early Modern England*. Cambridge: Cambridge UP, 2002.

Van Casselaer, Catherine. *Lot's Wife: Lesbian Paris, 1890–1914*. Liverpool: Janus Press, 1986.

Vapereau, Gustave. *L'Année littéraire et dramatique ou Revue annuelle des principales productions de la littérature française*. Paris: Hachette, 1864. Vol. 6.

Verel, Shirley. *The Dark Side of Venus*. New York: Bantam, 1962.

Verlaine, Paul. *Les Amies*. 1868. Translated by Norma Cole and Erin Mouré in Castle, *Literature*, 478–81.

– *Hombres*. [s.n.]: "Imprimé sous le manteau et ne se vend nulle part" [1904].

– *Œuvres poétiques complètes*. Paris: Gallimard Pléiade, 1962.

– *Selected Poems*. Trans. Martin Sorrell. Oxford: Oxford UP, 1999.

Vial, Henri. *La Raucourt & ses amies: Étude historique des mœurs saphiques au 18e siècle, les lesbiennes du théâtre et de la ville, Melpomène et Sapho, Lesbos à Paris, Courtisanes, Filles galantes et "Honnestes dames."* Paris: H. Daragon, 1909.

Vicinus, Martha. *Intimate Friends: Women Who Loved Women, 1778–1928*. Chicago: U of Chicago P, 2004.

– "'They Wonder to Which Sex I Belong': The Historical Roots of the Modern Lesbian Identity." *Feminist Studies* 18, no. 3 (1992): 467–97.

Vickers, Nancy. "Diana Described: Scattered Women and Scattered Rhyme." *Critical Inquiry* 8, no. 2 (1981): 265–79.

Vigny, Alfred de. "La Colère de Samson." 1864. *Poèmes antiques et modernes; Les Destinées*. Paris: Gallimard, 1973. 178–82.

Villarejo, Amy. "Forbidden Love: Pulp as Lesbian History." In *Out Takes: Essays on Queer Theory and Film*. Edited by Ellis Hanson. Durham, NC: Duke UP, 1999. 316–45.

Waelti-Walters, Jennifer. *Damned Women: Lesbians in French Novels*. Montreal: McGill-Queen's UP, 2000.

Wahl, Elizabeth. *Invisible Relations: Representations of Female Intimacy in the Age of Enlightenment*. Stanford, CA: Stanford UP, 1999.

Warner, John Harley. "The History of Science and the Sciences of Medicine." *OSIRIS* 10 (1995): 164–93.

Weil, Kari. *Androgyny and the Denial of Difference*. Charlottesville: UP of Virginia, 1992.

Weiss, Andrea. *Paris Was a Woman: Portraits from the Left Bank*. San Francisco: Harper, 1995.

Weisz, George. *Divide and Conquer: A Comparative History of Medical Specialization*. New York: Oxford UP, 2005.

Westphal, Carl. "Die Konträre Sexualempfindung." *Archiv fur Psychiatrie und Nervenkrankheiten* 2 (1869): 73–108.

White, Nicolas. "Paternal Perspectives on Divorce in Alphonse Daudet's *Rose et Ninette* (1892)." *Nineteenth-Century French Studies* 30, nos. 1–2 (2001): 131–47.

Wilkerson, William S. *Ambiguity and Sexuality: A Theory of Sexual Identity*. New York: Palgrave Macmillan, 2007.

Wilson, Stephen. *Ideology and Experience: Antisemitism in France at the Time of the Dreyfus Affair*. Hackensack, NJ: Fairleigh Dickinson UP, 1982.

Winn, Phillip. *Sexualités décadentes chez Jean Lorrain: Le Héros fin de sexe*. Amsterdam; Atlanta, GA: Rodopi, 1997.

Wittig, Monique. *The Straight Mind and Other Essays*. Boston: Beacon Press, 1992.

Ziegler, Robert. *Beauty Raises the Dead: Literature and Loss in the Fin de siècle*. Newark: U of Delaware P, 2002.

– "The Elitist Metaphysic of Joséphin Péladan." *Nineteenth Century French Studies* 16, nos. 3–4 (1988): 361–71.

Zimet, Jaye. *Strange Sisters: The Art of Lesbian Pulp Fiction 1949–1969*. New York: Viking Studio/Penguin Putnam, 1999.

Zimmerman, Bonnie, ed. *Lesbian Histories and Cultures*. New York: Routledge, 1999.

Zola, Émile. *L'Assommoir*. 1879. *Les Rougon-Macquart*. Vol. 2. Paris: Gallimard Pléiade, 1961.

– "Au couvent." In *Contes et nouvelles*. Paris: Gallimard Pléiade, 1976. 365–9.

– *Carnets d'enquêtes*. Edited by Henri Mitterand. Paris: Plon, 1986.

– *La Curée*. 1872. *Les Rougon-Macquart*. Vol. 1. Paris: Gallimard Pléiade, 1960.

– *Nana*. 1880. Edited by Colette Becker. Paris: Garnier Frères, 1994. Translation by George Holden. London: Penguin Classics, 2004. *ProQuest LLC*. http://literature.proquest.com. Accessed 26 March 2014.
– *Pot-Bouille*. 1882. *Les Rougon-Macquart*. Vol. 3. Paris: Gallimard Pléiade, 1964.
– *Le Roman expérimental*. 1880. Paris: Flammarion, 2006. *The Experimental Novel*. Translation by Belle M. Sherman. New York: Cassell Publishing, 1893.
– *Thérèse Raquin*. 1867. Paris: Gallimard, 2001.

Index

www.ingramcontent.com/pod-product-compliance
Lightning Source LLC
LaVergne TN
LVHW090152080826
844660LV00013B/768/J

* 9 7 8 1 4 4 2 6 4 6 7 2 8 *